THE ULTIMATE BOOK OF

GANGSTER

THE ULTIMATE BOOK OF
GANGSTER MOVIES

FEATURING THE 100 GREATEST
GANGSTER FILMS OF ALL TIME

GEORGE ANASTASIA & GLEN MACNOW

FOREWORD BY
JOE PISTONE
(A.K.A. DONNIE BRASCO)

RUNNING PRESS
PHILADELPHIA · LONDON

12 June
B+T
20 (14.-

© 2011 by George Anastasia and Glen Macnow
Published by Running Press,
A Member of the Perseus Books Group

Books published by Running Press are available at special discounts for bulk purchases
in the United States by corporations, institutions, and other organizations. For more
 information, please contact the Special Markets Department at the Perseus Books Group,
2300 Chestnut Street, Suite 200, Philadelphia, PA 19103, or call (800) 810-4145, ext. 5000,
or e-mail special.markets@perseusbooks.com.

ISBN 978-0-7624-4154-9
Library of Congress Control Number: 2011925144

E-book ISBN 978-0-7624-4370-3

9   8   7   6   5   4   3   2   1
Digit on the right indicates the number of this printing

Cover and Interior Designer: Josh McDonnell
Editor: Greg Jones
Researchers: Paul Jolovitz and Michael Regan
Typography: Akzidenz, Avenir, Boton, and Avenir

Photographs courtesy of Everett Collection

Running Press Book Publishers
2300 Chestnut Street
Philadelphia, PA 19103-4371

Visit us on the web!
www.runningpress.com

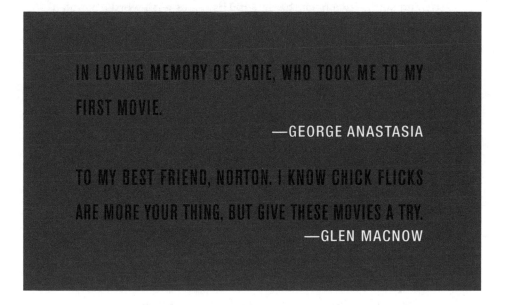

IN LOVING MEMORY OF SADIE, WHO TOOK ME TO MY FIRST MOVIE.

—GEORGE ANASTASIA

TO MY BEST FRIEND, NORTON. I KNOW CHICK FLICKS ARE MORE YOUR THING, BUT GIVE THESE MOVIES A TRY.

—GLEN MACNOW

ACKNOWLEDGEMENTS

Many people deserve our appreciation for their help in putting this book together. Greg Jones, our editor at Running Press, was enthusiastic and supportive from the outset. His talent with words, coupled with his vast knowledge of movies, proved invaluable—although his taste in films (*Cold Blooded?*) remains questionable. Thanks, too, to Joshua McDonnell at Running Press for his design work, which makes this book more readable.

Thanks to Frank Weimann, our agent at The Literary Group International, for fighting the good fight whenever it proved necessary.

Thanks to the agents and media representatives who helped us secure the interviews in this book, including Mike Amato, Ellie Martin-Sperry, Dan Ramm, Lynn Rawlins, Jay D. Schwartz and Stephen C. Thompson.

Special thanks to Joe Pistone, aka Donnie Brasco, for writing the foreword to this book and setting the stage for what we hope will be an enjoyable read.

And thanks, also, to Nick Caramandi, a mobster living in hiding, and Danny Provenzano, a mobster living large, for their thoughts, insights and perspective on the genre and how well it reflects life on the streets.

Many thanks, also, to scores of law enforcement and legal sources who will remain unnamed but who, over the years, have helped shape our view of the underworld.

And, finally, thanks to our fact-checker, Paul Jolovitz, who's the world's greatest nitpicker. And we mean that in a good way.

CONTENTS

FOREWORD

Everyone loves gangster movies. From the colorful characters and intense situations to the complicated plotlines and ultra violence—moviegoers can't get enough of the genre.

And it is true that gangster movies are the Westerns of this generation. White Hats vs. Black Hats; Law Enforcement vs. Made Men. It all comes down to the same basic theme of Good vs. Evil. And that battle has been a staple of storytelling for as long as people have told stories.

One of the greatest elements of gangster movies is the lineup of usual suspects that get fleshed out in unique ways in each new film. The power-hungry boss. The stone-cold killer. The industrious soldier. The beautiful moll. The lackeys and wannabes. The men in uniform. The undercovers. The innocent bystanders. Most of these types play a critical part in the making of just about every gangster movie.

Another common ingredient is the situational tension that drives gangster films—whether it's a robbery gone bad, a deadly shootout, a tense undercover operation, a shadowy sit-down, a sudden double-cross, or a bloody hit.

People especially like gangster movies that are based on real-life stories. Of course there is *Donnie Brasco*—the film based on my experiences as an undercover FBI agent infiltrating the New York City Mafia in the 1970s and 80s. A few other celebrated gangster movies based on real people and events are *GoodFellas*, *Casino*, and *The Departed* (which won the Best Picture Oscar in 2006). *GoodFellas* follows the rise of small-time wannabe Henry Hill; *Casino* documents the mob's overtaking of Las Vegas in the 70s and 80s; and in *The Departed*, Jack Nicholson plays a character based on over-the-top Irish gangster Whitey Bulger, who ran the Irish mob in Boston for years. These four films (and there are others) get the gangster life right—portraying the reality of violence, murder, envy and jealousy that members of the life deal with every day. Great gangster movies capture these things with fearless detail.

Of course the all-time gangster movie is *The Godfather*, followed closely by *The Godfather: Part II*. Another great gangster movie of note is *Mean Streets*—starring young actors Robert De Niro and Harvey Keitel, and directed by a young Martin Scorsese—which portrays the life of low-level gangsters and their struggle to make a name for themselves in the life. This is a great film to watch if you want to see a bunch of young guys creating their first film in the genre for which they'd all become famous.

Funny things happen on a movie set. While shooting the movie *Donnie Brasco*, a wiseguy I knew when I was undercover in the life showed up on the set. I confronted him as to why he was there. He told me he was not there on mob business, but because his son wanted to be an actor and he wanted to ask if I would give him a part in the movie. I spoke with the kid and could tell he really wanted to be an actor—so I put him in a couple of scenes. Every day the kid worked, the father showed up with Cuban cigars; we sat, smoked and talked about the old days in the life. If I had seen the same guy back in the day, the scene would have played out a lot differently—and if it was anything like in the movies, one of us might have ended up dead.

The Ultimate Book of Gangster Movies? Fuhgedaboudit!

—Joseph Pistone (a.k.a. Donnie Brasco)

INTRODUCTION

Walk into any bar where guys hang out and it's a good bet they are discussing one of three topics: sports, women or movies. It's also a good bet that most of those guys can speak with knowledge and intelligence about two of those topics.

This is a book about one of them—movies. More specifically, gangster movies.

Here's a little test. Ask any guy you know between the ages of 21 and 65 to complete the following movie quotes:

"Leave the gun, take ___."

"Say hello to my ___."

"Now youse can't ___."

"I coulda had class. I coulda ___."

These lines are part of the American lexicon, part of pop culture, part of every guy's experience interacting with other guys.

Indeed, gangster movies have influenced the culture since Hollywood first turned on the lights. Six decades before Joe Pesci's unhinged bantam tough guy terrorized the world in *GoodFellas*, Edward G. Robinson did exactly the same in *Little Caesar*.

The bad guy is always mesmerizing. We all want to believe we're rebels underneath our law-abiding skins. And so when we sit in a dark theater rooting for the gangster, we get the vicarious thrill of striking out at authority without, well, actually breaking the rules ourselves.

In some ways, the gangster represents the American dream come to life—he gets the money, he gets the power, he gets the women. This country was built on guts, vision, bloodshed and a good deal of criminality. It is no coincidence that each of those elements contributes to a solid gangster film.

Gangster movies are also the urban version of Westerns, that great early genre of film. As Americans moved from farms and small towns into the cities, Tom Mix became Tom Powers and, later, Tommy DeVito. The James Gang became the John Dillinger Gang and, later, the Corleones.

Even the real gangsters have always loved these movies. Dillinger was gunned down by lawmen in 1934 while leaving a theater showing *Manhattan Melodrama*, a film featuring Clark Gable as a racketeer. Decades later, infamous Gambino crime family hit man Sammy "The Bull" Gravano quoted lines from *The Godfather* to his allies and enemies.

There is also a *Godfather* connection to Joey Merlino, a young wiseguy long suspected of the attempted murder of fellow mobster Nicky Scarfo Jr. in an Italian restaurant on Halloween night in 1989. A gunman wearing a mask and carrying a trick-or-treat bag walked up to Scarfo's table in a South Philadelphia eatery and opened fire. Scarfo survived the hit, but that's not the point.

Merlino, according to law enforcement and underworld sources, deliberately dropped his gun as he walked out of the restaurant. The reason? He knew Scarfo's father, jailed mob boss Nicodemo "Little Nicky" Scarfo, was a big fan of *The Godfather* and especially liked the scene where Al Pacino blows away a mob rival and a corrupt cop in a Brooklyn restaurant. In that scene, Pacino drops his gun as he walks away.

In a case of art honoring art, the great HBO series *The Sopranos* often nodded to the mob films, including when Silvio Dante imitated Michael Corleone in *The Godfather: Part III* or when Christopher Moltisanti spouted another of his always-errant movie quotations, such as:

Christopher: "Louis Brasi sleeps with the fishes."

Big Pussy: "Luca Brasi. Luca."

Christopher: "Whatever."

Getting those lines correct is important. As part of our analysis in this book, we highlight both the quotes that "made" the gangster movies, as well as those that have made it into our national consciousness. We've transcribed these quotes directly while watching the films. In these days of fast-and-loose information dispersal via the Internet, you never know if a film quote referenced in informal discussion is accurate.

This book is designed to identify and discuss what we consider the Top 100 gangster movies ever made. It is not a book geared toward critics or film students; neither of this book's authors went to film school. Rather, it's a book for guys (and gals) who love the genre, who know what they call a Quarter Pounder in France, who would agree that while Pacino certainly earned the Oscar he won for *Scent of a Woman*, he probably deserved seven more for the roles he played in movies featured on our Top 100 list.

You may not agree with our choices. In fact, we would be disappointed if you had no quibble with our rankings or omissions. The point of a book like this is to spark debate. De Niro or Pacino? Coppola or Scorsese? *A Bronx Tale* or *Gangs of New York* or, for that matter, *King of New York*?

One of the biggest issues we dealt with was how to define a gangster movie, which is not as easy as defining a sports movie or a romantic comedy. To that end, we came up with this: a gangster movie is a film featuring an ongoing illegal enterprise conducted by a group of criminals; a movie in which the bad guys—not the police—are the central characters.

Under that litmus test, excellent films such as *L.A. Confidential* and *Bullitt* don't make the cut. Some entertaining caper films like *Ocean's Eleven* and *The Sting* also fail to meet our criteria due to their lack of an "ongoing" criminal enterprise.

Bottom line: Your definition may be different than ours. And sometimes we make exceptions to our own rule, such as our inclusion of *The French Connection*. We'll suggest that our label of "gangster film" mostly follows U.S. Supreme Court Justice Potter Stewart's inarguable characterization of pornography: "I know it when I see it."

In selecting our Top 100 gangster films, we considered both artistic merit and historical value. We looked for movies that had a powerful script, three-dimensional characters, memorable scenes and a good bit of action and violence. Because a movie where no one fires a gun is not much of a gangster movie.

Gangster movies can make you laugh (*Get Shorty*, *Snatch*). They can shock you with their brutality (*Scarface*, *Reservoir Dogs*). They can even make you cry (check out our 69th-ranked movie, the underappreciated *Let Him Have It*).

They often show a slice of history. *Gangs of New York* portrays the rise of street gangs in the Five Points area in the 19th century. *Kill the Irishman* accurately recounts the Cleveland mob wars of the 1970s, down to every last car bomb.

And they are sometimes just nonsense. Nobody's going to argue that Billy Crystal's attempt to pass himself off as a mob boss ("Benny the Groin, Sammy the Schnozz") in *Analyze This* bears any resemblance to reality. Still, it is damned entertaining.

———————————

Gangster movies date back to the onset of cinema. The first box-office success was 1912's *The Musketeers of Pig Alley*—D.W. Griffith's Dickensian look at the American immigrant experience, set in the squalor of Manhattan's Lower East Side.

The genre really gained traction two decades later because of changes in America. The Volstead Act, which mandated a prohibition of alcohol sales from 1920-33, didn't stop Americans from drinking so much as it led to bootlegging and the growth of organized crime. Mobsters like Al Capone and Lucky Luciano became celebrities, their stories luridly told by newspapers—and then by the cinema.

"Until Prohibition, mobsters were thugs who would hit you over the head and steal your money," said Nicholas Pileggi, the author of *Good-Fellas* and *Casino*. "Now they had opportunity. That's really how the genre started."

At the end of the 1920s, the nation was struck by the Great Depression. Americans were perplexed by an economic system that failed them. This helped make folk heroes out of outlaws like

John Dillinger and Bonnie and Clyde who robbed banks and shot their way to fame and fortune.

The executives at Warner Brothers—the major Hollywood studio that also owned movie theaters in America's big cities—wanted to provide the nation's urban immigrants with fare they liked. And so, starting in 1931, the studio created three landmark gangster films—*Little Caesar, The Public Enemy* and *Scarface.*

Police chiefs and censorship boards were appalled. But filmgoers were delighted, and often sympathetic to the bad guy—typically a young man trying to make his way in a country that didn't exactly embrace him.

Looking at the films now, they may seem a bit dated in everything from their dialogue to special effects. But if you can suspend your critical eye just a bit, they are still extremely entertaining.

Plus, they created a new art form. Calling *The Public Enemy* one of 15 films that "had a profound effect on me," Martin Scorsese wrote in 2010: "The shocking, blunt brutality; the energy of Cagney in his first starring role; the striking use of popular music (the song 'I'm Forever Blowing Bubbles')—this picture led the way for all of us."

Looking at the black-and-white classics of the 1930s and 1940s, you can still see the charisma of their stars—James Cagney, Edward G. Robinson and Humphrey Bogart. They were on-screen tough guys, sure, and were always headed for a fall at the movie's end. But they also allowed audiences to escape into the fantasy that somehow it would be fun to be a gangster. Their great work endures.

As America continued to change, so did its gangster films. After World War II, the old "ripped from the headlines" format seemed passé. Gangsters began to be portrayed less as gun-crazed killers than as businessmen running corrupt empires. You'll find some of those movies here, like *On the Waterfront* and *Underworld, U.S.A.*

You'll also find those that came out of a form called film noir, dark potboilers often taken from pulp fiction paperbacks of the era. The best of them, like *The Asphalt Jungle* and *The Killers*, tend to feature a disillusioned non-hero trying to survive in a world beset by greed and corruption.

The genre lagged for a while, until 1967's *Bonnie and Clyde*, starring Warren Beatty and Faye Dunaway, brought it back, more brutal and sexy than ever. That film reinvented the movie gangster as antihero and spawned a series of boy-girl "on the run" films that continued all the way through *True Romance*. Its graphic, slow-motion finale set a new standard for movie violence.

Of course, it was Francis Ford Coppola's *The Godfather* that created the modern gangster film in 1972. An epic, a family saga, a period piece, a Shakespearean tragedy, *The Godfather* got everything right. It showed organized crime—the Mafia—from the inside in a way approached by no film before it. Its script, with all those memorable lines, may be the most-quoted in history.

Two years later, *The Godfather: Part II* came close to equaling the original's brilliance. Sixteen years after that, *The Godfather: Part III* fell way short. You will still find it in this book, but you'll locate it quicker if you start thumbing from the back.

Since Coppola, three great directors have dominated the gangster genre. Brian De Palma created *Scarface, The Untouchables* and *Carlito's Way*, three very different looks at the subject.

Martin Scorsese, arguably the genre's greatest talent, created five movies that appear among our first 22, from 1973's *Mean Streets* to 2006's *The Departed*. The five masterpieces have much in common—deep, talented casts (including Robert De Niro in three of them), shocking violence (consider the baseball bat scene in *Casino*) and dense, evocative soundtracks (like the use of Derek and the Dominos' "Layla" during the mass killing scene in *GoodFellas*).

In the 1990s, Quentin Tarantino entered the scene as a writer and director. His version of organized crime features dark humor, stylized violence and nonlinear plotlines. His mobsters, like Vincent Vega and Jules Winnfield in *Pulp Fiction*, are seemingly regular guys who converse about fast food and foot rubs before blowing off the head of someone who did their boss wrong. Tarantino's brilliance is in making you sympathetic to the hit men, right up to the moment that they commit a heinous act.

Tarantino sparked a line of imitators, some talented, others not. One we like is Britain's Guy Ritchie, whose 1998 effort, *Lock, Stock and Two Smoking Barrels*, is up to Tarantino's standards. You'll also find Ritchie's follow-up film, *Snatch*, on our list.

Indeed, Great Britain is represented by seven films in our Top 100. There are four from France (starting with the great 1955 caper film *Rififi*), two each from Italy, Japan and Hong Kong, and one each from six other countries.

"I think people around the world are fascinated with gangsters," said British actor Tim Roth, who makes our book for his work in three films. (And don't miss our interview with Roth on page 82.) "Every country has got its version of the mob, right? And it doesn't matter where you're from. If you can slip into that dangerous underworld for two hours, have a few thrills and a box of popcorn, and then go home safe. . . . Well, that form of entertainment is never going to become passé."

There is a vast reservoir of movie information—some of it accurate, some of it not so accurate—in today's world of the Internet. We took advantage of some of the best websites, including the Internet Movie Database (www.IMDb.com), during our research. We also found articles and reviews—some decades old—that were helpful in giving context to films and adding background on actors and directors.

There is even a site (moviebodycounts.com) that offers "body counts" in action movies. And while we're on that topic, please note we tried our best to be accurate, but when bullets are flying and bodies are dropping, an exact count is sometimes impossible to come up with. Add to that the reality that not everyone who falls down after being shot dies and you see the problem. If you want to quibble with us about the number of kills in a given movie, well, go ahead.

Finally, a word about our take on foreign-language films. These were perhaps the most difficult to rank, in part because their stories take place in different cultures, but also because subtitles take something away from a movie. Consider this: how do you think the classic explanation for the meaning of the term "fuhgedaboudit" in *Donnie Brasco* would play with French or Japanese or German subtitles? So, when we're viewing a foreign film, we assume there's always a bit lost in translation.

1 THE GODFATHER (1972–R)

STARS: MARLON BRANDO, AL PACINO, JAMES CAAN, ROBERT DUVALL, DIANE KEATON
DIRECTOR: FRANCIS FORD COPPOLA

The Godfather changed everything. This milestone in cinema revived a genre that had languished for decades. Nearly every gangster movie produced since starts with *The Godfather* as its primary point of reference.

"It created the game," said Chazz Palminteri, whose film, *A Bronx Tale*, centers on growing up around mobsters. "Any of us today who make a movie about organized crime should realize that without *The Godfather*, we never would have had the chance."

But it did more than that. For better or worse, *The Godfather* changed how audiences view Mafiosi, elevating them from nasty thugs to a modern incarnation of Roman royalty. *The Godfather* does not present organized crime as an evil empire presided over by heartless men. Indeed, we never even see victims with lives destroyed by the mob's illicit activities. The treachery only occurs against traitors within the business, and the mob is a family enterprise presided over by a sympathetic patriarch. Decades later, Vito Corleone would become Tony Soprano.

The Godfather made careers, most notably those of Francis Ford Coppola and Al Pacino, despite the fact that both of them were almost fired during production. All these years later, it's still thrilling to watch Pacino as Michael, the Don's youngest son, evolve from an innocent outsider among his own family into a stone-hearted killer. Watch Pacino's eyes deaden over the course of the 175-minute film as he becomes the man his father never wanted him to be. It's why *The Godfather* is, ultimately, a tragedy.

Of course, it also revived Marlon Brando's career after he was deemed box-office poison. Brando's Vito Corleone is one of cinema's all-time greatest characters—gruff but charming, brutal but genteel. Brando and Coppola invented the persona—right down to the puffed-out jowls—and in doing so spawned a million imitators.

"It's the underworld and it's interesting to look on the dark side," actress Talia Shire, who plays Vito's daughter Connie, told *Vanity Fair*. "But in this darkness there is the Vito Corleone family. Remember when Vito says, 'There's drugs,' which he didn't want to touch? He's a decent man on the dark side who is struggling to emerge into the light and bring his family there. That's what still makes it dramatically interesting."

Indeed, the movie has aged better than any Barolo. Filmed in 1971 and set in the period of 1945-55, *The Godfather* still amazes, no matter how many times you've seen it before. The detail is awe-inspiring, from the beautiful tree-lined mountains of Sicily to that small moment when Enzo the Baker, after staring down assassins outside the hospital, cannot flick his cigarette lighter because of quavering hands.

There's a brilliant balance of action and drama, perhaps best exemplified by the baptism-massacre scene. Notice the rapid shift between shots of Michael at his nephew's baptism—vowing to renounce Satan—to shots of his enemies being gunned down all over town. The organ music swells as Michael becomes Godfather—by both definitions.

The Godfather is packed with rich characters, even in secondary roles. Clemenza (Richard Castellano), the jovial caporegime who teaches Michael how to cook the sauce. Fredo (John Cazale), the weakling brother who botches his father's protection. Moe Greene (Alex Rocco), the blustery Vegas casino owner who tries to dismiss Michael ("I made my bones while you were going out with cheerleaders") and ends up paying with a bullet through the eye.

Consider, too, what this movie brought to the modern vernacular: "I'll make him an offer he can't refuse." "Sleeps with the fishes." "Go to the mattresses." "This is business, not personal." Even the word "godfather" had no real meaning in modern culture until this movie. Now Google lists over three million references that start with "the godfather of…."

There is a scene in the movie *You've Got Mail* (a film you definitely won't find in this book's Top 100), where Tom Hanks' character describes *The Godfather* as "the *I-Ching* . . . the sum of all wisdom." Certainly, it provides life lessons:

"A man who doesn't spend time with his family can never be a real man."

"Don't ever take sides against the family."

"Women and children can be careless, but not men."

Okay, maybe that last reference seems dated. But the rest are words to live by. Not everyone, however, has used those lessons for the greater good.

"It made our life seem honorable," Salvatore "Sammy the Bull" Gravano, of the Gambino crime family, told the *New York Times* in 2000. "I would use lines in real life like, 'I'm gonna make you an offer you can't refuse.' And I would always tell people, just like in *The Godfather,* 'If you have an enemy, that enemy becomes my enemy.' It influenced the life, absolutely."

Well, we wouldn't endorse that. But if the real goodfellas buy into it, there must be something genuine there.

For all of those reasons, there is no doubt that *The Godfather* is the greatest gangster movie ever made. In fact, we would argue that it's the greatest movie of any type ever made. But that's for another book.

"I DON'T THINK PEOPLE REALIZE THE EXTRAORDINARY ALCHEMY: AN AGING STAR, A YOUNG ACTOR, A LOT OF PEOPLE IN THE RIGHT MOMENT IN THEIR CAREERS. IT WAS A GREAT MOMENT IN THE MOVIE BUSINESS— A GREAT ERA—AND IT ALL CRYSTALLIZED IN THIS TIME."

—PETER BART, vice president of production for Paramount Pictures, quoted in the book *The Annotated Godfather: The Complete Screenplay*

The Godfather was a sensation before its first scene was even filmed. Author Mario Puzo's novel spent 67 weeks on the *New York Times* bestseller list. Unfortunately for Puzo, he optioned the rights to Paramount before his book's release, getting a mere $12,500 advance, plus $80,000 more if a movie was actually made. Puzo later received more for cowriting the screenplay.

Despite owning the rights and despite the book's international buzz, Paramount shuffled its feet. Overblown epics fared poorly in the 1960s and mob movies did worse. *The Brotherhood*, starring Kirk Douglas as a Sicilian gangster, was a horrid flop in 1968.

As Paramount sat on the rights to *The Godfather*, others came sniffing around. Burt Lancaster, who loved the novel, tried to buy the property so that he could play Don Corleone. Eventually, Paramount executives decided to make the movie, but on a small budget. The template, believe it or not, was *Love Story* (1970), another Paramount project that had been filmed on the cheap and ended up turning a huge profit.

The first task was to hire a director. Richard Brooks (*The Professionals, Cat on a Hot Tin Roof*) declined because he thought Puzo's story glorified organized crime. Arthur Penn (*Bonnie and Clyde*) was committed to another film. Finally, after a dozen directors turned it down, Paramount approached Coppola. He was 31 years old and had yet to direct a major hit, although he was about to win an Oscar for cowriting the screenplay for *Patton.*

Coppola was also reluctant. He had read the novel and was put off by a major subplot involving Sonny's girlfriend, Lucy, and her abnormally "loose vagina." In the book, Lucy can only enjoy sex with the well-endowed Sonny. Coppola didn't want to create a movie about *that*.

His friend and business partner, George Lucas, recognized the commercial opportunity of *The Godfather* and urged him to find an element of the novel he liked and could build around. So Coppola reread it and latched onto the family dynamics, viewing the tale of a father and his three sons as a Shakespearean tragedy. He further saw the element of the mob struggling to adapt after World War II as a metaphor for capitalism.

Paramount hired the young director—and the battling began immediately. Cost-conscious executives wanted the story set in modern times because it would be cheaper to shoot a movie in contemporary settings than to create elaborate sets for a period piece. And they wanted it filmed either in a studio back lot or in an inexpensive Midwestern city, like Cleveland. Coppola, meanwhile, foresaw an epic. He fought to remain true to *The Godfather*'s time period and to film it in New York and Sicily. He got the studio to agree to a $2.5 million budget—and then exceeded it by $4 million.

The combat continued throughout the process. Bart, one of few Paramount executives who stuck up for Coppola, said afterward that the director was nearly fired five times—even as late as during the editing process.

The largest skirmishes were over casting. In Coppola's mind, just two men—the two he considered the world's best actors—could play Vito Corleone: Marlon Brando and Laurence Olivier. Sir Laurence was committed. And Paramount was adamantly against hiring Brando, calling him overbearing, overweight and over the hill. "I assure you that Marlon Brando will not appear in this motion picture," studio CEO Stanley Jaffe wrote to Coppola. "And furthermore, I order you never to bring the subject up again."

Jaffe preferred Ernest Borgnine or Anthony Quinn. George C. Scott and Richard Conte were considered, with Conte later landing the role of Don Emilio Barzini, Vito Corleone's rival. Comic actor Danny Thomas was even discussed, in what would have become *Make Room for Godfather*.

Coppola stuck to his guns. He met with Brando, who had to overcome his own doubts that he could play an Italian. Finally, the studio capitulated, and signed Brando at the bargain rate of $50,000 upfront and a back end of the gross, not to exceed $1.5 million. To his eternal dismay, Brando later sold back the royalties for a measly $300,000.

Casting the role of Michael proved as nettlesome. Higher-ups favored a star for the crucial role, suggesting Warren Beatty, Jack Nicholson or Robert Redford. Coppola wanted Pacino, who had yet to appear in a substantive movie role, but impressed the director by winning a Tony on Broadway. Robert Evans, Paramount's head of production, dismissed the five-foot-seven Pacino as "a runt." And when Coppola pointed out that Pacino's grandparents had immigrated to America from Corleone, Sicily, he was told that the actor looked "too Italian."

"The war over casting the family Corleone was more volatile than the war the Corleone family fought on screen," Evans wrote in his 1994 memoir, *The Kid Stays in the Picture*.

To his credit, Coppola stood by his choice for each major role—James Caan as Sonny, Robert Duvall as Tom Hagen, John Cazale as Fredo and Diane Keaton as Kay. The only time he deferred was hiring his sister, Talia Shire, to play Connie. Coppola did not want to be accused of nepotism. He also thought she was too pretty for the character.

Brando studied for his role by meeting with people connected to the Mafia who were relatives of actor Al Lettieri (Virgil Sollozzo in *The Godfather*). He designed the wide-jowled mien for his character, saying that Vito should "look like a bulldog." And he created the voice by listening to audiotapes of testimony from the 1950s Kefauver Committee hearings, which probed organized crime. "Important people don't need to shout," Brando concluded.

"I thought it would be an interesting contrast to play him as a gentle man, unlike Al Capone, who beat up people with baseball bats," Brando wrote in his autobiography, *Songs My Mother Taught Me*. "I saw him as a man of substance, tradition, dignity, refinement, a man of unerring instinct who just happened to live in a violent world and who had to protect himself and his family in this environment."

Caan, who grew up Jewish in Queens, modeled his character's mannerisms after gangsters he met over the years. He had a tougher time creating Sonny's machine-gun speech pattern until coming upon an unlikely muse.

"I started thinking of Don Rickles," he recalled to *Vanity Fair* in 2009. "Somebody was watching over me and gave me this thing: being Rickles, kind of say-anything, do-anything."

It shows through in Sonny's best line: "What do you think this is, the army, where you shoot 'em a mile away? You gotta get up close, like this—and *bada-bing!* You blow their brains all over your nice Ivy League suit." Caan says that "bada-bing," which became an iconic mantra, wasn't in the script. "It just came out of my mouth," he told *Vanity Fair*. "I don't know from where."

Improvisation like that played a huge role in *The Godfather*'s success. Consider, for example, Don Corleone's hard slap across the face of singer Johnny Fontane (Al Martino) and his barked instruction to "act like a man." That unscripted moment occurred because Brando felt Martino was acting stiffly, so he tried to get a rise out of him.

As the movie was being filmed in New York, an actual mob war broke out, initiated by Crazy Joey Gallo. The same week that the crew shot scenes of Michael ordering the execution of his enemies, real-life Mafiosi Joe Colombo Sr. was shot in the head at a Unity Day rally in Columbus Circle. Colombo (as you will read further down) had fought against *The Godfather*'s production until forging a deal with Paramount. He slipped into a coma after the shooting and lingered for seven years before dying in 1978.

The mob war only added to the buzz around the movie. *The Godfather* opened nationwide in March 1972 and, within months, became the highest-grossing film of all time, a distinction it held until "the summer of *Jaws*" in 1975. Stock in Gulf + Western, which owned Paramount, jumped $97 million within a month. Ticket prices, which averaged $1.50 at the time, were doubled or tripled for *The Godfather*. NBC bought the television rights for a then-record $10 million and later broadcast the film to an audience of 42 million Americans.

The Godfather won the Oscar for Best Picture. Coppola and Puzo won an Academy Award for Best Adapted Screenplay. Brando was announced as the Best Actor Oscar winner, a moment most remembered for Brando's sending of a faux-Native American named Sacheen Littlefeather to decline the award on the actor's behalf in protest. Overall, it was nominated for 11 Academy Awards. Pacino, Caan and Duvall all got bids for Best Supporting Actor, but split the vote—allowing Joel Grey to take home the prize for his work in *Cabaret*.

Perhaps the person most shocked at the film's success was Coppola, who had been told throughout that his dream would fail. "I fantasized that Mephistopheles popped out of the bushes and said: 'Francis, how would you like this movie to be the most successful movie ever made?' " Coppola said in *The Annotated Godfather*. "Something like that must have gone down, because the idea that this disastrous movie would be successful and remembered and even in the annals where it would be compared to movies that I thought were among the greatest, is so surprising."

⊙ **HIT:** One of Coppola's last fights was to keep intact the haunting score composed by Nino Rota. Fortunately, he won that battle, too.

⊗ **MISS:** There's nothing that misses in this epic film—except, perhaps, for the whiff of a punch Sonny aims toward brother-in-law Carlo as he beats him in the street. You'll hear the sound of a smack, but the swing misses Carlo by a solid foot.

✒ **WHAT THEY WROTE AT THE TIME:** "They have put pudding in Brando's cheeks and dirtied his teeth, he speaks hoarsely and moves stiffly, and these combined mechanics are hailed as great acting. . . . Like star, like film, the keynote is

inflation. *The Godfather* was made from a big best-seller, a lot of money was spent on it, and it runs over three hours. Therefore, it's declared important."—Stanley Kauffmann, *The New Republic*

☺ **GOOF:** The horse's head under movie producer Jack Woltz's silk sheets does not appear to be the head from his prized thoroughbred Khartoum. In an earlier scene, Khartoum is shown with a white patch between his eyes. The disembodied head in the bed is solid brown.

The head, by the way, is real and was supplied by a dog-food maker after earlier shots with a fake head looked, well, fake. The blood soaking Woltz's bed is made from Karo syrup, a technique conceived by makeup man Dick Smith. In his director's notes for this scene, Coppola wrote to himself, "If the audience does not jump out of their seat on this one, you have failed."

✔ **REALITY CHECK:** On his way to getting gunned down, Sonny's car radio is playing the October 3, 1951 broadcast of the Dodgers-Giants playoff game, which ends with Bobby Thomson's famed "Shot Heard 'Round the World." Only problem is the scene takes place in 1948. That's one hell of a radio Sonny's got.

◉ **REPEATED WATCHING QUOTIENT:** We'll take our cue from the great Pacino. "It's funny," he said in a 2004 interview, "but anytime I see it on TV, I still stop and watch it."

🎬 **PIVOTAL SCENE:** Young Michael's plan, of course, is to stay out of the "family business." That changes when his jaw is broken by corrupt police Captain McCluskey (Sterling Hayden) outside the hospital where Michael's father is recuperating.

The Corleone sons know the Don's enemies, while calling for reconciliation, will stop at nothing short of killing him. So a plan is concocted where Michael ("the nice college boy," as Sonny calls him) will agree to a meeting with McCluskey and Virgil Sollozzo (Al Lettieri), and then assassinate them.

They head to an Italian restaurant in the Bronx, where Corleone spies have planted a gun in the men's room ("I don't want him coming out of that toilet with just his dick in his hands," says Sonny). The backdrop is perfect—a neighborhood joint with a checkered tile floor and linen tablecloths. The three men sit around a small table and the waiter uncorks a bottle of red wine. "All I want is a truce," Sollozzo assures Michael.

As planned, Michael excuses himself to go to the bathroom. After a few panicked moments of groping for the hidden gun, he pulls it from behind an old box-and-chain toilet and tucks it into his belt.

Michael returns to the table. Sollozzo begins to speak, now in fluent Sicilian. His tone is reassuring, but his face is menacing. "Al [Lettieri] was perfect," Coppola says in the film's DVD commentary, "such a strong villain for Michael to play against."

An elevated train screeches by, obscuring Sollozzo's words. You also hear Michael's heart pounding. Suddenly, he pushes back from the table, stands and fires. A pink mist sprays from Sollozzo as the bullet burns through his forehead. Michael then turns on the dirty cop, firing twice and killing McCluskey as he lifts a forkful of veal ("the best in the city").

In that moment, the young man whose father dreamed of him being a doctor or senator has become a cold-blooded executioner. The smartest of the Corleone sons has taken his first step toward becoming Don.

The turning point for the plot was also a turning point for Pacino. Before this was filmed about a week into shooting, Paramount executives were displeased with what they saw from the young actor, and considered firing him. But his evolution in this scene—"kindly to menacing in a few minutes," says Coppola—floored everyone involved in *The Godfather*. "Al really showed his stuff," Coppola says.

One more note: Pacino sprained his ankle fleeing the restaurant and missed the next three days of shooting. If you spot a cane in the background of other scenes, it's the one he used between takes.

➡ **DON'T FAIL TO NOTICE:** The use of oranges as an omen of impending doom. There are six separate shots of oranges during *The Godfather*, and each time one of the characters in the scene winds up dead. See if you can spot all six.

➡ **DON'T FAIL TO NOTICE II:** The words Mafia and Cosa Nostra are never spoken in the film. This was part of an agreement between producer Al Ruddy and a pressure group called the Italian-American Civil Rights League, which was headed by the aforementioned Colombo.

◀ **CASTING CALL:** Robert De Niro, then an unknown 27-year-old, was cast in the small role of Paulie, the traitorous driver who calls out sick the day Don Corleone is shot. De Niro was released from his contract when he signed to appear in another mob movie, *The Gang That Couldn't Shoot Straight,* which proved to be a dud. Obviously, had De Niro stayed in this picture, he would not have been able to play young Vito in *The Godfather: Part II.*

🔫 **VIOLENCE LEVEL:** One of the amazing aspects of *The Godfather* is its ability to veer from beauty (say, the opening wedding scene) to brutality (Woltz awakening with the severed horse's head). Make no mistake; this is a bloody, sometimes sadistic film.

👊 **BET YOU DIDN'T KNOW:** Lenny Montana, who plays Luca Brasi, was a former professional wrestling champion who fought under the name "The Zebra Kid." He also reportedly worked for a time as a bodyguard for the Colombo family. Montana's fumbling of his lines when he thanks Don Corleone during the opening wedding scene was not rehearsed—it was the genuine result of a non-actor feeling intimidated sharing a scene with the great Brando. The shots of him nervously rehearsing were added later.

● BET YOU DIDN'T KNOW II: Caan was furious when he first saw the finished film, saying that more than 30 minutes of his scenes were cut out. Among those deleted was his personal favorite, which showed him too unnerved to sit in his father's power chair after Vito gets shot.

" BEST LINE: It's too easy to pick, "I'll make him an offer he can't refuse." The one we find ourselves repeating, often for no apparent reason, was improvised by actor Richard Castellano as Clemenza: "Leave the gun, take the cannoli."

● "I KNOW THAT GAL": The baby "boy" being christened is actually Francis Ford Coppola's infant daughter, Sofia. She appeared in all three *Godfather* films—as a child on the ship crossing the Atlantic in *Part II* and in the larger role of Michael and Kay's grown daughter, Mary, in *Part III*. Her subsequent acting career was not as impressive as her work as a director in such films as *The Virgin Suicides* and *Lost in Translation*.

    The Godfather is quite the Coppola family affair. In addition to daughter Sofia and sister Talia Shire, Francis' father, Carmine, wrote some of the music and appears as the piano player in the "go to the mattresses" scene. His cousin sings the aria at the wedding, and his mother appears as an extra during the christening.

● IF YOU LIKED THIS, YOU'LL LIKE: *The Godfather Trilogy: 1901-1980*, Coppola's 1993 re-editing of all three *Godfather* movies in chronological order. It runs 583 minutes and includes scenes edited out of the original movies. Our favorite added moment has Vito Corleone and his sons visiting the deathbed of wartime consigliere Genco Abbandando.

● BODY COUNT: Seventeen—fourteen by gunfire, two by garroting and poor Apollonia, who gets blown up in the car.

2 THE GODFATHER: PART II (1974–R)

STARS: ROBERT DE NIRO, AL PACINO, ROBERT DUVALL, DIANE KEATON, JOHN CAZALE, TALIA SHIRE | DIRECTOR: FRANCIS FORD COPPOLA

It's hard to imagine, but not everyone liked this movie when it was first released in 1974. In fact, two major critics, Roger Ebert and Vincent Canby, offered less than glowing reviews.

The film's 11 Academy Award nominations (and six Oscars) demonstrated that both the viewing public and the Hollywood cinephile thought differently.

So do we.

This is rightly considered one of the all-time best gangster films. And it is, without question, the best movie sequel ever made. Categorizing it as a sequel may not be exactly correct, however, since about a quarter of the movie is devoted to the early life of Don Vito Corleone, which would make it, technically speaking, a semi-prequel.

We're not here to quibble over semantics.

What *The Godfather: Part II* did was address the two major questions viewers were left asking after the stunning success of *The Godfather*:

Where did Don Corleone come from, both literally and philosophically?

And where was Michael Corleone going?

The answers come in dramatic fashion.

Al Pacino reprises his role as Michael and offers us an Ivy League Machiavelli. He has his father's cunning and guile, but somewhere along the way lost his compassion. How else do you explain his decision to have his own brother, Fredo (John Cazale), killed long after any damage Fredo has done to the family has been repaired?

Both his sister Connie (Talia Shire) and his consigliere and adopted brother Tom Hagen (Robert Duvall) try to negotiate a pass for the hapless and tragic Fredo (played again to perfection by Cazale).

Michael won't budge.

It was one thing not to give Tessio a pass. Michael's actions there, while cold and ruthless, were understandable. But there is nothing to gain by killing Fredo, no lesson to impart, no point to be made.

Still, Michael wants Fredo dead—although he kindly orders that the hit not be carried out until their mother has died. Talk about a family man!

When Tom, in frustration, tells him he's won and asks why he wants to wipe everyone out, Michael replies with ice, "I don't feel I have to wipe everybody out, Tom, just my enemies."

But by this point, enemies are all that Michael has.

He has isolated himself from nearly everyone he ever loved or who ever loved him. He has taken his children away from his estranged wife Kay (Diane Keaton), he has banished Fredo from the family and he has denigrated and belittled Tom Hagen.

Only his bodyguards and enforcers remain by his side, and they're obviously paid to do so.

Michael is clearly a victim of what Kay calls "the Sicilian thing that's been going on for 2,000 years." It destroyed their marriage and it destroyed his humanity.

Michael Corleone in *The Godfather: Part II* is a 20th-century prince corrupted by the machinations described in Niccolo Machiavelli's 16th-century political treatise. Does the end justify the means? If power corrupts, does absolute power corrupt absolutely?

Coppola and his script coauthor Mario Puzo explore those questions in both *Godfather I* and *II*, but it is the portion of Michael's story recounted here that drives home their answers. His father wanted things to be different for Michael. We know that from the first movie.

But the quiet and self-assured young Michael Corleone who says, "We'll get there, Pop" has disappeared by the time middle-aged Michael is sitting alone at his Lake Tahoe estate as *The Godfather: Part II* ends.

A flashback scene of the four brothers (including James Caan as Sonny) offers a glimpse of the way things used to be and shows us a young Michael full of hope and promise. But those days are gone, lost in the grab for power that included taking over another casino in Las Vegas, dealing with and battling against the sinister Hyman Roth (Lee Strasberg) in Cuba and matching wits and influence with a Senate subcommittee investigating the American Mafia.

Hope and promise, along with revenge (another Sicilian thing), are also what we get from the fascinating story of the early days of Vito Corleone, the young boy who came to America in 1901, fleeing the Mafia don in the town of Corleone who murdered his father, mother and brother. The boy loses his surname as he is processed through Ellis Island. It is a small, but touching moment in the film and one that surely resonated with many viewers. Like scores of other immigrants whose names were changed or bastardized, Vito Andolini became Vito Corleone when a clerk mistook his hometown for his surname.

Robert De Niro is masterful as he takes up the role of Vito Corleone as a young man with the wit and instinct of a Mafioso in the most favorable sense of that word. Despite being poor and struggling to make ends meet for his family in New York's Little Italy, he is a man of honor. He embodies *omerta*, the term that is most frequently associated with the Mafia's code of silence, but that in actuality means "to be a man." A man, in that world view, takes care of his own problems. He doesn't look to the authorities for assistance; doesn't complain.

The nobility that Puzo has transcribed in both his book and his screenplays—nobility that some sociologists and law enforcement officials contend never really existed—is captured in the Vito Corleone character that both De Niro and Marlon Brando portrayed.

One of the few lines that De Niro utters in English in *The Godfather: Part II* echoes a classic line from the original movie. When an incredulous young Clemenza (Bruno Kirby) asks how he intends to convince Don Fanucci to take less money than he has asked for, young Vito shakes his head knowingly and says, "I make him an offer he don' refuse. Don' worry."

Don Corleone has become an iconic figure in both the American underworld and in pop culture. "An offer he can't refuse" is now part of our lexicon.

In *The Godfather: Part II*, Young Vito's murder of Don Fanucci is one that we can appreciate, if not condone. While he and his associates will clearly benefit, he is ridding the neighborhood of the parasitic agent of the Black Hand. It is a victory over evil.

And later, his brutal slaying of Don Ciccio in Sicily to avenge the murders of his family members is one we can understand, if not celebrate.

Contrast those killings with Michael's decision, for example, to have a hooker brutally murdered in order to frame a senator and force him to do the family's bidding.

One generation removed from the hills of Sicily and from the teeming streets of Little Italy, Michael has lost his way.

He has, both Puzo and Coppola seem to be saying, become an American.

⊙ **HIT:** De Niro's performance as the young Vito Corleone on the streets of Little Italy is one of the high points of the movie. Nearly every scene foreshadows the development of the character we already know from Brando's performance in the original. We see the cunning and the ruthlessness in the plotting and the assassination of Don Fanucci. But there is humanity and genuine compassion as well. Young Vito's dealings with the landlord, for example, are both humorous and indicative of the way the don would operate throughout his life. The same can be said for the

way he developed a friendship and business relationship with Clemenza (Bruno Kirby).

⊗ **MISS:** What's not to like? But if you want to pick nits, there's one issue that doesn't ring true. It hardly seems likely that Tom Hagen would be permitted to visit Frankie Pentangeli (Michael Gazzo) in jail, let alone get permission to smoke a cigar with him on an Army base where the wiseguy-turned-government informant was being housed. And while we're on the subject, after Pentangeli reneges on his deal with the government and recants his testimony before the Senate subcommittee, why is he still being given special treatment by the Feds? In real life, he would have been moved to a high security wing of a federal prison for his own protection, but the cushy quarters at the Army base would have disappeared shortly after he failed to deliver what he had promised the subcommittee.

✎ **WHAT THEY WROTE AT THE TIME:** (File these under critics don't always know best): "It's a second movie made largely out of the bits and pieces of Mr. Puzo's novel that didn't fit into the first. It's a Frankenstein's monster stitched together from leftover parts. It talks. It moves in fits and starts but it has no mind of its own. Occasionally it repeats a point made in *The Godfather* (organized crime is just another kind of American business, say) but its insights are fairly lame at this point."—Vincent Canby, *New York Times*

And:

"What we're left with, then, are a lot of good scenes and good performances set in the midst of a mass of undisciplined material and handicapped by plot construction that prevents the story from ever really building."—Roger Ebert, *Chicago Sun-Times*

✔ **REALITY CHECK:** While the flashback scenes of Don Corleone's early life are based almost entirely on Puzo's original novel, the continuation of the Michael Corleone story is built around actual events. His appearance before a Senate subcommittee, for example, is reminiscent of the famous Kefauver Committee hearings that brought organized crime into America's living rooms via television news reports in the 1950s. One of the biggest gangsters called before the committee was Frank Costello, a New York City don not unlike Michael Corleone. The fall of Cuba's dictator Fulgencio Batista and the financial hit the mob took when it lost its casinos there is also based on actual events. And the character Hyman Roth is clearly built around legendary mob financial wizard Meyer Lansky. The "We're bigger than U.S. Steel" line uttered by Roth has often been attributed in real life to Lansky, who is credited with turning the American Mafia into an economic force in the 1950s and 1960s.

➡ **DON'T FAIL TO NOTICE:** De Niro got an Academy Award for Best Supporting Actor, which is noteworthy on several levels. Coupled with Brando's Best Actor Academy Award in *The Godfather*, it was the first time two actors won Oscars for portraying the same character.

Even more interesting—and often overlooked—is the fact that De Niro hardly spoke any English in the film. Almost every one of his lines is uttered in the Sicilian dialect, which he studied while living in Sicily in preparation for the role. And the lines he does deliver in English come with an Italian accent.

👁 **REPEATED WATCHING QUOTIENT:** Almost any scene, and especially those from the early days, is a set piece worth watching again and again. This is a movie that any fan of cinema can revisit repeatedly and come away impressed.

😈 **"I KNOW THAT GUY":** He's a lot younger and appears taller, but the voice is unmistakable. Johnny Ola, Hyman Roth's go-fer and the guy who turns Fredo against Michael, is played by Dominic Chianese who has done a lot of character acting but who is best known to younger viewers as Uncle Junior from the HBO series *The Sopranos*.

🍎 **BET YOU DIDN'T KNOW:** *The Godfather: Part II* was the first sequel in Academy Awards history to win a Best Picture Oscar. The film also garnered awards for Best Director, Best Supporting Actor (De Niro), Best Adapted Screenplay (coauthored by Puzo and Coppola), Best Art Direction/Set Decoration and Best Original Dramatic Score (Nino Rota and Carmine Coppola). Other nominations included Best Actor (Pacino), two for Best Supporting Actor, (Michael Gazzo and Lee Strasberg), and one for Best Supporting Actress (Shire).

🗩 **BEST LINE:** "My father always told me, 'Keep your friends close, but your enemies closer,'" Michael tells Tom, while explaining why he is dealing with Hyman Roth even though he knows Roth tried to have him killed. The American Film Institute rated the line number 58 on its list of the 100 most quoted movie lines.

🔫 **VIOLENCE LEVEL:** Controlled but constant. This was an underworld where murder was a negotiating tool employed both to settle disputes and send messages.

💀 **BODY COUNT:** Sixteen.

3 GOODFELLAS (1990–R)

STARS: RAY LIOTTA, ROBERT DE NIRO, JOE PESCI, LORRAINE BRACCO
DIRECTOR: MARTIN SCORSESE

Eighteen years after *The Godfather* portrayed a Mafia ethos based on family ties and a code of honor, *GoodFellas* came along to show the flip side.

There is no romance here. No looking out for one's people. No myth of a moral code. Instead, *GoodFellas* is about psychopaths who steal, kill and ultimately betray each other. It's two-and-a-half hours of blood, depravity and—that most American of vices—greed. Director Martin Scorsese summed up his subjects' wiseguy lifestyle in three words:

"Want. Take. Simple."

Oh, and by the way, it's a brilliant movie packed with dozens of colorful characters. The soundtrack of songs from the 1950s through the '80s compliments the action (and was, reportedly, among the most costly in movie history). *GoodFellas* is edited so tightly and flies by so fast that you may want to watch it again. Immediately.

Scorsese, in an interview with film critic Gavin Smith, applauded *The Godfather* as "epic poetry," while contrasting his film as "like some guy on the street corner talking." *GoodFellas*, he said, serves as an antidote to *The Godfather*, "in terms of [the characters'] attitude. They don't give a damn, especially when they're having a good time and making a lot of money. They don't care about their wives, their kids, anything."

The movie is based on the Nicholas Pileggi book *Wiseguy* (the title was changed for the movie to keep if from being confused with the 1987-90 television series *Wiseguy*). Pileggi, a renowned crime reporter, portrays the life of Henry Hill, a half-Irish, half-Italian drug dealer, arsonist, truck hijacker and extortionist. Hill, because of his non-Italian blood, could never become a "made man" in the Mafia. Or, as Pileggi told the *New York Times*, "He was an outsider, an observer. Henry was a thug, but he was a visiting thug."

The movie script, cowritten by Pileggi and Scorsese, doesn't stray far from the book's depiction of actual events. If anything, it's grubbier than real life.

GoodFellas opens with a jarringly violent stabbing-shooting of a guy in a car trunk. The scene ends with the camera frozen on the face of Henry, played by Ray Liotta. "As far back as I can remember," he calmly narrates, "I always wanted to be a gangster."

We then go back to Brooklyn in the 1950s, where Henry, age 12, gets his start as a go-fer for neighborhood capo and father figure Paulie Cicero (Paul Sorvino). He talks like a kid in love. "To me, it meant being somebody in a neighborhood that was full of nobodies." The wiseguys, he explains, "weren't like anybody else. I mean, they did whatever they wanted."

For his internship, the youngster firebombs cars and helps fence smuggled cigarettes (for which he takes his first rap). As he matures, he graduates into more serious crimes, like, say, murder one. At no point does Henry show remorse. This is entirely about business.

His mentor is Jimmy "the Gent" Conway (Robert De Niro), an amoral thief who, like Henry, cannot become a made man because of his Irish blood. His pal is Tommy DeVito (Joe Pesci), a punk prone to killing people who don't treat him with enough respect. Tommy's violent side shocks even his fellow mobsters. In one scene, Tommy degrades a young waiter named Spider (Michael Imperioli), forcing him to dance like "The Oklahoma Kid" and shooting him in the foot. Later, when Spider gives him lip, Tommy fires five shots into the poor kid's chest.

Henry also meets Karen (Lorraine Bracco), a nice Jewish girl from the suburbs he impresses by taking to the Copacabana. In perhaps the greatest Steadicam shot ever, the couple wind their way from the Copa's back door, through its kitchen, into the nightclub (all to the Crystals' "Then He Kissed Me"), to a front-row table, where they receive complimentary champagne and hear Henny Youngman crack, "Take my wife. Please." Good times.

This three-minute continuous shot—inspired by Scorsese friend/rival Brian De Palma and his wonderful tracking shot of Sean Connery's character getting murdered in *The Untouchables*—involved more than 400 precisely timed moments and is as graceful as a ballet. Henry greets everyone he passes—the maître d', gamblers, other goodfellas—and presses $20 bills into each waiter's hand. The scene establishes him as a big deal—at least in the eyes of the woman who soon becomes his wife.

Henry and the gang mature into some damned talented criminals. They reach their apex with the $5 million theft of cash and jewels stored in a vault at JFK Airport. The plot is based on the real December 1978 Lufthansa Airlines heist, the largest robbery ever committed on American soil at the time.

Of course, these being crooks, they eventually turn on each other. Rather than pay off the guys who actually stole the loot, Jimmy Conway whacks them (to the piano coda of "Layla"). "When they found Carbone in the meat truck," Henry notes, "he was frozen so stiff it took them two days to thaw him out for the autopsy."

Henry, by then a coke addict, becomes paranoid that he will be Jimmy's next victim. So when he gets busted by the Feds, he immediately becomes a snitch, testifies against his lifelong friends and gets a new life under the federal government's witness protection program. There is no soul searching because, as Pileggi wrote, "He has no soul. He has all the moral fortitude of a cheap-jack stockbroker trying to hustle."

Henry's only regret in the end is that the high life is over for him. *GoodFellas* closes with a shot of him walking out of a small suburban tract house in his bathrobe and leaning down to pick up a newspaper. In the purgatory where the government has relocated him, spaghetti and marinara sauce are replaced by egg noodles and ketchup. "I'm an average nobody," he complains. "I get to live the rest of my life like a schnook."

"He's angry about it," Scorsese said in an article in *GQ*. "And to a certain extent, I think that was a provocation of the audience, too—that these people lived this way, did these things, and he's complaining that he can't do it any more."

In its first public showing, *GoodFellas* bombed. A test audience in conservative Orange County, California gave it the worst preview grades in Warner Brothers' history.

"People got so angry they stormed out of the theater," Scorsese said. "They thought it was an outrage that I made these people so attractive."

The studio considered holding back the film or recutting its violent scenes. Eventually, Warner Brothers released it without changes in September 1990, but sent it to fewer and smaller theaters than originally planned. Word of mouth and strong reviews helped it develop legs. By Christmas, it proved to be one of the year's biggest hits.

Pesci won an Oscar for Best Actor in a Supporting Role and *GoodFellas* was nominated for five other Academy Awards, including Best Picture. That award was won by Kevin Costner's *Dances with Wolves*.

All these years later, you tell us—*GoodFellas* or *Dances with Wolves*?

⊙ **HIT:** So many great moments, we feel compelled to mention one more. The portrayal of Henry's final day as a wiseguy—the end of his downhill slide—is brilliant.

Strung out on cocaine, Henry's got a full agenda: collect his wheelchair-bound brother from the hospital, unload some hot guns, make the Sunday gravy, pick up a drug shipment and prepare it for distribution—all while dodging those helicopters that seem to be tailing him. In Henry's frenzied state, each chore takes on equal importance. It hits

the crash point when his drug mule, Lois, insists she must return to Rockaway to pick up her lucky hat before flying.

The scene is edited with fast, frenetic cuts. It's backed by hard-beating samples from a dozen artists—the Rolling Stones, the Who, Muddy Waters, and others. You feel as jumpy and paranoid watching it as Henry appears on screen.

"I've had a couple people come up to me who were users," Liotta told *GQ*. "And they said they would cue up that scene just to remember what that stuff could do to you."

⊗ **MISS:** We can't find anything to knock, so we'll leave that to misguided *Variety* critic Joseph McBride: "Dramatically unsatisfying. . . . Undercut by the off-putting, opaque characterization of Ray Liotta [who] develops a flashy, pretty-boy persona. . . . Scorsese misguidedly abandons his focus on the mob community to tell the unrewarding story of a lone wolf. . . . The film rambles seriously, wearing out its interest at least half an hour before it's over."

What was *he* watching?

◀ **CASTING CALL:** Al Pacino, John Malkovich and William Petersen all turned down the role of Jimmy Conway. Tom Cruise and Sean Penn were considered for Henry Hill. And Madonna was producer Irwin Winkler's first choice to play Karen Hill.

Think about that: Tom Cruise and Madonna. Slightly different movie, eh?

◉ **REPEATED WATCHING QUOTIENT:** What number is higher than infinity?

🎬 **PIVOTAL SCENE:** Henry deals drugs while imprisoned to keep his family from going broke on the outside. Upon his release, he's feted at a party at Paulie Cicero's house. After dinner, Paulie leads Henry into the backyard for a private chat.

"I know you did what you had to do in there. But I don't want any more of that shit," Paulie warns, his arm pulling Henry in tight. Paulie recalls another mob boss who received a 20-year sentence because one of his crew was selling behind his back. "Don't make a jerk out of me," he cautions.

"Just don't do it."

Henry looks his mentor in the eye. He emphatically vows to stay away from dealing.

Cut to the apartment of Henry's gumad, Sandy (Debi Mazar). As the soundtrack blares "Gimme Shelter," a bleary-eyed Henry dices a mound of cocaine with a playing card.

"I could see that this was a really good business," he says in narration, noting that he cleared $12,000 in one week. His betrayal of Paulie would prove to be their undoing.

✎ **WHAT THEY WROTE AT THE TIME:** "Watching *GoodFellas* is like going to the Bronx Zoo. You stare at the beasts of prey and find a brute charisma in their demeanor. You wonder how you would act if you lived in their world, where aggression is rewarded and decency is crushed. Finally you walk away, tantalized by a view into the darkest part of yourself, glad that that part is still behind bars."—Richard Corliss, *Time*

➡ **DON'T FAIL TO NOTICE:** At times, *GoodFellas* seems like an audition for *The Sopranos*. Nearly two-dozen actors appear in both this movie and that landmark HBO series. Most notable are Bracco (Dr. Jennifer Melfi), Imperioli (Christopher Moltisanti), Vincent Pastore ("Big Pussy" Bonpensiero), Frank Vincent (Phil Leotardo) and Tony Sirico (Paulie "Walnuts" Gualtieri). Actress Suzanne Shepherd plays the mother of both Karen Hill and Carmela Soprano.

One more almost made it. *The Sopranos* creator David Chase has said that he talked with Liotta about the role of Ralphie Cifaretto, which was ultimately played by Joe Pantoliano, and ranks as one of the show's all-time creepiest characters. (See *Six Degrees of Sopranos Separation* on page 30.)

😐 **"I KNOW THAT GUY":** That's Samuel L. Jackson in the minor role of getaway driver Stacks Edwards. Jackson was 41 years old when *GoodFellas* came out. The late bloomer did not become a Hollywood star until age 45, with the release of *Pulp Fiction*.

☹ **GOOF:** Henry Hill somehow goes from being right-handed to left-handed as he grows from a teenager to an adult. Of course, this is because the actor who played young Henry, Christopher Serrone, is a righty, while Liotta is a lefty.

🖤 **BET YOU DIDN'T KNOW:** Many of the small parts in *GoodFellas* are played by real mob figures. Scorsese felt they imparted genuineness to the film. "Mob guys love it, because it's the real thing and they knew the people in it," said Pileggi, "They say, 'It's like a home movie.'"

Watch, particularly, for the character of Fat Andy, who is played by Louis Eppolito, a former New York City cop who also worked for the Lucchese crime family. Years later, Eppolito was convicted of murder and racketeering, and received a life sentence.

🗨 **BEST LINE:** Could it be anything other than:

Tommy: "Let me understand this 'cause, you know, maybe it's me. I'm a little fucked up maybe. But I'm funny how? I mean, funny like I'm a clown? I amuse you? I make you laugh? I'm here to fucking amuse you? What do you mean funny? Funny how? How am I funny?"

The discomforting scene between Tommy and Henry was borne out of an incident Pesci had as a young restaurant worker when he complimented a mobster on his sense of humor. Scorsese allowed Pesci and Liotta to improvise their dialogue. The other actors in the shot were not told what would occur because Scorsese wanted their unrehearsed reactions.

🚩 **VIOLENCE LEVEL:** There's high, there's higher, and then there's Pesci in his prime. Just ask poor Billy Batts.

Batts (Frank Vincent) is a made man celebrating his release from prison in a bar owned by Henry. When Tommy also comes by, Batts takes a few verbal swipes, telling the one-time shoeshine boy to "go home and get your fucking shine box." It's major league ball busting but Tommy, as a relative youngster, is supposed to take it from an older guy who's his superior in the business.

He doesn't. Instead he leaves the bar, comes

back when the rest of Batts' party has gone, and—joined by Jimmy Conway—stomps Batts into near death (the final blows come later). As they wrap Batts' mutilated body in tablecloths, Tommy shows his only remorse, telling Henry, "I didn't mean to get blood on your floor."

⊛ **IF YOU LIKED THIS, YOU'LL LIKE:** *Shooting Henry Hill*, a 2007 documentary by Luke Heppner, who tracks the real Henry Hill. You learn that Hill was eventually tossed from the witness protection program for ongoing criminal activity. He battles alcoholism and works as a cook in an Italian restaurant.

⚔ **BODY COUNT:** Ten, but it feels like a whole lot more.

SIX DEGREES OF SOPRANOS SEPARATION

Watching the movies in this book can often seem like going to a *Sopranos* family reunion. In dozens of these films, you'll spot *Sopranos* cast members—sometimes in leading roles, sometimes as the guy in the back of the room pushing the rack of hot minks.

"If it hadn't been for *GoodFellas* or *Carlito's Way* or *A Brooklyn State of Mind*, I don't think there would have been a Big Pussy, at least for me," said actor Vincent Pastore, who is, in fact, the guy schlepping the furs in *GoodFellas*. His film *Brooklyn* doesn't make our Top 100, but you get his point.

It's fun to go back and watch Dominic Chianese playing Hyman Roth's henchman, Johnny Ola, in *The Godfather: Part II* long before he became Uncle Junior. Or see a younger James Gandolfini preparing for his role as Tony Soprano by portraying a bodyguard in *Get Shorty*.

By our count, 32 regulars and semi-regulars from *The Sopranos* appear in 27 of our Top 100 films. For the sake of this list, we set a minimum standard of five appearances on that landmark HBO series combined with at least one appearance in one of our Top 100 gangster films. That takes out a guy like Burt Young, who had one great *Sopranos* guest spot as Bobby "Bacala" Baccalieri Sr. and, of course, played bad guy Bed Bug Eddie in *The Pope of Greenwich Village*.

But plenty of other *Sopranos* cast members fulfilled the minimum criteria to make this list, which is ordered based on the number of our Top 100 films the actor appeared in. The name of the actor is listed first, with the name of his or her *Sopranos* character in parentheses, followed by the number and names of the Top 100 gangster movies he or she appeared in.

1. Paul Herman (Beansie Gaeta).
Seven—*Bullets Over Broadway, Heat, Casino, GoodFellas, At Close Range, The Pope of Greenwich Village, Once Upon a Time in America.*

2. Steve Buscemi (Tony Blundetto).
Four—*Pulp Fiction, Reservoir Dogs, Miller's Crossing, King of New York.*

3. Frank Vincent (Phil Leotardo).
Four—*Casino, Federal Hill, GoodFellas, The Pope of Greenwich Village.*

4. Vincent Pastore ("Big Pussy" Bonpensiero).
Three—*Made, Carlito's Way, GoodFellas.*

5. Tony Lip (Carmine Lupertazzi).
Three—*Donnie Brasco, GoodFellas, The Pope of Greenwich Village.*

6. Tony Darrow (Larry Boy Barese).
Three—*Bullets Over Broadway, GoodFellas, Kill the Irishman.*

7. James Gandolfini (Tony Soprano).
Two—*True Romance, Get Shorty.*

8. Joe Pantoliano (Ralph Cifaretto).
Two—*Bound, Midnight Run.*

9. Tony Sirico (Paulie "Walnuts").
Two—*Bullets Over Broadway, GoodFellas.*

10. John Cenatiempo (Anthony Maffei).
Two—*True Romance, The Departed.*

11. Edie Falco (Carmela Soprano).
One—*Bullets Over Broadway.*

12. Lorraine Bracco (Dr. Jennifer Melfi).
One—*GoodFellas.*

13. Michael Imperioli (Christopher Moltisanti).
One—*GoodFellas.*

14. Dominic Chianese (Uncle Junior Soprano).
One—*The Godfather: Part II.*

15. Drea de Matteo (Adriana La Cerva).
One—*Made.*

16. Steve Schirripa (Bobby "Bacala" Jr.).
One—*Kill the Irishman.*

17. Johnny Ventimiglia (Artie Bucco).
One—*Bullets Over Broadway.*

18. Federico Castelluccio (Furio).
One—*Made.*

19. Sharon Angela (Rosalie Aprile).
One—*Ghost Dog: The Way of the Samurai.*

20. Max Casella (Benny Fazio).
One—*Analyze This.*

21. Robert Funaro (Eugene Pontecorvo).
One—*American Gangster.*

22. Kathrine Narducci (Charmaine Bucco).
One—*A Bronx Tale.*

23. Suzanne Shepherd (Carmela's mother, Mary DeAngelis).
One—*GoodFellas.*

24. David Proval (Richie Aprile).
One—*Mean Streets.*

25. John "Cha Cha" Ciarcia (Albie Cianflone).
One—*GoodFellas.*

26. Richard Portnow (Attorney Hal Melvoin).
One—*Ghost Dog: The Way of the Samurai.*

27. Frank Pellegrino (FBI Bureau Chief Frank Cubitoso).
One—*GoodFellas.*

28. Marianne Leone (Joanne Moltisanti).
One—*GoodFellas.*

29. Louis Lombardi (Skip Lipari).
One—*The Usual Suspects.*

30. Elizabeth Bracco (Marie Spatafore).
One—*Analyze This.*

31. Lillo Brancato (Matt Bevilaqua).
One—*A Bronx Tale.*

32. Joseph Siravo (Johnny Boy Soprano).
One—*Carlito's Way.*

4 ON THE WATERFRONT (1954–NR)

STARS: MARLON BRANDO, EVA MARIE SAINT, KARL MALDEN, ROD STEIGER, LEE J. COBB | **DIRECTOR:** ELIA KAZAN

More than a half-century has passed since the release of *On the Waterfront*, a landmark film that captured eight Oscars for its gritty look at corruption on the docks of Hoboken, N.J. But the movie is still recalled today for so much brilliance—Marlon Brando's amazing performance as an inarticulate pug battling his union leader and his own conscience; an unparalleled supporting cast; an uncompromising screenplay; the outstanding—albeit politically motivated—direction of Elia Kazan.

Each of those facets is worth remembering. But there's something more here than just nostalgia. All these years later, *On the Waterfront* continues to

work as a magnificent bit of drama—and as a gangster movie. The story of a little man caught between principles and loyalties always resonates. And, last we checked, the problem of mob influence on America's labor unions hasn't gone away.

Watch it today—for the first time or for the 50th—and *On the Waterfront* still moves you. Some of the classics in this book—say, the original *Scarface* or *Bonnie and Clyde*—might seem dated, or at least products of their eras. But this script, this direction, even the musical score, could hit the box office today and still be fresher than anything out there. We just don't know who could match the work of the original cast.

For a moment, however, let's go back to 1954 to consider the film in the context of the times. Remember, *On the Waterfront* reached theaters around the tail end of the McCarthy era when the country—particularly Hollywood—was torn over the issue of people naming names to government committees. If the script is one about conscience, so is the story behind the script.

Kazan and screenwriter Budd Schulberg became Hollywood pariahs a few years earlier for fingering former associates (some of whom ended up blacklisted) to the House Un-American Activities Committee. When *On the Waterfront* came out, many filmgoers watched the story of a man betraying old friends and colleagues and deemed it an attempt by its two creators to justify their actions.

Kazan didn't disagree. "Every day I worked on that film, I was telling the world where I stood," he wrote in *A Life*, his 1988 autobiography. "And I was telling my critics to go and fuck themselves."

Regardless of where anyone stands on that issue, it should not detract from the film's brilliance—and its importance as a muckraking work of art. The screenplay is based on *New York Sun* reporter Malcolm Johnson's 1949 Pulitzer Prize-winning exposé of that city's waterfront and the influence of mob boss Albert Anastasia. Schulberg's adapted script is essentially true to real life.

The story opens with former boxer and current flunky Terry Malloy (Brando) unwittingly serving as bait in a murder trap set for a fellow longshoreman. The young man, named Joey Doyle, is pushed off a rooftop for speaking to a Waterfront Crime Commission panel investigating the methods of crooked union boss Johnny Friendly (Lee J. Cobb).

Friendly's got a hell of a gig. In addition to collecting dues from his own members, he forces them to kick back a further bit of their salaries for every day's work. Plus, he takes another illegal cut from any shipper running goods through "my dock-yards." If a worker protests, he is mangled by Johnny Friendly's goons.

"You get up in a [union] meeting," one down-trodden longshoreman explains. "You make a motion, the lights go out, and then you go out. That's how it's been since Johnny and his pals took over the local."

In a great bit of casting, three of those "pals" are played by real ex-boxers who fought Joe Louis for the heavyweight title—Tony Galento, Tami Mauriello and the gargantuan Abe Simon.

Anyway, Terry's inadvertent role in the murder has him chased by the Furies of remorse—personified by crusading waterfront priest Father Barry (Karl Malden) and Edie Doyle (Eva Marie Saint, in her movie debut), the sister of the man Terry set up. Of course, he falls for the girl, making things all the more complicated.

Eventually, Terry is subpoenaed to speak to that Crime Commission. Initially he blows off the investigators (look for a young Martin Balsam, also in his first movie), saying, "I've been on the docks and there's one thing I've learned: You don't answer no questions, you don't ask no questions."

The priest and the girlfriend keep talking into both of his ears, explaining things like compassion and a moral sense of right and wrong. "Conscience!" Terry screams out. "That stuff can drive you nuts."

Those angels on one shoulder are counterbalanced by Terry's loyalty to his own big brother, who works as a legal lieutenant to the corrupt union boss. "Charley the Gent" (Rod Steiger) apparently got all the family brains and fashion sense. He is accurately described by one lowly worker as "a butcher in a camelhair coat."

"They're asking me to put the finger on my own brother," Terry protests to Father Barry. "And Johnny Friendly used to take me to ball games when I was a kid."

"You've got a brother, eh?" the priest retorts. Pointing to the crowd of longshoremen, he adds, "Well you've got some other brothers. And they're getting the short end while Johnny's getting mustard on his face at the Polo Grounds."

Ultimately, Terry is pushed into a position that demands he betray someone. We already told you how Kazan's own McCarthy Era testimony impacted the story, so there's no great surprise where he's going. We can tell you that the real-life situation upon which the script was based did not have as triumphant an ending. In the movies, the good guys win. In life, well . . . not always.

In this story, the reluctant crusader topples corruption. There's a wonderful scene—far from the grimy docks—showing the bigger bigwig, the unnamed mob higher-up behind the seat of power (and listed in the credits as "Mr. Upstairs") viewing Terry's televised testimony to the Crime Commission. He is seen only from behind, sitting in a cushy chair, cigar in hand, as he angrily orders a butler to turn off the TV in his mansion.

"Anything else, sir?" the butler asks.

"Yes, Sidney. If Mr. John Friendly calls, I'm out."

"Anytime today, sir?"

"If he calls ever, I'm out."

That cuts to the final scene, in which Terry—ostracized after his testimony—heads back to the docks to demand his rights. He is brutally beaten by Friendly's henchmen, but the workers who witness it rally behind him. He becomes a working-class hero, Friendly gets tossed off the pier and we fade to black as Terry leads them all back to work and, presumably, a corruption-free union.

Brando was 29 when *On the Waterfront* was shot, and his character ranges from cocky to tortured to brutishly sexual. "Brando completely inhabits the role of a man trapped by his own life," wrote *Los Angeles Times* film critic Kenneth Turan. "The play of emotions on his face are as memorable as the iconic red and black plaid wool jacket he wears." Similarly, Roger Ebert of the *Chicago Sun-Times* wrote, "During the course of his career (especially the early portion of it), Brando gave some amazing performances, but nothing he did before or after rivals his depiction of Terry Malloy."

Brando won the Academy Award for Best Actor in a Leading Role, giving a mumbling 16-second speech when Bette Davis handed him the Oscar. (On a side note, call up that moment on YouTube, and you'll be treated to seeing Davis in an outfit that would make Lady Gaga envious.)

Overall, *On the Waterfront* was one of Hollywood's most-honored movies ever, garnering awards for Best Picture, Best Director (Kazan), Best Actress in a Supporting Role (Eva Marie Saint), as well as art direction, cinematography, editing and screenplay.

Steiger, Cobb and Malden were all nominated for the Best Supporting Actor. They split the vote, allowing the Oscar to go to Edmond O'Brien for *The Barefoot Contessa*. Given a ballot, we'd have gone with Malden.

⊙ **HIT:** Boris Kaufman's Oscar-winning black-and-white camera work is perfect for the story. Filmed on location in hardscrabble Hoboken, it colors the tenements, the piers and the puny little parks in bleak shades of gray. And watch how Kaufman films the faces of the workers—most of them actual longshoreman hired as extras. There's a genuineness that cannot be faked.

⊗ **MISS:** Not much to dislike here. If forced to criticize, we'd suggest that the ending gets a little too pat, as the "D and D" (deaf and dumb) longshoremen suddenly rally behind Terry and literally throw Johnny Friendly out of power. But, hey, that's a minor quibble and we're already 107 minutes in.

✎ **WHAT THEY WROTE AT THE TIME:** "Kazan succeeds in producing a shrewd piece of screen journalism, a melodrama in the grand manner of *Public Enemy* and *Little Caesar*. But he fails to do anything more serious—largely because he tries too hard. In searching for the general meaning in little lives, Kazan watches his characters through the magnifying glass of the old sentimental prejudice that ordinary people are wonderful no matter what they do."—Brad Darrach, *Time*

◉ **REPEATED WATCHING QUOTIENT:** Tremendously high. This richly textured masterpiece reveals fresh nuances upon every viewing.

▤ **PIVOTAL SCENE:** One of the cinema's classic moments occurs when Johnny Friendly dispatches Charley to ascertain whether his younger brother is going to turn against the gang and testify after being subpoenaed.

The two men meet in a cab, shrouded by venetian blinds. Charley tries to cajole Terry, to bribe him with a cushy union job, to bully him into keeping his mouth closed. But Terry isn't sure what he's going to do. Finally, frustrated, Charley impulsively pulls a gun on his kid brother. "Do you think," Charley shouts, "that Johnny's going to jeopardize his whole thing for one rubber-lipped ex-tanker who's walking on his heels?" And then, pleading, "Take this job, Terry."

Rather than being scared or angered by the gun, Terry pities his older brother. He pushes the gun away with, as Kazan put it, "the gentleness of a caress." Charley, embarrassed, tries to pull the conversation back to Terry's derailed boxing career, blaming his failures on "the skunk we got you for a manager (who) brought you along too fast."

But Terry reproaches his older, smarter brother for selling him out.

"It wasn't him, Charley, it was you," Terry retorts. "Remember that night in the Garden? You came down to my dressing room and you said, 'Kid, this ain't your night. We're going for the price on Wilson.' You remember that? 'This ain't your night.' My night? I coulda taken Wilson apart. So what happens? He gets the title shot outdoors in the ballpark and what do I get? A one-way ticket to Palookaville. You was my brother, Charley, you shoulda looked out for me a little bit. You shoulda taken care of me just a little bit so I wouldn't have to take them dives for the short-end money."

In that five-minute scene of lost love between the brothers, Brando's character—until then an inarticulate oaf—realizes his capacity for decency. Now, there is no doubt what he is going to do.

" BEST LINE: That cab scene ends with Charley suggesting that even though he forced his brother to take a dive in the ring, Terry got his payoff. "We had bets down for you," Charley says. "You saw some money."

"You don't understand," says Terry. "I coulda had class. I coulda been a contender. I coulda been somebody, instead of a bum, which is what I am, let's face it. It was you, Charley."

Those final lines were selected by the American Film Institute in 2005 as the third-best movie quote ever, behind only, "Frankly, my dear, I don't give a damn," (from *Gone with the Wind*) and, "I'll make him an offer he can't refuse" (from *The Godfather*).

⬙ BET YOU DIDN'T KNOW: Sometimes great art comes about by accident. Much has been made of the intimate mood created by those blinds in the taxi's rear window. Brilliant. Except that it was never planned. The camera department neglected to bring rear-projection equipment to the set that day (which would have allowed for a typical street-scene background), so the blinds were quickly rigged to keep the production moving.

☺ "I KNOW THAT GUY": There's no mistaking the skinny stooge named Slim following around Johnny Friendly. That's Fred Gwynne, the actor who would later play TV's Herman Munster, here making his film debut. That dumb look is merely a ruse—Gwynne graduated from Harvard as an English major and supported himself as a musician and book illustrator before becoming an actor.

➡ DON'T FAIL TO NOTICE: During his testimony at the Crime Commission hearing, Slim states his name as "Mladen Sekulovich." That happens to be the given name of Karl Malden, who, like many actors of his era, changed it for Hollywood. Malden always rued giving up his Serbian name, and persuaded Kazan to insert it into the film as a nod to his ethnic heritage.

◀ CASTING CALL: Lots of back story here. Grace Kelly was first offered the role of Edie, but turned it down to film *Rear Window*. Newcomer Elizabeth Montgomery (later of *Bewitched*) was also considered, but Kazan deemed her too sophisticated for the character.

The role of Terry was written for John Garfield, but he died in 1952 at the age of 39. Producer Sam Spiegel then petitioned Brando, who returned the script with a terse refusal. Meanwhile, Kazan approached Frank Sinatra, who eagerly accepted.

Spiegel, however, was adamant, in large part because he knew Brando would be better box office than Old Blue Eyes. So he and Kazan concocted a ploy to persuade Brando. They sent Malden—who had already signed on—to the Actors Studio (where Brando was learning his craft) and had Malden direct a scene from the movie with the role of Terry played by another young up-and-comer . . . named

Paul Newman. Brando watched the exercise and immediately changed his mind. It's debatable whether he was swayed by love for the script or potential envy over Newman landing the role.

☺ **GOOF:** Watch the body as Joey Doyle is hurled from the tenement roof to his death. It's clearly a stuffed dummy.

🐾 **BODY COUNT:** Three—one tossed from a building, one crushed by a falling load of whiskey bottles and one shot and hung on a meathook. Given the choice, we suppose, we'd pick the second option.

✹ **IF YOU LIKED THIS, YOU'LL LIKE:** *Force of Evil*, a 1948 potboiler starring the aforementioned John Garfield as a crooked lawyer who wants to take over New York City's numbers rackets—putting him into direct conflict with the brother he loves.

5 PULP FICTION (1994–R)

STARS: JOHN TRAVOLTA, SAMUEL L. JACKSON, UMA THURMAN, BRUCE WILLIS
DIRECTOR: QUENTIN TARANTINO

Pulp Fiction is more than a mere masterpiece. It's a force that produced new stars (Quentin Tarantino and Samuel L. Jackson) and revitalized careers (John Travolta and Uma Thurman). It kicked open Hollywood's doors to a new breed of writers and directors—wannabes aiming to duplicate the magic Tarantino created.

It generated more than $200 million at the box office, yet achieved a cult-like anti-mainstream status for millions of obsessive fans. Indeed, it became an arbiter of cool for the post-Boomer generation. Nearly two decades after its release, its characters, music and especially its dialogue are iconic.

Time ranked *Pulp Fiction* among the 100 best movies ever made. *Entertainment Weekly* named it the best film of the quarter-century between 1984-2008. Top critics Roger Ebert and Richard Corliss both called it the most influential film of the 1990s. And the American Film Institute ranked it No. 7 all-time among gangster films.

We think that's too low.

Pulp's brilliance is in how it draws you into the world of fundamentally dislikeable characters—hit men, dealers, and other assorted criminals—so that for two hours and 35 minutes, you are willing to suspend your moral judgment. They become sympathetic figures, regular folk debating the same

"YOU KNOW WHAT THEY CALL A QUARTER POUNDER WITH CHEESE IN PARIS? THEY CALL IT A ROYALE WITH CHEESE." FOX FORCE FIVE. VINCE'S 1964 CHEVELLE MALIBU. LANCE (ERIC STOLTZ) WATCHING THE THREE STOOGES WHILE MUNCHING ON FRUIT BRUTE CEREAL. ANTOINE ROCCAMORA (A.K.A. TONY ROCKY HORROR). "JUNGLE BOOGIE." THE GOLD WATCH. "BRING OUT THE GIMP."

mundane topics the rest of us argue about—although their exchanges are much wittier.

And, in a comedy that is darker than Michael Corleone's heart, you find yourself delighted at the most inappropriate moments. People are shot, raped and tortured, and you ask yourself: Should I be laughing? Should I be appalled? Sometimes, it's like chuckling at a gun being pointed at your face.

There's no real message to *Pulp Fiction*, which may be why some fans love it. It's not about family, like *The Godfather*. Or loyalty, like *Donnie Brasco*. Some of its bad guys win, some lose. Really, it's more amoral than immoral.

Part of the joy is not always knowing who the good guys are. Tarantino shot *Pulp Fiction* as a time-twisting weave of stories where villains can become heroes, or a guy peppered with bullets in one scene comes back from the dead, so to speak, in the next.

Behind it all is a hipness in everything from the wardrobe to the set design to the beat-heavy soundtrack that kicks off with Dick Dale's guitar classic "Misirlou" in the opening credits.

Pulp Fiction is a zigzagging symphony of three plots, none of them particularly original. "I wanted to start with the oldest chestnuts in the world," Tarantino told film writer Gerald Peary. "You've seen them a zillion times. The guy goes out with the mobster's wife—but don't touch her. The boxer who is supposed to throw the fight, but doesn't. Two characters go to kill someone."

What makes it work is the ingenious way the characters overlap, sliding from one segment to another. You don't really know how the puzzle is going to fit together until the end—so that you need to learn the legacy of Butch's gold watch to understand why he risks his life to retrieve it, which

leads to Vince Vega's death and that nightmarish scene in the basement of that pawn shop.

What *really* makes it work is the dialogue written by Tarantino and coauthor Roger Avary. The characters here are in bizarre situations (cleaning brains and skull from a car, for example), but their conversation is rarely used to explain what's going on. Instead, they engage in rapid-fire literate exchanges on everything from gourmet coffee to the relative cleanliness of pigs and dogs.

Samuel L. Jackson, who costars as hit man Jules Winnfield, recalled to *Total Film* magazine in 2006 his original reaction to seeing the screenplay. "I read it straight through, which normally I don't do," he said. "Then I took a breath and read it again, which I never do. Just to make sure it was true. It was the best script I'd ever read."

For our money, Jackson steals the movie as the Old Testament-quoting assassin who believes he has received a message from God. His eyes glow with ferocity, even as he delivers soliloquies that make him the deepest-thinking mobster you've ever heard. Plus, his comic teamwork with Travolta is the best we've seen since the heyday of Jack Lemmon and Walter Matthau.

Tarantino began writing the script in 1992 with a $900,000 advance he received based on the critical—if not box-office—success of *Reservoir Dogs*. He holed up in Amsterdam (thus all the references in *Pulp*), taking an apartment with no telephone. He spent nights in Holland's legal hash bars and days immersing himself in French gangster films.

Pulp Fiction was originally contracted to TriStar Pictures. But just before production was to begin, studio chief Michael Medavoy dropped the project, calling the script—according to coauthor Avary—"the worst thing ever written . . . too long,

"THE PATH OF THE RIGHTEOUS MAN IS BESET ON ALL SIDES. . . ." THE TWIST CONTEST AT JACK RABBIT SLIM'S. JULES' "BAD MOTHER FUCKER" WALLET. "HAMBURGERS, THE CORNERSTONE OF ANY NUTRITIOUS BREAKFAST." THE UC SANTA CRUZ BANANA SLUGS. PUMPKIN AND HONEY BUNNY HOLDING UP THE DINER. "FIVE LONG YEARS HE WORE THIS WATCH. UP HIS ASS. THEN HE DIED OF DYSENTERY."

violent, and unfilmable."

Fortunately, Miramax Films did not feel the same way about it. That studio, just taken over by Disney, of all corporate entities, picked up the project and assigned it an $8.5 million budget.

Typically, a budget that size would preclude signing major stars. But Bruce Willis, among the highest-paid actors at the time, viewed *Pulp* (wisely) as a chance to change his Hollywood image by appearing in a quirky indie film. He signed for a minimum salary to play Butch, the end-of-the-line boxer with his own plan to rip off the mob.

Tarantino wanted Uma Thurman for the role of mob wife Mia Wallace, partly, he said, because he fell in love with her feet (she does walk around barefoot a lot and there is that subplot about foot massages). Thurman was reluctant, having been shocked by the brutality she saw in *Reservoir Dogs*. "I found it rather terrifying," she said. "But I was just overwhelmed by Quentin's incredible energy."

The big casting surprise was Travolta, who had, by then, been reduced to playing second banana to a baby in the *Look Who's Talking* trilogy. Tarantino—over everyone's objections—insisted on hiring the faded *Saturday Night Fever* star to portray the coolest-of-cool gangsters. He even gave Travolta a dance scene, twisting away at Jack Rabbit Slim's.

A black tie and jacket replace Tony Manero's white polyester suit. And Vince Vega carries both a paunch and a heroin habit. But the role revived Travolta's career like *The Godfather* revived Brando's. He earned a Best Actor Oscar nomination (an award taken by Tom Hanks in *Forrest Gump*) and his per-picture salary grew from $140,000 in *Pulp* to $20 million for *A Civil Action* in 1998.

"Quentin will always be my guardian angel," Travolta later told *Cinecon.com*.

Pulp Fiction was nominated for seven Oscars, including Best Picture. It won just one, with Tarantino and Avary taking the Academy Award for Best Original Screenplay. It was also awarded the top prize at the 1994 Cannes Film Festival—an announcement that sparked some booing in the audience. Tarantino gave his critics the finger.

Its $212 million box-office gross is huge considering its dark nature. And, as we said, it launched some careers and revived others. More than anything, it made Tarantino into a pop icon.

All these years later, it still shines. The interwoven stories of junkies and murderers and petty thieves remains fresh and original. The quotable dialogue, the pumping soundtrack, the twists and turns still offer revelations upon each viewing. This is one Big Kahuna of a movie.

◉ **HIT:** Among all the great performances in *Pulp Fiction*, two actors who do cameos deserve special mention. First is Harvey Keitel as the tuxedoed Winston Wolfe, the Zen-like fixer whose specialty is getting rid of unwanted gore. "You've got a corpse in a car minus a head in a garage," he tells Vincent and Jules in his icy manner. "Take me to it."

Second is Christopher Walken as Vietnam POW camp survivor Capt. Koons, who hands young Butch Coolidge the gold wristwatch passed down four generations—and hidden for five years up Butch's dad's rectum and another two up the captain's. Walken rehearsed his three-minute monologue for eight weeks, creating a rhythm and cadence that makes it a spooky tweak of his role in *The Deer Hunter*. Brilliant.

"CHECK OUT THE BIG BRAIN ON BRETT." THE BAND-AID ON MARSELLUS WALLACE'S (VING RHAMES') NECK. THE WOLF IN HIS TUXEDO. "THAT'S 30 MINUTES AWAY. I'LL BE THERE IN 10." JIMMIE (TARANTINO) IN HIS BATHROBE. "OH MAN. I SHOT MARVIN IN THE FACE." "SON OF A PREACHER MAN." RED APPLE CIGARETTES. BIG KAHUNA BURGER. "I'MA GET MEDIEVAL ON YOUR ASS."

⊗ **MISS:** We cringe every time Maria de Medeiros comes on screen as Butch's girlfriend Fabienne (a.k.a. Lemon Pop), baby-talking about her desires for a pot belly and "bloooberry penkecks."

✎ **WHAT THEY WROTE AT THE TIME:** "You get intoxicated by it, high on the rediscovery of how pleasurable a movie can be. I'm not sure I've ever encountered a filmmaker who combined discipline and control with sheer wild-ass joy the way that Tarantino does."—Owen Gleiberman, *Entertainment Weekly*

✔ **REALITY CHECK:** Most of Jules' Ezekiel 25:17 speech ("The path of the righteous man. . .") is nowhere in the Bible. Rather, it is largely cribbed from the 1973 Japanese movie *The Bodyguard*, starring Sonny Chiba—one of Tarantino's all-time favorites.

Still, it's a really cool speech.

☺ **GOOF:** According to two doctors we consulted, injecting someone's heart with adrenaline to revive her from a heroin overdose (as Vincent does with Mia) would do no good. First, heroin overuse causes your respiratory system to shut down—not your heart to stop. Second, it's not the appropriate medicine for the problem. And even if it did work, the patient would not spring up like an alarm clock just went off, but slowly regain consciousness and sobriety.

Still, it's a really cool scene.

◉ **REPEATED WATCHING QUOTIENT:** Watch it three or four times to fully comprehend the intertwined, time-arcing plotlines. After that, just watch it again for its sheer brilliance.

🎬 **PIVOTAL SCENE:** The first scene of Vincent and Jules is mind-blowing. You see them driving, gabbing about McDonald's and foot-massage etiquette until they arrive at a nondescript apartment building. You know they're up to no good (especially when they pull guns from the trunk), but you're not sure exactly what.

They arrive at the apartment of the young dealers who have stolen from their boss, Marsellus Wallace. As a nervous Brett tries to talk his way out of trouble, Jules calmly samples his burger and Sprite. Then, almost as an aside, Jules shoots Brett's reclining cohort ("Flock of Seagulls") through the chest. This, of course, leads up to the brimstone Bible speech and the execution of poor Brett.

Chances are, you've seen the scene enough that its shock value is gone. But try to recall the first time. Vincent and Jules are two guys nattering about the topics guys talk about—food, sex, other guys' wives—when suddenly, without warning, they turn into brutal assassins. It's a stunner. And you realize, at that moment that *Pulp Fiction* isn't going to be like any movie you've seen before.

"AND I WILL STRIKE DOWN UPON THEE WITH GREAT VENGEANCE AND FURIOUS ANGER THOSE WHO ATTEMPT TO POISON AND DESTROY MY BROTHERS." "BUSTIN' SURFBOARDS." THE BONNIE SITUATION. "MMMM, THAT IS A TASTY BURGER." MONSTER JOE'S TRUCK AND TOW. BUTCH WITH THE SAMURAI SWORD. ZED'S CHOPPER. "ZED'S DEAD, BABY. ZED'S DEAD."

➧ **DON'T FAIL TO NOTICE:** At the end, you learn that Vincent and Jules are present in the diner while Honey Bunny (Amanda Plummer) and Pumpkin (Tim Roth) are scheming to rob it. This, of course, circles back to *Pulp's* opening scene.

But if you view that opening scene carefully, you learn right then that our hit men are in the house. Turn up the volume as Pumpkin talks about how easy it would be to rob a restaurant. You'll hear Jules in the background talking about quitting the gangster life and "walking the Earth." Then watch over Yolanda's right shoulder as Pumpkin suggests that no restaurant worker would "take a bullet for the owner." You'll spot Vincent, in his blue T-shirt, walking to the men's room.

◀ **CASTING CALL:** Co-executive producer Harvey Weinstein favored Daniel Day-Lewis for the role of Vincent and either Holly Hunter or Meg Ryan for the role of Mia. Fortunately, Tarantino ignored him.

Sylvester Stallone was considered for Butch—like he needed another boxing gig. And Ellen DeGeneres read for the role of Jody, the heroin dealer's wife. We would have loved to see her with all those piercings.

☛ **VIOLENCE LEVEL:** Well, other than the bondage and the rape and Jules driving with poor Marvin's brains splattered in his Jheri curls . . . other than that, yeah, it's still as violent as it gets.

♛ **BET YOU DIDN'T KNOW:** For the scene in which he is high on heroin, Travolta wanted to know what the experience was like without, you know, actually trying the drug. A recovering-addict friend of Tarantino's told Travolta to drink ten shots of tequila and lie down in a hot tub. Travolta later joked that this became his all-time favorite scene to rehearse for.

♛ **BET YOU DIDN'T KNOW II:** There has been much speculation about the mysterious orange-glowing contents of the briefcase that Jules describes as "my boss's dirty laundry." Essayists have suggested it contains everything from atomic explosives to diamonds to Marsellus Wallace's lost soul. According to Tarantino, however, the case is nothing more than a plot device and offers no explanation for its contents. "It's whatever the viewer wants it to be," he said during an appearance on *Inside the Actors Studio*.

♛ **BET YOU DIDN'T KNOW III:** The movie briefly became an issue in the 1996 presidential election when Republican candidate Bob Dole cited it as an example of Hollywood "peddling nightmares of depravity." Dole accused *Pulp Fiction*—which he had not seen—of "promoting the romance of heroin."

🤠 **"I KNOW THAT GUY":** That's Steve Buscemi as the Buddy Holly waiter in Jack Rabbit Slim's, taking the order for burgers—"bloody as hell"—and a $5 Martin and Lewis milkshake.

✹ **IF YOU LIKED THIS, YOU'LL LIKE:** *Pulp Fiction* spawned myriad copycats, as we said. Several of the best of them appear in this book's Top 100. Another good one is *Things to Do in Denver When You're Dead*, a 1995 ensemble film directed by Gary Fleder about an underworld caper gone bad.

⚰ **BODY COUNT:** Seven. We can only imagine the offscreen ending met by poor Zed.

6 | LITTLE CAESAR (1931–NR)

STARS: EDWARD G. ROBINSON, DOUGLAS FAIRBANKS JR., GLENDA FARRELL, STANLEY FIELDS | DIRECTOR: MERVYN LEROY

This is the movie that started it all.

At least that's the conventional wisdom among movie buffs and film critics who track the gangster genre.

Little Caesar—or more to the point, Edward G. Robinson's portrayal of the title character—churned new cinematic ground, creating a film type that has been matched in longevity and popularity only by the Western and the romantic comedy.

You have to wonder if this film—with a storyline that is somewhat melodramatic and concessions to the censorship standards of the day—would have had the same impact had someone other than Robinson been tapped for the lead.

But that's like asking what *Casablanca* would have been like without Bogey or *The Godfather* without Brando.

In a review after the film opened, a critic in the *New York Times* wrote that "Little Caesar [the character] becomes at Robinson's hands a figure out of a Greek tragedy, a cold, ignorant, merciless killer, driven on and on by an insatiable lust for power, the plaything of a force that is greater than himself."

Years later, in an essay that appeared in a gangster film encyclopedia, Phil Hardy wrote that *Little*

Caesar (the movie) "owes almost everything to Robinson's performance as a strutting bantam with a superman complex and paranoia to match."

Both critiques underscore one of the problems that director Mervyn LeRoy and screenwriter W. R. Burnett (who authored the novel on which the movie is based) had to deal with—censorship. There was a production code for the movie industry in the 1930s stipulating that movies were not to lower moral standards or celebrate or empathize with "crime, wrongdoing, evil or sin."

Lurking in the wings was the Catholic Legion of Decency that was founded in the early 1930s and would establish an even harsher code and rating system (although it turns out, the Catholic Church seemed to be more bent on the evils of sex and debauchery than the crimes of mobsters).

Because of this censorship, filmmakers had to be like the novelists of 18th-century France. They wrote stories in which their central figures engaged in all manner of sin and debauchery, but in order to avoid the wrath of the Church and others, the novelists made sure that their characters came to a terrible end, their punishment meted out by an all-seeing God delivering retribution on Earth with the burning fires of hell waiting in the beyond.

Neither Don Corleone nor his son Michael would have made it to the screen in the 1930s, at least not as they were portrayed almost a half-century later. Despite their faults, their flaws—yes, their sins—there was something to be admired about them.

Caesar Enrico Bandello had to be portrayed in such a way that neither his success nor his bravado could be celebrated. Yet Robinson was able to convey something in the character that would be echoed for generations to come in gangster movies.

Sine qua non was the phrase the Romans used centuries ago—"without which, there is none."

Enrico Bandello was the prototype for every film gangster who followed.

The tight-fitting three-piece suits, the high-collared shirt and tie, the fedora and the ever-present cigar—Rico brought it all to the big screen. There was also the tough-guy lingo, usually delivered out of the side of the mouth.

Who else could start the word "yeah" with an "n" and get away with it? It was a combination sneer and challenge, the classic Edward G. Robinson "Nnnnyeah!"

The storyline in *Little Caesar* isn't spectacular. By today's standards it's almost pedestrian. But its mood, the feel, the tension and the wanton violence accurately reflected the underworld of its day and captured the imagination of Depression-era audiences looking for a way to escape their daily grind and misery.

A small-time criminal who wants to make his mark in the big city, Rico—and his partner, Joe Massara (Douglas Fairbanks Jr.)—head for Chicago and the big time.

"Shoot first and argue afterwards," Rico says in explaining his underworld philosophy to his less-than-enthusiastic partner-in-crime. "This game ain't for guys that's soft."

Rico becomes a "torpedo" for Sam Vettori (Stanley Fields). Vettori's gang operates under the umbrella of mob boss Diamond Pete Montana (Ralph Ince) and the city's Big Boy (Sidney Blackmer)—a force in politics, business and the underworld.

Rico is the Sonny Corleone of his time. Ignoring the older mobsters counseling patience, he reaches for his gun to shoot his way out of almost any predicament. One of his victims is the head of the Crime Commission, who gets shot and killed during a New Year's Eve robbery of the Bronze Peacock, a supper club where the mob and the well-heeled intersect.

Rico's partner Massara, who wants to go legit, has helped set up the heist over the objections of his girlfriend and dance partner Olga (Glenda Farrell). Did we mention that Joe Massara's ambition was decidedly different than Rico's? One wanted to dominate the underworld; the other dreamed of a career as a ballroom dancer.

Go figure.

There is a shooting on the steps of a church, lots of plotting at the Club Palermo and a lavish funeral that foreshadows scenes in Little Italy from *The Godfather* decades later.

The loyalty between Rico and Joe is tested several times. Neither quite understands where the other is coming from, but their friendship prevails until Olga—"Love, soft stuff," Rico snarls after learning of their romance—convinces Joe to turn state's evidence and give up the gang. Even then, Rico can't bring himself to shoot Joe, who is wounded by one of Rico's associates.

By that point, Rico has worked his way nearly to the top of the underworld ladder, moving both Vettori and Montana aside and taking aim at the Big Boy himself. But his success quickly comes undone. Arrests, convictions and the execution of Vettori set the stage for the moralistic ending.

On the run, Rico is reduced to living in 15-cents-a-night flophouses. But he comes out of hiding when he reads newspaper articles in which Sergeant Flaherty (Thomas E. Jackson), his long-time law-enforcement nemesis, calls him a coward.

(All the cops, it seems, are Irish, while the gangsters are clearly Italian—a stereotyping in mob movies that to this day still drives the likes of the Sons of Italy wild.)

The final scene and the classic quote from Rico take place in the shadow of a billboard touting the "Tipsy, Topsy, Turvy" dance team of Joe and Olga.

Joe, who turned away from crime, has found success.

Rico, who embraced the gangster life, winds up riddled with bullets.

On screen in the 1930s, it couldn't have ended any other way.

⊙ **HIT:** The movie was rightly cited for its accurate depiction of the underworld of the 1930s. William Wolf said it concisely in an essay in the 1979 book *Landmark Films*: "Even when measured against today's more demanding standards, [*Little Caesar*] is extremely well made. It is taut, brittle, and involving. The violence crackles with realism and produces a sense of terror with its matter-of-fact killing. A vivid recreation of Chicago's underworld, it remains one of the best crime films ever made."

⊗ **MISS:** Early in the movie, Rico and Joe rob a gas station and then walk into an empty diner. Rico moves the clock back to 11:45 p.m. from midnight in order to set an alibi. When the diner owner enters from the kitchen, Joe orders two plates of spaghetti and two cups of coffee.

No way!

There isn't an Italian in America who's going to order coffee with his spaghetti. And there are very few Italians who will order spaghetti in a diner. And spaghetti isn't the kind of comfort food you're looking for around midnight. And when the plates are served (we never actually see what's on them), there is a shot of Rico cutting whatever is on his plate with a knife and scooping it up with his fork. Italians twirl their spaghetti; there is no need for a knife. Enough said.

✎ **WHAT THEY WROTE AT THE TIME:** "From *Little Caesar*, W.R. Burnett's much-admired novel about the rise and fall of a homicidal gang chieftain, comes the truest, most ambitious and most distinguished of all that endless series of gangster photoplays which have been inundating us in recent years. So many pictures celebrating the adventures of America's most picturesque banditti have been manufactured and their formula has become so stale that it is difficult to believe that a fresh and distinctive work on the subject is currently possible. But *Little Caesar*, by pushing into the background the usual romantic conventions of the theme and concentrating on characterization rather than on plot, emerges not only as an effective and rather chilling melodrama, but also as what is sometimes described as a Document. Chiefly, though, it is made important by the genuinely brilliant performance that Edward G. Robinson contributes to the title role."—Richard Watts Jr., *New York Herald Tribune*

✔ **REALITY CHECK:** Several scenes and characters in the movie were taken from the Chicago underworld of the day. The banquet "honoring" Rico and an earlier reference to a similar affair stem from a party that received extensive and less-than-favorable press coverage in which gangsters Dion O'Bannion and Sammy "Nails" Morton were feted by their underworld friends. Diamond Pete, the mob boss that Rico usurps, was fashioned after Big Jim Colosimo (who was rubbed out by Al Capone and Johnny Torrio). The Big Boy was believed to be a veiled reference to "Big Bill" Thompson, the corrupt mayor of Chicago during Prohibition.

◉ **REPEATED WATCHING QUOTIENT:** While the storyline isn't memorable, Robinson's performance is. This is the kind of movie that you pop into the DVD periodically just to watch a scene. Any scene, as long as Robinson is in it.

🍎 **BET YOU DIDN'T KNOW:** The Library of Congress, citing the film's cultural, historical and aesthetic significance, selected *Little Caesar* for preservation in the National Film Registry. And the American Film Institute in 2008 ranked it ninth on its list of Top 10 all-time gangster movies.

◀ **CASTING CALL:** Clark Gable was considered for the role of Joe Massara but Jack Warner, the head of the studio, decided the young, untested actor wouldn't do. Among other things, Warner thought Gable's ears were too big. That didn't seem to bother MGM, the studio that signed Gable and turned him into one of Hollywood's biggest stars.

❚❚ **BEST LINE:** "Mother of mercy, is this the end of Rico?" Robinson's last line in the film is one of the most quoted in the gangster genre. Ironically, the original line, in both the screenplay and the novel on which it was based, is: "Mother of God, is this the end of Rico?" Hollywood, ever conscious of the censors, opted to go with what was considered the less offensive line. Such thinking is hard to imagine today when, among other things, some movie websites track the number of "fucks" uttered in contemporary gangster films. (There were, for example, over 200 in Al Pacino's *Scarface*.)

🔫 **VIOLENCE LEVEL:** Lots of shooting, but as in all the films of this era, there is little gore and the gunplay is fairly antiseptic.

🦵 **BODY COUNT:** A censor-friendly six.

7 THE DEPARTED (2006–R)

STARS: JACK NICHOLSON, LEONARDO DICAPRIO, MATT DAMON, MARK WAHLBERG, MARTIN SHEEN | DIRECTOR: MARTIN SCORSESE

Where to begin?

Nicholson is diabolically brilliant as Boston mob boss Frank Costello.

Leonardo DiCaprio shows acting chops that he had only hinted at in earlier films as the troubled undercover cop Billy Costigan.

Matt Damon is perfectly cast as Colin Sullivan, the seemingly altar boy detective who is the mob mole inside the Massachusetts State Police.

And Mark Wahlberg, Martin Sheen, Alec Baldwin and the rest of the stellar cast make the most of whatever screen time is given them.

This is just a damn good movie, certainly one of the best of the decade and arguably one of the best of all time.

It won four Oscars, including Best Director, an award that had long eluded Martin Scorsese. It also was the first movie based on a foreign film (the Hong Kong gangland thriller *Infernal Affairs*, reviewed elsewhere in this book) to win for Best Picture.

Scorsese and screenwriter William Monahan took the outline of *Infernal Affairs,* grafted it onto actual events that had taken place in the New England underworld and delivered a classic. Their writing and directing do for the Irish underworld of Boston what Francis Ford Coppola and Mario Puzo did for the Italian underworld of New York three decades earlier. Like *The Godfather, The Departed* defines a time, a place and a subculture.

Writing for the *Boston Globe*, Ty Burr said *The Departed* is "the closest we've come yet to The

Great Boston Movie, a beast that requires more honesty than filmmakers (and audiences) have been willing to grant."

Scorsese opens his story with news clips from the turbulent 1970s and the school busing riots that helped give Boston its reputation for racial intolerance and polarization. Against that backdrop, we see Frank Costello in a corner store offering a young boy a handout—paying for groceries that the boy and his family obviously are hard-pressed to afford.

The boy is Colin Sullivan. The act of kindness is Costello's first recruitment pitch. He throws in a comic book for good measure as the boy's eyes light up.

Then, in the first of what seems like an endless stream of comments and one-liners that perfectly define his character, Costello asks the boy, "You do good in school?"

When Sullivan replies that he does, Costello grins (and here Nicholson offers one of those eye rolls that say so much more than the dialogue) and says, "I did too. They call it a paradox."

We get nearly 20 minutes of action before the opening credits roll and by that point the movie is off and running, a nonstop roller-coaster ride of lies, betrayal and double-dealing on the streets and inside police headquarters. Infused with equal parts cynicism and pessimism (stereotypical traits of the Irish-American experience, we're told), the dialogue is crisp, erudite and profane.

There are references to Hawthorne, Shakespeare and James Joyce. Conversely, and while we didn't keep count, the IMDb website notes that the film also includes 237 uses of the word "fuck" or its derivatives. According to IMDb, that's the most ever in a film that won the Best Picture Oscar.

There is a foray into Latin, when Baldwin's Capt. Ellerby tries to get at the motive behind a gangland hit.

"Que bono?" he asks Sullivan. "Who benefits?"

"Que gives a shit?" replies the detective, in dead-on accurate police speak.

There is also a reference, although not entirely accurate, to Freud's take on the Irish as "the only people who are impervious to analysis."

Scorsese used the alias of famous Italian-American gangster Frank Costello (born Francesco Castiglia) for Nicholson's character, but there is no doubt that he is the cinematic version of James "Whitey" Bulger, the notorious Irish mob boss from South Boston who terrorized the city for years. Bulger dealt in drugs, gambling, extortion, prostitution and murder. And on occasion, he ran guns for the IRA to enhance his stature in the poorer Irish neighborhoods of the city.

His brother William Bulger was, at different times, the President of the Massachusetts State Senate and the University of Massachusetts. Whitey clearly went in a different direction. But he managed to bob and weave in a violent underworld for three decades. Only later did it become clear that he had a get-out-of-jail card.

Bulger was a "top echelon" informant for the FBI, the highest and most secret rank of federal snitch. For years, he provided information about underworld rivals, helping the Feds make dozens of cases, most against traditional La Cosa Nostra gangsters. In exchange, two rogue FBI agents who were wined and dined by Bulger fed him the names of underworld figures who were providing law enforcement with information about him.

Some of those people turned up dead.

Both FBI agents were implicated in a criminal conspiracy. One is now serving a lengthy prison sentence. It was not the finest hour for the agency J. Edgar Hoover built.

That back story supports one of the best of many great lines in the movie. Wahlberg's Staff Sgt. Dignam is at a meeting with various law enforcement agencies who have set up a task force to go after Costello. Of the FBI, Dignam says, "My theory is . . . treat 'em like mushrooms. Feed 'em shit and keep 'em in the dark."

Whitey Bulger, who disappeared in 1995 shortly before he was indicted on federal racketeering and murder charges, spent nearly 16 years "in the wind" before being captured in Los Angeles in the summer of 2011. Bulger was on the FBI's 10 Most Wanted list for more than a decade and there were those who believed the feds weren't really interested in bringing him to justice because of the stories he could tell about the FBI's role in his criminal activities.

Some of the story has already surfaced and it's not pretty, although it is sometimes humorous. Much of it is detailed in a 600-page report filed by a federal judge assigned to get to the bottom of the FBI-Bulger relationship. There have also been several books written about it. The best one, for our money, is *Black Mass*.

One anecdote from real life could have been a scene in the movie: In 1985, the DEA had hidden electronic listening devices in Bulger's car. He learned about them (presumably from the FBI) and ripped them out. The DEA guys were listening when it happened and hightailed it over to Bulger's garage. At the very least, they wanted their expensive equipment—valued at about $20,000—returned.

Bulger was happy to give them their bugs, but was curious about what they were up to, telling them, "We're all good guys here. You're the good good guys and we're the bad good guys."

Costello's secret in *The Departed* is that he, too, is an FBI informant. That information changes the dynamic of the cat-and-mouse game that starts when Sullivan and Costigan begin their undercover work.

Matt Damon's Sullivan, a pristine State Police academy graduate, feeds Costello information from inside law enforcement, referring to him as "Dad" whenever he calls on a cell phone.

Meanwhile, DiCaprio's character Costigan is recruited by Capt. Queenan (Martin Sheen) and Sgt. Dignam from the same graduating class and goes undercover after he is bounced from the State Police and jailed on a trumped-up aggravated assault charge. Queenan, in turn, becomes a father figure to the angry, young cop who struggles to make sense of law enforcement, the underworld and his place in all of it.

Playing the role of a hothead with a short temper, DiCaprio works his way into Costello's organization at the same time Sullivan moves up the State Police ladder to a position in the organized crime investigating unit.

Eventually, both sides learn that the other has someone inside. The second half of the movie—full of dropping bodies, one literally from the roof of an abandoned warehouse, the rest falling under the constant spray of bullets—spins around the frantic attempts by Sullivan and Costigan to ferret out the identity of their counterpart.

Both also share a love interest in Madolyn (Vera Farmiga), a police shrink that Costigan is seeing as part of a court-ordered psychiatric evaluation after he is jailed on those phony charges. She eventually becomes the only person that Costigan can trust and indirectly sets up the movie's brutally cold, but satisfying, finale.

Through it all, Costello continues a dizzying commentary as he moves from one underworld gambit to the next, dealing stolen, high-tech microchip processors to the Chinese, moving shipments of cocaine, dismembering bodies and gunning down associates.

"She fell funny," he says offhandedly of a female victim after shooting her in the back of the head as she is kneeling in a field.

There are glimmers of humanity in Nicholson's character, as when he asks an associate about the man's ailing mother.

"She's on her way out," the associate sadly replies.

But then, returning to form, Costello replies, "We all are. . . . Act accordingly."

Whether he's sprinkling cocaine over two prostitutes with whom he is frolicking or berating a pedophile priest in a neighborhood restaurant, Costello is always in motion and constantly taking things to their limit. He is not immoral, but rather amoral, a mob boss who's chosen a life where good and evil no longer seem to matter.

"No one gives it to you, you have to take it," he says in a voice-over in which he decries the lack of initiative on the part of people looking for handouts and good will during the busing riots.

"A man makes his own way," he says at another point.

And, in perhaps his most telling and cynical take on the choice between good and evil, he asks rhetorically, "When you're facing a loaded gun, what's the difference?"

Costigan, Sullivan, Queenan, Ellerby, Dignam and the rest of the cops and gangsters all seem to share a version of that philosophy.

There are plenty of loaded guns in *The Departed* and just as many twisted and complex characters.

⊙ **HIT:** The interdepartmental rivalries that undermine the investigation of Costello are based on fact. For years, organized crime figures benefitted from disorganized law enforcement. There's a lot of that here, separate and apart from the fact that Sullivan is a mole. Again, Dignam nails it. When a surveillance operation goes bad, he gets into a shouting match with a detective from another agency, each asking whom the other thinks he is.

"I'm the guy doing his job," Dignam screams. "You must be the other guy."

⊗ **MISS:** It's hard to find anything not to like. But if we must, the final scene with the rat walking across the balcony railing outside Sullivan's apartment with the dome of the Massachusetts State House in the background was a bit much. It was unnecessary symbolism. We get it.

✔ **REALITY CHECK:** Over the years, Whitey Bulger "sightings" have been reported throughout the Western Hemisphere. At one point, he was "spotted" in Ireland (makes sense). At another, in Sicily (go figure). But the best was a report that he was seen walking out of a movie theater in Seattle. The film playing that night was *The Departed*.

💬 **BEST LINE:** There are so many that it's hard to pick one. We'll go with Frank Costello's (Nicholson's) opening lines, "I don't want to be a product of my environment. I want my environment to be a product of me."

✒ **WHAT THEY WROTE AT THE TIME:** "All the actors bring their A games to this triumphant bruiser of a film, its darkly wanton wit the only defense against complete chaos."—Peter Travers, *Rolling Stone*

◀ **CASTING CALL:** Both Ray Liotta and Denis Leary were considered for the role of Dignam, but each had prior commitments. Robert De Niro turned down the role of Queenan to appear in *The Good Shepherd*, a movie that DiCaprio dropped out of to play Billy Costigan here.

☺ **GOOF:** There's a brief scene in which a suburban police car drives by as the bodies of two mobsters are discovered. The police cruiser is marked with the words "Lynne Police." There is no "e" in Lynn, Massachusetts—the Boston suburb that is referenced.

◉ **REPEATED WATCHING QUOTIENT:** This should be an annual event for anyone who enjoys the genre. The writing, the acting and the directing all shine and get better with each viewing.

🍎 **BET YOU DIDN'T KNOW:** Nicholson, a staunch New York Yankees fan, refused to wear a Boston Red Sox cap for the film.

💀 **BODY COUNT:** Twenty-two.

8 DONNIE BRASCO (1997–R)

STARS: AL PACINO, JOHNNY DEPP, MICHAEL MADSEN, BRUNO KIRBY, ANNE HECHE
DIRECTOR: MIKE NEWELL

Al Pacino starred in more movies featured in this book than any other actor.

He gives a truly remarkable performance in creating and developing the character of Michael Corleone through the *Godfather* saga. He is over-the-top as only he can be as Tony Montana in *Scarface*. He is poignantly cynical and empathetic—despite an off-putting accent—as the tragic title character in *Carlito's Way*.

But his turn as Lefty Ruggiero in *Donnie Brasco* might be his best—and is certainly his most realistic—portrayal of a mobster. The glamour is gone. So is any hint of nobility.

There are times in those other films where it's impossible not to notice Pacino playing the character. In *Donnie Brasco,* he *is* the character. The only comparable Pacino performance is in *Serpico*, where the actor also disappeared into the persona.

Ruggiero is a street-level wiseguy who is always on the make. He never has enough money. He's got family problems (his son is a junkie) and FAMILY problems (he's aligned with the wrong faction during a turbulent period in the Bonanno crime family history).

Lefty is a soldier working in the crew of Sonny Black (Michael Madsen). His outfit is constantly overshadowed by a crew headed by Sonny Red (Robert Miano). Sonny Red's guys dress better and earn more money, giving them both style points and status in the New York underworld—where form is often more important than substance, but where nothing is more important than cold, hard cash.

An "earner" is someone of value.

A shooter—which is what Lefty has always been—is replaceable. Lefty may have 26 hits to his credit (a point he makes repeatedly), but too often he doesn't have 25 cents in his pocket.

Based on the true story of FBI undercover agent Joe Pistone's infiltration of the mob, *Donnie Brasco* provides an unvarnished account of what it's really like to be part of that world. It is a compelling story that Pistone first told in his book *Donnie Brasco: My Undercover Life in the Mafia* (written with Richard Woodley) and then repeated in detailed testimony before a U.S. Senate subcommittee in 1988, nine years before the movie was released.

"There is no honor among these thieves," Pistone told the subcommittee. "They deal in drugs, death, and deception. Though they continually claim to have rules of conduct that they live by, in reality their lives revolve around breaking these rules in a . . . never-ending life of trying to beat the system, both society's and the Mafia's."

Donnie Brasco captures that and more on the screen.

One of the reasons the movie works so well is the interplay between Pacino and Johnny Depp, who established himself as more than just a pretty-boy actor with his performance here as Joe Pistone. Using the undercover name Donnie Brasco (a name Pistone "borrowed" from a cousin), the street-smart, New Jersey-raised FBI agent manages to infiltrate a major New York crime family by posing as a jewel thief and hustler who knows how to make money. Ruggiero takes him under his wing, "vouches" for him with the crime family and begins to school him in the ways of the wiseguy.

Both men are, in their own way, outsiders.

Ruggiero is never quite part of the A-list within his own crew and within the broader organization. He is the butt of jokes and at one point is reduced to hacking off the tops of parking meters in an attempt to get some cash.

Pistone, who set out on what was supposed to be a six-month undercover operation, ends up living the life for six years, battling the bureaucracy that is the FBI and the handlers who never understand nor fully appreciate what he has accomplished.

Pistone also has to juggle his personal life around the 24/7 demands of life in the mob. His wife (excellently portrayed by Anne Heche) and young daughters often don't understand.

"Lefty Ruggiero, a Bonanno soldier who became my business partner when I was on the streets, took it upon himself to educate me in the ways of being a wiseguy," Pistone said in his Senate testimony. "He spent hours telling me about the proper conduct for mob members and associates while criticizing others for not complying with it. Nevertheless, he would then turn around and break the rules when it served his purpose, or if he could make an extra buck doing so. He best summed up this world of deception by once telling me that what was so great about being a wiseguy was that, 'You can lie, steal, cheat, kill, and it's all legitimate.'"

Screenwriter Paul Attanasio, who got an Academy Award nomination for best adapted screenplay, does a great job bringing that reality to the film. And director Mike Newell, with an all-star cast, is smart enough to let the story tell itself.

While the movie is a sprawling saga of the Mafia that stretches from New York to Miami, it is its small moments that say the most.

One of our favorites: Pistone stops by Ruggiero's home on Christmas Day and is forced by Lefty to stay for dinner. Lefty is cooking coq au vin, his specialty. Dressed in a fancy sweatsuit and with his wife and son hovering in the background, Lefty wants—in fact, needs—Pistone to stay. He is, in many ways, Lefty's only friend. So Pistone has to give up a holiday with his wife and daughters in order to share it with a mobster. He and Lefty exchange Christmas gifts, each handing the other an envelope stuffed with cash.

At the end of the night as Pistone is leaving, they embrace in the hallway outside Lefty's apartment. And then the gangster asks Pistone, "Could you spot me a couple a bills?"

With that, Pistone reaches into the envelope Lefty has given him and hands the wiseguy back the money that was his Christmas present.

Another classic moment comes when Pistone tries to explain to an FBI techie what "fuhgedaboudit" means.

"Forget about it is like if you agree with someone, you know, like, 'Raquel Welch is one great piece of ass. Forget about it!' But then if you disagree, like, 'A Lincoln is better than a Cadillac? Forget about it!' You know? But then, it's also like if something's the greatest thing in the world, like, 'Managia, those peppers, forget about it!' But it's also like saying, 'Go to hell' too. Like, you know, 'Hey, Paulie you got a one-inch pecker.' And Paulie says, 'Forget about it!' Sometimes it just means forget about it."

Donnie Brasco scores on so many different levels, in large part because of what Pacino and Depp bring to the screen. But it also works so well because the story doesn't try to be more than it is.

"One thing I will never forget . . . is the daily grind of trying to make a 'score' that they face from the time they wake up in the morning to the time they go to sleep at night," Pistone told the subcommittee. "This is not the romantic life of *The Godfather* or television drama but, rather, is a life of treachery, violence, and, ironically, boredom."

⊙ **HIT:** Along with *GoodFellas*, this may be the only movie that offers a realistic take on life in the underworld. *GoodFellas* is a more stylistic take, perhaps a reflection of the mob crew it depicts. *Donnie Brasco* is blue collar. *The Godfather*'s sense of honor and nobility is lost in the reality of everyday life. It's a struggle to survive. Good work is not always rewarded. There's lots of frustration and very little satisfaction.

⊗ **MISS:** The scene with the lion is almost cartoonish. While based on a real incident—Lefty was given a lion cub as a joke—the movie version has Donnie and Lefty feeding hamburgers through a partially opened window to a full-grown lion in the back seat of their car. New York is a tough town. But not even a wiseguy is going to be driving around with a snarling king of the jungle wedged into the back seat of his car.

✎ **WHAT THEY WROTE AT THE TIME:** "Contrary to movie myth, the Mafia is not made up of dignified men in tuxedos mumbling about honor. For the most part, it's guys in rumpled sport jackets knocking over parking meters, beating up truck drivers, hanging out in smoky men's clubs playing cards and wondering when they're going to get killed. It's made up of a lot of guys like Lefty, an aging Mafia soldier played by Al Pacino. Lefty isn't enough like Ratso Rizzo to be poignant: He's just a little threadbare, a little bit the loser—a true believer who has reached an age where he no longer believes in the institution he's given his life to. To watch Pacino here is to wonder how he knows what he knows. It seems more a matter of intuition than calculation that he understands, for example, the precise degrees of wisdom and smallness to give Lefty. And he knows how to show us."—Mick LaSalle, *San Francisco Chronicle*

✔ **REALITY CHECK:** The scene where Lefty and the crew dismember three rivals after ambushing them in the basement of a home is taken from the story of Roy DeMeo, a Gambino crime family soldier with a penchant for butchering the bodies of those he had killed. DeMeo was considered a psychotic and somewhat (somewhat?) out of control. His story is told in *Murder Machine*, a fascinating book by reporters Jerry Capeci and Gene Mustain. But DeMeo had no connection to the Bonanno family and the wiseguys Donnie Brasco dealt with.

⊙ **REPEATED WATCHING QUOTIENT:** Any time someone begins to wax poetically about the dignity and loyalty of the so-called men of honor, sit them down in front of a television set and pop this movie into the DVD player. Separate and apart from the high entertainment value and standout performances by Depp and Pacino, this is a lesson in underworld life, real and unvarnished.

♟ **BET YOU DIDN'T KNOW:** While the movie's ending implies that Lefty is going to be whacked, in fact he was arrested by the FBI, convicted and sentenced to 20 years in prison. He was paroled in 1992 because of his failing health. He died of cancer in 1994. Sonny Black, on the other hand, was whacked in retribution for bringing an FBI undercover agent into the family. When his body was found, both his hands had been cut off.

☺ **GOOF:** When the mobsters discuss the fact that John Wayne has died, there is snow on the ground in New York. Wayne died in June.

◢ **CASTING CALL:** Joe Pesci was considered for the role of Nicky that went to Bruno Kirby. Earlier in his career, Pesci lost the role of the young Clemenza in *The Godfather: Part II* to Kirby.

☻ **"I KNOW THAT GUY":** The FBI techie who asks Brasco/Pistone to explain what "fuhged-aboudit" means is Paul Giamatti. Giamatti is now renowned for his quirky roles in movies like *Duets* (2000), *Duplicity* (2009) and *Cold Souls* (2009) and his masterful performance as John Adams in the 2008 HBO series of the same name. He is the son of former Major League Baseball Commissioner and Yale University President A. Bartlett Giamatti.

🗩 **BEST LINE:** Brasco's explanation of the meaning of the phrase "fuhgedaboudit" is probably the most quoted from the movie, but we like two others that capture the essence of wiseguy life.

"A wiseguy's always right," Lefty tells Donnie early in their relationship. "Even when he's wrong, he's right."

And when Donnie compares the Mafia chain-of-command to the Army, Lefty bristles, "Bullshit. The army is some guy you don't know telling you to go whack some other guy you don't know."

🔫 **VIOLENCE LEVEL:** Relatively low, given the subject matter and the principal players.

🐌 **BODY COUNT:** Five.

AN INTERVIEW WITH MICHAEL MADSEN

Gravelly voiced actor Michael Madsen is the quintessential Hollywood heavy. He's played tough guys in *Sin City* and both *Kill Bill* films, as well as in two movies featured in this book—*Donnie Brasco* and *Reservoir Dogs*.

With Donnie Brasco *being a true-life story, what does that add to it from an actor's perspective?*

We had advisors around the set who knew the real-life character of Sonny Black. I kept going to them, because I wanted to pay respect to the guy when I portrayed him.

Was the movie close to the story in the book?

Yes, with some differences. For example, in the book, Sonny kept pigeons on the roof. I liked that and didn't understand why it wasn't used in the movie. Al Pacino explained to me that if Sonny had pigeons, the audience would develop sympathy toward him. And that couldn't happen.

What prep work did you do for the movie?

I read everything I could. I visited the grave where Sonny was buried. Turns out his real name is Dominick. Joe Pistone gave me an FBI cassette tape of conversations that he had with Sonny. I listened to those a lot. Don't tell Pistone, but I never gave them back.

We've heard that you almost didn't act in Reservoir Dogs *because people representing you recommended against it. Is that true?*

I was young and naïve, working with a large Hollywood agency that tended to not respond to people with low-budget material. I accidentally received Quentin's script through friends. So I called my agents, who said to me, "Oh yeah we passed on that without telling you." They weren't excited because it wasn't a big payday. But I knew it was something special.

You played the violent Mr. Blonde. Is it true that you lobbied to play Mr. Pink instead?

Yeah. I had done some scenes with Harvey Keitel in *Thelma and Louise*, but most got cut from the movie. I really enjoyed working with Harvey. When I found out he was Mr. White, I wanted as much dialogue with him as possible. Mr. Pink had the great exchanges with his character, so that's what I wanted. It turned out okay. My role worked for me, and Harvey and I became so close that he became godson to my son Max.

Do people still remember you from that movie for the cutting-off-the-ear moment?

That's spot on. It's kind of like the Richard Widmark scene in *Kiss of Death* when he pushes the wheelchair-bound woman down the steps. I'm sure he heard about that for the rest of his life.

How much of that scene was improvised?

I made up the moment when I talk to the ear, if that's what you're asking. When I stepped out with the bloody ear in my hand, Quentin was offscreen saying, "Throw it, throw it." But I didn't want to throw it. That seemed dismissive. So I spoke to it, because it was an ear after all. To be honest I didn't expect that to make it into the movie. Quentin can't take credit for that one. That was me.

What considerations do you put into playing a character as evil and unstable as Mr. Blonde?

I was a big Cagney and Bogey fan when I was a teen. I loved them as cool bad guys in black-and-white movies. Both had dual personalities. Just watch Bogart in *The Maltese Falcon*. He's a lot more than a guy with a pistol. I got a book about Cagney and remember that he said: "If you ever play someone who's evil, play it in a way that he doesn't think he's evil." That stuck in my mind. I threw in a couple of lines and gestures to make it so that Mr. Blonde didn't regard himself as a totally bad man.

Mr. Blonde's real name is Vic Vega. He's supposed to be the brother of Vincent Vega, played by John Travolta in Pulp Fiction. Is it true Tarantino planned a movie with both of them?

There was—a prequel where the brothers own a nightclub in Amsterdam and get in trouble together. After time went by and we got older, it became impossible to make a prequel. More recently, Quentin told me he came up with the idea to make it not a prequel but a present day thing. Vince and Vic each had twin brothers, and both are released from prison in different states. We head to L.A. to avenge the death of our brothers. It still hasn't happened, but Quentin tells me he's still interested.

We hear that mobsters love watching gangster films. Have any ever contacted you?

True story. While we were filming *Donnie Brasco*, I was contacted by a guy named Rocco, a real-life guy. He asked me to meet him at the St. Regis Hotel, which I did, reluctantly. He drove me to a suburban neighborhood and just dropped me off. I'm standing there confused, and here comes another car. It stops and lets off Johnny Depp.

Were you afraid?

We thought we were about to get plugged. Anyway, Johnny and I are let into a house, with seven or eight connected guys inside. One says to me, "Let's play a joke on Depp." They lead him into a dark closet and close the door. They're looking at me, laughing, and I'm telling them to let him out. Finally, after five minutes they open the door and he's all red-faced. There was one of those giant rubber rats in there, caught in a trap and wiggling, and when Johnny turned on the light in the closet he was really spooked.

So the goodfellas wanted to meet you guys just for a practical joke?

In part. After that, we drank some red wine and laughed and then they dropped us off. As I said, true story.

So what's your all-time favorite gangster movie?

I really liked *Angels with Dirty Faces*. When Cagney's character goes to the electric chair, you're wondering whether he's really scared or just acting that way for the priest and the boys. It's a question there's no answer to. That scene always stuck in my mind.

9 THE USUAL SUSPECTS (1995–R)

STARS: KEVIN SPACEY, GABRIEL BYRNE, STEPHEN BALDWIN, CHAZZ PALMINTERI
DIRECTOR: BRYAN SINGER

The genesis of this complex thriller was a magazine article, or—more accurately—the headline of an article. Director Bryan Singer was thumbing through *Spy* magazine in 1992 when he turned to a story entitled, "The Usual Suspects" after Claude Rains' classic line in *Casablanca*.

Hmm, thought Singer. Now *that* would make a good title for a movie.

Singer, then 27, contacted childhood friend Christopher McQuarrie, a struggling writer in Hollywood. The two men's first conception of the film was a visual—a poster of five guys in a police lineup.

From there, the creative process took over. What would happen, Singer wondered, if five felons met each other in that lineup? And what if a powerful hand far away had manipulated their introduction for a purpose?

McQuarrie blended those ideas with a screenplay he had been working on about a man who murders his family and escapes with a new identity. The script was loosely based on the true story of John List, a New Jersey accountant arrested in 1989 after nearly two decades as a fugitive.

And thus was born *The Usual Suspects*, a complicated underworld tale of changing identities and double-crosses, all centering on one mysterious question: "Who is Keyser Söze?"

Shot on a minuscule $6 million budget, *The Usual Suspects* was shown out of competition at the

Cannes Film Festival in 1995 and initially released in just a few art theaters. Word of mouth turned it into a cult hit and then a box-office success. The following year it won two Oscars—one for screenwriter McQuarrie and another for supporting actor Kevin Spacey for his portrayal of disabled conman Roger "Verbal" Kint. In his acceptance speech, Spacey joked, "Well, whoever Keyser Söze is, I can tell you he's gonna get gloriously drunk tonight."

The trick here is to write about *The Usual Suspects* without giving too much away. If you're reading this book, chances are you've already seen the movie once or twice or a dozen times. But if you haven't, our goal is to intrigue you into watching it without revealing the surprises that help make it great. So we're going to tread carefully.

Suffice it to say that *The Usual Suspects* joins classics like *Psycho, The Sixth Sense* and *Fight Club* in leaving you awed by its wonderful twist at the end.

The story, as we said, centers on five New York City criminals dragged into police custody one night for a truck hijacking that none of them actually participated in. While in the lockup, they decide to pull a job together. In a stunning daylight heist, they take down "New York's Finest Taxi Service," a ring of corrupt cops running a high-profit racket driving smugglers and drug dealers around the city.

The quintet includes: Dean Keaton (Gabriel Byrne), a disgraced former police officer trying to give up his life of crime; Michael McManus (Stephen Baldwin), a sharpshooter with a crazy side; Fred Fenster (Benicio Del Toro), McManus' sometime partner who speaks with an accent no one can understand; Todd Hockney (Kevin Pollak), a hijacker who's also good with explosives; and Verbal Kint (Spacey), a con artist and apparent weakling.

This is one dynamite crew and the actors don't disappoint. Del Toro, for example, worked with a speech coach to develop Fenster's unintelligible voice. He's alternately funny and confounding. And Spacey met with experts on cerebral palsy to study its effects. He filed down the heel of one shoe and glued together the fingers of his left hand during filming so that one side of his body seems paralyzed.

Spacey's character narrates much of the story from a police station—where he's being questioned by federal customs agent Dave Kujan (Chazz Palminteri, who's excellent in a small role). And, trust us, Verbal is an appropriate nickname for this yarn spinner.

Anyway, after the five take down the New York cops, they get talked into another job. This one, in California, doesn't go well at all. After its failure, they learn that the entire thing was manipulated by a mysterious lawyer named Kobayashi (Pete Postlethwaite).

Here's where the story takes its first great turn. Kobayashi, it turns out, works for a mysterious Turkish gangster named Keyser Söze. This is the scariest dude in the world—a man who killed his own family to show Hungarian mobsters that he could not be intimidated. A man so ruthless he murders not just his enemies, but also their children, their parents and their parents' friends. A satanic presence whose very name panics hardened mobsters worldwide.

That is, if he really exists. The great debate over Söze is whether the tales of his terror are true or just legend. "Spook stories," Verbal says, "that criminals tell their kids at night."

"Do you believe in him, Verbal?" asks Kujan.

"Keaton [Byrne's character] always said, 'I don't believe in God, but I'm afraid of him,' " Verbal replies. "Well, I believe in God, and the only thing that scares me is Keyser Söze."

Söze, working through Kobayashi, is the off-screen power that somehow pulled together the quintet of felons. We learn that each of the men had at one point in the past inadvertently wronged this criminal mastermind. In return for sparing their lives, Söze demands they pay him back.

And so, through Kobayashi, they are handed an apparent suicide mission, a payback crime that will leave them all rich—if they beat the odds and survive.

We're going to avoid telling you the details of that scheme for two reasons. One, as we've said, is we don't want to ruin the fun of this movie. And two, it's so complex that it might take 10 pages here just to lay it all out. Let's just say that it doesn't hurt to view this movie the first time with a pen and a notebook.

Long after *The Usual Suspects* arrived at and left the theaters, its tag line—"Who is Keyser Söze?"—stayed in the vernacular. The unseen character has come to represent two divergent concepts. First, the name is synonymous with a satanic and mysterious power, usually within organized crime. And second, Keyser Söze has come to mean being tricked, being made to believe in something that doesn't exist.

You may feel tricked the first time you watch this film. But you will not feel cheated. And when you watch it a second time—and you will—you'll delight in spotting the details and clues you missed the first time around.

◉ **HIT:** The aforementioned scene where our boys take down the dirty NYPD cops is a thing of beauty—in its inception and its presentation.

The scene opens with an emerald smuggler arriving at LaGuardia and climbing into the back of a two-man black-and-white. The smuggler hands forward a stuffed envelope.

"Is this enough to get me to Staten Island?" he asks.

"You kidding me?" responds one cop. "This will get you to Cape Cod."

The car winds its way though the city. On a narrow street, a white van stops short in front of it. Suddenly, another van crashes into it from behind, and a third pulls up alongside. Our guys, wearing stockings over their heads, draw guns. McManus leaps on top of the patrol car and pounds out the windshield with a sledgehammer. He snatches the jewels and the envelope from the stunned cops. Then he pours a jug of gasoline on top of the car and sets it afire as the gang peels away.

"Keaton made an anonymous phone call," Verbal says in the voice-over as we watch the cops and the smuggler stumble into the street—dazed and stripped of their riches. "The press was on the scene before the police. [The dirty cops] were indicted three days later, within a few more days 50 more went down with them. Everybody got it right in the ass, from the chief on down. It was beautiful."

⊗ **MISS:** Not much to dislike, although some critics disagree. Roger Ebert of the *Chicago Sun-Times* put *The Usual Suspects* on his list of all-time most hated films, saying, "To the degree that I do understand it, I don't care."

✎ **WHAT THEY WROTE AT THE TIME:** "The complicated plot makes sense if you're willing to pay attention. And if you're not, well, that's why God invented the rewind button. . . . For all its cross-plots and flashbacks, *The Usual Suspects* plays fair: When Keyser Söze is finally revealed, you can almost hear the satisfactory clunk of the last puzzle piece locking into place."—Ty Burr, *Entertainment Weekly*

☺ **GOOF:** During that great "New York's Finest" scene, the cop car drives past a palm tree. We've been to The Big Apple many times—still haven't located that flora.

◉ **REPEATED WATCHING QUOTIENT:** View it the first time just to take it in, the second time to see what you missed and the third time for the sheer pleasure.

🎬 **PIVOTAL SCENE:** Well, it's the ending of course. Without giving it away, we'll just repeat the line of Sgt. Jeff Rabin (Dan Hedaya) in explaining his messy office: "It's got its own system, though. It all makes sense when you look at it right. You just have to step back from it, you know?"

➡ **DON'T FAIL TO NOTICE:** There are clues along the way to that final twist. If you don't want to read them, skip to the next paragraph. . . . You've been warned. . . . Okay? . . . . Still here? Let's just say you should keep your eyes peeled for a gold watch and cigarette lighter. And take note of any references to urine. That's all we're going to tell you.

◀ **CASTING CALL:** Robert De Niro and Christopher Walken turned down the role of Special Agent Kujan. Al Pacino read for the part, but opted against it because he had already committed to *Heat* and didn't want to play a cop in back-to-back movies. Singer Johnny Cash declined an offer to play Redfoot, the L.A. fence.

😬 **"I KNOW THAT GUY":** The actor who ended up playing Redfoot is Peter Greene. He has more than 50 screen credits, but is best recognized as Zed, the disturbed—and doomed—motorcycle cop in *Pulp Fiction*.

🔫 **VIOLENCE LEVEL:** All in all, fairly low.

🍎 **BET YOU DIDN'T KNOW:** Screenwriter McQuarrie, who worked in the copy room of a Los Angeles law firm, based the name of the film's villain on a supervisor of that firm—Keyser Sume. Looking to tweak the name (perhaps to avoid a lawsuit), he thumbed through a Turkish dictionary and discovered the word *söze*, which means "to talk too much." Filmgoers in Istanbul might consider that a clue.

BET YOU DIDN'T KNOW II: The lineup scene, in which the five crooks end up laughing, was supposed to be played seriously. But the four other actors kept cracking up at Del Toro's bizarre delivery of his line, "Hand me the keys, you fucking cocksucker," as well as, according to Spacey, Del Toro's repeated flatulence. After a day of trying to shoot it straight, Singer gave up and used footage of the cast giggling.

🗨️ **BEST LINE:** Verbal Kint: "The greatest trick the Devil ever pulled was convincing the world he didn't exist."

✴️ **IF YOU LIKED THIS, YOU'LL LIKE:** Director Singer describes his film as *"Double Indemnity* meets *Rashomon."* So we recommend you see both of those classics.

🦴 **BODY COUNT:** Thirty-three—not including all the full body bags in one scene.

10 CASINO (1995–R)

STARS: ROBERT DE NIRO, JOE PESCI, SHARON STONE | DIRECTOR: MARTIN SCORSESE

In the opening shot of *Casino*, a man in a salmon-colored sports jacket climbs into his Lincoln Continental. He turns the key and the car explodes. Then, as director Martin Scorsese explains it, "You see him in slow motion, flying over the flames—like a soul about to take a dive into hell."

He's not going to hell—at least not yet. Instead, we later learn, Ace Rothstein survives this attempt on his life. For the next three hours, *Casino* shows how Ace reached the point where someone wanted to kill him.

The screenplay, written by Scorsese and author Nicholas Pileggi, is essentially the real-life tale of Frank "Lefty" Rosenthal, who ran casinos for the Chicago mob through the 1970s. Rosenthal is now remembered as the man who introduced sports betting to Nevada, although that element is barely mentioned in the movie. Rosenthal's Vegas ride ended when his car was firebombed in 1982. He survived that attack to tell his story to Pileggi.

And what a story it is. Power, corruption, money, infidelity—this epic has it all.

Robert De Niro stars as Sam "Ace" Rothstein, a brilliant handicapper from the Midwest whose ability to make money persuades the mob to hire him to run the fictional Tangiers casino in Las

Vegas. His job, essentially, is to skim enough from the enterprise so that a suitcase of cash can be flown back to the Kansas City bosses each week. This is an easy gig as long as Ace watches out for professional cheaters and greases the local pols.

There's a great early scene outlining the corruption that runs from parking valets to dealers to money counters to floor managers, all the way up the casino food chain. "What we show," says Scorsese, "is a bunch of cheats watching cheats watching cheats."

Everyone gets his share. To protect their investment in Ace, the Midwest bosses dispatch his childhood friend Nicky Santoro (Joe Pesci) to Vegas. Nicky's job is to both bodyguard Ace (which he does at one point by using a ballpoint pen as a stiletto) and to keep a wary eye on him.

But Nicky does more than that. He forms a crew and quickly becomes the most notorious gangster in Vegas. As Ace tries to keep his hands clean (at least publicly), Nicky's carelessness and zealous brutality attract unwanted attention. Soon enough, the FBI is listening to their every conversation.

(Nicky, by the way, is based on Anthony "Tony the Ant" Spilotro, a Chicago-born enforcer. His body is buried somewhere in an Indiana cornfield. More about that coming up.)

Adding to that dangerous mix is the high-end hustler Ginger (Sharon Stone), a stunner incapable of sobriety or loyalty. Ace first spots her swiping $1,000 chips from a john at the craps table—and immediately falls in love. When she balks at marrying him, he wins her with diamonds, furs and a key to the safe deposit box where he has stashed millions. This last move proves to be a mistake.

Casino bullrushes through a series of interwoven stories that ultimately lead to the three main characters being destroyed by greed and hubris. And there are meaty little subplots. Our favorite concerns a Kansas City underboss named Artie Piscano (Vinny Vella), who gripes that he never gets reimbursed after taking trips to Vegas to oversee the skimming operation. Piscano decides to keep expense records that are a bit too detailed. The cops bug his small grocery store, pick up his blabbing about bosses shortchanging him and discover his meticulous ledger when they raid the place. By the way, watch for Scorsese's mother in a brief but funny role as Piscano's no-nonsense mom.

The three lead actors are outstanding. Stone garnered her only Oscar nomination for portraying the devious and self-obsessed Ginger. Pesci's mien as Nicky Santoro is identical to the one he used to portray Tommy DeVito in *GoodFellas*, but, hey, when it works it works. And De Niro was really in a groove in the 1990s, filming *GoodFellas, Cape Fear, This Boy's Life, A Bronx Tale* and this movie all in the span of five years. Somehow, he took a wrong turn at *The Adventures of Rocky and Bullwinkle*, and now seems to accept any role that pays the bills.

There's also a wonderful supporting cast, led by James Woods as a vicious hustler/pimp, and including Frank Vincent, Kevin Pollak and comedian Don Rickles in a rare dramatic role.

Casino is one of eight film collaborations between De Niro and Scorsese, along with the likes of *GoodFellas, Taxi Driver* and *Raging Bull*. Think of the greatest actor-director pairings in history. John Wayne and John Ford? Humphrey Bogart and John Huston? Jack Lemmon and Billy Wilder? We'll take Bobby Milk and Marty Eyebrows over any of them.

There's one more star in the movie, and it's the city of Las Vegas. *Casino* shows the energetic town during the 1970s and '80s, which many consider its prime. "What interested me about Las Vegas was the idea of excess, no limits," said Scorsese. "People become successful there like no other city."

On the surface, it's all glitz and glamour—jewels and furs, neon and champagne. But underneath all that is the element of organized crime. As *Casino* brilliantly shows, the Mafia built the casinos with Teamster money, ran them beyond the purview of the law and used them to lure customers in, keep them playing and suck them dry.

Of course, Vegas doesn't work that way anymore . . . well, except for the sucking the customers dry part. The mob and the Teamster money were pushed out during the 1980s, replaced by Michael Milken and junk bonds and Steve Wynn. As Ace laments near *Casino*'s end, "The big corporations took over. Today, it works like Disneyland." It's debatable whether the current system is any cleaner.

⊙ **HIT:** The sound track is a tour de force of more than 50 songs, featuring music by everyone from Louis Prima to Roxy Music, from B.B. King to Devo. The songs aren't just random; they tie to moments and characters. Our favorite was the ominous introduction of dollars-and-diamonds obsessed Ginger through Mick Jagger's "Heart of Stone."

⊗ **MISS:** If *Casino* has a flaw, it's that it's a little too reminiscent of *GoodFellas*.

☺ **GOOF:** Take a close look at the opening scene of the car explosion. That's clearly a dummy behind the steering wheel.

◎ **REPEATED WATCHING QUOTIENT:** At three hours, it's a hefty time investment. But since many flights to Vegas take longer than that, we'd recommend you pick it up at the airport DVD rental kiosk to set the mood for your trip.

◣ **CASTING CALL:** Jamie Lee Curtis, Nicole Kidman, Michelle Pfeiffer and former porn star Traci Lords were all considered for the role of Ginger. Lefty Rosenthal wanted actor Richard Widmark to portray him, until he was reminded that Widmark was 80 years old at the time.

▣ **PIVOTAL SCENE:** As things spin out of control, Nicky, his brother Dominick and Nicky's No. 2, Frank Marino (Frank Vincent) drive to a cornfield for a clandestine meeting with associates. As Nicky steps from the car, Frank whacks him with a baseball bat. The other men then attack Nicky and his brother, clubbing them with aluminum bats.

Nicky is held down and forced to witness his younger brother getting pummeled. "Watch this," shouts Frankie, his longtime aide, as he swings at Dominick's skull.

Dominick is beaten semiconscious, stripped of his clothes and dragged into a freshly-dug grave as Nicky sobs. Nicky is next.

"The word was out that the bosses had enough of Nicky," Ace flatly says in a voice-over. "How much were they gonna take? So they made an example of him and his brother. They buried them while they were still breathing."

In an interview with *New York* magazine, Scorsese said the brutal scene (inspired by the real death of Tony Spilotro and his brother) was essential to show "where it really ends (for mobsters). It's your closest friend smashing you in the head with a baseball bat. Not even a gun. Not cutting your throat. You're going to get hit many times and you're still going to be breathing when they put the dirt on you. If you want to live that lifestyle, that's where you're going to go."

One final note: When Pesci was pushed into that dusty grave, he broke the same rib he had cracked filming *Raging Bull* in 1979.

✎ **WHAT THEY WROTE AT THE TIME:** "This is a disappointingly rudimentary tale about a love-smitten wimp, a cheating bitch and a deranged killer, who destroy everything for one another. It's clear Scorsese and Pileggi are trying to disinter the success of *GoodFellas*, their last collaboration. But they only come up with Raging B.S. *Casino* ends up like a few too many of its characters: face down in a shallow grave."—Desson Howe, *Washington Post*

☺ **"I KNOW THAT GUY":** Folk singer-comedian Dick Smothers takes a rare stab at drama, playing the corrupt politician known only as "Senator." Other Vegas regulars who show up onscreen include Rickles and Alan King, who have significant roles, and Steve Allen, Frankie Avalon and Jerry Vale, who play themselves in cameos.

♣ **BET YOU DIDN'T KNOW:** The Gaming Commission showdown between Ace and the Senator is based on a 1978 encounter between Rosenthal and current U.S. Senator Harry Reid, who headed the Nevada board at the time. Scorsese has insisted that the prostitute-loving, freebie-grubbing aspect of Smothers' Senator character has nothing to do with Reid.

➡ **DON'T FAIL TO NOTICE:** The attorney for Ace and Nicky is played by Oscar Goodman, who ran a winning campaign for mayor of Las Vegas four years after the movie's release and has served in that office ever since. Before running for office, Goodman spent three decades defending real-life mob figures, including Rosenthal and Spilotro.

🔫 **VIOLENCE LEVEL:** High enough that some critics thought the film deserved an NC-17 rating. Beyond the clubbing in the cornfield, three cringe-inducing scenes stand out: the multiple stabbing of a barroom wiseass by a ballpoint pen, the smashing of a cheat's fingers with a hammer, and the crushing of a hood's head in a carpenter's vise.

The third scene, which culminates in the poor guy's eye popping out, is based on a true episode that took place in Chicago in the 1960s. In that case, as in the movie, an unauthorized hit went down, angering mob bosses. To persuade one of the hit's participants to give up his partners, a mob enforcer embarked on two days of torture, ending with the vise.

💬 **BEST LINE:** Two actually, and they show the contradiction that is Sin City:

Early on, Ace is honored by the local Chamber of Commerce. "Back home, they would have put me in jail for what I'm doing," he marvels. "But out here, they give me awards."

But later, during a tense meeting in the desert, Nicky explains it all:

"I'm what's real out here," he lectures Ace. "Not your country clubs and your TV show. I'm what's real: the dirt, the gutter, and the blood. That's what it's all about."

✪ **IF YOU LIKED THIS, YOU'LL LIKE:** *The Cooler*, a great yarn about the transformation of Vegas. It centers on an old-school casino and a schmo (William H. Macy) whose job it is to bring bad luck to gamblers.

🔪 **BODY COUNT:** Twenty-five. Nicky is the league leader with eight kills.

11 SCARFACE: THE SHAME OF A NATION (1932–NO MPAA RATING)

STARS: PAUL MUNI, ANN DVORAK, GEORGE RAFT
DIRECTORS: HOWARD HAWKS, RICHARD ROSSON

Watching the original *Scarface* today, you may snicker at its clichéd characters and the hackneyed dialogue. The movie is dated in a way that *The Godfather* never will be. It's tough not to laugh out loud when Paul Muni, as mobster Tony Camonte, says: "What king of mug do you think I am? I don't know nothin', I don't see nothin' and I don't hear nothin'. And when I do, I don't tell a cop."

Still, there's something beyond the stereotypes and the arcane movie talk that makes this a great film. For one, the story it tells remains—as it was then—the American dream come to life: an immigrant from humble beginnings gets the money, gets the power, gets the women. The bad guy has always mesmerized audiences, and Muni is as magnetic as Robert De Niro and Al Pacino were a half-century later.

Beyond that, what you're seeing here is the birth of a genre. *Scarface: The Shame of a Nation* has direct connections to *GoodFellas* (note the scene where Tony asks the moll, "How do you mean, you think I'm funny?"), to *The Untouchables* (Muni's nod to Al Capone compares well to De Niro's) and, of course, to Brian De Palma's 1983 *Scarface* remake. Pacino's Tony Montana is an updated version of Muni's Tony Camonte—right down to the abnormal relationship with his sister and the wild-eyed final showdown.

"In that age of American film, there were no rules, and people had to find order in chaos," said screenwriter Robert Benton (*Bonnie and Clyde*) in the documentary *Public Enemies: The Golden Age of the Gangster Film*. Talking about pioneers like *Scarface* director Howard Hawks and screenwriter Ben Hecht, Benton said, "Those great storytellers did it. They invented an art form. That's an amazing thing to have done."

Not that it came easily. *Scarface* was the brainchild of aviation tycoon Howard Hughes (before he became a recluse). Hughes had previously produced only a few noncontroversial air show films. But with *Scarface*, he envisioned a gangster movie that was bolder and more violent than any previously made.

But his dream clashed with the Hays Office, the powerful federal censorship board. The Office battled Hughes on issues large (whether the movie would end with Tony being captured or shot) and small (whether Tony and his girlfriend could sit together on a bed).

Hughes alternately ranted and capitulated. To meet the guideline that movies had to discourage crime, he added the words "The Shame of a Nation" to the original title and tacked a moral statement to the opening that began, "This picture is an indictment of gang rule in America." The movie was anything but that and the censors saw through his linguistic ruse. After two years of battles and more than 30 script changes, Hughes still could not get Hays Office approval.

He finally decided to release *Scarface* without the panel's endorsement—a move similar to trying to market an NC-17 movie to general audiences today. The film was banned in seven states (including New York) and dozens of cities (including Chicago, where its story is based). Hughes was so frustrated that he stormed out of Hollywood and didn't produce another movie for more than a decade.

Still, the final product here is damned impressive.

Scarface's plot is a thinly veiled biography of Al Capone. It was written in just 11 days by Hecht, who learned his craft covering crime for Chicago newspapers. It is based on a 1930 novel with the same title by Armitage Trail (a pseudonym for Maurice Coons) and includes reenactments of real-life episodes like the St. Valentine's Day Massacre, the hospital shooting of Legs Diamond (you'll also note similarities to the hospital scene in *The Godfather*) and the 90th Street siege of "Two-Gun" Crowley in 1930.

The vehicle for the story is Muni's character, Tony, a vicious mob enforcer who guns down his local sponsor in order to please the big South Side boss. Tony knows from the start that he is destined for greatness—his motto is inspired by a tour company's neon advertising sign hanging across the street from his apartment reading, "The World is Yours."

Tony's violent streak sets off gang wars over the control of Chicago's bootlegging business. No one is safe—not small time saloon owners who get slapped around, not innocent bystanders caught in the crossfire of machine guns, not rival gangsters. The most notable victim is played by Boris Karloff, who looks like a cross between Abe Vigoda's Tessio and the Frankenstein monster. He gets gunned down while rolling a bowling ball. Gangsters bowled back then?

Anyway, Tony is rolling in dough, so he moves from a tenement he shares with his sister and mother—who keeps berating him as "a no-gooda boy"—into a townhouse with enough velvet and gold décor to stock a Vegas whorehouse. He kills his boss, steals that boss's mistress and decides to take her down to Florida for a month while things cool off in Chicago.

It's all going swimmingly—except for one hitch. Tony's got this thing for his sister, Cesca (Ann Dvorak). Midway through the movie, he goes to celebrate a victory at the Paradise Club, where he happens to catch his sister dancing with a man. He smacks the poor jerk around, and then takes Cesca home and beats her too, saying, "Next time I catch you in a place like that, I'll kill you."

Nothing more occurs, but Tony's leering look makes it clear that his motive is not exactly protecting his sister's honor. And given that incest was as taboo in 1932 as it is today, it's astounding that the censors' list of objections to *Scarface* apparently didn't include this thinly veiled relationship.

Later, upon his return from Florida, he discovers Cesca holed up with his best friend Guino (George Raft). Tony murders his pal in a rage—convinced that Guino has ruined his sister, as they used to say. Only after the murder does Tony learn that during the month he was tanning down South, Cesca and Guino fell in love, married and rented a place together. Sometimes, it pays to ask questions first.

It all sets off the climactic scene, back at Tony's place, where he and Cesca laughingly fight off dozens of cops until she dies in his arms of a gunshot wound. Alone and overwhelmed by tear gas, he surrenders to the police—sniveling like a coward—before making one last foolish dash for freedom. He is gunned down and dies under that neon advertising sign bearing his motto.

Censors weren't pleased with that ending and insisted on another one, in which Tony is captured, put on trial and executed for his sins. Director Hawks refused, so a stand-in director was hired—as well as a stand-in for Muni (filmed only from behind). Although Howard Hughes initially agreed to the Hays Office's demand, the revised ending eventually became the final straw for him. He reinserted the original ending and stopped seeking the censorship panel's seal of approval. In doing so, he guaranteed that *Scarface* would be a financial flop—although, by all accounts, Hughes didn't have to switch to a cheaper brand of Scotch over that.

Everything about *Scarface* is over the top—just as it was in the 1983 remake. While filming the latter version, Pacino studied Muni's scenery-chewing performance and decided to pay homage to it. Both men behave like animals—in fact, each is referred to as a "big ape." De Palma dedicated his version to screenwriter Hecht and director Hawks.

◉ **HIT:** Although he doesn't get many lines in his supporting role of Guino Rinaldo, young George Raft establishes a tough-guy persona that served him well for the rest of his career. Watch him as he habitually flips a coin—a trademark move he reprised in several movies, including the 1959 comedy *Some Like It Hot*.

Raft was a childhood friend of mobster Bugsy Siegel and was, by some accounts, a gangster himself. He was barred from entering Great Britain in 1966 because of alleged Mafia ties.

⊗ **MISS:** Even today, mob movies stereotype in disturbing ways. But *Scarface* really set the standard. With the exception of one character (detective Ben Guarino), every Italian-American man is hot-tempered, sociopathic and either slyly cunning or dumber than a tree stump. The most egregious is the gang secretary, who can neither read nor field a phone call, speaks with an exaggerated accent and wears an Alpine hat stolen from Chico Marx's wardrobe closet.

Remember, America was far less integrated and culturally sophisticated back in the 1930s. We can only imagine what an untraveled filmgoer from, say, Iowa, thought of Italian immigrants after viewing this film.

✎ **WHAT THEY WROTE AT THE TIME:** "*Scarface* contains more cruelty than any of its gangster picture predecessors, but there's a squarer for every killing. The blows are always softened by judicial preachments and sad endings for the sinners. . . . Presumably the last of the gangster films, it is going to make people sorry that there won't be any more."—*Variety*

☺ **GOOF:** Make sure to check out the score sheet that's shown right before Karloff's murder at the bowling alley. It defies all laws of math.

✔ **REALITY CHECK:** Let's see now, the Camontes live in poverty, with no apparent access to education or the fine arts. But when sister Cesca sits down at the piano, she can tickle the ivories like George Gershwin. Where'd she learn to do that?

◉ REPEATED WATCHING QUOTIENT: Once a decade or so, just to see where the genre was born.

🎬 PIVOTAL SCENE: After killing Louie, the local mob captain, Tony goes to collect his pay from the new South Side chief, Johnny Lovo. He is awed by Lovo's plush apartment, his silk bathrobe and—most especially—his icy blond girlfriend, who plucks her eyebrows and reveals shapely legs while buffing her toenails.

Ambitious Tony tries to persuade Lovo to make a move on his rival, but Lovo appears timid. Quickly, Tony concludes that rather than *work for* the man, he should *become* the man. He wants it all—including the blond.

Soon after, he boasts to a fellow hit man, "This business is just waiting for some guy to run it right. And I got ideas."

But we work for Lovo, his friend reminds him.

"Who's Lovo? Just some guy who's a little smarter than Big Louie, that's all. Hey that guy is soft. I could see it in his face. . . . Someday, I'm gonna run the whole works."

➡ DON'T FAIL TO NOTICE: The use of the letter "X" to foreshadow killings throughout the movie—almost as *The Godfather* later used oranges. In the bowling alley scene, Karloff is shot right after marking a strike on his score sheet. In another, Tony goes to kill a rival in an apartment, entering through a door marked by the Roman numeral X. And the St. Valentine's Day Massacre scene begins with the camera panning down from the roof of a garage supported by seven sets of intercrossing beams—one for each victim.

In another foreshadowing, Tony repeatedly prepares for his murders while whistling the beautiful theme from the Italian aria "Lucia di Lammermoor." We appreciate his musical taste, if not his moral compass.

🔫 VIOLENCE LEVEL: For all the gunshots and thrown punches, there really isn't much sadism or gore—in, say, a Pacino *Scarface* kind of way. Hughes had enough problems with the censors that he decided not to bathe victims in blood—or ink, considering this was a black-and-white film.

❞ BEST LINE: Early on, Tony's attorney gets him released from police questioning, leading the mobster to ask how he did it.

Lawyer: "A writ of Habeas corpus. Deliver the body. It means they can't hold you without booking you—no matter what they think you've done."

Tony: "That's a fine idea. You tell them I want lots of them writs of hocus pocus."

🗡 BODY COUNT: Twenty-eight on-screen, and at least that many implied off-screen.

☗ BET YOU DIDN'T KNOW: During production, Capone got wind that a movie was being made based on his story and sent henchmen to visit screenwriter Hecht. Somehow, Hecht convinced them that a film about a vicious Chicago bootlegger with a scar across his cheek had nothing to do with their boss. Ultimately, Capone is said to have loved *Scarface* so much that he owned a copy and watched it repeatedly during his stay at the federal penitentiary in Atlanta.

12 ONCE UPON A TIME IN AMERICA (1984–R)

STARS: ROBERT DE NIRO, JAMES WOODS
DIRECTOR: SERGIO LEONE

There are three versions of *Once Upon a Time in America*. There's the original six-hour movie conceived and directed by Sergio Leone. The famous Italian pioneer of spaghetti westerns envisioned releasing his coming-of-age saga in two parts; this version never made it to theaters.

Instead, Warner Brothers, the U.S. distributor, hacked *America* down to just over two hours and jerked around the chronology to make it all fit. And the result? No one understood the plot. "They took the essence out," protested Leone.

That version of *America* bombed. And then, sometime after it disappeared from theaters, Leone got back the rights to the film that would turn out to be his last. He restored more than 90 minutes, re-edited scenes so that the story revolves around flashbacks and released it on VHS. The film's beauty and sweeping drama finally became evident. "This was a murdered movie now brought back to life on home video," wrote *Chicago Sun-Times* critic Roger Ebert, who lauded the restored version as "an epic poem of violence and greed."

This third version by Leone—which runs 229 minutes—is the one you'll usually see on cable or available for rental or purchase today (we're assuming you've replaced your VCR with a DVD player by now). And while it still has flaws and gets convoluted at times, it ranks behind only the first two *Godfather* films as the most brilliantly stylistic gangster movie ever made.

Once Upon a Time in America tells the lifelong tale of a clan of Jewish mobsters. It has two main chapters—set in 1920 and 1933—plus a third chapter, set in 1968. Each chapter deals with power and sex and treachery.

Without giving away too much, we can tell you the central personality is David "Noodles" Aaronson (Robert De Niro), a gang member who goes into hiding in 1933 after a caper goes bad. He then leads a quiet existence for decades, until he suddenly receives a message aiming to pull him back toward his former life. He doesn't know who is seeking him or why.

That mystery provides the starting point for a tapestry of episodes that meander over the years. They tell the tale of childhood friends who grow up tightly bound by loyalty—at least until one double-crosses the gang. Only later do we learn that he was not the betrayer, but rather the betrayed.

The best scenes are those showing the urban jungle of Brooklyn's Williamsburg section, circa 1920. Five young friends, led by Noodles and Max Bercovicz, work the streets by rolling drunks and stealing watches. They're heartless from the start—torching the newspaper kiosk of a schlepper who has fallen behind on his payments to the local shyster.

But these are not just dumb thugs. They show their brains by devising a system to help bootleggers retrieve whiskey bottles that must be thrown overboard to avoid the Coast Guard. Now our kids are making serious money. They graduate to become genuine gangsters—even opening their own pension program.

Leone does a great job recreating the city of that era. Neighborhoods teem with diverse immigrants. Horse buggies jockey for position with backfiring cars. There's a rich texture here, created by elaborate sets, beautiful music and colorful faces.

By 1933, our boys are princes of New York's underworld. Noodles spends some years in prison and while he's gone, Max (James Woods) emerges as the gang's leader. But Max is too hot-tempered for the job (he's a lot more like Sonny Corleone than Michael Corleone). Some of his brainstorms

are downright irrational, like the suicidal notion of robbing a federal reserve bank.

America is a series of subplots and sequences. Some work better than others. There's a vicious diamond heist in which the victim's wife (Tuesday Weld) gets turned on by sexual brutality. There's a scene showing mob infiltration of unions, with Treat Williams playing an idealistic labor leader who learns he must make a deal with the devil. To pressure the local police chief (Danny Aiello) in that episode, the boys sneak into the neonatal ward housing his newborn son and switch the nametags on dozens of babies. Then they blackmail the chief—demanding his compliance before they'll correct the nametags. Of course, they end up losing the master list.

There's also Noodles' unrequited lifelong crush on neighborhood beauty Deborah (played as a child by 13-year-old Jennifer Connelly and as an adult by Elizabeth McGovern). In the movie's most disturbing scene, the grownup Noodles realizes he cannot possess Deborah and so he forcibly violates her.

The section of the film set in 1968 is its weakest, largely because it's downright implausible. Without giving away too much of the plot, lets just say that Noodles and Max—after splitting 35 years ago—come together. Except that Max is now a Rockefeller-like tycoon who serves in the White House cabinet and is caught up in a political scandal. Meanwhile, Deborah is a big-time Hollywood actress who miraculously hasn't added one wrinkle while everyone else has grown old.

It all leads to an illogical ending that film geeks have debated for nearly three decades. We won't spill it. Just watch out for that garbage truck.

There's a theory, hinted at by Leone himself, that all of the 1968 sequences are actually a dream. Be sure to notice that they begin after we see the 1933 Noodles escaping his fear and guilt at the neighborhood opium den. And, at the film's end, the camera cuts back to Noodles at the same spot, taking another deep puff and falling back onto a cot with a smile across his face.

We can only imagine what he's thinking in this pipe dream. But if one-third of the movie really is a fantasy that takes place in 1933, we'll give Noodles credit for envisioning late-model cars, television news reports and Vietnam-era protests. The guy is Nostradamus.

One fan of the movie who embraces the dream theory is Martin Scorsese, who knows a bit about the genre. He summed up *Once Upon a Time in America* this way: "It's a gangster picture, but extremely different from any of the films I was making or from Francis Coppola's *Godfather* pictures. *Once Upon a Time in America* is grand, operatic, and structured as a meditation on the passing of time and history—personal history, social history and economic history. There was no one else like Sergio Leone. This is one of his greatest films."

◉ **HIT:** Ennio Morricone's score ranks among the best in film history. The great arranger combines styles (from classical to Dixieland) and instruments (from horns to banjo to pan flute) to pull together the movie's three eras.

Morricone so precisely knew the sound he wanted that he finished most of the score before production began. His music was recorded early and played on the set to help create the mood for the actors. Despite universal applause, this score was not nominated for an Academy Award in 1984 because Warner Brothers neglected to put Morricone's name on the movie's credits.

⊗ **MISS:** Even in the restored 229-minute version, there are questions of context and moments of confusion. When did Noodles acquire this girlfriend? What's with the outline of the corpse in her bed? And how come Deborah never ages?

☺ **GOOF:** The scene at Miami Beach shows the sun setting over the Atlantic Ocean. Last time we checked, the sun sets in the west.

✎ **WHAT THEY WROTE AT THE TIME:** "To stupendous effect Sergio Leone, the Italian director who gave rise to the spaghetti western, uses what he remembers of Hollywood gangster movies of the Thirties to evoke a grandiose spectacle of a corrupt American dream."—Alexander Walker, *London Evening Standard*

✔ **REALITY CHECK:** We'll buy that Max goes underground and starts a new life with a new identity. But are we really supposed to believe that a notorious murderer can wind up as the U.S. Secretary of Commerce? What, the White House and Senate didn't conduct any background checks in the 1960s?

◎ **REPEATED WATCHING QUOTIENT:** There are enough great scenes here that it's worth going back to once a decade. Just make sure you have no other plans for the weekend.

🔫 **VIOLENCE LEVEL:** Very high. There are beatings and close-range shootings and two rape scenes. The second rape ranks among the most unsettling movie moments we've ever scene.

➡ **DON'T FAIL TO NOTICE:** The actor in the garbage truck scene at the end is not James Woods, but another man made up to look like Woods. "We used a body double because Sergio wanted it to be confusing," Woods says in the DVD commentary. "Sergio said he wanted the audience to think, 'It could be you, it could not be you. We know, but we don't know.' "

◄ **CASTING CALL:** Many names came up when this project was in development. Leone originally hoped to cast Gérard Dépardieu as Noodles, Richard Dreyfuss as Max and James Cagney as the older Noodles. Jodie Foster and Daryl Hannah turned down the role of Deborah. And somebody thought it a good idea to cast the virginal Julie Andrews as Carol, the Detroit woman turned on by her own rape. Andrews politely declined.

♟ **BET YOU DIDN'T KNOW:** Joe Pesci auditioned to play Max, but Leone didn't think Pesci could convince an audience he was Jewish. Leone offered Pesci his choice of any of the uncast roles. The actor picked mob associate Frankie, a meaty character in the original script. By the time the movie was edited to its final length, however, Pesci's screen time was cut to less than five minutes.

99 BEST LINE: Labor leader Jimmy Conway O'Donnell (Treat Williams) trying (unsuccessfully) to keep his union away from the mob:

Conway: "Our fight's got nothing to do with liquor and prostitution and dope."

Max: "You'd better get used to the idea, pal. The country is still growing up. Certain diseases it's still good to have when you're young."

Conway: "Well, you boys ain't a mild case of the measles. You're the plague."

"I KNOW THAT GAL": The frantic Jewish mother of teenaged trollop Peggy? Why, that's Estelle Harris, who eight years later began playing the frantic Jewish mother of George Costanza on *Seinfeld*.

✪ IF YOU LIKED THIS, YOU'LL LIKE: *King of the Roaring 20s: The Story of Arnold Rothstein*. TV's *Fugitive*, David Janssen, stars as the Jewish bootlegger and gambler who fixed the 1919 World Series.

🐾 BODY COUNT: Eleven. One little kid, one woman and nine guys who probably deserved it.

13 LÉON: THE PROFESSIONAL
(1994–R)

STARS: JEAN RENO, NATALIE PORTMAN, GARY OLDMAN, DANNY AIELLO
DIRECTOR: LUC BESSON

He's a highly efficient—but in many ways naïve—hit man who drinks milk, exercises religiously and seems obsessed with the care and maintenance of a houseplant.

She's a 12-year-old who smokes, curses and is wise way beyond her years.

Together they form an unlikely crime team in this fascinating and unusual look at the New York underworld.

Written and directed by Luc Besson, the French filmmaker who has built a career by combining Francophile introspection with over-the-top action, *Léon: The Professional* is a story about a heartwarming relationship that develops against a backdrop of murder, mayhem and corruption.

Spanish-born French actor Jean Reno plays the title character with just the right combination of menace and empathy. But Natalie Portman's Mathilda steals the movie. She is, at turns, street-smart and innocent, sassy and naïve, offering a performance that is touching without being melodramatic. Mathilda's seen too many bad things in her short life. And during her time with Léon, she sees many more.

The movie's less than 10 minutes old when her father, stepmother, stepsister and brother are wiped out by a group of corrupt DEA agents in a dispute over a drug deal gone bad. Léon, who lives in the apartment next door, saves her life. Sitting in his shabby living room, she asks what he does for a living. But we suspect she already has a pretty good idea.

"Cleaner," he says.

"You mean you're a hit man," she replies.

"Yeah."

"Cool."

Mathilda, who wants to avenge the death of her little brother (she could care less, she says, about her abusive father and the stepmother and stepsister he brought into her dysfunctional family), asks Léon to teach her his craft. At first, he resists, but then agrees.

The American version of the film shows Léon training his 12-year-old protégé. The European version includes scenes in which she actually takes part in the work. At one point, she even chides Léon, boasting that she is younger than he was when he carried out his first hit.

"Beat ya'," she says, as if she's discussing some athletic accomplishment.

There is a tough, urban edge to Mathilda that comes out in the matter-of-fact way she approaches the murder-for-hire business. But there is also an innate understanding on her part that a 12-year-old shouldn't be dealing with the things she has to deal with. Portman manages to convey all this in a stunning movie debut.

On the other hand, murder has always been Léon 's business. But in teaching Mathilda how to kill, he comes to appreciate the true meaning of life. That's the irony in the story—and the heart and soul of what otherwise would be just a hard-driving action drama.

Film critic Hal Hinson, writing in the *Washington Post*, described Léon as "a poetic brute, a man without humanity who has lived so close to darkness for so long that he has lost all connection to the light. The universe around him, too, is a symbolic construction, an interweaving of opera, film noir and existentialism, where the larger-than-life forces of innocence and corruption explode in blood and violence."

Mathilda brings him closer to the light, but also leads him to a new level of blood and violence.

There is the inevitable showdown between Léon and Stansfield (Gary Oldman), the leader of the dirty DEA unit that wiped out Mathilda's family. Oldman, the quintessential bad guy, is once again a cinematic force of nature, a pill-popping, classical-music-loving psychopath who casually deals in death and destruction.

Both he and Leon have dealings with Tony (Danny Aiello), a mobster/restaurateur. Over the years, Tony has provided Léon with his work assignments while "holding" Léon's money for him. The hit man gets $5,000 per body and has done enough work to fill a small cemetery.

Léon, who has lived a Spartan-like existence, has never required much money and has naively assumed that Tony has been stashing it away for him. At one point, he poignantly asks Tony to give his cash to "the girl" if anything happens to him. Leon may be the only one who actually believes that might happen.

Mathilda certainly doesn't.

Léon: The Professional ends with one of the most violent shootouts in gangster cinema history, as Leon matches fire with nearly 50 members of an NYPD SWAT team under the direction of the amphetamine-amped Stansfield. Their final scene together is a classic.

Mathilda, with Léon's houseplant lovingly tucked under her arm, manages to walk away from the carnage. No one else gets out alive.

◉ **HIT:** Besson does a good job conveying the idea of Léon's murderous work as a profession, a money-making proposition that has nothing to do with emotion. The character of Léon is almost mechanical—it's not for nothing that hit men are sometimes called "mechanics." And it is the juxtaposition of that life with the tenderness Léon comes to feel for the young girl in his care that makes the movie more than just another gangland story.

⊗ **MISS:** There's a lot of outlandish action here and we're inclined to just go along with most of it. Léon is a killing machine and the way he pops up shooting and dodging bullets is almost the stuff of a video game. But the one scene that had us screaming, "No way!" is when he busts into the DEA office in Manhattan to rescue Mathilda.

Getting past security is just not that easy. And having a cab waiting for the getaway took things that much further over the top.

✎ WHAT THEY WROTE AT THE TIME:
"Mathilda is like no New York City girl-child I've ever seen riding the subway. And I couldn't take my eyes off her. There's a lot that's rough and out of control in *The Professional*—Aiello is low on energy, while Oldman indulges in a performance so operatically unhinged you'd think the actor was galloping toward the playing fields of Mickey Rourke. But there's even more that crackles here in enjoyable homage to the city that never sleeps."—Lisa Schwarzbaum, *Entertainment Weekly*

🗩 BEST LINE:
We've got a few. But two in particular capture the essence of the characters delivering them.

When Léon is explaining his job as a cleaner, he tells Mathilda that there are limits: "No women, no kids. That's the rule."

When Stansfield traps Mathilda in the men's room of the DEA offices and realizes she planned to kill him, he pulls out his gun and confronts her. After popping a few uppers, he asks her if she likes life. When she says that she does, he tells her, "That's good because I take no pleasure in taking life from a person who doesn't care about it."

But the best line may come during the final "conversation" between Léon and Stansfield. Without giving up too much, we can tell you that a wounded Léon hands the DEA agent a gift and says, "This is for Mathilda."

🍎 BET YOU DIDN'T KNOW:
Reno made an appearance in Besson's *La Femme Nikita* (1990) as a "cleaner" named Victor. Like Léon, Victor wore a long wool coat, a knit cap and sunglasses.

☺ GOOF:
The private school where Mathilda eventually seeks refuge is supposed to be in Wildwood, New Jersey—a seashore town at the southern end of the state. But a scene from the school grounds shows Manhattan in the background.

◀ CASTING CALL:
Liv Tyler was considered for Mathilda, but at 15 was deemed too old for the role. The movie walks a fine line between Léon as father figure and Léon as potential sexual predator. When Natalie Portman tells a hotel desk clerk that Léon is her lover, we know that it's outlandish and not true. This is in part because Reno plays Léon as naïve, straight-laced and mentally slow. The older Tyler's presence would have heightened the sexual issue and distracted from the storyline. If she said they were lovers, we might have believed it.

🎬 PIVOTAL SCENE:
Léon watches through the peephole in his apartment door as the corrupt DEA agents wipe out the family living next door. Mathilda, returning home with a bag of groceries, has the presence of mind to walk past her own apartment, push Léon's door bell and quietly mouths the words, "Please open the door."

With one of the corrupt cops standing guard and watching, Léon has to choose between letting her in and ignoring her plea—which, he and she both know, is essentially an invitation to death. He opens the door and lets her in.

🔫 VIOLENCE LEVEL:
At the top of the charts. In part, because Léon is, after all, a professional assassin. But it's exacerbated by the fact that Stansfield is a certifiable psychopath. Both are armed and extremely dangerous throughout the movie.

☠ BODY COUNT:
We got to twenty-seven and stopped counting. The finale features so much gunplay and so many explosions that it's impossible to get an accurate total.

✵ IF YOU LIKED THIS, YOU'LL LIKE:
The aforementioned *La Femme Nikita*—which was written and directed by Besson—and its American remake, *Point of No Return* (1993), directed by John Badham and starring Bridget Fonda.

14 MEAN STREETS (1973–R)

STARS: ROBERT DE NIRO, HARVEY KEITEL, AMY ROBINSON, CESARE DANOVA
DIRECTOR: MARTIN SCORSESE

One of the best things about watching *Mean Streets* more than 30 years after its debut is that you know what's coming after this. And so you look and you watch and you listen for little signs—small scenes that are the roots and the seedlings of the Scorsese/De Niro oeuvre.

This was the first film in which they worked together. Down the road would be *Raging Bull* and *Taxi Driver* and *GoodFellas* and *Casino*.

Scorsese has gone on to become perhaps the greatest director in American cinema. De Niro is one of its finest actors.

So on one level, watching *Mean Streets* is like finding some old film of Joe DiMaggio and Mickey Mantle and Willie Mays during their first seasons in the big leagues. The raw talent is there. There are sparks and smoldering potential. And it's a

pleasure to watch because you know you are looking at the start of greatness.

Mean Streets also broke some interesting ground in the mob movie genre.

It was one of the first to tell the story from street level. This is not about a Mafia don or the capo of a crew. It's about a bunch of guys from the neighborhood who are "connected," some directly and some, as is more often the case in real life, through a series of vague relationships.

Charlie (Harvey Keitel) is connected. His uncle Giovanni (Cesare Danova) heads a crew that runs part of New York's Little Italy—where the movie is set. He makes collections for his uncle and is on a career path that could lead to bigger and better things.

On the immediate horizon is a chance to take

over a restaurant whose owner, deeply in loan shark debt to Giovanni, is ready to give up the establishment to settle his financial score.

"Honorable men go with honorable men," Giovanni tells Charlie, who understands the concept but is pulled in other directions by his personal ties. The first is his loyalty to Johnny Boy (Robert De Niro), a boyhood friend. Johnny Boy isn't very connected and is hardly honorable. The other is his love interest in Johnny's cousin Teresa (Amy Robinson). She's considered "sick in the head" by Giovanni because she suffers from epilepsy.

Scorsese, who cowrote the script, weaves his story about the mob and street life around those characters and those relationships. There's a lot of Catholicism built in as well, with talk of guilt and redemption and burning in hell—all hallmarks of the Catholic Church in Scorsese's formative years.

In an interview in London's *Telegraph* in 2010, Scorsese described how the story and its conflicts came from his own background.

"The world I came from was very much based on loyalty and trust," said the director, who grew up on Elizabeth Street in the heart of New York's Little Italy. "And I think that's why so many of the stories I've done are rooted in a kind of tribal behavior that has to do with betrayal. When a person does 'betray' the other—he or she—why does that happen? What puts that person very often in a place where they have no choice, they couldn't do otherwise—and where the decision is not good either way."

Charlie has to choose, and in the end he, Johnny Boy and Teresa pay a price.

De Niro's Johnny Boy, a neighborhood screwup constantly bobbing and weaving away from loan sharks, is the primary reason Charlie finds himself in that place of conflict that Scorsese described.

Time and again, Charlie sides with his friend, even though he knows it flies in the face of the rules of the street and, more importantly, that it violates the rules of the honored society that his uncle is so much a part of.

Johnny Boy, a free agent and a force of nature who bounces around the neighborhood to the beat of a drummer only he can hear, could care less about the mob. His confrontation with Michael (Richard Romanus), a wiseguy loan shark trying to collect, establishes his character early in the movie.

"Michael, you make me laugh," says Johnny Boy in a scene that hints at the acting chops we see writ large in *Taxi Driver* and *Raging Bull*. "You see, I borrow money all over this neighborhood, left and right from everybody. I never pay them back. So I can't borrow no money from nobody no more, right? So, who would that leave me to borrow money from but you? I borrow money from you because you're the only jerk-off around here who I can borrow money from without payin' back, right?"

Somehow, in Johnny Boy's twisted logic, it's Michael's fault that he owes him money.

Go figure.

But that's life on the streets. It doesn't have to make sense. *Mean Streets* captures that rhythm.

So we see the guys hustling a couple of teenagers out of $40 by selling them bogus fireworks. And we follow them to a pool hall where they intend to collect a $235 debt, but instead get into a fight over the meaning of the word "mook." Or we listen as Charlie and his friend Tony (David Proval) discuss St. Francis of Assisi, a hero in Charlie's angst-ridden Catholic mind. There is a part of Charlie that wants to do good. And a part of him that wants to be a gangster.

"Francis of Assisi had it all down," Charlie says.

"St. Francis didn't run numbers," Tony replies.

All of this comes from the neighborhoods where Scorsese and De Niro grew up. *Mean Streets* brings it to life.

A soundtrack that includes classics like "Be My Baby" by the Ronnettes, "Please Mister Postman" by the Marvelettes, and a pulsating "Jumpin' Jack Flash" by the Rolling Stones (the topic of a recent Scorsese documentary) goes a long way in helping set the mood.

But it's the acting in the film's series of character studies and small dramas that drives the story.

Vincent Canby, writing in the *New York Times*, praised Scorsese for creating a script that "faces its characters and their world head-on.

"It never looks over their shoulder or takes a position above their heads in order to impose a self-conscious relevance on them. There is no need to."

That, Canby wrote, is what filmmaking is all about.

Mean Streets helped define a genre. But more important, it marked the start of something extraordinary in the American cinema.

⊙ **HIT:** Pick almost any scene and there's something worth watching. Scorsese made slicker, better-crafted movies as his career progressed, but the nuts and bolts of who he is and what he's about are here.

⊗ **MISS:** In that same vein, some of the camera action is disconcerting. This film was made on a limited budget—about $600,000—and primarily shot with hand-held cameras. This added to its almost documentary feel at times. But at other times,   it was both dizzying and off-putting, like a home movie. A small nit to pick, but there none the less.

✎ **WHAT THEY WROTE AT THE TIME:** "Instead of developing these characters and their complex interactions, [*Mean Streets*] remains content to sketch in their day-to-day happenings. But Scorsese is exceptionally good at guiding his largely unknown cast to near-flawless recreations of types. Outstanding in this regard is De Niro."—*Variety*

❝ **BEST LINE:** "You don't make up for your sins in the Church. You do it in the streets. You do it at home. The rest is bullshit and you know it," muses Charlie in a voice-over of his thoughts as the movie opens. The comments set the tone for what's to come. (Scorsese, rather than Keitel, did the lines.)

◄ **CASTING CALL:** Scorsese's mentor, independent filmmaker Roger Corman, was willing to finance the film but wanted Scorsese to change the story and use an all-black cast. Scorsese turned down the offer.

☺ **"I KNOW THAT GAL":** Scorsese's mother, Catherine, has a cameo as the apartment neighbor who comes to Teresa's aid when she has an epileptic fit. She is also the woman seen closing the window at the end of the film. Scorsese has used his mother in several of his films. She was, for example, cast as Joe Pesci's mother in *GoodFellas,* playing the classic kitchen scene in which her son asked to borrow a knife.

♟ **BET YOU DIDN'T KNOW:** Scorsese and Mardik Martin wrote the script while driving around New York's Little Italy, stopping to write and absorb scenes and settings. The screenplay was originally called *Season of the Witch*, but was changed to *Mean Streets*, a title taken from a line in a Raymond Chandler essay called "The Simple Art of Murder."

◎ **REPEATED WATCHING QUOTIENT:** A classic that the Library of Congress has included among films worth preserving in the National Film Registry, *Mean Streets* is worth a second, third and fourth look. Once a year, at least.

☛ **VIOLENCE LEVEL:** Lots of shouting. Plenty of cursing. Not much shooting,

⚰ **BODY COUNT:** Three.

⊕ **IF YOU LIKED THIS, YOU'LL LIKE:** Scorsese's first full-length film, *Who's That Knocking on My Door* (1967), is another story about life in Little Italy. Keitel also plays a major role in this one, again portraying a young Italian-American trying to figure out life.

15 RESERVOIR DOGS (1992–R)

STARS: HARVEY KEITEL, TIM ROTH, MICHAEL MADSEN, STEVE BUSCEMI
DIRECTOR: QUENTIN TARANTINO

Reservoir Dogs is an action film without much action. A crime drama in which you never see the main crime take place. A comedy that makes you sometimes feel uneasy about laughing. A buddy movie where the buddies end up killing each other.

What is it exactly?

"It's a heist film," says writer-director Quentin Tarantino, "about a bunch of guys who get together to pull a robbery and everything goes wrong. It all leads to violence and blood, but it ends up being black, gallows humor."

All true. And *Reservoir Dogs* is more than that. It's the movie that launched Tarantino's career at age 29, and turned American cinema on its (severed) ear. Tarantino's idea was to focus his story on

the robbers, not the cops. And, rather than discuss their caper on-screen, they would spend most of their time—as guys do—engaged in small talk about pop culture or fast-food joints or women they want to sleep with.

That dialogue has the sneaky effect of putting the audience on common ground with the gangsters. Turns out, we listen to the same oldies on the radio, crack the same jokes and have the same debates about issues like tipping. In a strange way that prompts you—as the viewer—to feel sympathy for these dark-hearted characters.

Mix into that Tarantino's creative use of time arcs and unconventional pacing. It all made *Reservoir Dogs* a sensation—with critics and filmmakers at least—when it came out in 1992. And so this movie begat *Pulp Fiction*, of course, as well as *The Usual Suspects* and *Memento* and *Suicide Kings*. Not to mention dozens of copycats that don't match up.

But you needn't care about all that. You just have to enjoy *Reservoir Dogs* as a powerful movie.

The story centers on six crooks hired by gang leader Joe Cabot (played by old-time Hollywood tough guy Lawrence Tierney) and his son Nice Guy Eddie (Chris Penn) to pull off a big diamond heist. None of the crew knows each other going in, and that's deliberate. This way, as Joe sees it, anyone who gets caught cannot rat out his mates.

Each is assigned a color-coded alias—Mr. Blue, Mr. Brown, Mr. Blonde, etc. There's a great little moment when Steve Buscemi's character balks at being given the name Mr. Pink. "Be thankful you're not Mr. Yellow," barks Joe.

There's a strong cast here, led by Harvey Keitel (who helped find funding for the film) as Mr. White. As a group they joke, they posture, they bond and they prep for the crime.

But something goes wrong. The diamond robbery (which, again, we never see) is interrupted by an army of cops who obviously got tipped off. The job blows up, leaving one of the gang dead, one missing and one—Tim Roth's Mr. Orange—bleeding to death from a shot to the belly.

The survivors rendezvous at an empty warehouse and try to figure out what went wrong. They engage in some paranoid finger-pointing, assuming that one among them must be working with the cops. And they try to beat an explanation out of an unfortunate LAPD rookie taken hostage by the psychotic Mr. Blonde (Michael Madsen).

The movie leaps around in time. It opens with the characters arguing over the lyrics to Madonna's song "Like a Virgin." Then it moves to the opening credits, with our antiheroes rambling down the street in slow motion, all decked out in black suits and sunglasses. Then we cut to the getaway car, where Mr. Orange writhes in pain in the backseat as Mr. White tries to comfort him, figure out where things went awry and drive away from the scene of their crime.

It all requires you to pay close attention. Not that doing so is a challenge. You, as an audience member, know the bottom line of the botched heist before the movie's characters do. The fun is seeing who on-screen will figure it out and how many will kill each other along the way.

Reservoir Dogs borrows a lot from Stanley Kubrick's 1956 classic *The Killing*, a film you'll find later in this book. That film also uses flashbacks and fast forwards to flesh out the characters and show how the caper got botched.

Tarantino mulled over *Reservoir Dogs* for eight years before writing the script in less than a month in a spiral notebook (no typewriter). He expected to make the movie himself on a minuscule budget of $30,000. But an acting coach who knew somebody who knew Keitel agreed to show the script to the prominent actor. Keitel was enthused, agreeing both to act in it and find $1.5 million to finance it.

What makes *Reservoir Dogs* snap is Tarantino's terrific dialogue. In a news conference at Cannes after the movie premiered, the screenwriter/director was asked how he comes up with his on-screen conversations.

"I just keep a notebook with me at all times," he said. "So, if we're discussing Pam Grier or Madonna or macaroni-and-cheese or Coca Cola, I just write it down. Everything you see in the movie is just a conversation I've had in real life."

◉ **HIT:** One of the joys of watching a Tarantino movie is catching inside references to his other works. So we have Mr. White being asked about formerly working with a woman named Alabama. That character, played by Patricia Arquette, actually shows up in Tarantino's next script, *True Romance*.

There's also a reference to *Pulp Fiction's* big boss Marsellus Wallace as a fence for the stolen diamonds. Notice, too, that Mr. Blonde's real name is Vic Vega. It's the same surname, of course, of John Travolta's Vince Vega in *Pulp Fiction*. Tarantino envisioned doing a prequel to both of those films called *Double V Vega*, but scrapped it when Madsen and Travolta got too old for the roles.

⊗ MISS: We appreciate Tarantino's gritty dialogue. But maybe, in just one of his movies, could he back off the incessant use of the N-word? The blanket of racial epithets has been questioned by many, including Spike Lee, who told *Variety*, "I'm not against the word. I've used it. But Quentin is infatuated with the word. What does he want—to be made an honorary black man?"

For his part, Tarantino—like Lenny Bruce a half-century ago—says that by repeating a loaded word so frequently and randomly, he hopes to defuse its impact.

✎ WHAT THEY WROTE AT THE TIME:
"*Glengarry Glen Ross* with guns, *Diner* with gore, *GoodFellas* minus girls."—*Village Voice*

▤ PIVOTAL SCENE: Few movie moments make you cringe like Mr. Blonde's seven-minute torture of Marvin the cop.

Left alone in the warehouse with Marvin and a dying Mr. Orange, Mr. Blonde announces he will torture the hostage officer—not because he thinks it will yield helpful information, but simply because he will enjoy it.

As the helpless cop sits taped to a chair, his tormentor turns on the radio. Mr. Blonde begins to dance to the '70s hit "Stuck in the Middle with You" by Stealers Wheel. Then he pulls out a straight razor, struts up to Marvin and slices off his ear. Even as his victim gasps in pain, Mr. Blonde mocks him by talking into the now-severed ear. "Hey, what's going on?" he says to the bloody flesh. "Can you hear that?"

The scene was shot so that the camera pans away from the action right as Mr. Blonde begins his razor surgery—although most viewers swear afterward they witnessed the actual cutting. The DVD contains deleted scenes that are even more graphic, including one where blood begins to spurt from poor Marvin's ear hole.

After the attack, Mr. Blonde douses the cop with gasoline, a prelude to burning him alive—until those plans are interrupted. We don't want to give away that part.

A FEW OTHER THINGS YOU SHOULD KNOW ABOUT THE SCENE:

• Madsen had a tough time carrying through with his sadistic role. At one point, actor Kirk Baltz, playing Marvin, improvised the line where he begs for his life by saying he has a child at home. Madsen, a new father himself, had to stop and leave the set.

• Tarantino deliberately chose a sugary Top 40 song for the scene to give the audience false comfort before the violence. "You're tapping your toe, you're enjoying Michael Madsen doing his dance and then, voom!—it's too late, you're a co-conspirator," he said in the book *Quentin Tarantino: The Cinema of Cool* by Jeff Dawson.

• Right before release, Miramax Films head Harvey Weinstein pleaded with Tarantino to delete the scene, telling him it would prompt audiences to walk out. "And that happens every single screening," Tarantino later told the *Seattle Times*. "For some people the violence is a mountain they can't climb. That's okay. It's not their cup of tea. But I am affecting them. I wanted that scene to be disturbing."

⚑ VIOLENCE LEVEL: You're kidding, right?

☺ GOOF: During that torture scene, Marvin the cop's legs are alternately duct-taped to the chair and kicking in the air.

✔ REALITY CHECK: We can't imagine Mr. Orange would survive for all those hours after being shot. He's spilling enough blood to supply an Army hospital.

➨ DON'T FAIL TO NOTICE: The scream heard when Mr. Pink pushes a woman to the sidewalk during his escape from police. The sound is the so-called "Wilhelm Scream," a Hollywood effect that has been dubbed into more than 200 films—from *Star Wars* to *Batman Returns* to *Toy Story*. Tarantino, a Hollywood history buff, edited it into this movie, as well as into *Kill Bill: Vol. I*.

Although no one is sure, most believe the scream was first heard in 1951's *Distant Drums*, and was voiced by Sheb Wooley. You might recognize Wooley as the kindly but weak-hearted principal in *Hoosiers*, or as the singer of the old novelty song "The Purple People Eater." You can see a three-minute compilation of more than 30 movies using the Wilhelm Scream by going to www.youtube.com/watch?v=cdbYsoEasio.

➡ **DON'T FAIL TO NOTICE II:** The film doesn't have a single woman in a speaking part.

◀ **CASTING CALL:** Christopher Walken and Vincent Gallo declined roles, while George Clooney, Samuel L. Jackson and David Duchovny auditioned but were turned down. Tarantino sought James Woods, making five separate offers to his agent. It later came out that the agent never forwarded the offers to Woods—prompting Woods to fire the man.

🍎 **BET YOU DIDN'T KNOW:** Right before filming started, all eight of the principal actors met at a dinner party hosted by Keitel. It came out in conversation that each of them had spent time in jail—most notably Edward Bunker (Mr. Blue), a convicted bank robber who made the FBI's Ten Most Wanted list.

"Whatever they had done in their lives to get there," said producer Lawrence Bender, "all of that energy was about to be put to good use."

🤠 **"I KNOW THAT GUY":** Deadpan comedian Steven Wright provides the disc jockey's voice for "K-Billy's Super Sounds of the 70s," the radio show constantly playing in the background.

👁 **REPEATED WATCHING QUOTIENT:** Extremely high. This is a richly textured film that reveals further nuances upon each viewing.

🟦 **BEST LINE:** Mr. Pink (Buscemi), suggesting that there is a rat among the group: "Somebody's shoved a red-hot poker up our ass, and I want to know whose name is on the handle."

✵ **IF YOU LIKED THIS, YOU'LL LIKE:** *Kaante*, Indian director Sanjay Gupta's 2002 reimagining of this film. In the Bollywood version, the six conspirators also favor black suits and sunglasses, and spend much of their time in restaurants engaged in small talk. Unlike the bad guys in *Reservoir Dogs*, they also sing and dance.

🔪 **BODY COUNT:** Twelve that you see, plus four offscreen that are referenced.

AN INTERVIEW WITH TIM ROTH

Actor Tim Roth, a favorite of Quentin Tarantino, plays undercover cop Mr. Orange in *Reservoir Dogs* and the restaurant stickup man known as Pumpkin (or occasionally Ringo) in *Pulp Fiction*. He has acted in more than 50 movies and played the lead character in the TV show *Lie to Me*.

We heard you got cast for* Reservoir Dogs *even after refusing to read for the movie. Is that right?

True story. I got called to meet with Quentin and Harvey Keitel, which, of course, was very exciting. They wanted me to audition and I wouldn't—not because of snobbery, but because I've always been bad at reading. I figure I lost 50 percent of the roles with bad auditions. We went for sandwiches at a deli, and Harvey was disappointed I wouldn't try out. Afterward I took Quentin to my favorite pub. He's talking about the movie, and we're getting drunk. He started writing lines from the script on napkins. We're snockered and I'm reading dialogue off a beer-soaked napkin. And that was my audition.

When you got the script the roles weren't assigned. Did you want to be a particular character?

My agent suggested I look at Mr. Blonde and Mr. Pink. But reading it, I loved the role of Mr. Orange, because I loved the idea of an Englishman playing an American playing a cop playing a gangster. All those layers. But Quentin liked me for Mr. Orange for a different reason. I was unknown in the United States at the time. So in casting, he wanted me to look like the spare guy who the audience would expect to get killed in the opening scene because,

hey, who knew Tim Roth? As the movie reveals characters, you don't think they're going to come back to this guy. So my anonymity back then helped me get the role.

Your character spends most of the movie lying on the ground drenched in blood. What challenges did that present?

For one, they had to hose me down every day just to get me off the floor. For five weeks of filming, I was stuck to that floor, which was in a very hot room at the back of a funeral parlor. They used syrup for the blood, which wasn't really pleasant after all those days.

The greatness of* Reservoir Dogs *and* Pulp Fiction *is in the dialogue, the conversations between the characters. How much of that was improvised by the actors?

None of it. It feels organic, like it came out at the spur of the moment, right? But the dialogue went unchanged from script to the final movie. Quentin's dialogue sounds like spontaneous conversations about tipping waiters or banging Madonna, but it's written out word for word. And often it has nothing to do with the plot per se, but everything to do with the characters. It's not just shoe leather. It makes the characters real.

You worked with some terrific actors in those two movies. Did any of them particularly impress you?

That would be Harvey (Keitel). Our characters in *Reservoir Dogs* have an echo of a father-son relationship, which ends with my betrayal. I was always a huge fan of his going back to *Mean Streets* with De Niro. He's an interesting guy, a consummate professional. To be able to play scenes with him was extraordinary.

The other one who impressed me was Michael Madsen. He was a guy I didn't expect to get along with, a real man's man, a tough guy. I didn't grow up in that world. But he was so much deeper than that. We talked about poetry—which he writes— and about novels. I loved him and still do.

To what do you attribute the enduring popularity of those Tarantino films?

The brilliance of the writing. The novelistic structure. A novel can go in any order, why not a film? That, plus the humor, especially in *Pulp*. Very dark but very funny.

What are your all-time favorite gangster movies?

Anything with (James) Cagney. He's the all-time great. Look at him in *White Heat*, he eats chicken and then throws the character in the trunk. That's a great scene, the juxtaposition—like one Quentin would have done. That and *The Public Enemy* might be my two favorites.

As a native of England, what do you see as a difference between British and American gangster films?

Well, Guy Ritchie's films are looking at Quentin— and maybe a little too closely. I think the big difference is that British gangster films show less glamour. Our filmmakers go for more anger and dirt. They are filled with nasty people you definitely don't want to be around. The Americans go more for family and the romance of it all. But in either country, if you can put the audience in fear of being in the same room as the guy, that's a successful gangster movie.

Is it true that as a teenager you wrote letters to famous directors, trying to get into the business?

I did. I was 15 and wanted to get into acting. I sent handwritten letters along with my photo to Scorsese, Stanley Kubrick, Coppola. The amazing thing was that 30 years later I got to work with Coppola (on 2007's *Youth Without Youth*). The first day of shooting he brought the letter. He saved it all those years. Imagine that.

Would you like the opportunity to act in another gangster film?

I did. I was a hit man in *The Hit* (1984), directed by Stephen Frears, which I am proud of. I was going to be involved in a sequel to *The Long Good Friday*, but that didn't get off the ground. And maybe you missed me in *Hoodlum* (1997). That didn't work as well. I played Dutch Schultz—kind of half Cagney and half Bugs Bunny.

16 SCARFACE (1983–R)

STARS: AL PACINO, STEVEN BAUER, MICHELLE PFEIFFER, MARY ELIZABETH MASTRANTONIO | DIRECTOR: BRIAN DE PALMA

Critics had mixed reactions to this gangland epic when it was released.

But the early negative reviews did little to keep *Scarface* from becoming an American pop culture phenomenon.

Three decades later, posters, video games and online quote boards keep the buzz going.

A remake of the 1932 classic of the same name starring Paul Muni, Al Pacino's *Scarface* is more often compared to his other underworld epics, *The Godfather* and *The Godfather: Part II*. All four movies are about the immigrant experience and a

charismatic figure from the underclass using any means possible to realize the American dream.

The dream, of course, becomes a nightmare.

Pacino's Tony Montana lacks the style and grace of Michael Corleone. But then Michael is a second-generation ethnic who has been educated at an Ivy League school. Montana is literally up from the streets. Director Brian De Palma, with a script by Oliver Stone, made no attempt to sugarcoat what that meant.

Montana is arrogant, bombastic, self-indulgent, ruthless and a cold-blooded killer. His story is about power—how to get it, how to use it and how to hold onto it.

Sprinkled with street-level philosophy that is as much a reflection on the American economic and political systems as it is about the drug subculture, *Scarface* is a story about the United States in the 1980s. And like Stone's other morality tale from that decade, *Wall Street* (1987), it embodies a mantra from those turbulent times that Gordon Gekko made famous—"Greed is good."

But whereas the greed in *Wall Street* inspired insider trading and hostile takeovers, *Scarface*'s greed leads to murder and mayhem. Released from a Cuban prison and sent to America in the controversial Mariel boatlift, Montana and his best friend Manny (Steven Bauer) end up in Miami as struggling sandwich shop workers. But they've got big dreams.

They graduate to become low-level enforcers for Frank Lopez (Robert Loggia), a drug kingpin who has clearly made it. Lopez—with his wealth, power, status and beautiful American ice goddess mistress Elvira Hancock (Michelle Pfieffer)—has everything Tony wants.

The first half of the film is Montana maneuvering to get it. Never subtle, Tony makes his plans clear in a discussion with Manny while they're still struggling.

"Me, I want what's coming to me," he says.

"What's coming to you?" a skeptical Manny asks.

"The world, chico, and everything in it," Montana replies.

While Pacino's Cuban accent is sometimes disconcerting (much like his attempt at a Puerto Rican accent in *Carlito's Way*, a film also reviewed in this book), his performance in the first half of the movie is compelling.

We shouldn't like Tony Montana, but we do. On a certain level we want him to succeed.

His balls-to-the-wall confrontation with a chainsaw-wielding drug dealer in a raunchy motel bathroom showcases Montana as the ultimate tough guy. His nonchalant, let's-do-business reaction after his associate, Omar Suarez (F. Murray Abraham), is hung by the neck from a helicopter circling a South American cocaine kingpin's com-

pound is cool and calculating. His wooing of Elvira combines arrogance and sweetness.

All three incidents offer hints at who Tony Montana is and who he might become.

At first, the sultry and aloof Elvira wants nothing to do with him and says as much in one of the classic movie putdowns of all time: "Even if I were blind, desperate, starved and begging for it on a desert island, you'd be the last one I'd ever fuck."

Tony, of course, ends up in bed with—and eventually married to—Elvira.

He also gets the money, the power and the status that comes with being a cocaine kingpin in 1980s Miami, a world populated by corrupt cops, fast women and hairy-chested wannabe gangsters dressed in open-collared shirts, gold chains and three-inch-heeled boots.

He has figured out the way the game is played.

"In this country, you gotta make the money first," he tells Manny. "Then when you get the money, you get the power. Then, when you get the power, you get the women."

Strip away the violence and the bravado, however, and *Scarface* offers a rather mundane storyline about how power corrupts.

Tony's fall is telegraphed during one of his first meetings with Lopez and Elvira.

"Rule number one," Lopez tells his young protégé. "Don't ever underestimate the other guy's greed."

"And don't get high on your own supply," Elvira adds.

The second half of the movie deals with the repercussions of Tony's failure to heed those words of advice.

His relationship with Gina (Mary Elizabeth Mastrantonio), a sister he hasn't seen in years, adds a bizarre, familial twist to the story with hints of incestuous desire. After she and Manny become lovers, their fates are sealed. This is not a marriage made in heaven, but rather in the violent underworld of Tony Montana. Their separation is bloody and final.

Pacino, as is his wont, begins to chew the scenery as the movie rushes toward its gun-blazing finale. Hopped up on coke, rejected by his Cuban immigrant mother because she sees him for what he is and at war with his South American cocaine supplier, Tony is armed and dangerous in the extreme.

Movie critic Leonard Maltin, who offered a less-than-favorable comparison to the original *Scarface*, wrote that this version "wallows in excess and unpleasantness for nearly three hours and offers no new insights except that crime doesn't pay. . . . Even so, this has become a pop culture phenomenon with Pacino's Tony Montana an underdog hero."

Another critic referred to Montana as a character "cut from inch-thick cardboard."

Oliver Stone had a different take on his lead character. Speaking to the American Film Institute at a banquet to mark Pacino's receipt of an AFI Lifetime Achievement Award, Stone said, "You'll never see a bad guy like this again."

⊙ **HIT:** The violence and degradation of the cocaine underworld are captured in both the writing and the acting. While *Scarface* was clearly a reference to the 1930s classic on which it was based, a more accurate description comes in the Spanish title for the film, *El Precio del Poder*—"The Price of Power."

⊗ **MISS:** There are several over-the-top moments, but none compare with the finale. As Tony's body floats in the pool in front of the statue, we see the words "The World Is Yours." The irony is lost, as is any attempt at subtlety. This point has already been made about a dozen times.

✎ **WHAT THEY WROTE AT THE TIME:** "De Palma's update of the 1932 classic is the most stylish and provocative—and maybe the most vicious—serious film about the American underworld since Francis Ford Coppola's *Godfather*. In almost every way, though, the two films are memorably different. *Scarface* contains not an ounce of anything that could pass for sentimentality, which the film ridicules without mercy. *The Godfather* is a multigenerational epic, full of true sentiment. *Scarface* has the impact of a single, breathless anecdote, being about one young hood's rapid rise and fall in the southern Florida cocaine industry."—Vincent Canby, *New York Times*

✔ **REALITY CHECK:** The Mariel boatlift, which sets the movie in motion, was an actual event that lent credence to the film's story. There were about 125,000 Cubans brought to the United States at the time. Of those, about 12,500 were criminals. Fidel Castro emptied his prisons, increasing the number of "refugees" seeking freedom in America.

◉ **REPEATED WATCHING QUOTIENT:** This film has taken on cult status. If you're a fan—and we know there are tens of thousands of you out there—you can't see it enough. For others, an occasional revisit will do.

➜ **DON'T FAIL TO NOTICE:** The film is dedicated to Howard Hawks and Ben Hecht, the director and writer of the original *Scarface* from 1932. A lot had changed in regards to censorship standards in the half-century between the two films. But De Palma still had to fight to keep his *Scarface* from receiving an X rating. He won that battle despite all the movie's gory, graphic violence and foul language after experts testified before the Motion Picture Association of America that the film accurately depicted life in the drug underworld. The word "fuck" and its derivatives are used more than 200 times.

🍎 **BET YOU DIDN'T KNOW:** Writer Oliver Stone picked the name Montana because he was a big fan of San Francisco 49ers quarterback Joe Montana. Tony Montana is called "Scarface" just once during the film—in an early scene when immigration officials refer to him as "Caracicatriz," which is Spanish for "Scarface."

🙶 **BEST LINE:** "Say hello to my little friend!" is one of the most frequently quoted lines from any gangster movie. It made the American Film Institute's list of Top 100 all-time quotes (ranking 61st). The line has come to define the Tony Montana character created by Pacino, a hopped-up kingpin, standing alone against the world, brandishing an assault rifle equipped with a grenade launcher. This, we know, is not going to end well.

We also like Tony's take on life: "All I have in this world is my balls and my word. And I don't break 'em for no one."

Stone, at the aforementioned AFI ceremony, had this to say about his script: "No matter how many screenplays I write, I think 'Fuck you' and 'Say hello to my little friend' may well live on as my contribution to the culture."

◀ CASTING CALL: John Travolta was considered for the role of Manny. Steven Bauer, who got the part, is the only Cuban cast in a major role. Several actresses were considered for or turned down the role of Elvira. Rosanna Arquette, Melanie Griffith and Kim Basinger were among those who passed on the chance, while Geena Davis, Carrie Fisher and Sharon Stone auditioned but didn't get the part.

☛ VIOLENCE LEVEL: Off the charts, from the chainsaw scene to the final shootout, this is one of the most violent gangster movies of all time.

⚰ BODY COUNT: Forty-two.

17 WHITE HEAT (1949–NR)

STARS: JAMES CAGNEY, VIRGINIA MAYO, EDMOND O'BRIEN, MARGARET WYCHERLY
DIRECTOR: RAOUL WALSH

James Cagney returned to Warner Brothers to make this movie, still considered one of the best gangster films of all time. In the 1930s, Cagney had helped establish the genre—which became the studio's franchise—with leading roles in *The Public Enemy* and *Angels with Dirty Faces* (both of which also made this book's Top 100).

On one level, *White Heat* was a return to that successful style. Both Cagney and Warner Brothers were mending their fences after a contract dispute had ended their relationship and hurt him in the pocketbook and the studio at the box office.

But Raoul Walsh took the typical gangster-prison movie to another level with this story of Cody Jarrett, a mentally unstable and chillingly violent mob leader with an Oedipus complex. Cody's relationship with his mother (Margaret Wycherly) gave Walsh a turbulent and troubling back story that positioned *White Heat* as part of a new wave of movie making.

This was film noir, movies where evil not only exists, but flourishes. Cagney's Cody Jarrett isn't a charismatic outlaw who viewers could vicariously admire, but rather a despicable embodiment of immorality, a man who takes what he wants whenever he wants it, mocking and abusing all those he comes in contact with—including the cops, members of his own gang and his less-than-virtuous wife, Verna (Virginia Mayo).

Ma, in fact, is the only woman whom Cody cares about. And it is her comfort he seeks when the rush of a migraine headache—the "white heat" from which the movie's title is derived—staggers him.

Several reviewers later compared *White Heat*'s mother-son relationship to the one developed by Alfred Hitchcock in *Psycho*.

"Never would we see a stronger or more bizarre mother-son relationship . . . until Hitchcock stretched the situation . . . a decade later," John Puccio wrote in an excellent review of *White Heat* published in 2005. David Thomson, writing in the (London) *Guardian,* said of Ma Jarrett, "there wouldn't be a better killer mother until *Psycho*."

Thomson, who included *White Heat* in his list of all-time, Top 10 gangster movies, also raised a question that is sure to generate debate among 21st-century gangster movie buffs: who is nastier—James Cagney or Joe Pesci?

Cagney's performance here is the precursor to Pesci's in *GoodFellas*. Both portrayed gangsters whose trademark was violent behavior fueled by a viciousness born of an internal turmoil that burst to the surface unexpectedly—and seemingly without logical justification.

Jarrett's actions underscore that viciousness in scene after scene. At one point, he kidnaps Roy Parker (Paul Guilfoyle), an associate who had tried to kill him. Parker is placed inside the trunk of a car and Jarrett asks him how he's doing.

Parker replies that it's a "little stuffy."

"I'll give ya' a little air," Jarrett cackles, pulling out a gun and pumping four bullets into the trunk.

Members of Jarrett's own gang refer to him as a "crackpot," but can do little about it. When his second-in-command, Big Ed Somers (Steve Cochran), implies that he is ready to take over, another gang member quips, "Where do ya' want the body sent?"

Everyone knows that to cross Cody Jarrett is to court death.

During the California train robbery that sets the movie in motion, Jarrett coldly guns down the train's engineer and fireman because they have heard an associate refer to him by name. The associate, who gets burned by steam from the engine during the getaway, is later marked for death by Jarrett after he and the rest of the gang decide to abandon their mountain hideout. Left behind in a cabin, the disfigured gangster freezes to death.

The discovery of his body—and a cigarette pack from which a fingerprint is taken—give U.S. Treasury agents evidence linking the train heist and murders to the Jarrett gang. (The use of forensic evidence and "sophisticated" tracking and tailing techniques were emphasized by Walsh in a storyline that at times has the gritty feel of a documentary. The device worked well at the time, but today seems somewhat dated.)

The rest of the movie is built around the Feds' attempt to nail Jarrett and Jarrett's battle with his personal demons as he cleverly stays one step ahead of those pursuing him.

White Heat is sprinkled with some good, tough-guy dialogue. "You wouldn't kill me in cold blood, would ya', Cody?" a gangster who has betrayed Jarrett asks. "Nah, I'll let ya' warm up first," Cody replies. The film is a character study that becomes more intense as the story unfolds, with Max Steiner's musical orchestration heightening that tension.

Jarrett's relationship with his mother first surfaces in the mountain hideaway, when he suffers a seizure. She takes him into a bedroom and strokes his head. After he comes out of it, she pours a glass of whiskey and offers it to him.

"Top of the world, son," Ma Jarrett says, setting up the film's signature phrase.

Ma Jarrett is the brains and stabilizing force behind the gang. Cody's wife, Verna Jarrett, plays the opposite role, always pushing for more.

"I'd look good in a mink coat," she tells Cody, who is insisting that none of the $300,000 taken in the train heist be spent.

"You'd look good in a shower curtain," he replies.

Later, still complaining about cash, Verna says, "Money's only paper if you don't spend it."

After Cody cleverly ducks the train heist investigation by confessing to an Illinois bank robbery that occurred at the same time (explaining that he couldn't be in two places at once), he is sentenced to three years in jail.

Ma Jarrett takes over the gang, but Big Ed and Verna have other ideas.

Treasury Department investigators who don't buy Cody's alibi put an undercover agent (Edmond O'Brien) into the prison to get close to the gang boss and find evidence that will tie him to the train robbery and murders.

A series of penitentiary scenes play like set pieces from a dozen other prison movies that were made in the 1930s and 1940s. But they have their moments, one classic one coming when one of Jarrett's cellmates is meeting with his lawyer. The lawyer goes on in great detail about the different legal moves he is attempting to get his client out of jail.

"Jerry," the inmate finally says in disgust, "you couldn't get me out of here if I was pardoned."

Jarrett's last contact with Ma occurs during a prison visit in which she tells him that Big Ed and Verna have taken off together. She blames herself and says she will make it right, but Jarrett tells her to leave it alone, that he will deal with them when he gets out.

Later, while planning an escape, he learns that Ma has died. He flips out and is taken to a prison infirmary. From there, he plots a new escape with a decidedly different agenda.

The ensuing mayhem stems from the death—murder—of the only woman who ever meant anything to him. His plans for revenge coupled with a Trojan horse scheme to knock off a chemical plant and its $426,000 payroll led to one of the most dramatic finales in crime film history.

White Heat was ranked fourth in the American Film Institute's list of 10 greatest gangster films. *Time* magazine has listed it as one of the Top 100 films of all time.

⊙ **HIT:** Cagney. Cagney. Cagney. His performance became the template for movie gangsters for the next 20 years.

⊗ **MISS:** What passed for high tech in 1949 looks hokey in 2011. It's like comparing those old *Flash Gordon* serials to *Avatar*. This is not a fault of the movie, but one that a 21st-century viewer will have to make allowances for while watching the film.

🎬 **PIVOTAL SCENE:** Sitting at the prison mess hall table with dozens of other inmates, Jarrett spots a new arrival and passes word down the line seeking news about Ma. Word comes back, inmate to inmate, "She's dead." When Jarrett gets the message, he goes nuts and the film takes on an even darker hue.

❞ **BEST LINE:** "Made it Ma! Top of the world!" Jarrett shouts in his final lines in the film. The quote was listed at #18 on the American Film Institute's list of greatest movie quotes. And like many others ("Play it, Sam," in *Casablanca* for example), it is often misquoted. "Top of the world, Ma," is how most people incorrectly remember the line, just as most usually say, "Play it again, Sam."

✎ **WHAT THEY WROTE AT THE TIME:** "Let us soberly warn that *White Heat* is . . . a cruelly vicious film and that its impact upon the emotions of the unstable or impressionable is incalculable. . . . Mr. Cagney achieves the fascination of a brilliant bullfighter at work, deftly engaged in the business of doing violence with economy and grace."—Bosley Crowther, *New York Times*

➡ **DON'T FAIL TO NOTICE:** One of the burly prison inmates who helps pass word to Jarrett along the dining table that his mother has died is former All-American Jim Thorpe, who briefly tried his hand at acting after his sports career had ended.

😀 **"I KNOW THAT GUY":** Fred Clark, who played Daniel "The Trader" Winston (the fence who Jarrett employed to turn his stolen money—with traceable serial numbers—into usable cash), was just beginning his career. He had a small part in *Flamingo Road*, the Joan Crawford melodrama that came out the same year as *White Heat*. He later appeared in over 100 films and television series, usually as the bumbling associate or foil of the film's male lead. His film credits include *How to Marry a Millionaire* (1953), *Don't Go Near the Water* (1957) and *Auntie Mame* (1958).

🍎 **BET YOU DIDN'T KNOW:** The character of Cody Jarrett was loosely based on Francis "Two Gun" Crowley, an Irish gangster and convicted murderer from New York City. Crowley was arrested in 1931 after a two-hour shootout with police in Lower Manhattan that attracted a crowd of over 15,000, according to news reports from the day. Convicted of murdering a police officer, his last words before being executed a year later were, "Send my love to my mother."

🔫 **BODY COUNT:** Seventeen, with sixteen dying by gunfire and one freezing to death.

18 A BRONX TALE (1993–R)

STARS: CHAZZ PALMINTERI, ROBERT DE NIRO, LILLO BRANCATO
DIRECTOR: ROBERT DE NIRO

A *Bronx Tale* is more than a wonderful portrait of growing up around the mob in the 1960s. Written by Chazz Palminteri, directed by Robert De Niro and starring both, the movie is a primer on life. No film this side of *The Godfather* provides as many valuable life lessons. Such as:

"You want to see a real hero? Look at a guy who gets up in the morning and goes off to work and supports his family. That's heroism."

Those words come from Lorenzo Anello (De Niro), a bus driver trying to scrape by in New York's Fordham neighborhood. They are meant to inspire his son Calogero (Lillo Brancato). Lorenzo leads the straight life, staying within his means (which

means sitting in the nosebleed seats at the fights), cleaning up his bus each day and constantly preaching morality to his boy.

But the nine-year-old is intrigued by the gangsters living around him, particularly Sonny (Palminteri), the charismatic boss. "In my neighborhood he was a god," Calogero says in narration. "I would sit on my stoop and watch him all day and night."

One afternoon, Calogero witnesses Sonny shooting a man in a confrontation over a parking spot. Despite police pressure to pick the killer out of a lineup, Calogero refuses to rat. This impresses Sonny. Soon enough, he has the young boy running his errands and rolling his dice in the backroom craps game at his bar, the Chez Bippy. The blessed

Calogero even makes 11 passes in a row.

"The working man is a sucker," pronounces Sonny. This sets up a decade-long tug of war between Calogero's two role models. It's tough to stay loyal to Dad when the flashiest guy in town gives you $600 in spending cash.

"The saddest thing in life is wasted talent. You can have all the talent in the world, but if you don't do the right thing, nothing happens."

Lorenzo again. A connoisseur of jazz and baseball, Lorenzo is a believer in the American dream. If you work hard and believe in yourself, great things can happen. You can even become the next Mickey Mantle.

The words are really a father's hope that his son will resist the allure of gangster life, that he will see how Sonny has squandered his abilities and chosen to go for the easy buck. After discovering the $600 Calogero has received for carrying drinks at the craps game, Lorenzo confronts Sonny in front of his men at the bar. This is, of course, a risky move. But Lorenzo gets Sonny to concede—kind of—that interfering with a man's son is off limits, even for a Mafiosi.

Even though Calogero (nicknamed "C" by Sonny) sees his father's courage, he still can't stay away from the goodfellas. By age 17, he's hanging with the local juvenile delinquents at their own social club, the Deuces Wild—a kind of Chez Bippy with training wheels. The aspiring wiseguys dress like hoods, toss rocks at black bus passengers riding through the neighborhood and buy guns, anticipating with glee the day they'll get to shoot someone.

Sonny, for his part, doesn't see this issue much differently than Lorenzo. He declares C's friends "jerkoffs" and warns the boy not to aspire to his status. "Don't do what I do," he warns. "This is my life, not yours."

"Mickey Mantle don't care about you. So why care about him? Nobody cares."

This is Sonny's advice to C after the boy talks about how crushed he is by the Yankees' loss in the 1960 World Series. He hates the Pittsburgh Pirates, C says, because they made "The Mick" cry. Mantle is a deity to him.

"Mickey Mantle makes $100,000 a year," Sonny says. "How much does your father make?"

"I don't know."

"You don't know? Go ask Mickey Mantle to help if your father can't pay the rent."

"From that day on," the kid concedes, "I never felt the same about the Yankees."

The point is not to waste your time believing in idols. The "nobody cares," part means not to think that others are looking out for you. You need to act for yourself, Sonny preaches. This comes into play as C's friends grow older and noticeably more stupid. One night, the others use peer pressure to rope C into going along with them on a violent escapade that will prove fatal. Fortunately, Sonny sees what's occurring and pulls C from the car just in time, saving his life.

"Give her The Test."

This is Sonny's method of determining whether a woman is worthy of a young man's affections. The Test is simple: If you're picking up a girl for a date, get out of your car and lock both doors. Let her in on the passenger side and then walk behind the car toward the driver's side.

"Look through the rear window," Sonny advises. "If she doesn't reach over and lift up that button for you so you can get in, dump her. She's a selfish broad and all you're seeing is the tip of the iceberg. Dump her fast."

(Yes, we know The Test has become passé since power door openers came into being. But in 1968 this was an excellent measuring stick—much better than the Mario Test, which you'll also see in this movie.)

In *A Bronx Tale*, C crosses racial lines by dating a black girl from school named Jane (Taral Hicks). Their relationship is threatened in a *West Side Story* way by hatred between their Italian and black neighborhoods (and by Calogero's lying over his involvement in some violence). But ultimately it works out. And she passes The Test.

"Is it better to be loved or feared?"

"If I had my choice I would rather be feared. Fear lasts longer than love."

Had he not been a mob leader, Sonny would have made a great philosophy professor. Here he preaches life according to Machiavelli's *The Prince*. Sonny knows that everyone laughs at his jokes not because they are funny, but out of respect.

"Fear keeps them loyal to me," he says. "The trick is not being hated. I treat my men good. But if I give too much, I'm not needed. I give just enough where they need me but don't hate me."

While the rest of the neighborhood lives in fear of Sonny, C comes to love him. In the end though, the 17-year-old cannot save his mentor. During a party, as everyone is laughing, a young man nursing a longtime grudge sneaks up behind Sonny and shoots him dead.

In the closing scene, C attends his hero's funeral. He notices the huge bouquets, observing, "Gangsters have this thing about flowers. Whoever sends the biggest arrangement cares the most." And he notices the other mobsters cracking jokes and gossiping about how Sonny fell after he was shot.

"It was just like Sonny said it would be," C says in narration. "Nobody cares."

There's a lot to be learned from *A Bronx Tale*. And there's a lot to enjoy.

◉ **HIT:** At times, this is a downright funny movie. You'll laugh at the great side characters like Tony Toupee, Frankie Coffeecake, JoJo the Whale (so fat that "legend has it his shadow once killed a dog"). Our favorite is Eddie Mush, the walking jinx. The man cast in that role, Eddie Montanaro, is the real-life Eddie Mush from Palminteri's youth. On Montanaro's first day of shooting, it rained.

✖ **MISS:** The biggest downside to *A Bronx Tale* is that it's virtually impossible to find. Licensing rights were exclusively sold to Amazon.com in 2010, which means that the DVD is unavailable through Netflix or most video stores, if you can still find a video store in business.

✏ **WHAT THEY WROTE AT THE TIME:** "*A Bronx Tale* is a joy, a film that comes unerringly from someone's heart and experience, and not from a power lunch of agents with clients to be packaged."—Jay Carr, *Boston Globe*

☺ **GOOF:** Nine-year-old Calogero wears a baseball jacket bearing the emblems of Major League teams, including the Mets. Problem is, the scene is supposed to be taking place in 1960. Any good baseball fan—especially a New Yorker—knows that the Mets didn't become a franchise until 1962.

◉ **REPEATED WATCHING QUOTIENT:** We've watched it enough times to memorize every line of dialogue. We suggest you do the same.

▤ **PIVOTAL SCENE:** A gang of tough-guy bikers roll into the neighborhood, landing in Sonny's bar. These are most unwelcome outsiders.

Sonny, who's been chatting outside, comes in to keep the peace. Have a beer on me and leave, he says with a smile. At the same time, he whispers to his aides, telling them to prepare.

The bikers get their beers—and spray them over the barkeep. Clearly, they intend to bust up the joint. When Sonny orders them out, the gang's leader—an enormous red-bearded lug—tells the neighborhood's protector, "I'll tell you when the fuck we'll leave. . . ."

Not a smart move. Sonny calmly locks the bar shut from the inside and tells the bikers, "Now youse can't leave."

The fight is won before the first punch is thrown. The bullies are intimidated. "All the courage and strength was drained from their bodies," Calogero says in narration. "In that instant, they knew they made a mistake. They walked into the wrong bar."

Sonny's guys burst in from an adjoining room. They pummel the bikers with chairs, bats and bottles. The frenzy is reminiscent of the Billy Batts stomping in *GoodFellas*—multiplied by 10. In the end, the bikers are dragged outside and further beaten by neighborhood teens. Their choppers are bashed and overturned.

"Look at me," Sonny says to the gang's leader as his pulls his face off the ground. "I'm the one who did this to you."

The bottom line is that the pros always know how to beat the amateurs. And no one messes around in Sonny's neighborhood.

CASTING CALL: Gangster movie staple Frank Vincent (Billy Batts in *GoodFellas*) was originally set to play a mob don. His part was cut from the script before filming, but Vincent still got paid.

VIOLENCE LEVEL: Other than the scene with the bikers in the bar, not overly high.

DON'T FAIL TO NOTICE: The music that's used whenever Sonny holds court at Chez Bippy. It's all Tony Bennett and Dino and Ol' Blue Eyes, suggesting that this is one cool character.

BEST LINE: We already gave you a bunch, but here's one more. Nine-year-old Calogero goes to church to confess that he lied to police about witnessing a murder. When the priest presses for details, Calogero says, "No, Father, I'm not telling nobody nothing."

"Don't be afraid, my son," the priest says. "Nobody's more powerful than God."

"I don't know about that," answers Calogero. "Your guy's bigger than my guy up there, but my guy's bigger than yours down here."

"You've got a point," concedes the priest. "Five Our Fathers and five Hail Marys."

BET YOU DIDN'T KNOW: Lillo Brancato, the actor who plays Calogero at age 17, was unable to establish himself in Hollywood and eventually fell into using cocaine and heroin. In 2005, he was shot while engaging in a drug-fueled burglary in which a policeman was killed. He was acquitted of second-degree murder, but convicted of attempted burglary and sentenced to 10 years in prison.

In a 2009 interview on the show *20/20*, Brancato said he ignored advice from De Niro and squandered his opportunities. "Bob told me, 'A lot of people are going to want to be your friends, you know, and they don't have your best interest at heart.' I kind of shrugged it off. . . . I am ashamed."

Talk about wasted talent.

"I KNOW THAT GAL": Calogero's mother is played by Kathrine Narducci, whom you may recognize as Charmaine, the shrill wife of henpecked restaurateur Artie Bucco in *The Sopranos*. Narducci was not a professional actress before this movie and came to the open casting call to audition her nine-year-old son. De Niro spotted her and asked her to read.

IF YOU LIKED THIS, YOU'LL LIKE: Chazz Palminteri's one-man show, *A Bronx Tale*, on which this movie is based. Palminteri masterfully plays 18 different roles over 90 minutes. He still occasionally tours the country performing the show.

BODY COUNT: Six, although four are just seen in body bags.

AN INTERVIEW WITH CHAZZ PALMINTERI

Chazz Palminteri grew up on the corner of East 187th Street and Belmont Avenue in the Bronx. That upbringing provided the stories for his autobiographical *A Bronx Tale*, which began as a stage play before being made into a movie in 1993.

What inspired you to write A Bronx Tale?

Well, I wasn't doing very well as an actor. I landed a few guest roles in shows like *Dallas* and *Hill Street Blues*, but I had to take a job as a doorman at a nightclub in L.A. to get by. One night, a guy I didn't recognize tried to push by me into the club. I asked him to wait a second, and he gave me a hard time. He threatened to have me fired, which I didn't appreciate. Turns out it was [powerful talent agent] Swifty Lazar and, 15 minutes later, I actually was fired.

So now I'm in my dump of an apartment in North Hollywood, with $187 in the bank. Very depressed. Suddenly, the advice that my father always gave me came to my mind.

What was your father's advice?

Lorenzo Palminteri always said, "The saddest thing in life is wasted talent." He put it on an index card when I was about nine and tacked it on my bedroom wall. I thought of that message that night and decided that if no one was going to hand me a great role, I had to write one myself. I was determined not to waste my talent.

How much of the story is autobiographical?

Almost all of it. I was that young boy, Calogero, who saw a man kill someone six feet away from me. And I remember it as it was in the movie—slow motion with the murderer staring at me and me staring back. Nobody said a word. My father heard the gunshots and came running downstairs to grab me and drag me inside. The only embellishment is that in real life I never went back to look at a suspects lineup. My father just told the police, "He didn't see nothing," and that was that.

I did date a black girl in high school and my father was a bus driver. So it really is my story. And the message is my father's message: "It doesn't take strength to pull a trigger; the real tough guy is the working man." That's what he instilled in me.

A Bronx Tale *started as a one-man stage play. Give us a little of the history.*

After I got fired from the nightclub, I went to a drug store and bought five big yellow legal pads and started writing. First, I wrote about witnessing that murder. I performed it for my theater workshop and it went over well. So I added parts about my boyhood infatuation with those wiseguys and my relationship with my father. After about nine months I had 90 minutes of material. I started performing it on stage in Los Angeles (in 1990) and it was a big hit.

So those characters in the story are real?

All of them. I didn't invent Frankie Coffeecake or JoJo the Whale or Tony Toupee. They were all part of my childhood. It was quite a neighborhood. I play 18 different roles in the play.

Did you get offers for the movie rights?

Lots of them. It's kind of like Stallone and *Rocky*—every studio head wanted the property, but not me. I was an unknown with a great story. They offered me a quarter million for the rights, but I insisted that I write the screenplay and play the role of Sonny. They didn't go for that. Then they offered me a half-million. In the end I turned down one million, which they would give me if I walked away. And trust me, I had no money in the bank then.

So how did it come to be?

Robert De Niro came to see the show and loved it. He came backstage and said, "Let's make this movie. You write the screenplay, because it's your story. You should play Sonny and I'll play your father and direct it." It was the moment I had waited for. We shook hands and that was that.

A year after* A Bronx Tale*, you costarred in* Bullets Over Broadway*, getting an Oscar nomination. What was it like working with Woody Allen?

That was great because Woody really let me improvise a lot and play the role as I saw fit. The character I play in the movie, Cheech, the mob guy who likes to write, is really me in terms of being a street guy with an artistic side. So it came naturally.

Then in 1995, you were in* The Usual Suspects, *as the detective who learns too late that he's been duped. What do you remember about making that movie?

What I remember is that I loved the script, but wasn't sure if it would work. There were a lot of twists and turns. As we were shooting it, the actors would turn to each other and say, "This is good, but are people going to understand it?" Turns out the audience loved it.

You've revived the one-man play of* A Bronx Tale *recently. Your father would be proud that his message still gets out there.

Well, his passion stayed with me. I hand out a card to young people who see the play, saying, "The saddest thing in life is wasted talent." I sign it and have the kids sign it, like a contract. I think the play and the movie touch people because the story is really about doing something with your life. And that, really, was my father's message.

19 BONNIE AND CLYDE (1967–R)

STARS: WARREN BEATTY, FAYE DUNAWAY, GENE HACKMAN
DIRECTOR: ARTHUR PENN

Bonnie and Clyde may not boast the epic story of *The Godfather*, the churning violence of Pacino's *Scarface* or the underworld insight of *GoodFellas*. But if you love those masterpieces, raise a little toast of Anisette—or perhaps Texas moonshine—to this biopic about Depression-era bank robbers Bonnie Parker and Clyde Barrow.

Because *Bonnie and Clyde* is not just a classic about thieves in love and on the run. It also revived the gangster movie genre.

You can thank Warren Beatty for that. As a young movie star hoping to break into producing,

Beatty bought the script for $10,000 in 1966. According to Hollywood lore, he then implored legendary studio head Jack Warner to front him the money for the project, going so far as to beg on his hands and knees.

Warner reluctantly ponied up a paltry $1.8 million—as long as Beatty agreed to play the male lead. Warner had no faith in a period piece about notorious bandits Bonnie Parker and Clyde Barrow. But he figured anything putting the heartthrob Beatty's face on-screen at least stood a chance to break even.

To this day, Beatty denies the tale—at least the part about crawling before Jack Warner. But he also saved a letter the studio chief wrote to other Warner Brothers executives. It reads: "What does Warren Beatty think he's doing? How did we ever get us into this thing? This gangster stuff went out with Cagney."

Warner, of course, was right. By and large, the American gangland movie disappeared from the 1940s through the mid-60s, which is why you'll find so few films from that era in this book.

But Beatty's instincts were also correct. *Bonnie and Clyde* was a box office smash. Its success led—directly or indirectly—to the green-lighting of dozens of future projects, from outlaw films (*Reservoir Dogs, Natural Born Killers*) to gangster biopics (*Dillinger, The Untouchables*), to, yes, those masterworks at the front of this book.

It was also a critical success, although not universally.

"A milestone in the history of movies," wrote Roger Ebert of the *Chicago Sun-Times*. "A work of truth and brilliance. It is also pitilessly cruel, filled with sympathy, nauseating, funny, heartbreaking, and astonishingly beautiful."

Meanwhile, Bosley Crowther of the *New York Times* called it, "a cheap piece of bald-faced slapstick comedy that treats the hideous depredations of that sleazy, moronic pair as though they were as full of fun and frolic as the jazz-age cutups in *Thoroughly Modern Millie*."

Crowther was soon removed from his spot as the *Times'* lead critic—a position he held for 27 years. His editors cited that review as evidence he was out of touch with modern tastes.

It wasn't Bosley Crowther's peers, but the under-30 audience that made *Bonnie and Clyde* a hit during a turbulent decade when every issue seemed to split down a generational divide.

"Young people understood this movie instantly," director Arthur Penn told the *Los Angeles Times*. "They saw *Bonnie and Clyde* as rebels like themselves. It was a movie that spoke to a generation in a way none of us had really expected."

In part, that's because Beatty and Faye Dunaway portrayed the title characters as populist outlaws celebrated in the press for fighting the establishment—as represented by Depression-era banks. The two are 1930s Robin Hoods, heroes to the downtrodden. In one scene, they decline to rob an elderly man during a bank stickup, prompting him to say that if they are ever caught and executed, he will bring flowers to their funeral.

More than that, *Bonnie and Clyde* was considered a landmark movie because of its sex and violence. Consider the opening scene, where the nearly nude Bonnie peers out the second-story window of her ramshackle West Texas home and spots Clyde trying to steal her mother's car. Rather than being frightened or outraged, she is turned on—as she demonstrates when she comes downstairs and literally strokes Clyde's pistol.

A hood out on parole, Clyde takes her into town, where he robs a grocery store. This really arouses her. Problem is, Clyde cannot perform in bed. Or, as Bonnie puts it, "Your advertising is just dandy. Folks would never guess that you don't have a thing to sell."

Beatty's willingness to play a pathologically violent criminal plagued by sexual dysfunction was daring for a leading man in those times. He did insist on one change in the original script, which portrayed Clyde as a gay man having an affair with gang getaway driver C.W. Moss (Michael J. Pollard, an actor Beatty met during his tenure on the 1960s TV show *The Many Loves of Dobie Gillis*).

Anyway, Clyde promises to whisk Bonnie away from her dreary life as a roadhouse waitress, "serving greasy burgers to truckers with tattoos who keep trying to get into your pants." And so begins life on the run, as they alternately stick up banks, shoot some cops, hide out for a few days and try to get their pictures published.

Fame is a major goal here, making Bonnie and Clyde the forerunners of every modern "reality show" pseudo-celebrity from Jon and Kate to Snooki and The Situation. Bonnie writes poems that she mails to the papers (those are Ms. Parker's real works that Dunaway recites) and Clyde is always poised with the Kodak. They somehow come to believe that their purpose in life is to bring excitement to a dreary nation beaten down by the Depression.

Along the way, the Barrow gang is joined by

Moss, as well as Clyde's brother Buck (Gene Hackman) and Buck's wife Blanche (Estelle Parsons). It's a terrific cast of actors who were largely unknown before this. For Hackman and Dunaway, the movie provided breakout roles. For Parsons, a veteran stage performer, it provided an Oscar for Best Supporting Actress. *Bonnie and Clyde* was nominated for 10 Academy Awards and won two—one for Parsons and one for cinematographer Burnett Guffey.

We don't think we are giving away too much here telling you that it doesn't end well for these outlaws. The first half of the movie is often played for laughs, with Keystone Kops chase scenes executed over banjo-picking bluegrass music. But as the law draws closer, the mood of the film darkens. First, you get to laugh with the gang, then you get to watch as its members are picked off, one by one.

The final scene was shocking at the time, and became the inspiration for many to follow—including the slaughter of Sonny in *The Godfather*. Bonnie and Clyde are double-crossed and a Texas posse pounces on them after they stop their car to help a man posing as a stranded motorist on a rural road. The pair are shot an estimated 150 times, their bodies writhing in super-slow motion. Clothes and flesh fly off with every machine gun blast.

"We did that shot in one take," Beatty told the *Los Angeles Times*. "We had one car and one load of squibs [tiny special-effects explosives], so we had to keep it together. We shot off more bullets than had ever been used in movie history. . . . There were squibs all over me, there was a makeup guy, off-camera, who was going to pull my scalp off when it exploded. I was just hoping I did it right."

It's riveting stuff. No final words, no postscript. Just the two young outlaws convulsing for minutes until they lie there lifeless.

Today, *Bonnie and Clyde* stands as a cultural touchstone. It was selected for preservation in the United States National Film Registry for being "culturally, historically or aesthetically significant."

◄ **CASTING CALL:** Beatty knew he would play Clyde the moment he signed on as producer. But Bonnie? The list of those considered sounds like a stroll down Hollywood's Walk of Fame.

Beatty's real-life girlfriend at the time, Leslie Caron, wanted the part. She later insisted that she convinced Beatty to buy the script. But Beatty refused to give her the role, leading to their breakup. Others mentioned for the role included Natalie Wood and Jane Fonda (both declined), Tuesday Weld (who inconveniently got pregnant) and Cher (whose then-husband, Sonny Bono, didn't want her taking part in such a controversial project).

Dunaway, the daughter of a Florida dirt farmer, auditioned and got the gig. "Never have I ever felt so close to a character," she later told Ellis Amburn, author of *The Sexiest Man Alive: A Biography of Warren Beatty*. "Bonnie was a yearning, edgy ambitious Southern girl who wanted to get out of wherever she was. . . . That was me."

Bonnie and Clyde also marks the debut (of sorts) of Morgan Fairchild, although you won't recognize her. She was hired as Dunaway's stand-in.

◉ **HIT:** *Bonnie and Clyde* was as much a pop phenomenon as a movie. The maxi skirts and berets worn by Dunaway became fashion trends. The bluegrass soundtrack featuring Flatt and Scruggs (who also played the *Beverly Hillbillies* theme song) climbed into the Top 10. And two separate pop songs were written about the duo—one rose to No. 7 in the United States, the other to No. 1 in France.

⊗ **MISS:** Penn curiously calibrated the soundtrack so that the volume moves up and down with the intensity of the action on the screen. It varies from ear-splitting during gun battles to, "Huh? What'd he say?" during small conversations. Make sure you keep the remote control at hand.

BET YOU DIDN'T KNOW: As opposed to Dunaway, who stands five-foot-seven, the real Bonnie Parker was just four-foot-ten. And her appearance, unlike Dunaway's, was anything but glamorous.

DON'T FAIL TO NOTICE: In the final death scene, Clyde is driving in socks, with no shoes, and Bonnie is eating a pear. According to newspaper accounts, that is how it went down on May 23, 1934.

"I KNOW THAT GUY": That nervous undertaker Bonnie and Clyde decide to kidnap after stealing his car is 33-year-old Gene Wilder in his movie debut.

REALITY CHECK: A movie like this strays from the facts, although many of the portrayed incidents did occur. The broadest poetic license involves the character of lawman Frank Hamer (Denver Pyle), who hunts down Bonnie and Clyde—but only after they have captured, photographed and humiliated him by tying his hands and shoving him into the middle of a pond in a rowboat. In real life, Hamer was a retired and legendary Texas Ranger who never met the outlaw pair before he gunned them down. Hamer's family sued the producers, including Beatty, for defamation of character and received an out-of-court settlement.

BEST LINE: "This here's Miss Bonnie Parker. I'm Clyde Barrow. We rob banks."

PIVOTAL SCENE: Bonnie insists on visiting her mother even as the law draws closer. In a scene shot through a romanticized haze, the duo shares a picnic with her extended family, deep in the woods. Bonnie is initially ecstatic.

Clyde tries to charm Mrs. Parker, suggesting that he and Bonnie hope to settle down just a few miles away. But the wise mother won't have any of it, predicting that if they were ever spotted in the area, her daughter "won't live very long."

Forget settling down, she says. "No, you'd best keep running, Clyde Barrow. And you know it."

Hearing this, Bonnie turns ashen. This joy ride will inevitably end in her bloody death, and now she realizes it.

"When I started out, I thought we was really going somewhere," she tells Clyde as they drive away. "But this is it—we just going, huh?"

VIOLENCE LEVEL: Fluctuating. Because the movie is told from the lead characters' delusional point of view, their victims die without suffering or spilling blood. But when the Barrow Gang members are hit by bullets, wounds open and blood seeps. Their pain feels genuine, in part, because we watched these people tell jokes or play checkers in the last scene. It all culminates, of course, in the slow-motion, bullet-spewing climax which, at the time, was considered among the most violent scenes in movie history.

BODY COUNT: Twelve—eight cops, one bank manager, and three gang members.

REPEATED WATCHING QUOTIENT: Dunaway's seminude scene at the beginning—daring as it was in 1967—is still impressive, and the bloody finale is riveting. You can probably fast forward through the other 100 minutes the second time around.

IF YOU LIKED THIS, YOU'LL LIKE: *Big Bad Mama*, a 1974 shoot-'em-up in which Angie Dickinson leads a dysfunctional family driven to bootlegging and bank robbing by the Depression. Same attitude, same banjo-plucking, same car chases.

20 CARLITO'S WAY (1993–R)

STARS: AL PACINO, SEAN PENN, PENELOPE ANN MILLER, JOHN LEGUIZAMO
DIRECTOR: BRIAN DE PALMA

Brian De Palma was worried about doing another Hispanic drug kingpin movie after *Scarface*. But the story and the acting in *Carlito's Way* go in such a different direction that there ended up being few similarities between the two films. This is a personal look at one man's attempt at redemption. *Scarface*, on the other hand, is a saga about one man's one-way trip to hell.

Carlito's Way and *Scarface* do share a couple of important things. They both succeed at what they are trying to do and have Al Pacino as the primary reason to thank for it.

While *Carlito's Way* was not a box office smash, Pacino's portrayal of the title character, Carlito "Charlie" Brigante, is in many ways

stronger, and certainly more simpatico, than his portrayal of *Scarface*'s Tony Montana a decade earlier.

Critics were not overwhelmed by this De Palma/Pacino effort, with one suggesting the story would have played better and leaner as a *Miami Vice* episode. That's harsh. Pacino, as he does on occasion, chews some of the scenery (see: *Scent of a Woman, Dog Day Afternoon* and *And Justice for All* for other examples). But if you like Pacino—and what gangster film fan doesn't?—then his spurts of overacting can easily be ignored. Or even savored.

Using voice-overs throughout and told in flashback after Carlito is shot on a train platform, *Carlito's Way* offers an interior view of the drug underworld. Carlito provides cynical commentary about the greed, corruption and treachery that simply come with the territory.

It is territory that Carlito hopes to leave behind after having his conviction and 30-year prison sentence for drug dealing overturned. His dream is to go to the Bahamas, where a friend has opened a car rental business and has promised him a piece of the action.

"I'll tell you something, car rental guys don't get killed that much," he says in explaining his desire for the seemingly inexplicable career makeover.

But like another Pacino character that we're all familiar with, Carlito can't seem to find his way. Just when he thinks he's out, forces keep pulling him back in.

Those forces include a wannabe kingpin who starts out idolizing Carlito but ends up gunning for him and a coked-up lawyer/best friend who once helped spring Carlito from jail on a legal technicality. The friend now needs Carlito to help him deal with a mob boss who is less than pleased with the legal service he has been receiving.

Sean Penn gives a pulsating performance as attorney David Kleinfeld, who spends more time snorting coke and chasing broads than filing legal briefs. With a frizzed-out, red mop of hair and tight-fitting, three-piece suits that scream shyster, Kleinfeld looks more at home in Carlito's nightclub than he does in a courtroom.

John Leguizamo's Benny Blanco ("Benny from the Bronx") gives Charlie a chance to see what he used to be, even if he doesn't want to accept or admit it. And that vision reinforces his desire to put that life behind him and leave New York.

When they first meet, Blanco calls Carlito the "J.P. Morgan of the smack business." Benny thinks he's paying a compliment. But Carlito doesn't like the reminder.

But there are flashes of the old Carlito. A second meeting with Blanco ends with a confrontation. Carlito and his bodyguards throw the young drug dealer down a flight of steps.

"Dumb move, man, dumb move," Carlito says in a voice-over as Blanco tumbles down the concrete stairway at the back of the nightclub. "But it's like them old reflexes comin' back."

When his bodyguards want to finish the job in the alley behind the club, Carlito calls them off and tells them to let Blanco live. That, from an underworld perspective, turns out to be an even dumber move.

Honor and loyalty (or the lack thereof) and betrayal drive the rest of the movie.

"Fuck you and your self-righteous code of the street," Kleinfeld says in an early argument that hints at what is to come.

"Favor gonna kill you faster than a bullet," Carlito muses at another point, letting us know that he knows that he has lost his edge.

Viggo Mortensen makes a brief appearance as Lalin, an old drug-dealing friend now confined to a wheelchair as the result of a gangland shooting. His conversation leads Carlito to quickly surmise that he's wearing a wire for the cops. When Charlie confronts him and rips the wire from his chest, Lalin is reduced to tears and says he'd be better off dead than confined to the chair wearing diapers.

While trying to maneuver through his old world and legitimately build up a stash that can finance a move to the Bahamas, Charlie rekindles his romance with Gail (Penelope Ann Miller). In the novels on which the movie is based, Gail was a teacher. De Palma, reaching into a bag of urban movie clichés, makes her a struggling dancer who moonlights at a strip joint.

Reluctant at first to get involved again with Carlito, Gail buys into his dream, but then realizes it is going to play out like a nightmare.

"I know how this dream ends," she says while urging him not to help Kleinfeld deal with the mob boss.

But Carlito's sense of honor trumps his common sense.

"Dave is my friend," he says. "I owe him. That's who I am. That's what I am. Right or wrong, I can't change that."

Gail turns out to be the only person close to Carlito who doesn't betray him. His final wish is for her to get out of New York.

"No room in this city for big hearts like hers," he says.

In an attempt to recapture this film's magic, Michael Bregman, one of the producers here, directed a 2005 prequel called *Carlito's Way: Rise to Power*. It was a bust. Or as Carlito might have said, "No mas."

◉ **HIT:** The running gun battle/chase scene through the subway and train station that takes up nearly 10 minutes at the end of the film is a cinematic classic that echoes some of the great film noir finales from the past. Taut and nerve-racking, it perfectly sets up the climax.

⊗ **MISS:** Pacino doesn't quite nail his character's Puerto Rican accent. At times it seems he's back in *Scent of a Woman* and at other times he sounds like Michael Corleone doing Tony Montana.

➡ **DON'T FAIL TO NOTICE:** The exterior of the hospital where Carlito goes to visit Kleinfeld after he is stabbed by the mobsters is the same hospital exterior used in *The Godfather*. In that movie, as we all know, Pacino's character, Michael, goes to visit his father, Don Corleone, after he was shot. And it's in front of that hospital that Michael Corleone has the confrontation with police that eventually leads to his exile in Sicily. The ramifications of the hospital visit here are just as interesting.

❞ **BEST LINE:** "I don't invite this shit, it just comes to me," Carlito says after he tries to help his cousin and, instead, gets caught in a drug deal gone bad in a Harlem pool hall. The scene, early in the movie, sets the stage for all that follows.

✎ **WHAT THEY WROTE AT THE TIME:** "*Carlito's Way* harks back to the gangster flicks of yore, where the molls were window-dressing and all the real action belonged to the hombres. De Palma's vibrant, visceral crime drama is hombre hoo-ha—and a whole lot of fun."—Steven Rea, the *Philadelphia Inquirer*

◄ **CASTING CALL:** In an earlier attempt to make the movie, there was talk of Marlon Brando playing Kleinfeld, a move that would have teamed the two principals from *The Godfather* in a decidedly different on-screen relationship.

☺ **GOOF:** At the end of the movie, Carlito and Gail plan to flee New York on a train to Miami. They meet at Grand Central Station in Manhattan. The only trains out of New York to Miami depart from Penn Station.

🍎 **BET YOU DIDN'T KNOW:** The movie is based on two novels by Judge Edwin Torres, *Carlito's Way* and *After Hours*. Pacino met the judge while filming *Serpico*. He later read and liked the novels. Torres, who cowrote the screenplay, took Pacino around Spanish Harlem to get a sense of the place and his character before filming began.

🔪 **BODY COUNT:** Twelve.

21 THE POPE OF GREENWICH VILLAGE (1984–R)

STARS: MICKEY ROURKE, ERIC ROBERTS, DARYL HANNAH
DIRECTOR: STUART ROSENBERG (WITH AN UNCREDITED ASSIST FROM MICHAEL CIMINO)

To appreciate just how well director Stuart Rosenberg and writer Vincent Patrick captured wiseguy street corner ethos in this classic mob tale, you have to understand the meaning of an Italian phrase that has come to define the way certain mobsters act.

The phrase is *faccia una bella figura*. Literally, it means "make a good impression." But in fact the phrase conveys much more. It describes an attitude, an approach to life that is more typically found in the southern half of Italy, especially in Naples and points south.

It's part of a philosophy built around the idea that while it may be important to be good at what you do, it's even more important to look good while you're doing it.

Faccia una bella figura is what *The Pope of Greenwich Village* is all about. You have to understand it to understand where Charlie (Mickey Rourke) and Paulie (Eric Roberts) are coming from.

Take the classic scene (one of dozens in this film) between Paulie and his hospitalized father (Philip Bosco). They're walking down a hallway, the father in a flimsy hospital gown, Paulie dressed to the nines, discussing Paulie's investment—with borrowed shylock money—in a racehorse. From there, the conversation shifts to life and success and how you have to make it on your own.

"Your mother's not doing you no favor bringing you manicotti twice a week and washing your laundry," Paulie's father tells him as he wonders whether he and his wife have spoiled their son.

He then holds up Paulie's cousin Nicky, who has his own house and buys a new Oldsmobile every year, as an example of success.

Paulie wants no part of it.

"Nicky the Nose is better off?" he asks, his voice rising. "He don't go for spit. The Nose shines his own shoes, Pop. That's no big success."

When his father asks how he would define success, Paulie doesn't miss a beat.

"Knowing how to spend it," he says. "I never ordered a brandy in my life wasn't Cordon Bleu. I took 500 from a shylock, pay to see Sinatra at the Garden. Sat two seats away from Tony Bennett. That's success, Pop."

The performances of Rourke and Roberts are nearly perfect in this story of honor, betrayal and family. And with a rich and talented supporting cast (Geraldine Page was nominated for a Best Supporting Actress Oscar even though she appeared in just two scenes and had a total of about eight minutes of screen time), it is hard to understand why the film was a box office bust.

Nearly three decades later, the film has status as a cult and video favorite. It's a classic wiseguy buddy movie with a message that resonates long after the film has ended.

Rourke, who was touted as the next De Niro after stellar performances in *Body Heat*, *Diner* and this film, was never able to recapture the screen presence he had here. He was quirky good in movies like *Barfly* and *Angel Heart*, but then drifted in films like *Wild Orchid* and *Harley Davidson and the Marlboro Man* while earning the reputation as an actor who was "difficult to work with." It's hard to imagine he's the same actor whose current comeback was launched in *The Wrestler*.

Roberts, whose sister Julia has churned out one box office hit after the other, never again reached the level of performance he offered here in a mesmerizing turn as a fast-talking street hustler who isn't quite able to figure the angles.

Charlie and Paulie were quintessential New Yorkers, the kind of guys you find in a bar on Sullivan Street or grabbing a meal at a restaurant on Bleecker. They're from the streets, part of a rich and storied neighborhood that includes places like the Caffe Reggio (where Kerouac, Burroughs and the other beats used to hang) and Village Vanguard (where dozens of jazz greats made their bones) and Washington Square Park (with its chess games and dog runs and street musicians gathered around a fountain that is more European than American).

The Pope of Greenwich Village plays to the grit and the vibe that is Lower Manhattan. And while Sinatra's "Summer Wind" is heard at three different times during the movie, it's the rhythm of the streets that is the real soundtrack here.

Charlie and Paulie are cousins and both lose their jobs at a local restaurant after Paulie, a waiter, is caught stealing. Charlie, a host who has aspirations of owning his own joint, tells Paulie it's all his fault. But Paulie, in the logic of the neighborhood, says that's not true. If he had thought he was going to be caught, then he would be responsible for Charlie losing his job. But since he didn't. . . .

To make up for it, Paulie brings Charlie into a deal he's working. He's borrowed money to invest in a racehorse secretly sired by a champion. It's all in the genes, he tells Charlie. The horse really has nothing to do with it. This horse, the product of "artificial inspiration," is a sure thing, a longshot with a big payoff.

Charlie, who's got alimony payments, a pregnant girlfriend Diane (Daryl Hannah) and a restaurant in the country that he wants to buy, agrees to help Paulie rob a safe in order to get cash to bet on the horse.

Barney (Kenneth McMillan) is the Irish locksmith/safecracker with failing eyesight Paulie has also brought into the deal. He lives in the Bronx with his wife and their mentally challenged 20-year-old son. And he's looking for "one nice score" before retiring.

They bust into the safe and get the cash—$150,000.

Along the way, there's a dead cop on the take to the mob and wearing a body wire. And a vicious mob boss, Bed Bug Eddie Grant (Burt Young) who happens to be the owner of the safe and the money that was inside it—two facts that Paulie has neglected to mention to Charlie.

Honor, loyalty and family ties—not the Mafia version, but the street-corner kind—drive the rest of the story.

Diane ends up choosing the money—Charlie's end was $50,000—over their relationship. She takes off after realizing that Charlie is never going to change. That they literally come from different worlds is driven home when Diane, her WASPish, New England roots showing, tells Charlie that he's "outgrown" Paulie and doesn't need him around anymore.

Charlie tells her that may be the way things are where she comes from, but it's not the way things are for him.

"Italians outgrow clothes, not people," he says. The look on his face says that he knows this relationship is doomed as well.

Bed Bug Eddie wants his money back. More importantly, he wants revenge. And with his reputation for carving up people, the threat sends Barney scrambling to safety in Chicago, costs Paulie his thumb and sets up a final confrontation with Charlie at the mobster's clubhouse in the Village.

Charlie prepares for his meeting with the mobster by picking out his best suit of clothes and most expensive shoes. Then he heads for a barbershop where he gets a shave, his hair cut, his nails manicured and his shoes shined.

As he walks down the street, the camera pans up from the sidewalk, capturing the shoes, the clothes, the strut. Charlie doesn't know if he's going to come out of the meeting with Bed Bug Eddie alive.

But whatever happens and whatever he needs to do, he's going to look good doing it.

Faccia una bella figura.

HIT: The "members only" mob clubhouse with the storefront windows and door painted black is a dead-on replica of the clubhouse on Sullivan Street in Greenwich Village out of which Vincent "the Chin" Gigante used to run the Genovese Crime Family, one of the biggest and without question the most powerful of the five New York families.

Gigante dodged the Feds for years by pretending to be crazy. He used to roam the neighborhood during the day in a bathrobe and slippers mumbling to himself. Sometimes, the Feds would tail him heading to a late-night rendezvous in an Upper Eastside apartment with his mistress. Gigante was finally convicted of racketeering in 1997. The jury rejected his insanity defense. He died in prison in 2005. If there ever was a Pope of Greenwich Village it was The Chin. (His brother, by the way, Father Louis Gigante, was a priest.)

MISS: The stick ball game in the schoolyard goes from being funny to being ridiculous when Charlie and his teammates, dressed in suits and sport jackets, begin to sway to the beat as Sinatra's "Summer Wind" provides background music.

WHAT THEY WROTE AT THE TIME: "A generic New York street movie, about a couple of guys from the neighborhood who get into a lot of fucking trouble with the fucking mob and yell their fucking heads off at each other but in the end they love each other because . . . well, shit, they're a couple of guys from the neighborhood, after all."— Dave Kehr, *Chicago Reader*

BET YOU DIDN'T KNOW: Michael Cimino, who had hits like *The Deer Hunter* and flops like *Heaven's Gate* on his resume at the time, played a role in directing *The Pope of Greenwich Village*, but what that role exactly was has never been made clear. Some reports say that he was originally tapped to direct, but had a falling out with the lead actors and was fired. Others indicate that when director Stuart Rosenberg (*Cool Hand Luke*) fell ill during filming, Cimino, as a favor, stepped in and directed a few scenes.

BEST LINE: Paulie: "Charlie, they took my thumb!"

REPEATED WATCHING QUOTIENT: This is one of those movies that surprises and entertains every time you watch it. If you turn on the television and happen to catch it already in progress, you sit and watch a scene or two, waiting for the line that you already know, but can't wait to hear again.

GOOF: Charlie's hairstyle changes from damp moptop to swept-back to moptop again in the scene where Diane tells him she's pregnant.

DON'T FAIL TO NOTICE: The name of the horse Paulie has invested in—Sorry Hope.

"KNOW THAT GUY": Jimmy the Cheese Man, who invests with Paulie in the horse and whose mozzarella is the topic of ridicule, is veteran character actor Joe Grifasi. The actor with the ethnic face has over 100 screen and television credits. He was Yogi Berra in *The Bronx Is Burning* cable series; had dozens of appearances on *Law & Order*; played a nebbish Jewish accountant opposite George Clooney in *One Fine Day* and had a small role as a waiter in *Moonstruck*.

BODY COUNT: One dead cop, but it was an accident. And one severed body part.

22 GANGS OF NEW YORK (2002-R)

STARS: LEONARDO DICAPRIO, DANIEL DAY-LEWIS, CAMERON DIAZ
DIRECTOR: MARTIN SCORSESE

Before there was John Gotti, before Carlo Gambino, before Lucky Luciano, there was Bill "the Butcher" Poole.

The 19th-century boxer, fixer and, yes, actual butcher, was a forerunner of the mobsters who later controlled New York City. Poole began as a thug with the Bowery Boys street gang and rose to become a massive figure in the 1850s. He enswathed himself in the Stars and Stripes, squeezing his corrupt grip over the Five Points area and steering the xenophobic Know-Nothing Party, whose political agenda didn't amount to more than terrorizing Irish-Catholic immigrants.

Martin Scorsese tells Poole's story—dramatically if not always accurately—in *Gangs of New York*, an epic undertaking that presents Lower Manhattan in the mid-19th Century as a cross between Hell's Kitchen and the Wild West. *Gangs* is based on a 1928 book of the same name that Scorsese discovered as a young man. He was stunned to learn that he grew up just blocks from its setting and yearned to tell the story for 30 years (keep reading to see the odd casting choices he considered along the way).

The movie strays from the more factual book, but that's to be expected. Bill Poole becomes Bill Cutting—the perfect name for a butcher. The character of Amsterdam Vallon is invented to build story and allow for the casting of box-office giant Leonardo DiCaprio. And the requisite love triangle is created between DiCaprio, Bill the Butcher and a saucy pickpocket played (unconvincingly) by Cameron Diaz.

The film's most egregious factual flaw? Most of *Gangs* takes place during the Civil War, and the inevitable showdown between the main characters occurs as New York burns during the Draft Riots of 1863. Problem is, Poole was actually murdered in 1855. Bill the Butcher had as much to do with that draft uprising as Joe the Plumber.

But so what? You're not watching a documentary; you're watching an engaging look at the genesis of organized crime in America. Think of it as *Roots* meets *The Departed*.

DiCaprio does a fine job as a Dickensian character who becomes Cutting's protégé, but eventually rebels and forms the Dead Rabbits gang (not named after the furry rodent, but a corruption of the Gaelic word *ráibéad*, meaning "a man to be feared"). There's a strong supporting cast that includes Brendan Gleeson, John C. Reilly, Liam Neeson and Jim Broadbent, who's charmingly smarmy as Tammany Hall boss William Tweed. Other historical figures make brief appearances, including editor Horace Greeley and showman P.T. Barnum.

But the real reason to watch the film is to witness the gargantuan performance by Daniel Day-Lewis. As Bill the Butcher, he preens, he struts, he rants. Dressed in a stovepipe hat and checkered pants, he carves enemies with a meat cleaver and picks his teeth with a steak knife. He's got a handlebar mustache, slicked-down hair and a glass eye—which he taps with a stiletto. This is what you want in your prehistoric godfather—a cross between *Oliver Twist*'s Bill Sikes and *Scarface*'s Tony Montana.

Day-Lewis, as always, immersed himself in his role. He perfected the 19th-century *Noo Yawk* inflection by listening to early recordings (including some by poet Walt Whit man) and talking in the accent for eight months—on and off the set. He hired circus performers to teach him knife throwing and apprenticed in a butcher shop to learn how to incise and gut carcasses. He *became* Bill the Butcher—so much so that after a few days, he got into some celebrated post-shooting fistfights.

If *Gangs of New York* has shortcomings, it's that it tries to be too much. Essentially, Scorsese presents old Gotham as a battleground among three groups. The first—represented by The Butcher—is the working-class natives, English and Dutch descendents whose gangs hold sway over the town's day-to-day running. The second—their sworn enemies—are the new Irish immigrants, who form their own gangs just to scrap for survival. And the third is the establishment, represented by corrupt cops and politicians; they are the least noble of the three.

"The country was up for grabs," Scorsese said in an interview soon after *Gangs'* release. "New York was a powder keg. . . . It was chaos, tribal chaos. Gradually, there was a street-by-street, block-by-block working out of democracy as people learned somehow to live together. If democracy didn't happen in New York, it wasn't going to happen anywhere."

Perhaps, but you won't see much of the democratic process in this film. Mostly there's fighting—vicious, close-up hand-to-hand brawling with clubs and fists and knives. Lots of knives. And lots of factions: rich against poor, white against black, gang against gang.

The film opens with a *Gladiator*-like battle between natives and immigrants. That culminates with the death of the Irish leader, "Priest" Vallon (Neeson), whom we come to see as the only honorable man in New York. Priest's young son, Amsterdam, witnesses the slaying at the hands of Bill the Butcher. And that sets up the rest of the story—the son must avenge his father.

Flash forward 16 years, and the little boy comes back as DiCaprio. Not exactly the intimidating sort (especially when he shares screen time with Day-Lewis), but sharp enough to work his way into Bill's inner circle where he can plot his revenge. He becomes the Butcher's surrogate son and even takes on the boss's ex-mistress (Diaz) as a lover. Shrinks would have had a field day with this if they'd existed in 1862.

The story is slow to unfold—hey, this movie runs nearly three hours—and you watch it all through a Hieronymus Bosch-like underworld of bar brawls, bareknuckle fights and toothless people betting on a caged showdown between a dog and a pack of sewer rats.

It all leads up to that final face-off between the two main characters, yoked to those infamous draft riots. You'll have to see the movie to see how that plays out, but we were disappointed in the payoff—or lack thereof.

◉ **HIT:** *Gangs of New York* presents the city as a smoky, claustrophobic tangle of brick streets, sagging tenements and intricate catacombs. These are complex sets with no digital shortcuts or computer-generated backgrounds. Surprisingly, Scorsese decided that the best way to recreate New York City of the 1860s was to travel 4300 miles to the Cinecitta Studio in Rome, where a five-block neighborhood was built. *Gangs* cost $100 million (twice the budget of any Scorsese film to date) and took eight months to film. It shows.

⊗ **MISS:** Cameron Diaz seems out of place as Jenny, the weathered and scarred 19th-century grifter. With those straight white teeth, she's a little too cute for the neighborhood.

✐ **WHAT THEY WROTE AT THE TIME:** "This historical epic fudges a few facts, tacks on a pandering love story and trips on its own grand ambitions. And yet here is a film I give the highest rating. Nuts? I don't think so. *Gangs of New York* is something better than perfect: It's thrillingly alive . . . [Scorsese] makes us see ourselves in the immigrant tribes who fought with knives, picks, axes and shovels to carve out a piece of turf on the mean streets of New York."—Peter Travers, *Rolling Stone*

◀ **CASTING CALL:** When he first conceived *Gangs*, Scorsese wanted to cast John Belushi as Bill the Butcher and Dan Aykroyd as Amsterdam Vallon. Imagine what *that* would have become. As the project evolved over the years, other possibilities included Robert De Niro and Mel Gibson as Amsterdam, and Willem Dafoe as Bill the Butcher. Sarah Michelle Gellar was hired to play Jenny, but had to quit over a shooting conflict with her TV show, *Buffy the Vampire Slayer*.

😊 **"I KNOW THAT GUY":** Take a close look at Johnny, the friend who betrays Amsterdam. Try to picture him 20 years younger. Yep, that's Henry Thomas, who peaked as an adorable 10-year-old playing Elliott in *E.T.: The Extra-Terrestrial*.

✔ **REALITY CHECK:** Several items that appear in the movie were not available in America in 1863, including latex balloons, a microphone and bananas.

➡ **DON'T FAIL TO NOTICE:** The blue American eagle design on Bill the Butcher's glass eye. Very cool.

👁 **REPEATED WATCHING QUOTIENT:** At 167 minutes, *Gangs* is a bit of a project to undertake. Just be thankful that Scorsese cut it down from its original four hours.

✂ **BODY COUNT:** We stopped keeping score at 100, about one hour into the film.

🎬 **PIVOTAL SCENE:** Amsterdam plans to kill Bill the Butcher to avenge his father's death. But working undercover, he becomes more like Bill's protégé than his enemy. The men attend a theater showing of *Uncle Tom's Cabin* one night, and a stranger walking up the aisle suddenly pulls out a gun and shoots at Bill.

The Butcher is wounded, but Amsterdam's quick action—tackling, wrestling and killing the assassin—saves Bill's life.

"It's a funny feeling being taken under the wing of a dragon," Amsterdam muses in narration. "It's warmer than you'd think."

🔫 **VIOLENCE LEVEL:** Far higher than any of Scorsese's four other movies in this book. Throats are slashed, arms get hacked off by cleavers, throats are crushed. Watch for the large jar of souvenir severed ears, kept on a bar top like pickled eggs.

💬 **BEST LINE:** Bill the Butcher: "I'm 47 years old. You know how I stayed alive this long? All these years? Fear. The spectacle of fearsome acts. Somebody steals from me, I cut off his hands. He offends me, I cut out his tongue. He rises against me, I cut off his head, stick it on a pike, raise it high up so all on the streets can see. That's what preserves the order of things. Fear."

🍎 **BET YOU DIDN'T KNOW:** The final scene shows the development of the New York skyline from 1863 on, and closes with a view of the World Trade Center towers. The movie was completed before the attack on the towers, but not released until a year after. There was debate over whether to leave the shot in, with Scorsese having the final word:

"It had to end with that, or the movie shouldn't have existed," he said. "The people in the film and the people of New York—good, bad, and indifferent—were part of the creation of that skyline, not the destruction of it."

✳ **IF YOU LIKED THIS, YOU'LL LIKE:** *The Musketeers of Pig Alley*. Well, maybe not, but Scorsese has always said that the 17-minute silent-era short by D. W. Griffith influenced his crime movies more than any other. (See the following chapter.)

THE FIRST GANGSTER MOVIE EVER MADE

Before the Tommy guns and speakeasies of the 1920s, before drugs and gambling became the fuel for gangster films, long before "Leave the gun, take the cannoli," there was *The Musketeers of Pig Alley*.

Released in 1912, the 17-minute silent is believed to be the first film ever made about organized crime. It includes many of the gangster movie elements still used today—the smiling evil guy, the battle over territory, corrupt police.

Mostly, it's melodrama. Movies back then didn't have a lot of time to build plot or develop character, so they hit you hard and fast with emotion. The movie centers on "The Little Lady," a child of the slums married to a struggling musician. She is played by Lillian Gish, a major star of the silent era.

Early on, the musician husband takes to the road for a gig, leaving her alone and depressed. She winds up meeting a local gangster called "The Snapper Kid." You can tell he's a bad guy because he dresses more nattily than everyone else. The Kid takes the naïve young thing to a dance, where a rival gangster attempts to slip her a mickey and steal her virtue. Her husband returns from his road trip with a wallet full of money, which is immediately stolen by the Kid's gang. Not a good day for nice people on the mean streets.

Musketeers was directed by film pioneer D. W. Griffith (*The Birth of a Nation*), who was popping out one-reelers at the rate of one a week back in 1912. This one is notable for its attempts to show urban squalor as it was in the day, with bleak scenes of guys drinking booze from a jug, kids dressed in rags and women who just might be hookers. The milieu is enhanced by real-life hoods Griffith paid (perhaps in protection money) to serve as extras.

Griffith's message here appears to be that poverty breeds crime—not a universally accepted insight back then.

There's more to the plot, and if you're interested, just Google the title. Several websites carry the movie, which is now in the public domain and can be viewed in its entirety almost before the microwave popcorn is ready.

23 THE PUBLIC ENEMY (1931–NR)

STARS: JAMES CAGNEY, EDWARD WOODS, JEAN HARLOW
DIRECTOR: WILLIAM A. WELLMAN

Hollywood was in flux at the start of the 1930s. Even as the Great Depression put a quarter of the country out of work, more Americans than ever saved their nickels for a weekly all-day trip to the theater.

That audience was changing as the population became increasingly urban. Westerns were geared at rural audiences. The new filmgoers, sons and daughters of immigrants who had settled in America's growing cities, were more excited about the nascent breed of gangster films showing characters more familiar to them than, say, Hopalong Cassidy.

Warner Brothers, which owned hundreds of theaters in the big cities, was smart enough to make movies aimed at that working class audience. They created stories about less-than-admirable antiheros who stirred viewers' sympathies by trying to make it in a strange and hostile land.

Into that era walked young James Cagney. He was an unlikely Hollywood star—short, uncouth, distinctively New York. And he was the right man for the right time.

Cagney, along with Edward G. Robinson, Paul Muni and, later, Humphrey Bogart, invented the film gangster. Each brought a sense of the street and gritty realism. For Cagney, that came naturally. He grew up on Manhattan's Lower East Side and had to drop out of college after one semester when his father died. He knew how to be tough, in an argument or in a rumble.

The Public Enemy is Cagney's breakout film. As bootlegger Tom Powers, he is the punk pup who grows up to be a wolf-like predator.

"The audience loves Cagney because he's a character who will fight," said Mike Newell, director of *Donnie Brasco*. "He would not accept the world the way it was. That was a good thing to be in the '30s, when so many people were squashed by the system."

It's easy to recognize that now. But it almost didn't happen. *The Public Enemy*, based on the factual novel *Beer and Blood* by Chicagoan John Bright, began filming in 1931. Edward Woods, a better-known and more genteel actor, was cast in the lead, with Cagney in the second banana role as best friend Matt Doyle.

After three days of shooting, director William Wellman realized, as he later said in an interview in *Film Comment*, "We'd made a frightful mistake. We had the wrong man playing the wrong part. This Cagney is the guy."

Wellman called producer Darryl F. Zanuck, who approved of Wellman's idea to have the two actors swap roles. And Cagney's career as a leading man was launched.

A technical circumstance also greatly aided Cagney's rise to film stardom. The sound equipment in *The Public Enemy* was better than anything used in the first few years of talking pictures. Prior to this, film actors had to speak slowly and over-enunciate to be understood. Cagney brought a machine-gun vocal delivery to his role. Before this movie, his staccato speaking style would have sounded like a jumble to film audiences.

The Public Enemy was filmed in four weeks for just $151,000 and released three months after Warner Brothers' first gangster hit, *Little Caesar*. It was among the first bargain-basement productions to gross more than $1 million. For weeks, a theatre in New York City's Times Square ran it 24 hours a day to packed houses.

The simple plotline tracks the lives of two young men as they progress from petty theft to bootlegging and murder. *The Public Enemy* was among the first movies to show how environment contributes to crime. Cagney's Tom Powers grows up with an emotionally absent father whose solution to parenting problems is to beat the boy with a leather strap. Tom is lured by the corruption of the streets, even as his older brother Mike stays straight by joining the Army and serving in World War I.

Tom rises from apprentice to gang leader by being more ruthless than his friends and rivals. He's also quite the babe magnet, working his way through a series of trollops.

Cagney's character is modeled after Chicago mobster Dion O'Banion, a rival to Al Capone. Many of the film's plot elements were inspired by true incidents, including the part where Tom and Matt shoot a horse that tosses and kills their associate, Sam "Nails" Nathan. According to the *Encyclopedia of American Crime*, two Chicago gangsters did exactly that in 1923 after bootlegger Sam "Nails" Morton died in a riding accident.

Mostly, *The Public Enemy* is remembered for two scenes. Foremost is the controversial breakfast table moment when Tom's irritation with girlfriend Kitty (Mae Clark) prompts him to smash a grapefruit in her face. More than anything, the action shows Tom's lack of human regard. The scene was a shocker at the time, perceived as one of crudest acts ever committed against a woman in film. Women's groups demanded it be edited out.

There are many versions of how the scene came to be, with everyone from Zanuck to Wellman to screenwriter Bright taking credit for it. Both actors in the scene, however, insist it was Cagney's spur-of-the-moment idea. In her autobiography, Mae Clarke wrote that Cagney whispered his plan to her right before filming, mostly as a joke to get a reaction from the crew. Neither actor expected the shot to stay in the finished film. But Wellman liked it so much he kept it in. Mae Clarke's ex-husband, Lew Brice, reportedly enjoyed the scene so much that he went to the theater each day for weeks just to watch that moment. As soon it ended he would leave.

The film's other iconic scene is its finale. After he is badly injured in a shootout, Tom's enemies kidnap him from the hospital. Back at their apartment, Tom's brother and mother get a phone call saying he is returning home. His mom cheerfully goes upstairs to make up his room, while his brother puts a record ("I'm Forever Blowing Bubbles") on the Victrola.

The doorbell rings. Mike opens the door and there's Tom, trussed up in rope and wrapped in a blanket, looking like a zombie. For a moment, you think he's alive—until his bloody, bullet-riddled body teeters and then crashes face first onto the floor. The needle reaches the end of the record and it skips, sounding like a heartbeat.

It's a horrifying scene, especially by 1931 standards. According to Wellman, producer Zanuck had to fight—literally—to keep it in. "(Jack) Warner said, 'Cut it out, it will make everyone sick. It made me sick,' " Wellman recalled in the documentary *Public Enemies: The Golden Age of the Gangster Film*. "Zanuck hauled off and slugged him. Knocked the cigar out of his mouth. Warner said, 'Well, if you feel that strongly, keep it.' "

The story may or may not be true. But the scene is a fittingly great ending to a great film.

⊙ **HIT:** The DVD release contains terrific commentary from gangster film heavyweights, including Martin Scorsese.

"My father took me to see it when I was 10," Scorsese says. "The impact stayed with me for many years. Of all the films, it's the toughest in its depiction of that world and how people behave in it and the nature of what a young killer really is. I must have watched it a dozen times as a kid. I was studying it, I guess."

⊗ **MISS:** Several actors in key roles are poor at, well, acting. Tom's war veteran brother Mike (Donald Cook) shows, to steal a line from Dorothy Parker, an emotional range from A to B. His mother (Beryl Mercer) alternates between fretting and crying. And as Gwen the floozie, platinum bombshell Jean Harlow, who went on to stardom, appears to be reading her lines—and not very well—from cue cards.

◉ **REPEATED WATCHING QUOTIENT:** The early classics are worth viewing to learn how they established the genre. But they don't have the texture or complexity to inspire a contemporary film fan to keep going back.

✔ REALITY CHECK: The movie is set in Chicago, but half its characters speak like they're from the South Bronx.

✎ WHAT THEY WROTE AT THE TIME: "A grim and terrible document, with no attempt to soften or humanize the character. Of all racketeer films it is the most brutal and least like movie fiction. For this reason it is the most arresting. Cagney triumphs."—Norbert Lusk, *Picture Play* magazine

PIVOTAL SCENES: Although young Tom shoots a cop to escape a botched robbery early in the movie, the extent of his viciousness is not revealed until later. Out at a nightclub, Tom and Matt stumble upon their old mentor, the aptly named Putty Nose. The two have never forgiven Putty Nose for leaving them exposed during that bungled holdup.

They follow Putty Nose back to his plush apartment and corner him. "I've always been your friend," the older man protests.

"Sure, you taught us how to cheat, steal and kill," Tom snaps. "Then you lammed out on us."

Putty Nose begs for his life. He runs over to the piano and reminds the two how he sang for them when they were boys. His voice quavers as he plays a silly old song. Tom, standing behind the piano, raises his revolver.

The camera tracks across the room to Matt. You hear, but do not see, as the song ends with a gunshot and the sound of Putty Nose's head hitting the piano keys. Matt, who merely wanted to scare the man, looks on with horror.

Tom crosses the room, shoots his cuffs as only Cagney could, and matter-of-factly says, "Well, I guess I'll go call Gwen." The coldblooded killer is unfazed by his cruelty.

➡ DON'T FAIL TO NOTICE: The scene where Mike Powers slugs Tom in the mouth. Wellman, wanting an authentic reaction, whispered to Cook that he should really sock Cagney. Cook obliged, cracking one of Cagney's teeth. To his credit, Cagney stayed in character and finished the scene, albeit in great pain.

☛ VIOLENCE LEVEL: Not high, other than that grapefruit. To keep censors from chopping the movie, Wellman placed most of the bloodshed off-screen. He created the illusion of more brutality through facial reactions and screams.

● BET YOU DIDN'T KNOW: Because of lax safety standards, Cagney had a close call during filming. Wellman hired sharpshooters to fire real machine guns in a scene where Tom ducks around the corner to avoid gunfire. If you watch, you'll see the bullets hit the wall just feet from Cagney's head. One bad ricochet and the great actor's career may have had an early ending.

❝❝ BEST LINE: Mike Powers, just back from World War I, discovers that his brother and brother-in-law are mobsters. He confronts them at the dinner table, the characters separated by a keg of fresh beer:

Mike: "You murderers. There's not only beer in that keg. There's beer and blood. The blood of men."

Tom: "Ahh, you ain't changed a bit. Besides, your hands ain't so clean. You killed and liked it. You didn't get them medals by holding hands with them Germans."

⊛ IF YOU LIKED THIS, YOU'LL LIKE: *The Roaring Twenties*, *'G' Men* and *Each Dawn I Die*. All are Cagney movies that could merit inclusion in our Top 100.

⚜ BODY COUNT: Three on-screen, a few more (and one poor horse) offscreen.

24 SEXY BEAST (2000–R)

STARS: RAY WINSTONE, BEN KINGSLEY, IAN MCSHANE
DIRECTOR: JONATHAN GLAZER

Don Logan is a frighteningly malevolent mobster. He urinates on your floor, describes in detail his old sexual bouts with your best friend's wife and rousts you from sleep with a heel stomp to the head.

Logan has the hair-trigger violent streak of *Casino's* Nicky Santoro. He stabs you with words like Frank Costello in *The Departed*. The mere mention of his name instills gape-mouthed fear like *The Usual Suspects'* Keyser Söze.

And this monster, this beast, is brilliantly created by a kind-faced, five-foot-eight English gentleman best remembered for his textured portrayal of the world's foremost practitioner of nonviolence in *Gandhi*.

Sir Ben Kingsley becomes the ruthless Logan in *Sexy Beast*, and he's 90 percent of the reason to watch the movie. The plotline here is straightforward, nothing special really. The action is sporadic. The supporting cast is strong—led by British veteran Ray Winstone, who's actually the film's lead, and Ian McShane, who can always dial up ominous.

But it's Kingsley—throwing off Gandhi's loincloth and round spectacles—who becomes the savage bully you'll remember long after viewing *Sexy Beast*. A former Shakespearean actor, Kingsley nuanced the gentle accountant in *Schindler's List* and the regal Persian ex-patriot in *House of Sand and Fog*. There's nothing gentle or regal, though, about Kingsley's portrayal of Don Logan. He fires insults with a bullet's speed and a carving knife's edge. He is a rabid dog, gnawing at your leg until it buckles. Friends, wives, strangers—

no distinction matters as he hurls obscenities.

It's a joy—albeit a frightening one—to watch the character at work. Even the way he sits on a chair. The smallest man in the room intimidates criminals twice his size with his posture—perfectly erect, all 90-degree angles. He radiates terror, even when he's perfectly still.

Kingsley earned a Best Supporting Actor nomination (the Oscar went to the obscure Jim Broadbent from the even more obscure movie *Iris*). In 2006, his work in *Sexy Beast* was ranked No. 97 among *Premiere* Magazine's "100 Greatest Performances of All Time."

And whom did Kingsley draw on to create this character?

"My maternal grandmother," he told IFC's *Escape from Hollywood*. "She was an extremely violent and unpleasant woman. She was racist, fascist and anti-Semitic. When I play great heroic Jews and great heroic dark people, I'm sticking two fingers up at her. When I played Don Logan, I was channeling her."

Logan is a recruiter for the London mob assigned by his boss, Teddy Bass (McShane), to put together a team for a bank heist. The caper requires the skills of Gal Dove (Winstone), an expert safecracker.

Gal, however, is out of the business. He's living in a villa on the Costa del Sol in Spain with his wife, Deedee (Amanda Redman), a retired porn star. He has plenty of money socked away. The last thing he wants to do is go back for one more job.

Sexy Beast's opening scene shows Gal baking in a chaise lounge by his pool, a few empty Heinekens nearby. You hear what's going through his mind: "People say, 'Don't you miss it, Gal?' I say, 'What, England? Nah. Fucking place. It's a dump. Don't make me laugh.' Grey, grimy, sooty. . . . What a toilet. . . . They say, 'What's it like, then, Spain?' And I'll say, 'It's hot. Oh, it's fucking hot.' Too hot? Not for me, I love it."

Into this paradise steps Logan, the houseguest from hell with a job offer that is not exactly cast as a proposition Gal has the option of declining. Logan puts Gal and Deedee—along with another retired mobster and his wife—through a torment that escalates from anxious courtesies to threats and gut punches. Winstone, often cast as a heavy (*The Departed, Edge of Darkness*), seems downright huggable by comparison. His character of Dove withstands Logan's cruelty, trying to save his manhood without losing his life.

The duel of wills and wits grows increasingly ugly and violent. We won't tell you how that portion of the movie ends—it's a stunner—but Gal does return to London to assist in the bank heist. It's a waterlogged caper in which the crooks drill into a safe-deposit vault from the pool of a Turkish bath adjacent to the bank. The vault, predictably, fills with water, leading to a strange scene in which stacks of money and priceless jewelry float through the murk as the robbers try to grab what they can.

Sexy Beast was directed by Jonathan Glazer—a native Londoner known mostly for his work on music videos and Guinness Beer commercials. We're not sure why he's only directed one motion picture since this—the confusing *Birth,* the story of a woman who becomes convinced that a 10-year-old boy is the reincarnation of her late husband. Here's hoping Glazer gets more chances with films like this.

⊙ **HIT:** Other than the brilliant performance by Kingsley, the best thing about this movie may be its edgy soundtrack. It starts—as Gal lazes by his pool—with the song "Peaches" by the Stranglers ("Walking on the beaches, looking at the peaches"), and closes with Dean Martin's "Sway" ("Dance with me, make me sway, like a lazy ocean hugs the shore"). The songs aren't just great to listen to, they perfectly fit their scenes.

⊗ **MISS:** The strong Cockney accents can be difficult for an untrained ear to comprehend. Fortunately, the DVD offers English subtitles.

✒ **WHAT THEY WROTE AT THE TIME:** "Ben Kingsley looks like a shaved weasel—fresh skin and a bleached goatee. He is Don Logan, a fear-of-God-inspiring bloke who, as inhabited by Kingsley, reaches for the scope and menace of Don Corleone, Keyser Söze and Bill Murray in *What About Bob?*"—Wesley Morris, *San Francisco Chronicle*

☺ **GOOF:** The plot of the film is about robbing an exclusive bank billed as having "the most elaborate security system in Europe." If that's the case, how do you explain the black-and-white monitors? The lack of motion sensors? The masonry wall—rather than hardened steel—that protects the back of the vault? Not exactly Fort Knox.

👁 **REPEATED WATCHING QUOTIENT:** Worth stumbling upon anytime, if only to see what a powerful and dynamic actor Kingsley can be.

🗨 **BEST LINE:** Don Logan to Gal: "Shut up, cunt. You louse. You got some fucking neck ain't you? Retired? Fuck off. You're revolting. Look at your suntan, it's leather. It's like leather man, your skin. We could make a fucking suitcase out of you. Like a crocodile, fat crocodile, fat bastard. You look like fucking Idi Amin, you know what I mean?"

This is not Logan's vilest outburst, just his first of many.

👅 **BET YOU DIDN'T KNOW:** The word "fuck"—and its derivatives—is used 115 times in this 89-minute film, or an average of once every 46 seconds.

PIVOTAL SCENES: After failing to bully Gal into the heist, Logan heads to the airport to get back to London. On the plane, he berates other passengers and responds to a stewardess's request to put out a cigarette by blowing smoke in her face. He is removed from the flight and detained at the airport for a few hours.

Set free, he immediately heads back to Gal's house—where, one more time, Gal tries to tell him he will "pass up the opportunity."

"Not this time, Gal," shouts Logan. "Not this fucking time. No. No, no, no, no, no, no, no, no, no! No! No, no, no, no, no, no, no, no, no, no, no, no! No! Not this fucking time. No fucking way. No fucking way, no fucking way, no fucking way!"

That's 29 repetitions of the word "no," if you're scoring at home.

When spitting invective doesn't work, Logan resorts to violence, punching Gal in the face. This time, he does not intend to leave for London alone.

➡ **DON'T FAIL TO NOTICE:** The closing credits, which include the words, "Good-bye, sweet Cavan." That's a tribute to actor Cavan Kendall, who plays Gal's buddy Aitch. He died of cancer at age 57, passing away between the time the movie was shot and released.

◀ **CASTING CALL:** Anthony Hopkins was considered for the role of Don Logan.

🔫 **VIOLENCE LEVEL:** Sporadic. Most of the movie's shock effect is in the dialogue, but occasionally Logan will smack a teenager with the butt end of a rifle or wake someone by literally kicking him out of bed.

🦴 **BODY COUNT:** Just two, although one is a glorious, bloody death scene.

✴ **IF YOU LIKED THIS, YOU'LL LIKE:** *The Limey,* director Steven Soderbergh's 1999 crime thriller with the same tense pace and occasional incomprehensible Cockney-accented dialogue. It's about a British prison parolee who comes to the United States to investigate the suspicious death of his daughter.

25 ROAD TO PERDITION (2002–R)

STARS: TOM HANKS, PAUL NEWMAN, JUDE LAW, DANIEL CRAIG, TYLER HOECHLIN
DIRECTOR: SAM MENDES

There was a story circulating in the New York underworld back in the 1980s about a meeting between Gambino crime family boss John Gotti and Vincent "the Chin" Gigante, the secretive, old-world style leader of the more powerful Genovese organization.

Gotti, according to reports that filtered back to law enforcement from mob informants, was boasting about how his son, John A. Gotti, had been formally initiated into the crime family. His son, Gotti said proudly, was now a made man, a "friend of ours" in the lexicon of the American Mafia.

Gigante was less than impressed.

"I'm sorry to hear that," he said.

Fathers and sons and the mob. The smart ones don't want the legacy to pass from one generation to the next.

Road to Perdition, a period piece about one branch of the Chicago crime family in the 1930s, is really a story about fathers and sons.

Paul Newman, in his last movie role, plays John Rooney, the patriarch of a mob family located just outside of Chicago. The organization is under the umbrella of Al Capone's syndicate, but as is and was the case in Chicago, the mob—which is known as the Outfit—is more like a loose federation than a traditional Mafia family.

Rooney has a biological son named Connor (Daniel Craig) and a surrogate son named Michael Sullivan (Tom Hanks)—an orphan he raised. Sullivan is a hit man for the Rooney organization. Connor is a hothead who lacks his father's intelligence and patience. His shortcomings prove deadly.

Told in flashback through the voice of Sullivan's son Michael Jr. (Tyler Hoechlin), *Road to Perdition* examines the relationship between fathers and sons and the sense of honor, family and loyalty that both the traditional mob and blood relationships engender.

Can a gangster father keep his son from following in his footsteps?

And how far would he go to do so?

Those are the fundamental questions at the heart of this fascinating story. There's plenty of violence and treachery, two staples of most classic gangster films. But there is another level to the narrative that makes *Road to Perdition* a different kind of mob movie.

Hanks is surprisingly good as the pragmatic and vengeful assassin who uses the skills developed in Rooney's service to turn the aging mob boss's world inside out. And Newman brings just the right blend of menace and cynicism to his character. Their scenes together are some of the best in the film.

Their verbal confrontation before Sullivan sets out on his one-man (plus a boy) crime spree defines the story.

"There are only murderers in this room, Michael, open your eyes," Rooney says as he entreats his adopted son to reconsider his plan. "This is the life we choose, the life we lead. And there is only one guarantee: none of us will see heaven."

"Michael could," Sullivan says of his 12-year-old son.

"Then do everything that you can to see that that happens," says a resigned and saddened Rooney.

What follows is not exactly what the aging mob boss had in mind.

Michael Sullivan, the hit man and orphan, chooses *his* family over *the* family, a decision that lends a level of nobility to what he sets out to do.

The plot is set in motion several scenes earlier as Michael accompanies Connor to a meeting with Finn McGovern (Ciaran Hinds), another mobster whose brother has been killed. The typical Irish wake for the dead gangster allows director Sam

Mendes and writer David Self to set up the relationships and hint at the treacherous nature of the organization.

John Rooney toasts his dead associate with the hope that "he gets to heaven at least an hour before the devil finds out he's dead." Much drinking and dancing follow.

No one is quite sure why McGovern's brother has been killed, but McGovern clearly holds Rooney responsible.

At a warehouse meeting the next night, Connor Rooney is supposed to iron out the problem with McGovern. Michael Sullivan is there to back him up. Unbeknownst to either, Michael Jr., in an attempt to learn what his dad does for a living, has slipped into his father's car. He watches the meeting unfold by looking through a warehouse window.

What he sees is the short-tempered Connor fly off the handle and gun down McGovern. Michael Sullivan Sr. then kills two of McGovern's associates to protect Connor Rooney.

It's what he does.

As they leave, they discover young Michael. In one of several rain-soaked scenes that add to the film's gloomy atmosphere, Michael Sr. tells his son, "You are not to speak of this to anyone."

Connor is not comfortable with that arrangement, however, and a short time later goes to Sullivan's home. He mistakenly kills Sullivan's younger son Peter (Liam Aiken) and then guns down Sullivan's wife Annie (Jennifer Jason Leigh).

This sets up the father-son dynamic that defines the rest of the movie.

Michael Sullivan first goes to John Rooney for justice, but is told instead that they are all murderers and to let it go. In fact, Rooney has chosen his own blood, Connor, over the son he loves better, Sullivan.

Michael Sullivan then travels to Chicago with his one surviving son and namesake to meet with Frank Nitti (Stanley Tucci) and ask for permission to do what he has to do—kill Connor Rooney. Tucci, in a well-acted supporting role, tells him that while the organization is sorry for what happened, Connor Rooney is being protected.

It's business, he says.

With that, Michael launches his father-son crime spree, setting out to rob banks where the mob has stashed its money. This, he reasons, will force Capone to grant him his wish.

Along the way, young Michael learns how to drive a car so that he can handle the getaways and father and son, who have never spoken that much, learn about one another.

Feeling guilty and responsible for what has happened, Michael Jr. asks his father if he loved his brother Peter more than him, pointing out that he always treated Peter differently.

"Well, I suppose it was because Peter was just... such a sweet boy," Michael Sr. says. "And you, you were more like me. And I ... didn't want you to be."

In another conversation that underscores how their relationship is developing, the younger Michael, after a bank robbery, asks what his take will be. His father asks how much he wants.

"Two hundred dollars," the boy says.

"Okay, deal," says his father.

Michael Jr., who is eating at a diner at the time, stops to consider, then asks, "Could I have had more?"

"You'll never know," says his father.

The Sullivans rob several banks while staying one step ahead of a psychotic hit man, Harlen Maguire (Jude Law), sent by the Capone organization.

In addition to avenging the murders of his wife and youngest son, Michael Sullivan's goal is to get to Perdition, a lakeshore town where his wife's relatives live and where he hopes to find safety for his surviving son. This allows for the less than subtle double-entendre that is the movie's title.

Michael Sr., the Rooneys, Nitti, an unseen Al Capone and all the other gangsters have clearly chosen a life that drives them down the road to hell.

Michael Jr. has a chance to go in a different direction. And his father will do everything in his power to help make that happen.

HIT: The movie captures the bleak, film noir feel of the 1930s gangster genre. This is due in large part to cinematographer Conrad L. Hall, whose work was recognized with an Academy Award.

MISS: The premise of robbing banks and only taking the mob's money is a bit of a stretch. It's hard to imagine gangsters like Capone letting a banker off the hook after he explains that we've been robbed of your money, but no one else's. Those guys don't need the Feds to insure their deposits.

✔ REALITY CHECK: Newman wanted his John Rooney character to speak with the hint of an Irish accent. So he got a tape made by Irish-born author Frank McCourt (*Angela's Ashes*) and studied his voice inflections and speech patterns.

❞ BEST LINE: "Natural law: sons are put on this earth to trouble their fathers," says Rooney as he complains about his hotheaded son Connor to Michael Sullivan, the orphan he has raised as a son and who is, in many ways, closer to him than his own blood.

✎ WHAT THEY WROTE AT THE TIME: "*Road to Perdition* ponders some of the same questions as *The Sopranos,* a comparably great work of popular art, whose protagonist is also a gangster and a devoted family man. But far from a self-pitying boor lumbering around a suburban basement in his undershirt, Mr. Hanks' antihero is a stern, taciturn killer who projects a tortured nobility. Acutely aware of his sins, Sullivan is determined that his son, who takes after him temperamentally, not follow in his murderous footsteps."—Stephen Holden, *New York Times*

◀ CASTING CALL: Anthony LaPaglia was cast as Al Capone and was in one scene, but the scene was cut after Mendes decided that Capone was a more ominous presence unseen.

➡ DON'T FAIL TO NOTICE: Jude Law had a make-under before he appeared as the psychotic photographer/hit man Harlen Maguire. He was given a sallow, almost yellow skin tone, his gum line was lowered and his teeth were made to look rotten.

🎬 PIVOTAL SCENE: When the Sullivans avoid Maguire, the hit man sent to kill Michael Sr. at the diner, they realize that the mob has not only refused Michael's request, but has now decided to eliminate him. At that point, Michael has two choices, flee or fight back. He decides to fight back and launches the crime spree—bank robberies and shootings—that dominates the second half of the movie.

🍎 BET YOU DIDN'T KNOW: In the novel on which the movie is based, Michael Sullivan's character is so violent he is known as the "Angel of Death." The movie script softened the character, partly at Hanks' request. And the hit man character played by Law was created for the movie.

🔫 BODY COUNT: Twenty-one.

26 GET SHORTY (1995–R)

STARS: JOHN TRAVOLTA, GENE HACKMAN, DANNY DEVITO, RENE RUSSO
DIRECTOR: BARRY SONNENFELD

One year after reviving his career in *Pulp Fiction*, John Travolta gracefully slipped back into the role of a mobster. Like Vincent Vega, *Get Shorty*'s Chili Palmer is ultracool, sharp-witted and drawn to dressing in black. He can shatter your nose with a punch or fire his Colt Detective Special accurately enough to add a part to your hairline.

But he'd rather not. Because this is a reluctant thug—or loan shark, to be specific. What Chili is really looking to do is get out of the rackets and into Hollywood. From one dirty business to another.

"In *Pulp Fiction*, we played characters who were hell-bent on death . . . high all the time and killing people," Travolta told the *Times* of London. "In [*Get Shorty*], we are hell-bent on life."

That's the setup for this quirky film, based on an Elmore Leonard bestseller. There is a three-pronged, interweaving script involving an insurance scam, a drug-smuggling sting and a movie-making venture. Each, it turns out, is a cesspool. And throughout, Travolta plays the charming criminal who never raises his voice and never loses his shy smile.

Rather than bust jaws, Chili moves you with his confidence. "Look at me," he keeps telling his adversaries. "Look at me like I'm looking at you."

He then calmly persuades even the toughest-minded adversary to repay a debt, back off a fight or go into business with him.

You can't help but root for this guy surrounded by a cast of oddball characters.

Those characters—and the sharp dialogue—are what make *Get Shorty* work. Beyond Travolta's Chili, there's Harry Zimm (Gene Hackman), a schlock producer (his finest work is *Bride of the Mutant*) trying to spin financial misfortune to his advantage. There's Martin Weir (Danny DeVito), a self-absorbed screen superstar who sits in the same restaurant seat each day so that he can gaze at the billboard touting his latest film.

Actors in smaller supporting roles also shine. Delroy Lindo plays a menacing drug dealer who, like Chili, is owed a debt by Zimm and is looking to break into movies (who isn't?). Dennis Farina steals a few scenes as a mid-level mobster who tries to bully Chili, but keeps getting his face disfigured as a result. Bette Midler, Harvey Keitel and Penny Marshall all show up, as does one particular paragon of gangster actors—before he struck it big. More about that guy later.

Overall, this cast (through 2010) has combined to be nominated for nine Oscars, 27 Golden Globes and 12 Emmys—lugging home more than a few. Unfortunately, *Get Shorty* garnered no Academy Award nominations (we certainly would have taken it over *Babe* as a Best Picture hopeful), although Travolta collected the Golden Globe for best performance by an actor in a musical or comedy.

To be honest, the dense plot is difficult to describe in a few paragraphs. In short, Chili heads from Miami Beach to Las Vegas to Hollywood, chasing a $150,000 casino debt run up by Hackman's character Zimm. Chili confronts the producer at his home one night, and persuasion turns into conversation about Hollywood.

Chili, who is looking for a lifestyle change, pitches a story to Zimm about another case he's working on—a deadbeat dry cleaner (David Paymer) who faked his own death and skipped town with $300,000 in insurance money. Chili must track down the guy and collect the debt for inept Miami Beach mobster Ray Barboni (Farina).

Zimm loves the idea, but he's got other concerns. Drug-dealing limo executive Bo Catlett (Lindo) has made a large investment in the producer's next film. Unfortunately, Zimm has already blown that money. So Bo decides, as compensation, he will muscle his way into Chili's new venture.

There's also an international cocaine deal being monitored at the airport by obvious and jumpy DEA agents. That angle is complicated by the disappearance of a Colombian lord's nephew. And there's the repeated riff on Hollywood, convincing you that the best preparation for becoming a film producer is a stint in the underworld.

Truth be told, the satire in *Get Shorty* barbs the film industry much more sharply than it does the crime industry. We learn about movie stars that never pick up the check, never order from the menu, rarely know their own phone number or zip code and often sit facing the sun as an excuse to show off fancy sunglasses. And they're sheep. There's a wonderful little thread running through *Get Shorty* that begins with Chili seeking to rent a Cadillac at the airport and settling for an Oldsmobile Silhouette, which is described as "the Cadillac of minivans." By the end of the movie, he has convinced all of Hollywood to drive the soccer-mom vehicle.

The patter, much of it taken straight from Leonard's novel, will remind you of a lot of *Pulp Fiction*. In one scene—evocative of *Pulp's* French McDonald's vs. Burger King discussion—mobsters debate the use of "i.e." vs. "e.g." as a conversational tool. In another, one of Chili's 25-watt cohorts reads an article stating that most Americans die in bed, so he decides to start sleeping on the couch.

◉ **HIT:** Even before he was Jersey mob boss Tony Soprano, actor James Gandolfini knew how to play a tough guy (*8MM*, *True Romance*). Here, however, he's anything but menacing as Bear, a bodyguard and former stuntman. Gandolfini's Southern-bred character alternately dotes on his young daughter and keeps getting throttled as he tries to protect his boss. Still, even as he gets beat up, you can see some of Tony Soprano's classic gestures in their formative stages—like the one where he girds his chin and stares dead-fish eyes at a challenger.

⊗ MISS: Veteran actress Rene Russo seems like she's just along for the ride, playing an aging B-movie scream queen.

✐ WHAT THEY WROTE AT THE TIME: "This playful, thoroughly entertaining spoof of Hollywood moviemaking stems from the more bitter [though equally entertaining] novel by Elmore Leonard. The famous crime writer, apparently disgusted by the mediocre movies Hollywood has made from his previous novels, had the ingenious notion to compare the capricious, dishonorable nature of organized crime to the movie business."—Ralph Novak, *People Weekly*

◉ REPEATED WATCHING QUOTIENT: High. The acting is terrific, Leonard's script is witty and the plot twists get better with each viewing.

➡ DON'T FAIL TO NOTICE: At several points, characters are seen reading a copy of *Newsweek*. Look closely and you'll spot DeVito's character of Martin Weir on the cover. The headline, "Napoleon, Solo," touts Weir's supposed biopic on the French emperor—which, come to think of it, would make a great role for DeVito.

◀ CASTING CALL: Bruce Willis, Michael Keaton, Al Pacino and Robert De Niro all turned down the role of Chili. In addition, Quentin Tarantino declined an offer to direct—a decision he regretted. Two years later, Tarantino directed another Elmore Leonard story, *Jackie Brown*.

⚑ VIOLENCE LEVEL: Decent. Ray Barboni (Farina) is the leading psychopath, stepping on an old man's head and socking a woman in the jaw. Plus, you get to see Gandolfini get picked up by the balls and tossed down a flight of steps.

🍎 BET YOU DIDN'T KNOW: The undersized, indecisive, self-obsessed movie star character DeVito plays is based on Dustin Hoffman, according to Leonard. The author met Hoffman when they attempted to make a deal on a movie treatment of Leonard's book *La Brava*.

Hoffman and director Martin Scorsese kept the author shuttling from his Detroit home to New York, each time looking to rework the script, Leonard recalled to the *Guardian* of Great Britain. "Finally I said to them: 'Look, it's okay for you guys, but I'm not getting paid for this.' Hoffman told me, 'Don't worry, you'll be paid retroactively.' My agent rolled on the floor laughing when I told him this. He said, 'They'll never make the picture.' "

Which, of course, they didn't.

BET YOU DIDN'T KNOW II: In an alternate version of *Get Shorty*—edited to be shown as an in-flight film—the fiery plane crash scene leading to the insurance scam was chopped out. All the dialogue about it was altered to describe a train wreck.

☻ "I KNOW THAT GUY": The mob boss enjoying a massage on his yacht? That's Moe Greene, dammit! Actually, it's actor Alex Rocco, whose Moe Greene character in *The Godfather* had the gall to tell off Michael Corleone ("Do you know who I am?!"), leading to him getting a bullet through the eye during his daily rubdown. You would think he'd know better than to climb back onto the massage table in another movie.

⚰ BODY COUNT: Three. One guy is shot, one gets pushed over a railing and one poor sap gets both shot *and* sent over the railing.

⊛ IF YOU LIKED THIS, YOU'LL LIKE: *The Player*, Robert Altman's 1992 nasty send-up of Hollywood. The twisting plot focuses on a studio executive (Tim Robbins) caught up in blackmail and murder.

27 RIFIFI (1955–NR)

STARS: JEAN SERVAIS, CARL MOHNER, ROBERT MANUEL, JANINE DARCEY
DIRECTOR: JULES DASSIN

Film critics have tagged this as one of the best French crime movies ever made, with some even putting it at the top of the list. We haven't seen *every* French gangster film, but our initial reaction is to agree. And, ironically, were it not for the infamous Communist witch hunt that drove dozens of talented actors, directors and writers out of Hollywood in the 1950s, *Rififi* might have never been.

Rififi was the brainchild of banished American director Jules Dassin, who at first didn't want to do the film. In fact, he found the novel on which it was based—with its brutal beatings, blatant racism and a dash of necrophilia—both bizarre and repulsive.

But in a fascinating interview that is part of the DVD package, Dassin said he finally agreed to direct because he needed the work.

Before he was driven from Hollywood because of his membership in the Communist Party in the 1930s, Dassin, the son of Russian-Jewish immigrants, was considered one of the up-and-comers in the then-emerging film noir genre. His works included *Brute Force* (1947) and *The Naked City* (1948).

In *Rififi,* Dassin used the skeleton of Auguste le Breton's novel and literally made the story his own. Along the way, he took some of the elements of film noir, added a more personalized and internalized characterization of the central figures, and helped launch a new style in filmmaking that became known as the French New Wave.

The word *rififi* is French slang that in the movie is translated as "rough and tumble." In actuality, rififi is more an attitude than an adjective. It's a macho, tough guy, in-your-face approach to life that could be described as gangster existentialism. Things are what they are and if you're rififi, you deal with them.

The novel was a graphic story of French Algerian gangsters in the Paris underworld, but the producers were worried about a potential backlash. (This was, after all, the time of the French-Algerian conflict. See the *Mesrine* chapter on page 197, for reference.) So they asked Dassin to make it a story about American gangsters.

He had a better idea. Why not make it about Frenchmen?

Out of that came what is now considered a classic.

The storyline is taut and the acting near perfect.

Tony le Stephanois (Jean Servais) is an aging gangster who comes home from prison to find that his girlfriend Mado (Marie Sabouret) has taken up with Louis Grutter (Pierre Grasset), the leader of another crime group.

Tony's not happy with that development nor with the fact that he can barely make ends meet. His young protégé and friend, Jo le Suedois (Carl Mohner) suggests a jewelry store heist to solve Tony's financial woes.

Jo's friend Mario Ferrati (Robert Manuel), an Italian living in Paris, has cased the high-class Mappin & Webb jewelry store and declares it the perfect target.

At first, Tony balks at the idea. But after an encounter with Mado that ends badly (he beats her with a belt), Tony decides to direct the heist. He says, however, that they have to do it his way. There will be no guns and they will go for the safe, not the jewels under the display cases.

To that end, Mario agrees to recruit his friend, the renowned safecracker Cesar le Milanais (Dassin played that role, using the name Perlo Vita).

The first half of the film revolves around the elaborate and painstaking planning that sets up the dramatic robbery. The way the thieves disarm the jewelry store's alarm system is ingenious. (The movie was banned in Mexico and several South American countries after thieves began to employ the same methods in real life.)

While dramatic is an overused word, it applies here.

The four-man team breaks into an apartment above the jewelry store, ties up the elderly couple living there and then begins to cut a hole in their living room floor to gain access to the jewelry store below.

That these guys are, as the French say, *sympathique*, is evident from the beginning of the robbery when Tony tucks a pillow behind the head of the elderly woman to make her more comfortable after she and her husband have been gagged and tied up.

A clock ticking on a mantel provides a time line for the heist, which begins shortly before midnight and doesn't end until six the next morning. In film time, the robbery takes about 30 minutes. And during those minutes, not a word NOT ONE WORD—is spoken. The robbers go about their business efficiently, the tension conveyed by their nods, shrugs and the sweat dripping from their foreheads. The only noises come from the tools used to pull off the job.

Dassin said that both the producer and the musical director were aghast when he first suggested going 30 minutes without any dialogue. The musical director said he would write a lengthy piece that could be played as the backdrop. When he supplied the music, Dassin said he showed him a clip with the music and another without it. The musical director agreed that the lengthy scene was better when presented in silence.

The heist goes off without a hitch, but Tony's problems are just beginning.

The thieves have made off with gems worth 240 million francs, screams a newspaper headline. Cesar has also grabbed an expensive diamond bracelet on his way out and later gives it to Viviane, the nightclub chanteuse he has been wooing since his arrival in Paris.

She thinks the bracelet is a fake, but when she laughingly shows it to the club owner—the gangster Pierre Grutter—he immediately realizes the piece came from the sensational robbery.

Grutter, Tony and their various associates now begin a game of cat-and-mouse, one trying to hide the loot and the other trying to find it. This leads to murder, kidnapping and a less-than-happy ending for almost everyone involved.

Dassin, on the other hand, used the success of the film to rebuild his career, first in Europe and then back in the United States. He met the Greek actress Melina Mercouri at the Cannes Film Festival in 1955—the year *Rififi* came out. They eventually married. While Dassin no longer identified himself as a Communist, he remained an advocate of liberal causes and his work and politics continued to make headlines. He and Mercouri left Greece in 1966 and later were suspected of helping finance a failed coup aimed at overthrowing the country's dictatorship. They returned in 1974 after Greece's military dictatorship fell.

In films, Dassin went on to direct Mercouri in the classic *Never on Sunday* (1960). He also received high praise for his work in *Topkapi* (1964), another heist film.

◉ **HIT:** Filming in standard black and white, Dassin said he made a point to never shoot in sunlight, much to the consternation of the film's producer, who became upset with the delays. But the dark, rainy, cloudy atmosphere coupled with the Paris street scenes (is there a better city in the world in which to film a movie?) added just the right touch.

As a reviewer for the *New York Times* noted (see below), you can almost smell the atmosphere.

⊗ **MISS:** There's a scene at the nightclub early in the movie in which Viviane does a jazz number entitled "Rififi." It's clearly a way to explain the French argot and the meaning of the word, but given the tone and mood of the rest of the movie, it seems somewhat out of place to be singing about this lifestyle.

✎ **WHAT THEY WROTE AT THE TIME:** "This is perhaps the keenest crime film that ever came from France, including *Pepe le Moko* and some of the best of Louis Jouvet and Jean Gabin. . . . This beautifully fashioned black-and-white film . . . has a flavor of crooks and kept women and Montmartre 'boites' that you can just about smell. . . . But there is also a poetry about it—and a poetic justice, too. Mr. Dassin has got the tender beauty of Paris at dawn, when there is no one stirring but milkmen, street cleaners, gendarmes—and thieves. And he has ended his film with a feeling for the pathos of the comédie humaine that would do justice to a story with a more exalting theme."—Bosley Crowther, *New York Times*

✔ **REALITY CHECK:** The scene in which Cesar admits that he has betrayed his friend Mario and asks for forgiveness was not in the novel. Dassin, who played Cesar, added that part of the story with the Hollywood witch hunts in mind. He was one of the people who had been betrayed and his message was that there could be no forgiving.

👁 **REPEATED WATCHING QUOTIENT:** A classic in the foreign film noir genre, this is a movie worth revisiting from time to time.

🍎 **BET YOU DIDN'T KNOW:** Dassin met with Auguste le Breton, the author of the novel on which the script was based, shortly before starting to shoot the movie. He was not happy with Dassin's adaptation. "I have read your screenplay," said the author, who showed up for the meeting dressed in gangster-like garb, including a fedora. "I would like to know, where is my book?" Dassin tried to explain that he only took parts of the book and expanded on them. Le Breton again asked the same question, "Where is my book?" Then he pulled out a gun and placed it on the table. Dassin said all he could do was laugh at the ludicrousness of the situation. Luckily, the author joined in and they became friends.

◀ **CASTING CALL:** Dassin had to operate with a small budget. Servais was a well-known French actor who hadn't had much recent work, so he came cheap, as did Carl Mohner, who was an unknown. Dassin saved additional money by casting himself as Cesar.

🙿 **BEST LINE:** "There's not a safe that can resist Cesar and not a woman that Cesar can resist," says Mario in describing his Milanese friend and his skills. They need him for the heist, but the comment also foreshadows the romantic entanglement that leads to the betrayal.

🔫 **VIOLENCE LEVEL:** Low-key, but effective. The shootings were standard for the time. Nothing flashy or outlandish. The beating scene, even though it takes place offscreen, was the most disturbing.

🦂 **BODY COUNT:** Eight.

28 THE UNTOUCHABLES (1987–R)

STARS: KEVIN COSTNER, SEAN CONNERY, ROBERT DE NIRO
DIRECTOR: BRIAN DE PALMA

The Untouchables should not be celebrated for its plotline, which basically boils down to: straight-laced cop chases charismatic criminal, catches him, roll credits. It certainly doesn't earn points for historical accuracy, telling a wholly contrived story of Eliot Ness vs. Al Capone in Prohibition Era Chicago. And there's not a lot of character development in this one. The good guys—led by Kevin Costner as the overly prim Ness—are all saintly, while the bad guys have no redeeming qualities.

That said, the film deserves its rating here. The reason? Over the course of 119 minutes, *The Untouchables* presents four of the iconic scenes in gangster movie history.

Count 'em:

1. The Baseball Bat Scene. In the midst of a dinner party in his honor, Capone (Robert De Niro) takes out a Louisville Slugger and delivers a tribute to baseball as the All-American sport. As his underlings smoke cigars and chuckle in agreement, Capone circles a huge round table—finally stopping behind one nodding toadie. He briefly speaks of betrayal and then applies a few Ruthian swings to the employee's skull.

It's jarring stuff—for the audience, as well as for Capone's flunkies. They sit aghast at the table as their cohort's blood seeps across the white linen. And it really happened. In 1929, Capone learned that two of his hit men were hatching a plan to kill him. He called a dinner party and battered them to death in front of the entire gang.

"The point here," director Brian De Palma explains in the film's DVD commentary, "is that Capone is the king, the god. He makes people live, he makes people die."

2. The Death of Agent Oscar Wallace. Charles Martin Smith plays the Treasury accountant who conceives the idea of nabbing Capone for tax evasion, rather than for his more hideous—but less prosecutable—crimes. Over the course of the film, we watch Wallace transform from a nebbishy money cruncher into a real cop. He comes to enjoy carrying a gun, throwing a punch and, yes, even sneaking a nip of Canadian whiskey.

Entrusted with protecting Capone's bookkeeper, Wallace escorts the man onto an elevator in the police station. We, the audience, can spot that the elevator operator is Capone's henchman, Frank Nitti—but Wallace does not know. The door closes and—BANG! BANG! By the time the other Untouchables reach the scene, the open door reveals that the bookkeeper has a bullet through his head, Nitti has fled and Wallace has been shot dead. His body hangs from a hook in the elevator, with the taunting word "Touchable" painted in his blood on the wall.

Two things you should know about the scene. First, De Palma, who never shies away from gore, looked at the scene's setup and said, "No, too much blood." Second, it ends with Sean Connery's character of Jimmy Malone pulling Wallace from the hook and gently laying down his body. "When Sean did that beautiful gesture," Smith recalled, "the other actors were all so emotionally touched that we started crying. We had to shoot it again."

3. The Shooting of Jimmy Malone. Connery's gruff Irish cop meets his end when a knife-wielding intruder lures him out onto the front steps of his home and he is gunned down by Nitti. The so-called "creeper scene" that sets up the shooting is a De Palma trademark, in which the camera follows the victim as if seeing him through the eyes of his hunter. It builds up the tension, in that the audience knows what's waiting for Malone—but he doesn't.

"Sean hated the scene," De Palma says on the video commentary. "He was hurt by the [blood] pellets the first time and had to go to the hospital. He didn't want to reshoot it."

But De Palma wasn't satisfied with the first take and made the legendary actor endure it a second time. He needed to, said the director, "because we had to make it a shocking moment." Connery won an Oscar for Best Supporting Actor for the movie.

On a personal note, a friend of the authors originally watched *The Untouchable*s in a South Philadelphia movie theater, a few rows away from some notorious Philly wiseguys. The real-life mobsters cheered each murder by Capone's men and erupted into raucous applause as Malone lay dying.

4. The Train Station Sequence. Sure, it's cribbed from that Film 101 standard—the Odessa steps massacre in *Battleship Potemkin* by Russian director Sergei Eisenstein. But the scene at Chicago's Union Station where the Untouchables nab Capone's accountant—as a baby's carriage rumbles down the steps—is riveting stuff.

And it was largely improvised. Originally, De Palma and writer David Mamet's script called for the scene to involve a crash of two vintage-era trains, but Paramount Pictures didn't want to pony up for that. Studio executives simply told the director that old trains could not be located. So De Palma took his cast and crew to the train station, which they had already rented out, and spent a few nights making it up as they went along. It works, right down to music director Ennio Morricone's effect of the baby's music box tinkling as bullets whiz by his pram.

There are other memorable moments in *The Untouchables*—the cross-border raid into Canada (which resembles something out of an old John Ford Western) comes to mind, as does Ness pushing the snide Nitti off a 10th-story rooftop.

So while we can't say that *The Untouchables* breaks any new ground in the genre or stands as a great film, we can say this: if you pop it into your DVD player and grab a bucket of popcorn, there are enough creative and well-acted scenes to keep you well entertained for two hours.

⊙ **HIT:** Although filmed in the mid-1980s, *The Untouchables* really evokes the Great Depression era with its vintage cars, clothing and street scenes. To keep modern skyscrapers from showing up on screen (before the days when they could be digitally removed), De Palma shot most scenes at night and paid the owners of the post-1930 buildings huge fees to keep all their lights off.

⊗ **MISS:** Ness's relationships with his wife (Patricia Clarkson) and daughter are beyond saccharine. The wife puts love notes in his brown-bag lunches before he goes into battle. There are butterfly kisses and bedtime prayers and eyes batting to syrupy string music. Not to sound unromantic, but we were ready to use Ness's lunch sack as a barf bag.

🙿 **BEST LINE:** Capone on the lunacy of Prohibition: "People are gonna drink. You know that, I know that, we all know that, and all I do is act on that. And all this talk of bootlegging—what is bootlegging? On a boat, it's bootlegging. On Lake Shore Drive, it's hospitality."

🎬 **PIVOTAL SCENE:** Initially, Malone refuses Ness's request to help him nail Capone—largely because he has no faith that the by-the-book outsider has any prayer of success. Still, he agrees to meet with Ness—away from the police station, where "the walls have ears." The two kneel in conversation in the front row of a Catholic church.

"Do you *really* want to get Capone?" asks the skeptical beat cop. "You see, what I'm saying is, what are you prepared to do?"

"Everything within the law," answers Ness.

Malone scoffs. The only way to win the fight, he says, is to go way *outside* the law. "He pulls a knife, you pull a gun. He sends one of yours to the hospital, you send one of his to the morgue. *That's* the Chicago way."

Ness—who likely has never even jaywalked—accepts the unholy deal. The two shake hands—"a blood oath," as Malone terms it. Ness now has a streetwise mentor.

The scene was filmed by cinematographer Stephen H. Burum from a low angle that shows the men's hands in front, their faces next and an intricately painted church ceiling in the background. Burum said the shot of their hands almost touching reminded him of Michelangelo's famed *Creation of Adam* mural on the ceiling of the Sistine Chapel. We don't know about that, but it is visually grabbing.

✔ **REALITY CHECK:** Oh, almost everything, starting with the fact that the real-life Ness had nothing to do with pinning tax evasion charges on Capone. Regard this movie as entertainment, not as anything approaching actual history.

✒ **WHAT THEY WROTE AT THE TIME:** "*The Untouchables* is not a realistic recreation of Chicago during Prohibition. Nor is it a typical effort from Brian De Palma, who has often put his awesome technique and his admirable sense of film history to trashy (*Dressed to Kill*) or trivial (*Wise Guys*) ends. Instead, it goes to that place that all films aspiring to greatness must attain: the country of myth, where all the figures must be larger and more vivid than life."—Richard Schickel, *Time*

◀ **CASTING CALL:** Paramount did not envision *The Untouchables* as a big-budget movie, so executives turned down De Palma's ideas of casting Jack Nicholson, Mel Gibson or Michael Douglas for the role of Eliot Ness. Instead, they selected Costner, a relative unknown at the time. De Palma was reluctant until he spoke with Steven Spielberg, who had directed Costner in a TV episode and was enthused over the young actor.

Paramount also balked at De Niro's exorbitant fee for two weeks of shooting and hired British actor Bob Hoskins (*The Long Good Friday, Who Framed Roger Rabbit*) to play Capone. De Palma drew the line, said he would quit the project if De Niro wasn't cast, and won the chance to work with an actor he had discovered as an unknown in the 1960s (and once paid $50 for a role).

Hoskins got $200,000 to walk away. He later called De Palma and asked, "Are there any other movies you don't want me in?"

♟ **BET YOU DIDN'T KNOW:** De Niro, a notoriously meticulous method actor, anguished that he could not gain sufficient weight to portray Capone in time for filming, so he wore a body suit during most scenes. He also insisted on wearing exactly the style of clothes that Capone wore in 1930—right down to hand-sewn silk underwear.

◎ **REPEATED WATCHING QUOTIENT:** Connery and De Niro always deserve an encore. Beyond that, it's worth seeing again to watch the film that launched Costner's once-thriving career.

☺ **GOOF:** As Malone lay dying, Ness hugs his ally's bullet-riddled body and hears his last words, directing Ness that he can capture Capone's fugitive accountant at the train station. Ness immediately leaves—with a stainless and well-pressed suit. It's a neat trick for a man who was just rolling around in blood.

☞ **VIOLENCE LEVEL:** No shortage of blood, bombs and bullets. And baseball bats. This is, after all, a Brian De Palma film.

➡ **DON'T FAIL TO NOTICE:** How many scenes the white-suited Nitti appears in, usually without speaking and often in the background. In the video commentary, De Palma says he wanted Nitti as a "constant evil force" passing through the film.

☻ **"I KNOW THAT GUY":** Nerdy mob accountant Walter Payne is played by nerdy-looking Jack Kehoe. You may recognize the spectacle-wearing, mustachioed actor from his roles in *Serpico, The Sting* and *Midnight Run*. We'll always remember him as the unlikely outside shooting star "Setshot" from *The Fish That Saved Pittsburgh*.

🦶 **BODY COUNT:** Twenty-three, starting with a ten-year-old girl being bombed and ending with Nitti flying off a roof.

✸ **IF YOU LIKED THIS, YOU'LL LIKE:** The original 1959-63 television series of the same name, starring Robert Stack as the incorruptible Ness and featuring the memorable narration of Walter Winchell. The show was created by Desilu Productions, the studio owned by Desi Arnaz and Lucille Ball (of *I Love Lucy* fame). It struck such a nerve that a mob informer later told the government there was a Mafia hit temporarily ordered on Arnaz.

Sonny Corleone (James Caan) in *The Godfather*

GREATEST MOB HITS

We estimate the combined body count of the movies in this book at well over 2,000. There are murders by meat cleaver (*Gangs of New York*), by lye-infested coffee (*The Pope of Greenwich Village*), by hand grenade (*Léon: The Professional*) and one in which a poor fool gets smothered in his own stash of cocaine (*American Me*).

So picking a list of the greatest killings in the history of gangster films was a tough task. But here's our stab. We ranked them on the basis of their impact on their stories, their originality and their setups. Oh, and we limited it to one entry per movie to keep the first two *Godfather* films from dominating.

10. Miller's Crossing. Big city boss Leo O'Bannon (Albert Finney), his house set afire and his bodyguard murdered, calmly climbs out of bed, stubs out his cigar and guns down four rivals aiming to assassinate him. All to the tune of "Danny Boy."

9. Bugsy. Knowing he's going to get hit for squandering the mob's money, Warren Beatty's Bugsy Siegel awaits his fate in his living room chair, reading the newspaper. Suddenly, nine rifle shots fly through the picture window, riddling Siegel's body. The last one sends his eye flying across the room. Rather grotesque but, by all accounts, consistent with how the real Bugsy Siegel met his end.

8. Bonnie and Clyde. One for the law. In a forerunner to this list's No. 1 selection, our lovable gangsters on the run are waylaid by cops on a dirt road. There's no invitation to surrender, just a half-dozen machine guns peppering bullets into their writhing bodies for 23 seconds. They roll around in slow motion, they die, the scene cuts to the closing credits.

7. The Public Enemy. Tom Powers (James Cagney) is coming home from the hospital, and his family couldn't be more excited. Problem is, Tom has been beaten, shot and bound. So when his brother eagerly opens the front door, poor Tom's body lists for a moment—his eyes open—then falls face down to the floor. Homecoming ruined.

6. Casino. We cover the cornfield murders in the main chapter, so let's go with the killing of Tony Dogs, the fool who shoots up one of Remo's bars. "For two days and two fucking nights, we beat the shit out of this guy," says Nicky (Joe Pesci) in narration. "We even stuck ice picks in his balls." In the end, squeezing Dogs' head in a tool shop vise finally persuades him to give up his accomplice. "Charlie M!?" shouts Nicky. "You make me pop your fucking eye out of your head to protect that piece of shit?"

5. The Departed. Justice appears imminent as Costigan (Leonardo DiCaprio) handcuffs his enemy, Sullivan (Matt Damon), and hauls him down an elevator at gunpoint. As the humiliated Sullivan implores Costigan to "just kill me," the elevator door opens and—Bang!—Costigan is blasted by another dirty cop laying in wait. "Did you think you were the only one he had on the inside?" the murderous cop (actor James Badge Dale) calmly asks, referring to mob boss Frank Costello. For jump-from-your-seat surprise, this one tops them all.

4. The Untouchables. It's a lovely formal dinner as Al Capone (Robert De Niro) presides over a table of 20 underlings, extolling the virtues of baseball. At the end of his treatise on teamwork as his toadies nod in agreement, Capone pivots and swings his Louisville Slugger—four times—into the back of the head of a disloyal gang member. No one moves a muscle as the dead man falls face first to the table, his cigar still in his mouth, his blood seeping across the nice linen tablecloth.

3. GoodFellas. The one that gets us every time is the shooting of Tommy (Pesci) as he goes to his "made man" ceremony. First, Tommy puts on his best shiny suit, kisses his mom good-bye and drives off to a quiet suburban neighborhood. It almost feels like he's headed to his confirmation. Instead, two mobsters lead Tommy into a wood-paneled den and then—BAM!—right in the back of the head. Instead of being made, Tommy pays for his unauthorized hit on Billy Batts. We sure didn't see that one coming.

2. The Godfather: Part II. Fredo in the boat. We understand that the stupid older sibling conspired with Hyman Roth to take down Michael. And we know Michael heeded his father's advice to keep his enemy close until the time seemed right. But ordering the death of your brother? That's as cold as it gets. The scene is set up brilliantly, with Fredo praying the "Hail Mary" (which he believes provides him luck while fishing) before Al Neri pumps a shot to the back of his head in the night shadows. Runners up: young Vito going back to Italy for revenge and his shooting of Don Fanucci in the tenement hallway.

1. The Godfather. Remember the first time you saw it? Sonny, the hotheaded son of Don Corleone, gets lured to a remote toll booth. You sense something's not right with the toll taker, who fumbles for change and then drops to the floor. Suddenly, eight guys pop up and open fire with Tommy guns. Sonny does the dance of death as he staggers from his car and is hit—by actual count—with 110 bullets. Actor James Caan's body was covered with explosive-filled brass casings and tiny packets of fake blood for the scene. He said afterward, "I wouldn't be honest if I said it didn't make me a little nervous." Runners up: Michael's double murder at the Italian restaurant, Luca getting stabbed through the hand and then garroted, and Moe Greene taking a bullet in the eye.

29 EASTERN PROMISES (2007–R)

STARS: VIGGO MORTENSEN, NAOMI WATTS, VINCENT CASSEL, ARMIN MUELLER-STAHL
DIRECTOR: DAVID CRONENBERG

An organized crime investigator once tried to explain what it was like tracking Russian mobster immigrants in his East Coast city. His only comparison, he said, was to an earlier generation of American cops in the last century and their efforts to keep tabs on newly arrived Italian gangsters.

"It's like tracking the Sicilians back in the 1920s," he said of the Russians settling into his city's Eastern European ethnic neighborhoods—where police are neither welcomed nor trusted. "They speak a different language. They have a different culture. And even honest citizens in their community don't want anything to do with us."

He and others in law enforcement estimate it will take at least another generation before they really have a handle on the Russian mobsters in their midst.

Today *Vory v Zakone* (thieves in law), as the Russian mob is known, is as mysterious and impenetrable as the Mafia used to be. Once a highly secretive society, today the Italian-American crime syndicate is part of our pop culture. Indeed, the word "mafia" is now a generic term applied almost arbitrarily to any ethnic criminal group, including the Russians. Google the words "Russian Mafia" and you'll get nearly three million hits.

But the Russian mob in America doesn't have a face. There is no Al Capone or John Gotti, no Vito Corleone or Tony Soprano.

While set in London, *Eastern Promises* takes a first step toward introducing the American general public to the Russian underworld. In this well-crafted and superbly acted film, director David Cronenberg uses a narrow focus to tell a much broader story, a technique that pays huge dividends.

The diary of Tatiana (Tatiana Maslany), a 14-year-old, drug-addicted prostitute who dies while giving birth to a daughter in a London hospital, sets the film in motion. Her account of how and why she came to London—provided by periodic voice-overs as the diary is translated from Russian—offers a back story of the mob's involvement in white slavery and English brothels.

Anna (Naomi Watts), a half-Russian, half-English midwife who finds the diary after helping deliver the young teen's child, hopes to use it to locate family members of the now orphaned baby.

Instead, the diary and a business card for the Trans-Siberian Restaurant leads her to Russian mob boss Semyon (Armin Mueller-Stahl), his bumbling gangster son Kirill (Vincent Cassel) and Kirill's associate and driver, Nikolai (Viggo Mortensen).

"I'm driver," Nikolai tells Anna during the first of several brief encounters that Cronenberg skillfully uses to establish a relationship between the two. "I go left. I go right. I go straight. That's it."

But Nikolai is clearly much more than just a driver.

Mortensen, who spent time in the Urals "absorbing" the Russian temperament before filming began, was nominated for an Academy Award for Best Actor (Daniel Day-Lewis won for *There Will Be Blood*). His performance dominates the movie.

As in his earlier work with Cronenberg in *A History of Violence*, Mortensen portrays a complex character with a murky past. And like that earlier film, *Eastern Promises* raises a fundamental question about violence: can it ever be justified?

Joe Morgenstern, writing in the *Wall Street Journal*, noted that Mortensen's "mercurial portrayal makes it equally plausible that Nikolai is a guardian angel with dirty wings or a suave thug with surface sanctity." Either way, Nikolai is a gangster who "meets brutality with brute force," Morgenstern wrote.

Early in the film, he helps dispose of the body of a Chechen mobster Kirill has had killed. But first, he decides to hinder future identification of the corpse using pliers and a knife. Before he begins that gruesome task—and with a twinkle in his eye—he tells an associate, "Now I'm going to do his teeth and cut off his fingers. . . . You might want to leave the room."

Then he casually puts a cigarette out on his own tongue before beginning the process.

This is one tough Russian.

His body, covered in tattoos from his days as a prisoner in Russian jails, further enhances his status with Semyon and other members of *Vory v Zakone*.

He is cold and uncaring as he dismisses the fate of Tatiana and that of her daughter during one conversation with Anna. But in another, he seems genuinely concerned as he cautions her not to pursue the issue of the prostitute's death with Semyon.

"Anger is very dangerous," he says after Anna shouted about the need to know what happened to Tatiana and why. "It makes people do stupid things. Stay away from people like me."

Anna, of course, cannot. And that drives the story. Her Russian uncle Stepan (Jerzy Skolimowksi) and her English mother Helen (Sinead Cusack) both caution her to let it go.

"This isn't our world," her mother tells her. "We are ordinary people."

But Anna won't hear it.

German actor Armin Mueller-Stahl is both avuncular and heartless as Semyon, the man most responsible for Tatiana's plight. His posh, old world-style restaurant offers vodka, borscht and violence in equal measures as the story unfolds.

In the meantime, Semyon's incompetent (and perhaps sexually conflicted) son Kirill blunders his way through the London underworld. Think Fredo with a Russian accent. His penchant for screwing up nearly costs Nikolai his life and sets up one of the most dramatic fight scenes in gangster movie history. Naked in a steam bath, his tattooed torso fully exposed, Nikolai takes on two knife-wielding Chechen hit men. The pair has come to London to avenge the murder of their brother—whose toothless, fingerless body was recovered by authorities after it had been dumped in the Thames.

The fight scene, wrote critic Roger Ebert (more from him below), "sets the same kind of standard that *The French Connection* set for chases. Years from now, it will be referred to as a benchmark."

As more is learned about Russian organized crime in England and the United States, the same may be said for *Eastern Promises*. It is a fascinating story and one that introduces a new facet of the gangster genre to American pop culture.

"I need to know who you are," Anna says to Nikolai during one of their last encounters.

So do we.

◉ **HIT:** The foreign and brutal nature of the *Vory v Zakone* comes across throughout the film. Nikolai has to renounce his own family during the equivalent of a making ceremony. He also very cavalierly dismisses the death of Tatiana and the fate of her infant when he tells Anna, "Slaves give birth to slaves." This is a cold and uncaring underworld.

✕ **MISS:** Rowdy soccer fans on the way to a match are used as a cover for the Chechen hit men's first murder. The gory and graphic throat slitting occurs in broad daylight as the crowd surges toward the stadium. This takes soccer violence to a new, and somewhat unrealistic, level.

❚❚ **BEST LINE:** "I fear you more than I fear them," says Azim (Mina E. Mina) after he double-crosses the Chechen hit men by telling Semyon what they are planning.

✎ **WHAT THEY WROTE AT THE TIME:** "The actors and the characters merge and form a reality above and apart from the story, and the result is a film that takes us beyond crime and London and the Russian mafia and into the mystifying realms of human nature."—Roger Ebert, *Chicago Sun-Times*

➜ **DON'T FAIL TO NOTICE:** While the movie is graphic in its violence, it is one of the few genuine gangster films in which there is no gunplay. Knives are the weapons of choice.

◉ **REPEAT WATCHING QUOTIENT:** This is the kind of movie that is worth revisiting regularly. Mortensen's performance provides new surprises each time and the character relationships are richer with each new look.

♠ **BET YOU DIDN'T KNOW:** Mortensen, a huge NHL fan, based his character's voice and mannerisms on those of Russian hockey player Alex Kovalev.

☺ **"I KNOW THAT GUY":** Vincent Cassel, the French actor who played Kirill, appeared as "Night Fox," the international thief François Toulour in *Ocean's Twelve* and *Ocean's Thirteen*.

⚔ **BODY COUNT:** Five, counting Tatiana's death during childbirth.

30 THE FRENCH CONNECTION (1971–R)

STARS: GENE HACKMAN, FERNANDO REY, ROY SCHEIDER
DIRECTOR: WILLIAM FRIEDKIN

We'll admit it: *The French Connection* is a movie more about the cops than the bad guys. The film that earned Gene Hackman a Best Actor Oscar largely spotlights the exploits and foibles of Jimmy "Popeye" Doyle, a driven but reckless New York City narcotics detective.

But taken from the other side, it's a damned good story about the mobsters. Popeye's target is Alain Charnier (Fernando Rey), a suave heroin importer from Marseilles. *The French Connection* traces how Charnier tricks a naïve friend into smuggling a large stash of drugs through the Port of New York, lines up a buyer and attempts to put $32 million of smack onto the streets.

Okay, maybe we're reaching just a little to call this a gangster movie. But *The French Connection* so vividly shows how drug trafficking worked back in the 1960s that we felt we had to include it here.

Much of its potency stems from the fact that it's all based on a true story. Hackman's Popeye Doyle and his partner Buddy Russo (Roy Scheider) are modeled after larger-than-life NYPD detectives Eddie Egan and Sonny Grosso. That duo busted an organized crime ring spanning two continents in 1961, seizing a then-record 112 pounds of heroin. Their story was told in a bestselling book by Robin Moore that became the template for this movie. Egan and Grosso, by the way, have small roles in the film as police supervisors.

Mostly, *The French Connection* focuses on pursuit. It opens in Marseilles with a detective tracking our drug kingpin and getting killed in the process. From there, the smugglers and the cops engage in a dance of circling and evading through a series of stakeouts, peek-a-boo chases through New York and the famous scene where a car pursues an elevated train. More about that coming up.

The subjects of all this police attention are Charnier (called "Frog One" by the narcs) and the Lincoln Continental he has managed to sneak through U.S. customs. Inside the car is 170 pounds of pure, uncut heroin, dubbed by Charnier's impressed chemist as "Junk of the Month Club (quality). Sirloin steak. Grade-A poison. Absolute dynamite."

At one point, the suspicious cops impound the Lincoln and take it apart, piece by piece, looking for the haul. They tear up the trunk, the lining, the glove box, but can't find anything. Finally, they check the deep recesses of the rocker panels—where they find dozens of colorfully wrapped packages filled with heroin worth millions.

Charnier's American contacts are Brooklyn deli owner Sal Boca (Tony Lo Bianco), who's looking to graduate into big-time crime, and Upper East Side real estate magnate Joel Weinstock (Harold Gary), who's seeking to diversify his portfolio. It's an unlikely drug cartel, but it is based on real characters from that 1961 bust.

The star, of course, is Hackman as Popeye Doyle. There's no glamour to this character. Popeye is racist and violent and amoral. He cruises Bedford-Stuyvesant in a ridiculous porkpie hat, strutting into bars to brutalize the soul-brother patrons and bust the street junkies.

Popeye's got a shaky history and knows he needs a major bust to redeem himself. There's a subplot about other cops not wanting to work with him. Apparently, a good officer was killed during one of his operations and the others think Popeye was to blame.

A shocking moment occurs toward the end of the film, and Popeye's lack of remorse after it takes place will stay with you. You realize that his motivation all along hasn't been about helping right triumph over wrong. It's been about winning at all costs.

While Popeye is all single-minded obsession, the drug dealer Charnier is calm and calculating.

And the contrast between the two antagonists goes way beyond their personalities. Charnier lives with a sexy young girlfriend in a stone castle so close to the Mediterranean that he can fish from his front yard. Popeye, meanwhile, lives by himself in a blue-collar public housing apartment cluttered with trash.

There's a terrific scene midway through the movie in which Popeye stakes out Charnier. On a cold and dirty corner, the detective blows into his hands and stuffs his face with a limp slice of pizza and coffee from a Styrofoam cup. Meanwhile, the drug dealer luxuriates across the street in a four-star hotel, dining on a multicourse feast by a fireplace. Life just isn't fair.

The *French Connection* was a huge hit when it came out in 1971. Made on a budget of just $1.8 million, it grossed more than $50 million, the third-best box office tally for any movie released that year.

Hackman was already a respected actor at the time, having been nominated for a Best Supporting Actor Oscar four years earlier for his work in *Bonnie and Clyde*. His Best Actor Oscar for this movie, however, established him as a major star for decades to come.

The movie also won the Best Picture Oscar (topping *A Clockwork Orange* and *The Last Picture Show*) and took home three other Academy Awards, including one for Best Director for the 36-year-old William Friedkin.

And beyond all that, *The French Connection* can be credited with helping create the tough-but-flawed-working-class-cop film character that flourished in the 1970s and remains prevalent to this day. And this movie can certainly be seen as the root of more-recent efforts like *Prince of the City, Training Day* and *The Departed*.

Oh, and one more thing. We told you the movie is based on an actual case. It ends with the freeze-frame postscript scenes that tell you what happened to each of the major characters. But it doesn't tell you this—a year after *The French Connection* was released, it was revealed that all of the heroin confiscated in the original case had been stolen from the NYPD's property department.

⊙ **HIT:** New York City is more gritty than pretty in this period piece, which was shot before the Big Apple's late-20th century revival. The skies are gray, vacant lots are strewn with debris and there's a doomed look to the city—right down to the rusty Rheingold beer signs. It's not attractive, but the urban tangle is a genuine representation of a time and place.

⊗ **MISS:** *The French Connection* was shot on a minuscule budget and sometimes it shows. Watch, for example, when the French detective gets gunned down early in the film. You can see a hose at the bottom of the screen squirting blood up at his face.

✎ **WHAT THEY WROTE AT THE TIME:** "There is only one problem with the excitement generated by this film. After it is over, you will walk out of the theater and, as I did, curse the tedium of your own life. I kept looking for someone who I could throw up against a wall."—Gene Siskel, *Chicago Tribune*

🎬 **PIVOTAL SCENE:** Popeye loses his tail on Charnier's henchman, Pierre, as Pierre climbs into an elevated train. So the desperate detective commandeers a passerby's car and threads through crowded city streets trying to keep pace with the train while staying under the El tracks.

It is, quite simply, the greatest chase scene ever. Popeye rumbles into oncoming traffic, smacks several cars along the way and nearly runs over a woman pushing a baby stroller.

The scene was shot live in Brooklyn and without the permission of New York City authorities. Stunt driver Bill Hickman (who also appears in the movie as federal agent Mulderig) essentially did it on a dare from Friedkin, who challenged Hickman to top the great chase scene he had engineered three years earlier in *Bullitt*.

According to an interview Friedkin did with the American Film Institute, the director himself climbed into the backseat to operate the primary camera while Hickman girded himself with a shot of Jack Daniels. Hickman then raced 26 blocks at 90 miles per hour, as a second unit car with Hackman at the wheel trailed behind. The squealing cars and endangered pedestrians you see along the way did not know they were part of a movie shoot.

"It was a terrible thing for us to do," Friedkin conceded in the AFI interview. "Really, it was life threatening. We were lucky to come out of it without being arrested."

👜 **BET YOU DIDN'T KNOW:** The accidents during that chase scene were not scripted. In one, the lead stunt car sideswiped a transit bus. In another, a man who lived a few blocks away drove across the path of the chase at 86th Street and Stillwell Avenue and was run into by the trailing car carrying Hackman. The man was reimbursed for his damages.

◉ **REPEATED WATCHING QUOTIENT:** Worth a viewing every five years or so.

99 BEST LINE: "Do you pick your feet in Poughkeepsie?"—Popeye's trademark line to suspects, designed to rattle them.

◀ **CASTING CALL:** Quite a few actors *almost* got to play Popeye Doyle. Lee Marvin, James Caan and Peter Boyle all turned down the role— Boyle because his agent predicted the movie would flop. Paul Newman was contacted, but his fee was too high. Jackie Gleason was considered. And New York columnist Jimmy Breslin actually rehearsed on the set for three weeks before he was let go—in part because he couldn't drive a car for the chase scene.

Meanwhile, Fernando Rey was cast as the French smuggler by mistake. Director William Friedkin confused Rey with Francisco Rabal, an actor he wanted to hire after seeing him in the movie *Belle de Jour*. Once Rey was brought over from France, though, Friedkin decided to keep him.

☺ **GOOF:** In the opening scene, Popeye and Buddy go into a dive bar to roust potential drug users. When they enter, it is dusk. When they chase a suspect out onto the sidewalk a few minutes later, it is a sunny midday.

➡ **DON'T FAIL TO NOTICE:** In the scene of the drug-laden car being unloaded at the Port of New York, you can catch a glimpse of the World Trade Center towers under construction in the background. This is believed to be the first appearance of the towers on film.

🔫 **VIOLENCE LEVEL:** Moderate, although it was considered extremely violent back in 1971.

✪ **IF YOU LIKED THIS, YOU'LL LIKE:** The *French Connection II*, which is an adequate sequel. A better suggestion, however, is *The Seven-Ups*, starring Scheider as a NYPD detective who discovers a plot to kidnap mobsters for money. It was written by ex-cop Sonny Grosso, costars Lo Bianco and features another great car chase.

🦴 **BODY COUNT:** Twelve.

31 THE PETRIFIED FOREST (1936–NR)

STARS: HUMPHREY BOGART, BETTE DAVIS, LESLIE HOWARD
DIRECTOR: ARCHIE MAYO

The Petrified Forest was a hugely successful stage play in the early 1930s. The story of a diverse group of people held hostage one night by an escaped gangster at an Arizona road stop, it seemed a perfect candidate for transformation to celluloid.

So Leslie Howard, who drew raves on Broadway, signed to reprise his role as the pacifist drifter who winds up at the café that night. Bette Davis, a 27-year-old who had already won an Oscar, was cast as Howard's romantic interest—the waitress with wanderlust and dreams of being an artist. And, for the role of fugitive con Duke Mantee, Warner Brothers hired Edward G. Robinson, as reliable a tough guy as there was in Hollywood.

Except that Howard balked. He threatened to drop from the film if his Broadway costar, Humphrey Bogart, was not brought along to continue in the gangster role. Warner Brothers executives were not keen on the idea, since Bogart hadn't made much impact in his first dozen movies. But Howard had clout, so the studio heads relented:

That turned out to be the best thing—for the movie and for Bogart. *The Petrified Forest* became a critical and box-office success, in large part because the fifth-billed member of the cast stole the show as the brooding desperado with the simmering anger.

It also jumpstarted Bogey's stalled career. Before this movie, Bogart told friends that he was frustrated and considered quitting the business. After *The Petrified Forest*, he became, at age 37, a rising star. Five years later, another movie in this book—*High Sierra*—would further elevate his Hollywood status.

Watching *The Petrified Forest* you can see Bogey developing his craft. Riffing off of John Dillinger, he holds his arms at a curious angle, like

he is about to reach for a gun. (For decades, Bogey impersonators would ape that posture.) Bogart studied films of Dillinger and tries here to recreate the famous bank robber's battered facial expression and insolent demeanor. His clothing and hairstyle in *The Petrified Forest* are designed to make him look more like Dillinger. Even the setup for the plot (a daring bank robber escapes from prison and kills four in a shootout) is patterned after Dillinger's 1933 breakout from a jail in Lima, Ohio.

On a side note, Bogart never forgot how Howard helped his career, later naming his daughter Leslie in tribute. Howard, who went on to play Ashley Wilkes in *Gone with the Wind*, died in 1943. His camouflaged plane was shot down over the Bay of Biscay by German fighter aircraft.

In truth, Howard's character of failed writer Alan Squier is the center of this movie's story. It's just that Bogart's morose and menacing mobster overshadows him.

The story largely takes place at a café/gas station on the edge of Arizona's Petrified Forest National Park. Gabrielle Maple (Davis) lives there with her father and grandfather. It's not much of a life. Dad keeps reminiscing about his glory days in World War I (even donning the old uniform for a VFW-like meeting) and Gramp keeps repeating yarns of the Old West and his time spent running with Billy the Kid. There's also the station's gas jockey, an oaf named Boze who won't stop hitting on Gabrielle.

Into this world steps Squier, the self-described intellectual ("brains without purpose"). He's wandering the earth after his first novel sold just 400 copies. He's fatalistic, he's been to Europe and he quotes poetry. What girl wouldn't fall for that?

Over the next few hours, the road stop is overrun with various characters, all with a good story. The plot is based on a stage play (written by Robert Emmet Sherwood). Everyone gets to speak at length, and *The Petrified Forest* is guilty of getting a little chatty. But in a very short time, you get to know each of the people who wander into the Black Mesa Bar-B-Q.

The payoff comes a half-hour into the film. Barging through the doors with guns held high comes our escapee and his gang of three. "This is Duke Mantee, the world famous killer," announces the henchman Ruby (Adrian Morris—who looks like a 1930s version of John Candy). "And he's hungry."

Mantee's got a plan to carry out—well, after he fills his belly. He's going to hole up at the Black Mesa, waiting for his moll and the rest of his crew. Then they'll use the nine hostages in attendance as human shields to escape to Mexico.

Squier has a plan as well. He's got a $5,000 life insurance policy in his backpack, which he signs over to Gabrielle. Then he asks Duke to shoot him ("What's one more murder? They can't execute you twice."), so that the frustrated girl can use the money to go to France and *really* learn how to be an artist. This guy knows how to win over a woman.

There's some terrific dialogue here, as you'd expect from an adapted play. The pace moves slowly and there's not much action, but *The Petrified Forest* runs just 82 minutes, so you'll never get bored.

The script's undercurrent themes of existentialism, classism, pacifism, women's liberation and black pride have had critics atwitter for more than 75 years. But, hey, we're not here to teach a film class. We're just recommending a solid, entertaining movie.

⊙ **HIT:** *The Petrified Forest* differs from most movies in this book in its desert setting. And Bogart's take on the gangster as a resident of the Old West, rather than a big city, gives it a unique spin.

"He ain't no gangster," argues the sympathetic, albeit jingoistic, Gramp at one point. "He's a real old-time desperado. Gangsters is foreigners and he's an American."

⊗ **MISS:** We understand that the original play was largely set inside one claustrophobic room. But a film called *The Petrified Forest* should have made at least some use of the beautiful Arizona outdoors. In the few external scenes, the cacti are clearly made of plywood.

✒ **WHAT THEY WROTE AT THE TIME:** "There should be a large measure of praise for Bette Davis, who demonstrates that she does not have to be hysterical to be credited with a grand portrayal; and for Humphrey Bogart, who can be a psychopathic gangster more like Dillinger than the outlaw himself."—Frank S. Nugent, *New York Times*

☺ **GOOF:** Toward the beginning of the film, Boze the masher tells Gabrielle he has never been married. That would have been more believable if someone had told actor Dick Foran to remove his wedding ring.

◉ **REPEATED WATCHING QUOTIENT:** At 82 minutes, sure, why not.

🎬 **PIVOTAL SCENE:** Being held hostage—and already through with the world—Squier decides to have Mantee kill him so that Gabrielle can cash in his $5,000 life insurance policy. He explains this to Mantee while Gabrielle is out of earshot.

"Dead, I can buy her the tallest cathedrals, golden vineyards and dances in the streets," he rationalizes. "One well-placed bullet will accomplish all that. And it will earn a measure of directed glory for him that fire it."

Holding up his insurance policy, he adds, "This document will be my ticket to immortality. It will inspire people to say, 'there was an artist who died before his time.' "

➡ **DON'T FAIL TO NOTICE:** Hanging on the café's wall is a Native American headdress highlighted by buffalo horns. Several times in the movie, the shot is framed so that the horns appear to be coming out of Duke Mantee's head like the devil's horns.

VIOLENCE LEVEL: As low as any movie in this book. You might, however, get talked to death.

BET YOU DIDN'T KNOW: Nearly every Depression-era movie had a happy ending, so Warner Brothers executives were concerned how audiences would respond to this film's downbeat finish. They filmed an alternate happy ending. When they tested both with audiences, the unhappy ending always scored higher. So it was left intact, much to director Archie Mayo's relief.

BEST LINE: Squier: "So tell us, Duke, what has your life been like?"

Mantee: "You know the story. Since I've been a grown-up, I've spent most of my life in prison. I'll probably spend the rest of it dead."

"I KNOW THAT GUY": Gramp Maple, the garrulous codger, is portrayed by Charley Grapewin, who three years later would play Uncle Henry in *The Wizard of Oz*.

IF YOU LIKED THIS, YOU'LL LIKE: *The Taking of Pelham One Two Three*. We recommend the 1974 version over the 2009 effort and the 1998 telemovie. It's the story of an armed gang (led by Robert Shaw) hijacking a New York City subway car and demanding a ransom for the passengers' release.

BODY COUNT: A mere two.

32 CITY OF GOD (2002–R)

STARS: ALEXANDRE RODRIGUES, LEANDRO FIRMINO DA HORA, HAAGENSEN, SEU JORGE. | DIRECTOR: FERNANDO MEIRELLES

City of God has been referred to by some movie critics as the Brazilian *GoodFellas*. It's not a bad comparison.

Like *GoodFellas,* there's a voice-over from the main character, Rocket (Alexandre Rodrigues), that keeps the story moving. And one of the lesser characters here, like Spider in *GoodFellas*, gets shot in the foot. But the chaos, the wanton violence and the sense of despair are more reminiscent of *Mean Streets*, Martin Scorsese's 1973 breakout gangster film.

Based on the semi-autobiographical novel of the same name by Paulo Lins (who grew up in Cidade de Deus—the housing project from which the book and movie took their title), this is a story of life in one of the most violent slums on the fringes of Rio de Janeiro. What we find here is a Brazil far removed from Carnival and the beaches of Ipanema. While some of the women are, indeed, tall and tan and lovely and while the movie's recurring musical themes echo the sambas and bossa nova beats that define the carefree Brazil of travel agents, *City of God* offers a gritty and harrowing look at life in the *favelas*.

Those notorious shantytowns have spawned some of Brazil's most violent street gangs and kingpins and were the killing fields for a bloody drug war in the 1980s that is captured in the brutal, final scenes of the movie.

A reviewer writing in the London *Guardian* after Lins' novel had been translated and published in English in 2006 raved about the book, but described it as a "postcard from hell."

Director Fernando Meirelles, who was nominated for an Academy Award for his work here, managed to turn that sprawling, 496-page novel into a fast-paced underworld saga about the young (some of the characters are nine- and ten-year-old street urchins), violent and disenfranchised who populate the underbelly of Brazilian society.

"I smoke, I snort, I've killed and robbed . . . I'm a man," says a teenaged wannabe gang member named "Steak & Fries" (Darlan Cunha) as he petitions for admission into one of the drug crews that run the slum.

The hand-held camera work of cinematographer Cesar Charlone helps create a documentary feel to the movie. This is further enhanced by Meirelles' decision to recruit more than 100 boys and young men from the slums of Rio as his cast. Few of the actors had any film experience. They were put into a theater group set up by the director about a year before he began shooting the film.

In an interview published online shortly after the film was released, Meirelles, who was born and raised middle class in São Paulo and studied architecture in college, said he became involved in the lives of his young actors—sometimes feeding and housing them, other times settling disputes that had nothing to do with the movie. To his credit, the director didn't hesitate to tap into and use the insights and backgrounds of his troupe as he was filming.

Prior to a scene depicting one of the big gang confrontations, for example, one of the actors playing a minor character asked the director if they were going to pray before going into battle. This, he said, was what they used to do when he was a gang member. Meirelles instructed the actor to lead the others in prayer, and filmed the unscripted scene.

The movie is told in three parts—chapters, if you will—tracing the housing project known as Cidade de Deus from its sun-baked inception in the 1960s through the gloom, doom and oppressive overcrowding that had come to define the area by the 1980s.

Rocket, a preteen when the story begins, is one of the few characters who makes it out of the ghetto, using his talent as a photographer to chronicle the turmoil around him and win the chance to work for a newspaper.

As the narrator, he provides a straightforward account of the events that shape life in the favela, starting with the gritty, Robin Hood-like tale of the Tender Trio (who rob and then share their booty with the poor) and ending with the rise and fall of Li'l Ze (Leandro Firmino da Hora), the psycho-pathic drug kingpin and one of the chief protagonists in the gang war.

Li'l Ze starts out as Li'l Dice, changing his name as he grows both physically and in stature within the criminal underworld. Along the way, cocaine replaces marijuana as the drug of choice for those both using and selling. Coke offers a bigger kick and more power—as does the ever-expanding arsenal of guns used by the teen and preteen gangsters.

Li'l Dice's fascination with violence surfaces early in life when he is assigned the job as lookout while the Tender Trio rob a motel/brothel. He's told to fire a warning shot if the police show up.

Angry at not being included in the actual heist, he fires the shot even though there are no cops. Then after the Tender Trio scatter, Li'l Dice walks into the motel and starts blowing people away. He keeps shooting through a series of confrontations and drug wars, including a battle with a group of ambitious nine- and ten-year-old junior gangsters called the Runts.

These are the Dead End Kids, but with a nasty, totally amoral violent streak. But they are just part of life, along with corrupt cops, greed, treachery and rape, in the *City of God*.

And things have only gotten worse since the writing of the book the film was based on, according to its author.

"The world of the favela today is much more cruel than when I was growing up there or even as I show it in my book," Lins said in a 2004 interview. "If I were to write about the way things are today, I would start the book with a pile of rubber tires, gasoline and someone being burned alive."

Mean streets, indeed.

◉ **HIT:** The frantic pace and relentless violence drive home the promotional tagline that so accurately described the film: "Fight and you'll never survive. . . . Run and you'll never escape."

✖ **MISS:** This is a general complaint about gangster movies with subtitles, and there's really nothing that can be done about it. In fact, it probably applies to any movie with subtitles. But we often miss the subtle things that can define or refine a foreign film. For example, nicknames are crucial to the characters, but most get lost in the translation here. The character called Knockout Ned (who came up with that?) is called Mane Galinha in the original. It translates as "Chicken Mane" and refers to the character's penchant for stealing chickens as a boy and indirectly relates to the opening scene in the movie. But it was decided that "chicken" has the connotation of cowardice in English, so the name was changed in the subtitles. L'il Dice is another nickname that has no connection to the original. The character has nothing at all to do with dice. Go figure.

✔ **REALITY CHECK:** While the movie was filmed in several *favelas* around Rio, it was not shot in the Cidade de Deus housing project because it was considered too dangerous to film there.

🗩 BEST LINE: "To be a real hood, you need more than just a gun, you need ideas," says Rocket in a voice-over early in the film.

✐ **WHAT THEY WROTE AT THE TIME:** "The latest and one of the most powerful in a recent spate of movies that remind us that the civilized society we take for granted is actually a luxury . . . law and order are as scarce on these means streets (just minutes away from one of the world's most glorious beaches) as they are in the slums of 1860s Manhattan depicted in Martin Scorsese's *Gangs of New York*."—Stephen Holden, *New York Times*

🍎 **BET YOU DIDN'T KNOW:** Seu Jorge, who plays reluctant gang leader and hero Knockout Ned, is a popular samba-soul singer in Brazil.

BODY COUNT: Forty-two. Everyone's got a gun and is ready to use it.

🔫 **VIOLENCE LEVEL:** Among the highest of any movie in this book.

⊕ **IF YOU LIKED THIS, YOU'LL LIKE:** *City of Men,* a sequel produced by Meirelles in 2007. The sequel followed a highly acclaimed television series in Brazil of the same name that Meirelles put together after the success of *City of God*.

33 AMERICAN GANGSTER (2007–R)

STARS: DENZEL WASHINGTON, RUSSELL CROWE, JOSH BROLIN, ARMAND ASSANTE
DIRECTOR: RIDLEY SCOTT

Based loosely on the life and times of Harlem drug kingpin Frank Lucas, *American Gangster* was an attempt to do for America's black underworld what the *Godfather* films did for the American Mafia.

That director Ridley Scott falls somewhat short of that goal doesn't detract from the value of this film. It's not a classic, but it's one of the best of this emerging genre, light years better than earlier works like *New Jack City* or *King of New York* (both of which are ranked in this book).

Scott used a screenplay by Steven Zaillian to tell parallel stories about the business of dealing heroin and the business of investigating that business.

Frank Lucas (Denzel Washington) and Richie Roberts (Russell Crowe) are the entrepreneurial kingpin and the too-honest-for-his-own-good cop whose lives, we know, are eventually going to intersect. Both deal in worlds steeped in corruption. And both decide there is a better way to go about their business.

Lucas corners the heroin market in Harlem by cutting out the middle men and establishing his own supply and distribution networks. His is a basic Wharton School of Economics approach.

"I sell a product that's better than the competition at a price that's less than the competition," he explains.

The product, branded "Blue Magic," is high-grade heroin imported from Thailand. Most of it came into the United States during the height of the Vietnam War. Lucas traveled to Thailand himself to set up the supply system, and then brought his brothers and cousins up from North Carolina to handle sales and distribution in Harlem and in parts of North Jersey.

Interspersed with actual television news reports about the war and footage of press conferences from then-President Richard Nixon, *American Gangster* captures the chaotic mood of the 1960s as Lucas builds his empire—and the turbulence of the 1970s as he fights to keep it.

Roberts is a struggling Newark, N.J., police detective who finds himself ostracized after he turns in nearly $1 million in cash that he and a partner find in the trunk of a drug dealer's car. Labeled a "fuckin' Boy Scout" by less-honest fellow cops, Roberts catches a break when he is tapped by a supervisor to head an elite drug squad in New Jersey's largest city. He is also attending law school at night and is involved in a protracted custody fight with his former wife Laurie (Carla Gugino).

Both Roberts and Lucas also intersect with the local wiseguys. Roberts' boyhood friend is Joey Sadano (Ritchie Coster)—a character not unlike Joey Sodano, a Newark-based member of the Philadelphia mob killed gangland-style in 1996. He tries to steer Roberts away from investigating Lucas. It would be, he says, in no one's best interest to pursue the investigation. But Roberts, after threatening his friend with arrest, continues full steam ahead.

Lucas, in turn, deals with Sadano's uncle, mob leader Dominic Cattano (Armand Assante) who suggests that Lucas would be wise to share the wealth and ease up on his monopoly control of the heroin market in Harlem. It seems like Assante has played this role in a dozen movies, but he's always a pleasure to watch.

During a meeting at Cattano's country estate—where both men wear tweed jackets with leather arm patches and shoot skeet—the mob leader cautions Lucas about his business tactics.

"What about your fellow dairy farmers out here, Frank?" Cattano asks. "Are you thinkin' . . . of them?"

"I'm thinking of them, Dominic, about as much as they've ever thought about me," Lucas coldly replies.

Frank Lucas lived his life and ran his business on his own terms, using violence whenever he felt it was necessary. Like the old-time mobsters who once dominated the underworld, he believed in maintaining a low profile and not calling attention to himself. The idea was to make money, not headlines. *American Gangster* makes that point again and again.

When his brother Huey (Chiwetel Ejiofor) shows up at a party dressed like a pimp, Frank, in a conservative business suit, pulls him aside and asks, "What's this?"

"This is a very, very, very nice suit," Huey says with a smile.

"That's a clown suit," Frank replies. "That's a costume with a big sign that says, 'Arrest me.' You understand? You're too loud. You're making too much noise. Listen to me. The loudest one in the room is the weakest one in the room."

Frank Lucas, who inherited the drug business of his mentor Bumpy Johnson and who clashed with rival kingpin Nicky Barnes (Cuba Gooding Jr.) emerges in *American Gangster* as a charismatic and complicated figure, not unlike Vito or Michael Corleone.

The contradictions in his lifestyle are captured in a series of vignettes that are reminiscent of the baptism scene in *The Godfather*. It opens with the Lucas clan gathered at the sprawling New Jersey estate Frank has purchased for his mother (played perfectly by veteran actress Ruby Dee). They are there to celebrate and share Thanksgiving dinner. As they join hands to say grace, the movie cuts to scenes of:

• Roberts slapping a sandwich together in a dingy apartment.

• Corrupt Det. Trupo (Josh Brolin), who has tried to shake down Lucas, answering the door at his expensive home to find a caged, live turkey on his doorstep. As he looks out to his driveway, his prized Mustang Shelby blows up.

• Junkies in a squalid Harlem tenement shooting heroin into their veins.

The problem with a film based on real characters is its tendency to overhype or overdramatize. There is some of that here. Shortly after bringing his brothers and cousins north, Lucas is sitting in a diner in Harlem having breakfast with them and discussing business. In between bites, he gets up, walks out onto the street and shoots a rival in the head. Then he goes back to the restaurant to finish eating.

"Now, what was I saying," he says as his startled family members look on.

The message the scene delivers to the country bumpkins: welcome to New York. It's powerful, but over-the-top. No way, in Harlem or anywhere else, does a hit go down like that with the shooter calmly walking back into a nearby restaurant to finish his meal.

American Gangster was "one percent reality and 99 percent Hollywood," a federal judge and former prosecutor who helped convict the real Frank Lucas told CNN after the movie was released. Judge Sterling Johnson Jr. said Lucas was illiterate, vicious and violent, "everything that Denzel Washington was not."

Which is why we say the movie was "loosely" based on his life.

⊙ **HIT:** The soundtrack from Def Jam Records—featuring Bobby Womack, the Staple Singers, Sam & Dave and John Lee Hooker—is a perfect mix of blues and soul that evokes the 1960s and 1970s.

⊗ **MISS:** The custody battle between Roberts and his wife seems contrived—like a soap opera attempt to provide a back story that helps explain a troubled character. In fact, Roberts and his wife didn't have any children when they divorced and he later complained about that element of the story line.

◀ **CASTING CALL:** Benicio Del Toro was originally signed to play Roberts. After production delays, he dropped out. Crowe, who had worked with Ridley Scott in *A Good Year* (2006), was then tapped for the part.

" BEST LINE: Lucas tells an associate, "See, you are what you are in this world. That's either one of two things. Either you're somebody or you ain't nobody."

🍎 BET YOU DIDN'T KNOW: The movie was based on the *New York* magazine piece "The Return of Superfly" written by Mark Jacobson and published in 2000.

🎬 PIVOTAL SCENE: Lucas shows up at the Ali-Frazier fight in a chinchilla coat and hat given to him by his wife. The get-up attracts Roberts, who is there taking surveillance photos. Up until that point, Lucas was a virtual unknown to the drug task force. After that, he became its prime target. (Lucas later throws the coat and hat in a burning fireplace, realizing he has violated his own low-key dictum and has paid a price as a result.)

✔ REALITY CHECK: At the end of the film, Roberts, who now has his law degree, switches hats and becomes the prosecutor in the Lucas case. No state would permit an investigator to prosecute a case he has worked. The move is fraught with legal inconsistencies.

(In real life, Roberts spent several years as a county prosecutor before switching to defense work. One of his first clients was Frank Lucas, by then serving time in jail. That was permissible because the new charges against Lucas had nothing to do with the case Roberts had worked on as a cop.)

☺ GOOFS: Lucas' nephew is touted as a pitching prospect, a southpaw who wants a tryout with the Yankees. But when we see the kid playing catch at a family picnic, he's throwing right-handed.

🔫 VIOLENCE LEVEL: High and brutal. The movie opens with a victim being tortured, burned and shot. It also includes the aforementioned street shooting and several other violent scenes.

☠ BODY COUNT: Thirteen, but it seems like more.

AN INTERVIEW WITH DANNY PROVENZANO

Danny Provenzano is an actor, director, writer and a gangster—which for the purposes of this book makes him a crossover artist. It also puts him in a unique position to talk about what's real and what's *reel*.

He's the nephew of the late Anthony "Tony Pro" Provenzano, a Genovese crime family capo who was a notorious Teamsters Union leader and one of the prime suspects in the disappearance of Jimmy Hoffa.

Danny, who spent more than six years in a New Jersey state prison after pleading guilty to a racketeering charge in 2003, has the right "family" bloodlines, so to speak. He's also got a movie resume. Early in his career, he did a couple of horror films. More recently, he wrote, directed and starred in *This Thing of Ours*, which came out just before he went to prison. He played a young, disillusioned wiseguy who reported to his uncle, played by Frank Vincent. James Caan was the crime family boss. Vinny Pastore also had a key role.

The movie did okay. It got some notice at a few small film festivals, had a short run in theaters and is now available on DVD.

One scene in the movie shows a deadbeat who owes the mob several thousand dollars getting punished by two mobsters. They grab him and smash his thumb with a hammer. It was art imitating life. The racketeering charges against Danny included several allegations that he used violence and threats to collect debts. Danny says he was simply going after what was his; that people owed him and wouldn't pay. So he had to force the issue. In one instance detailed in the indictment, a former associate was assaulted in a dispute over $7,000. The man was kidnapped on Danny's orders and his thumb was smashed with a hammer.

Danny doesn't deny the allegation. Nor does he shy away from the obvious conclusion that he used some of his own "life experiences" to write his movie script. But he points out that the real-life victim was dropped off at the entrance to a hospital emergency room by his assailants.

A wiseguy with a heart. And also with a love of movies.

Here's what he had to say about gangster films.

You make a distinction between a mobster and a gangster. From your street-level perspective, what's the difference?

A mobster, the best way to describe it, would be the politician of organized crime. Look at a guy like Paul Castellano [the late boss of the Gambino crime family]. Castellano was a mobster. John Gotti [who was convicted of murdering Castellano] was a gangster, somebody who was willing to put in work. Most of the time, the guy who's willing to put in work doesn't have the brains for the politician part. And vice versa. The politician doesn't have the stomach for the gangster part. When it comes to violence, they want no part of it. A true gangster

lives for it, knows what his calling is. Vito Genovese was a gangster. Castellano wanted to talk things out. He would take a lot of time. Vito would say this is our problem, let's kill him.

Why do you think people are fascinated with mobster/gangster movies?

People wish they could do what gangsters do. But we're a civilized society. People go to court to solve their problems. You ever look at *Judge Judy* [the television show]? It's friends robbing friends, an exfriend doing something to somebody. You got a problem, you take it to court. But most people don't want to be in front of Judge Judy. They want to do what I did: dress in black, ride with some guys and get people to pay me the money they owe me. . . . I guarantee you, most people, what they really want to do is slap the piss out of the motherfucker who robbed them. That's what I did and it's why I went to jail. Most people wish they could solve their problems that way. But they can't. That's why they watch gangster movies.

What's your favorite gangster movie?

The movie HBO did about John Gotti [*Gotti: The Rise and Fall of a Real Mafia Don*, 1996]. I liked it because the movie was made without disrespecting John or his family. Armand Assante nailed John. He played him perfectly. And the movie just felt real, unlike some of the stuff I saw in *The Sopranos*. Everything that was in the Gotti movie could happen or did happen in real life.

When you made This Thing of Ours, what was the message you wanted to deliver? How close to reality were you able to keep the story?

I used a few of the incidents that I was indicted for and the character I played, Nicky, was based a little on my own life. People thought I was little ballsy or arrogant to do that. I probably was both.

In the movie, two of Nicky's friends get killed and he's disillusioned by that. . . . The message was that my character, Nicky, should have known better. He should have known that's what that life was about. And while he felt betrayal, it was the life. There was nothing disloyal about it. The murders were part of the business. Loyalty and honor only exist among friends. Maybe five or six guys are loyal to one another. But to find that kind of loyalty amongst organized crime in general? No. It doesn't exist. It never did.

There are movie critics who have said that while The Godfather (Parts I and II) are probably the all-time best mob movies, the most realistic are Donnie Brasco and GoodFellas. Would you agree with that?

As a filmmaker, I totally agree that cinematically, *The Godfather I* and *II* are the greatest gangster movies ever made. But the content was more about the Corleone family than organized crime. . . . But what it did—and Francis Ford Coppola will take the trophy for this—was open up filmmakers to movies about the Mafia. *GoodFellas* I love. It's extremely realistic and well made. That movie exposed the Mafia a lot more for what it was than *The Godfather*. And it told the story of Henry Hill to a T. *Donnie Brasco*, I didn't like as much because the director and the writer took a lot of creative license. That scene where they cut up the bodies, that was (mobster) Roy DeMeo. He was with the Gambino family. [See the book *Murder Machine* by Gene Mustain and Jerry Capeci for the full DeMeo story.] It had nothing to do with any of the guys Donnie Brasco was involved with.

Women don't seem to play a major role in most mob movies. Are they not part of the life or have the movies missed something?

The movie people are not missing a thing. The percentage of women in the game, other than being a *goomah*, is almost zero. . . . The fear factor is not there. And without that, you can't enter that world. I ain't scared of a woman. It may be chauvinistic, but that's the way it is.

Harold Shand is a patriot. Fiercely loves his native England. Proudly shows visitors around London. Toasts the Queen. Hates the Irish Republican Army (IRA).

Harold's also the head of London's East End mob. He's pugnacious and vicious. When he believes informants are holding out on him, he has them brought to a meat-packing plant, where they are hung upside-down from hooks and punched like the sides of beef in *Rocky*.

There's a fascinating blend of flag waver and felon in the English bulldog character created by Bob Hoskins in *The Long Good Friday*. Comparing his homeland with that of a visiting American Mafiosi, Shand says, "Look what England has given to the world: culture, sophistication, genius. A little bit more than the hot dog, know what I mean?"

The intersection of crime and nationalism is the focus of this underrated, low-budget effort. The movie, now largely forgotten, created controversy when it was shot in Great Britain in 1979 because the script pits Shand's mobster against the terroristic IRA.

Some British political leaders—as well as the film's original financier, media mogul Lew Grade—deemed it too kindly to the IRA. "They thought it was unpatriotic, disparaging of the British Army and promoting terrorism," director John Mackenzie told London's *Sunday Independent* in 2006. "And Grade was frightened that bombs would go off in his cinema. Crazy."

Mackenzie admitted that he had some compassion toward Shand's IRA enemies in the film. "I was not sympathetic to the violence," he said. "But I was sympathetic to the sense that they are committed people who do something for a cause."

Release was held up 18 months. The film was re-edited, shelved, and finally sold to a distribution company headed by former Beatle George Harrison. Then, shortly after it hit theaters, Harrison said he regretted backing such a violent movie.

Well, Harrison was a pacifist. Despite the violence—or perhaps because of it—*The Long Good Friday* can be regarded three decades later as a sharply written, well-acted film with a provocative plotline. And you don't get the sense today that it glorifies terrorism or makes the IRA look attractive—beyond casting a dashing young actor as that group's most visible face. More about him later.

The story opens with Shand basking on his houseboat on the Thames, enjoying small talk and Bloody Marys with his wife, Victoria (Helen Mirren). This is a boss on top of his game. He is proud to have kept the underworld peace for a full decade. And now he is aiming to convince a visiting counterpart from New Jersey to invest in a casino project he's got planned for London's Docklands.

Suddenly, however, his perfect life is shattered. While his mother attends church on Good Friday, her Rolls Royce is blown up and the chauffeur is killed. Soon after, one of his best men is stabbed to death in a public bath. A bomb (which fails to detonate) is discovered at another of his casinos. Finally, a pub that he owns is firebombed, just as he drives up to eat there.

Someone is after Shand, but who? "What blokes might have an old score to settle with me?" he wonders aloud. "Well there was a few. . . . Nah, they're all dead."

The middle part of the movie shows Shand and his gang torturing half of London trying to determine the enemy's identity. There are some tough scenes to watch, but you'll admire how Hoskins can shift from charmer to sadist and back again. You'll also find yourself admiring his nastiest henchman, a thug covered with scars and knife wounds known as Razors—"or as the youth of today call him, the human Spirograph," Shand notes.

Also worth mention is the great Helen Mirren

as Victoria. Mirren accepted the role only when director Mackenzie consented to make her more than the typical moll. She's amiable, shrewd without being a shrew and able to mollify the monster just by giving him the look that most wives seem to know.

Eventually, Shand discovers that his stalker is the aforementioned IRA. Turns out that his young chief lieutenant has been paying off the group for years—without Shand's knowledge. It's the only way, the aide insists, to ensure labor peace among the Irish workers Shand employs.

Fine idea, at least until the bagman in the operation shortchanges the IRA by $5,000. That same night, three of the IRA's top men are wiped out, leading that group to believe—erroneously—that Shand is behind their deaths. Shand is the last to find out.

"All this anarchy is over five poxy grand?" Shand fumes. "I'll crush them like beetles."

But, of course, he cannot. For three decades, starting in 1969, the Provisional IRA waged a paramilitary campaign aimed at ending British rule in Northern Ireland. The English Army couldn't stop them. Even the toughest of London hoodlums stands no chance. You will, however, enjoy watching Shand try.

◉ **HIT:** Hoskins is a well-tailored pit bull in what proved to be his breakout role. He's alternately charismatic and ferocious in a manner that evokes James Cagney in his prime. Stay tuned for the final scene, where the camera focuses on his face for a full two minutes. His shifting of emotions from fury to frustration to helplessness could serve as a teaching moment for any aspiring actor.

Hoskins revealed that he learned from real-life criminals hanging around the set to act more like a Roman emperor than a thug. "They said, 'Naw, Bob, don't shout. Remember the man's dignity.' They wanted the boss to be a proper boss, not a prat."

⊗ **MISS:** Between the muddled sound and the rapid-fire Cockney slang, the dialogue in *The Long Good Friday* is incomprehensible at times to American ears. The film's producers considered overdubbing Hoskins' voice for U.S. audiences, but backed off when he threatened to sue. We wouldn't want that, but English subtitles on the DVD would have helped.

✎ **WHAT THEY WROTE AT THE TIME:** "Mr. Hoskins' character of Harold emerges as an unexpectedly captivating man, even in a movie that concentrates on his savagery. In a scene that shows him rounding up all possible suspects and hanging them, upside-down from meat hooks to interrogate them, Harold still maintains his aplomb. Mr. Hoskins makes the mobster as clever and understandable as he is abhorrent."—Janet Maslin, *New York Times*

◀ **CASTING CALL:** Veteran television actor Anthony Franciosa was cast as the visiting American mob boss. He quit the movie after three days of arguing with the director.

◉ **REPEATED WATCHING QUOTIENT:** May warrant a second viewing just to enjoy Hoskins' performance.

⌐ **VIOLENCE LEVEL:** One poor guy is interrogated while having his buttocks slashed with a knife. Another has his hands nailed to the floor. And another is punched in the face while suspended upside down. So, yeah, we'd say high.

🍢 **BEST LINE:** "No one's heard nothing?" Harold fumes after pressuring his sources brings no new information on the killings. "That just ain't natural. It's like one of them silent, deadly farts. No clue, and then pow, you go cross-eyed."

▤ PIVOTAL SCENE: After a horrible day of carnage on Good Friday, Shand confronts Jeff, his protégé and the man who has been paying off the IRA behind his back.

"Don't lie to me," Shand says. "I can smell your lies. And I can smell something else—your greed and ambition."

Jeff finally fesses up, insisting that he did it for Shand because without the terrorist group's tacit support, all of Shand's empire would come to a standstill. Jeff then says they need to stop the IRA's revenge campaign.

"Revenge?" Shand shouts. "It's me who's gonna take revenge."

"They're an army of ants," Jeff yells back. "You can't beat them."

Shand flies into a frenzy. He feels betrayed by his favorite underling and enraged over his disloyalty to Shand's beloved England. He picks up a broken bottle and stabs Jeff in the neck, slicing his carotid artery. Blood spurts, and Shand realizes what he has done. He embraces Jeff, who dies in his arms.

It's a shocking outburst. And it's made better because you get the sense that Shand is as horrified by his own actions as you are.

☻ "I KNOW THAT GUY": That's 26-year-old Pierce Brosnan making his film debut as an IRA assassin. Brosnan had no scripted dialogue in the movie. He improvised his first-ever on-screen line: "Hi."

✵ IF YOU LIKED THIS, YOU'LL LIKE: *Mona Lisa*, a 1986 British effort in which Hoskins plays a mobster who can't regain his former status after a prison stretch. He ends up as a driver for an expensive call girl, creating problems with the local kingpin, played by Michael Caine.

❧ BODY COUNT: Eight.

STARS: COLIN FARRELL, RALPH FIENNES, BRENDAN GLEESON
DIRECTOR: MARTIN MCDONAGH

Phil Leonetti, a mob hit man who became a government witness, was asked in court if he thought he was ruthless. Leonetti, who had admitted to 10 gangland murders for the Philadelphia mob, said he didn't think so.

"I know what it means to be ruthless," he said. "But I don't remember ever doing anything—as a matter of fact, I know for sure—I never did nothing ruthless besides, well, I would kill people. But that's our life. That's what we do."

Willard "Junior" Moran, a hired gunman for the same mob, offered a similar explanation while describing his life as a contract killer.

It was like being a soldier in a war, he said. Everyone involved in the underworld knew the rules and knew that murder came with the territory.

"I never killed an innocent person," Moran said.

But what if a hit man does kill an innocent person?

Does he feel remorse? Or guilt? Or shame?

Does his conscience bother him?

And if it does, can he do anything about it?

Those are the questions that drive Irish writer/director Martin McDonagh's *In Bruges*, a dark and sobering story about loyalty, honor and relationships in the underworld.

Two Irish hit men, Ray (Colin Farrell) and Ken (Brendan Gleeson), are sent to Bruges, a picturesque medieval city in Belgium, to hide out after a hit in London goes awry.

McDonagh, who got an Oscar nomination for Best Original Screenplay, underscores the moral dilemma at the heart of his narrative by making the target of the hit a priest. But that's not the problem. Ray successfully blows away the good father after visiting him in confession. Their dialogue, part of a flashback as Ray ponders what he has done, establishes the cold and calculating nature of the business Ray, Ken and their boss, Harry Waters (Ralph Fiennes), are engaged in.

Ray, in the confessional, tells the priest he has murdered someone. The priest asks why.

"For money, father."

"For money? You murdered someone for money?"

"Yes, father. Not out of anger. Not out of nothing. For money."

"Who did you murder for money, Raymond?"

"You, father."

"I'm sorry?"

"I said you, father. What are you, deaf?"

With that, Ray raises his gun, tells the priest, "Harry Waters says hello," and fires a shot through the confessional.

The priest stumbles out into the church and Ray fires several more shots. One strikes a young boy, praying nearby. The boy, shot in the head, and the priest, riddled with bullets, both collapse dead on the church floor.

Ken grabs Ray and hustles him away.

The death of the boy, not the murder of the priest, haunts Ray as he and Ken sit in Bruges waiting for further instructions from Harry.

Fiennes is particularly effective as the no-nonsense mob boss. For the first two-thirds of the movie, he is only a voice on the phone, but his conversations are chilling.

At one point, he tells Ken, "If I had killed a little kid, accidentally or otherwise, I wouldn't have thought twice. I'd of killed myself on the fucking spot. On the fucking spot. I would have stuck the gun in me mouth. On the fucking spot."

When Harry finally appears in person in Bruges, he hasn't warmed up a bit. He's ice cold and brutal, but in a matter-of-fact, it's-strictly-business kind of way.

By that point Ken, about 20 years older than

Ray, has undergone a change. Bruges has given him a different perspective. He appreciates the history and the architecture of the beautiful city and is content to spend time visiting sites and museums, taking a boat ride on the canal, meandering about the cobblestoned streets and taking in a view of the gothic buildings from the city's famous bell tower. Bruges, he tells Harry in one of several phone calls, "looks like a fairy tale."

Ray, on the other hand, just wants to go home.

While he waits, he romances a female drug dealer named Chloe (Clémence Poésy), blinds her ex-boyfriend in one eye by shooting him in the face with a blank gun and punches out a Canadian tourist that he mistakes for an American.

"That's for John Lennon," he says after decking the tourist who complained about Chloe blowing smoke from her cigarette in a restaurant where they were having dinner.

There's also a racist midget who is acting in a movie being shot in the city and a pregnant innkeeper who refuses to allow a shootout in the stairwell of her bed and breakfast.

"You're both crazy," she tells the gunmen after they have politely asked her to get out of the way.

In Bruges provides a sometimes comedic, but just as often somber picture of a violent criminal underworld. There are rules. There is logic. There is, in fact, a twisted morality. But, McDonagh seems to say, there is little room for humanity.

Ruthless?

Harry dismisses that thought after a murderous chase through the cobblestone streets in one of the movie's final scenes.

"You've got to stick to your principles," he says as he stands over the bodies of two victims, brandishing his gun.

It's a line that Leonetti and Moran would appreciate.

◉ **HIT:** Brendan Gleeson is perfect as the hit man who, struck by the beauty and peacefulness of Bruges, quietly reevaluates who he is and what he has done. He realizes that it's too late for him to change, but maybe not too late for Ray.

⊗ **MISS:** Americans. Canadians. To the Brits, we're all the same. Too many cheap clichés.

✎ **WHAT THEY WROTE AT THE TIME:** "*In Bruges*, at its best, works like *Pulp Fiction* with Irish (and Belgian) accents, digressing into weird discourse and giving a bunch of actors the occasion to shine in small, peculiar roles."—Steven Rea, *Philadelphia Inquirer*

◀ **CASTING CALL:** Three of the principle actors have recurring roles in the *Harry Potter* series. Clémence Poésy first appeared as Fleur Delacour in *Harry Potter and the Goblet of Fire* (2005). Brendan Gleeson has a recurring role as Prof. Alastor "Mad Eye" Moody and Ralph Fiennes is Lord Voldemort in several of the Potter films.

➡ **DON'T FAIL TO NOTICE:** The black-and-white movie Ken is watching on his hotel room television while waiting for a call from Harry is the Orson Welles film noir classic *Touch of Evil*. Welles' movie, by the way, also turns up as one of Chili Palmer's (John Travolta) favorites in *Get Shorty*.

⚰ **BODY COUNT:** Five, maybe six depending on where you think the ending is going.

36 PEPE LE MOKO (1937–NR)

STARS: JEAN GABIN, GABRIEL GABRIO, MIREILLE BALIN, LUCAS GRIDOUX
DIRECTOR: JULIEN DUVIVIER

Jean Gabin was already one of France's top leading men when he made this film. But the role of Pepe solidified his standing in the annals of his country's cinematic history.

Pepe le Moko is described as a foray into poetic realism and as the precursor to what became known as film noir. The movie works in large part because of Gabin, who portrays the gangster Pepe as a multidimensional character whose flaws are also his charms.

Humphrey Bogart gave off the same vibe as Rick in *Casablanca* (1942), a movie that in several ways echoed the exotic, inexplicable and fascinating world of French North Africa portrayed here.

Later French film stars like Yves Montand and Jean-Paul Belmondo dipped into the Gabin playbook in their portrayals of street-tough but sympathetic rogues whose love of life was matched only by their love of women.

The film's impact on cinema in both Europe and the United States should not be underestimated. It is considered one of the finest films from the early days of French cinema and a classic example of the gangster movie, no matter the country.

More than 70 years after *Pepe le Moko*'s release, critics still can barely contain themselves when writing about it.

Michael Atkinson's breathless analysis, in an

essay for the Criterion Collection of film reviews, is typical: "Seasoning post-WWI fatalism with what would become film noir's sense of criminal doom, the movie stands as the pivotal cave-painting template upon which an entire cultural identity has been formed. With its casually comfortable exoticism, abstruse locale . . . and it's oddly, beautifully sympathetic anti-hero . . . *Pepe* established a narrative paradigm that persists today, on and off the screen.

"Without its iconic precedent there would have been no Humphrey Bogart, no John Garfield, no Robert Mitchum, no Steve McQueen, no *Chinatown* . . . no movie-star heritage of weathered, cool, vulnerable nihilism, bruised masculinity-as-culture syndrome."

Who knew?

While on the surface a story about a gangster hiding out in the Casbah of Algiers, *Pepe le Moko* is actually a story about a man's willingness to risk everything in order to find himself.

Pepe (le Moko is slang for someone from Marseilles) is at home in the Casbah, a labyrinth of streets and alleyways populated by gangsters, con men, hustlers and molls.

It's *Arabian Nights* meets *Guys and Dolls*. On the run for crimes committed in France, Pepe has an almost Robin Hood-like existence there, planning heists and scams with a band of loyal followers while surrounded by a populace that won't give him up to police.

His chance meeting with Gaby (Mireille Balin), the beautiful mistress of a Parisian businessman, sets the course for Pepe's ultimate, self-inflicted demise. Gaby is literally slumming it with some tourist friends in the Casbah when she meets the notorious—and by definition romantic—Pepe.

Their mutual infatuation blossoms into a love affair after both realize that they come from the same place, literally and figuratively. Memories of Paris, where they both grew up, make Pepe realize that while he's not in prison, he is a prisoner.

Gaby's jewels, fine clothes and studied manners belie an ambition and a drive that Pepe knows all too well. While Pepe's associates see Gaby as a mark—"She's a walking ice palace, the sparkles she's got on her," says one—Pepe is interested in wooing, not robbing her.

"What did you do before?" he asks during one intimate moment.

"Before what?" she asks.

"Before the diamonds," he says.

"I dreamt of them," she replies.

Bogart and Bergman couldn't have uttered the lines any better.

Getting what you want at whatever the cost serves as a theme for the film and many of its characters, including the entertainingly inscrutable Algerian Inspector Slimane (Lucas Gridoux) who is set on forcing Pepe out of the Casbah so that he can be arrested.

Slimane, unlike the French police, understands both his prey and the culture of the Casbah. He is patient, treacherous and a master of the double-cross, turning the game of cops-and-robbers into a Romeo and Juliet tragedy that leads to Pepe in handcuffs and Gaby on a ship heading back to Paris.

Pepe has one last move to make, however. He may not get what he wants, but then neither does the good inspector.

⊙ **HIT:** The recreation of the Casbah on a studio set in France embodied the claustrophobia, the intrigue and the uncertainty that were key elements in the movie. The Casbah is as much a character as any of the actors.

⊗ **MISS:** The shootout with the police who have come to The Casbah to arrest Pepe doesn't ring true. This may be a result of applying 21st-century movie sensibilities to 1930s cinema, but the action seemed more like a bunch of kids playing cops-and-robbers.

"Gotcha." "No ya' didn't." "Yes I did."

Pepe doesn't help when, in the middle of the gunplay—and before he takes a grazing shot in the forearm—he tells his gang to just "aim for the legs" in order to avoid killing anyone.

✎ **WHAT THEY WROTE AT THE TIME:** "Perhaps there have been pictures as exciting on the 'thriller' level as this before . . . but I cannot remember one which has succeeded so admirably in raising the thriller to a poetic level."—Graham Greene, the [London] *Spectator*

☺ **GOOF:** When Pepe gets drunk while mourning the death of his good friend Pierrot, he sprawls in a chair, his sports jacket falling open to show the monogram on the pocket of his black shirt. The initials "JG" are clearly visible. This, obviously, was Gabin's shirt, not something that came from wardrobe.

✔ **REALITY CHECK:** The movie is based on a novel of the same name written by Henri La Barthe. The author, perhaps trying to hint at verisimilitude, wrote the book under the name "Detective Ashelbe." If you sound out "Ashelbe," it is the French pronunciation for La Barthe's initials—HLB.

◉ **REPEATED WATCHING QUOTIENT:** For any serious film buff, especially anyone fascinated with film noir, this is a movie worth studying.

🍎 **BET YOU DIDN'T KNOW:** The American remake, *Algiers*, starring Charles Boyer in the title role, was spoofed in a Warner Brothers cartoon and launched a classic character that you may remember—Pepe le Pew. The romantic skunk is often remembered for his famed quote, "Come wiz me to ze Casbah."

◀ **CASTING CALL:** It wasn't enough for American film producers to remake this movie. They had to do it twice. The second time was a less-than-memorable musical called *Casbah* starring Tony Martin, Yvonne DeCarlo and Peter Lorre. One remake was enough.

🔫 **VIOLENCE LEVEL:** Understated, if not underplayed.

❞ **BEST LINE:** "He's God up there, you don't arrest God," says Inspector Slimane, explaining to the French police why it's impossible to capture Pepe in the Casbah.

Or this exchange between Pepe and L'Arbi (Marcel Dalio) who is adamantly denying that he is an informant:

"I swear on my father's head," says L'Arbi.

"No risk," Pepe replies. "He was guillotined."

⊛ **IF YOU LIKED THIS, YOU'LL LIKE:** *Algiers,* the 1938 remake starring Boyer and Hedy Lamarr, or *Bob le Flambeur* (1956), a story about a gangster who, like Pepe, chooses to act despite the high risk of failure.

🦿 **BODY COUNT:** Three.

37 A HISTORY OF VIOLENCE (2005–R)

STARS: VIGGO MORTENSEN, MARIA BELLO, ED HARRIS, WILLIAM HURT
DIRECTOR: DAVID CRONENBERG

Joey Cusack was the nastiest guy in Philadelphia's Irish mob. He killed dozens, sometimes without the go-ahead from his bosses. Had a real vicious side. Carved up a made man with barbed wire once, scraping out his eye.

And then, he wanted out. But you can't opt out of the mob. So Joey Cusack disappeared. Walked into the desert and emerged three years later as a whole new man. Literally.

That's the setup for this fine movie. But the story, of course, is that you can never escape your past. History always catches up—specifically, in this case, a history of violence.

Early in the movie, you get no hints that actor Viggo Mortensen's character was once that brutal mobster. Instead, he is the ultimate Middle

American—mild Tom Stall who runs a friendly diner in small-town Indiana. He ties on an apron each morning, serves up pie and smiles at customers' stories. At home, there's pretty wife Edie (Mario Bello), an angst-filled teenaged son and an adorable six-year-old daughter. One night, he comforts the girl after a nightmare, telling her, "There's no such thing as monsters."

But, of course, there is. A pair of evil killers have already wandered into this Norman Rockwell painting. They reappear one evening to terrorize Tom's diner. Tom is initially passive, directing them to the cash register. But when one of the bad guys threatens his waitress, Tom snaps into ferocity. He tosses a hot coffee pot at the first man, grabs his gun and blows away both thugs, while sustaining just a stab in the foot. And Tom Stall becomes the kind of local hero adored by the 11 o'clock news.

He's a reluctant idol, however. Tom wants nothing to do with the people carrying cameras or notepads. Back at the diner, when a packed house applauds his vigilantism, he dismisses it with an "aw shucks." Even at home, where his family craves details, he says, "Aren't you as sick of hearing about me as I am?"

By now, the world has heard of him—including the guys he left behind 20 years ago.

Limousines arrive at the diner one morning, carrying menacing strangers from Philadelphia in sunglasses and black suits. They seem to know Tom—they keep calling him Joey—and they're downright intimidating. Their leader, Carl Fogarty (Ed Harris), carries a gruesome scar on his face and suggests that our small-town superman was the cause of it long ago.

Tom denies it all. Just mistaken identity, he insists, as the men in black dog him and his family around town. Eventually, however, it becomes clear—in a bloody showdown with more shock value than the diner murders—that Tom Stall and Joey Cusack are one and the same.

Without giving away too much of the movie, let's just say that the illusion becomes impossible to sustain and Tom/Joey must return to Philadelphia to make things right. There, he confronts his mob-boss brother Richie, played by William Hurt, who's apparently attempting to parody every bad gangster performance ever. More about that later.

The plotline of a mob guy trying to get out is not unique. We've seen it in movies from *On the Waterfront* to *Sexy Beast* to *Road to Perdition*. But *A History of Violence* is different in that we revisit the criminal two decades later, long after he figured he had put his old life in the rearview mirror. He is so far removed from it that he is asked, at one point, whether when he dreams he thinks of himself as Joey Cusack or Tom Stall. He's not sure of the answer.

There's another interesting angle in the movie examining what happens to a family when it finds out that dad used to work as a hit man. For Edie—terrifically played by Bello—the transformation is bracketed by two terrific sex scenes between hus-

band and wife, the second suggesting that she is both repulsed and turned on by the discovery.

Meanwhile, Tom's son Jack (Ashton Holmes) has it no easier, being cruelly picked on at school. He tries disarming the menace with humor and self-deprecation. But when pushed too far, he batters the bully with a shocking brutality that suggests the history of violence has been implanted in his gene pool.

Director David Cronenberg (*Eastern Promises, The Fly*) does a strong job with this Jekyll and Hyde story, although at times the bloodshed becomes more cartoonish than realistic. That may stem from the story's roots—a popular graphic novel by John Wagner and Vince Locke.

◀ **CASTING CALL:** Harrison Ford turned down the chance to play Tom Stall.

◉ **HIT:** Cronenberg resists the temptation to turn the Stalls into the Waltons here. It would have been too easy to make everything sunny in Indiana until the scary truth emerges. Instead, life is more mundane than idyllic—right down to breakfast coming out of a cereal box.

"I didn't want to go overboard with the sunniness of it all," Cronenberg told Salon.com. "The scene in the kitchen, in the beginning, is not flooded with yellow light. It's warmish, but not warm. . . . There are things that are not so nice and not so stable, lurking under the surface."

This is a normal family with normal family joys and anxieties—well, at least at first.

✘ **MISS:** William Hurt is a talented actor with an Academy Award on his mantel and, in fact, received a Best Supporting Actor Oscar nomination for his work in this movie. We don't get it. Man, does he chew up—and spit out—the scenery. Hurt plays the head of Philadelphia's Irish mob, using an inflection that sounds more Brooklyn than Broad Street. Hurt said he studied the accent listening to members of Maria Bello's family, who live in the Philadelphia suburb of Norristown. We'll take him at his word, but he sure sounds like a Big Apple drunk trying to imitate Rocky Balboa.

BET YOU DIDN'T KNOW: Cronenberg changed the Italian-sounding surnames in the original script to Irish names. According to the DVD's audio commentary, he did not want the audience to anticipate Tom's past mob ties early in the film. And he said neither Mortensen nor Hurt seemed able to play convincing Italian-Americans.

"I KNOW THAT GUY": Stephen McHattie—the older of the traveling killers who meet their end in the diner—is recognizable for his roles as Hollis Mason, the wise Nite Owl in *Watchmen*, and as the Grand Inquisitor in *The Fountain*. But if you want to see him in a great movie, check out *The Rocket: The Legend of Rocket Richard*, a little-known biopic about the French-Canadian hockey great. McHattie plays Montreal Canadiens coach Dick Irvin.

GOOF: Check out the Canadian speed limit sign as Tom drives from Indiana to Philadelphia. That's one circuitous route. (The "Philadelphia" scenes were all shot near Toronto, by the way.)

BEST LINE: Angry teenager Jack Stall to his dad, after learning of his true past: "If I rob Mulligan's Pharmacy, are you going to ground me if I don't give you a piece of the action? If I go to Sam [the sheriff] about you, will you have me whacked?"

PIVOTAL SCENE: After Tom refuses to voluntarily return to Philadelphia, Fogarty and his men decide to get tough. They kidnap his son, and—showing him to Tom—say they will exchange him in return for Tom's cooperation.

"Don't make us hurt the kid," Fogarty says, as one of his men holds a gun to Jack in front of Tom's house. "We just want you to take a trip down Memory Lane. Come with us."

Tom agrees, and his son is released to run inside the house. Alone, facing three enemies, Tom shows no fear—in fact, he starts to morph into the mobster he was years ago. You see it in Mortensen's face—his mouth hardens, his eyes sharpen. Suddenly, he's Joey Cusack again. It's a terrific moment of acting.

"It will be better if you just leave now," he warns

Fogarty in a dead, flat voice. His body clenches.

Fogarty chuckles at the advice. And then. . . .

Well, you'll have to watch the movie.

VIOLENCE LEVEL: Very high, as you would figure from the title. It's actually even higher in the European version of the film, which provides more gushing blood and louder bone-crunching effects during two beat-down sequences.

BODY COUNT: Thirteen—ten from gunshots, three from some impressive martial arts moves.

WHAT THEY WROTE AT THE TIME: "Is Canadian director David Cronenberg the most unsung maverick artist in movies? Bet on it. Cronenberg knows violence is wired into our DNA. His film shows how we secretly crave what we publicly condemn. This is potent poison for a thriller, and unadulterated, unforgettable Cronenberg."—Peter Travers, *Rolling Stone*

(Note: Travers named *A History of Violence* the fourth-best film made between 2000–09.)

REPEATED WATCHING QUOTIENT: Worth viewing about once a year to see Mortensen's transformation, the high-quality violence sequences and—we'll admit it—Bello's nude scenes.

IF YOU LIKED THIS, YOU'LL LIKE: *Boy A*, a 2007 indie film about a 24-year-old who is released from prison for a murder he committed as a child. He tries to establish himself in a new life, but people he befriends learn his terrible secret and he cannot escape his past.

AN INTERVIEW WITH VIGGO MORTENSEN

Since debuting as an Amish farmer in *Witness* in 1985, actor Viggo Mortensen has appeared in more than 30 movies, most notably the *Lord of the Rings* trilogy. He stars in two films directed by David Cronenberg that make our Top 100 gangster films—*Eastern Promises* and *A History of Violence*. We talked to him about his experiences making those two films.

In A History of Violence, your character is a former hit man who became a peaceful family man. Eventually he must shift back to being the hit man. Can you tell us about the transformation—what did you attempt to do in your voice, your face, your gestures?

We all prepare for public display of a particular persona on any given day, depending on who we meet and how we feel about them. Some people are better able to isolate their preoccupations, regulate their moods and control the persona they present. My character in this movie is very good at this. He managed to keep his former—perhaps fundamental—persona under wraps for many years.

In the situation where Carl Fogarty (Ed Harris) confronts my character, Tom Stall, in front of his home and family, the buried side of the Tom's personality—the Joey Cusack persona—is flushed out. Tom is forced to revert to Joey in order to protect himself and his loved ones, openly employing all Joey's ruthless characteristics.

So how did you attempt to show that?

David Cronenberg and I agreed that the transition ought not to appear to be an obvious transformation. In this pivotal scene, what needed to happen was a delicate reveal, a shedding of a pretense rather than an imposition of another layer of personality. This sort of gradual unveiling is all the more shocking due to its lack of superfluous histrionics or obvious physical alteration. It could only be accomplished with the help of an extremely attentive director who possesses a light, intelligent touch on the set and in the editing room.

Likewise, compare the two sex scenes with Maria Bello, who plays Tom's wife, Edie. In the first, she is the aggressor—Tom is almost passive. In the second, he assaults her on the steps. What's your view of what those scenes were showing?

The difference between the scenes is that, in the second one, the cat is already out of the bag. The Joey character has been revealed, and there is nowhere to hide for either Edie or Tom. That is not to say that the aggressiveness only comes from Tom/Joey. The forceful nature of the scene is prompted by both characters. This has as much to do with vulnerability and affection as it does with a vengeful impulse to control the other person physically. I believe that both partners are attempting to wrestle with and perhaps preserve what essentially binds them—emotionally, as well as physically. Maria Bello was brave and extremely focused in this scene. A more tentative actress would not have been able to help this scene work as Maria did.

Do you think the movie audience is supposed to become complicit in the violence? We found ourselves cheering at your character's outbursts.

I do not think that it was a specific goal. But we were certainly aware, during the moments in which the movie shows physical violence, that the audience might be co-opted. We all have these impulses, and we all, to some degree, show at least the potential for psychic or physical violence. We could even feel it a little bit on the set from the crew. There was a sense of vicarious thrill in the air at times. And [because the movie was shot in Canada] we are talking almost exclusively about Canadians in that instance, people who by and large—with the exception of some ice hockey players and fans—are renowned for their civility.

At the end of the movie, Tom/Joey returns to his family. There's a terrific gesture of his young daughter pushing his dinner plate in front of him at the table. What do you think happens to the Stall family after that final scene? Can it work for them?

The little girl, played by Heidi Hayes, had that brilliant impulse of serving her father, even placing his silverware upside-down (right-side-up from her point of view) by his plate. I do not know what happens to the family after that final dinner scene. I do not think anyone can say for sure. It could work for them, but the odds against that are high.

In Eastern Promises, how would you describe the difference between a Russian gangster and an American gangster?

I would not say they are inherently different, even generally speaking. Nor would I say that all American gangsters are the same or that all Russian gangsters are the same.

Did you prepare differently for Eastern Promises?

For Nikolai, I felt a specific need to learn to speak Russian convincingly, and to understand something about the culture and physical environment in which he was raised. I always try to figure out for myself an answer to the question of what happened to the character since he or she was born.

Tattoos are highly significant with the Vory v Zakone. We're told you researched that issue. How authentic were yours in the film?

With regard to the manner in which the specific tattoos are earned, where they are placed on the body and what they represent, what we did was quite authentic. I did as much research as possible, observing and, when feasible, speaking with individuals bearing tattoos similar to those we used. I also read all the literature and photographic documentation I could find on the subject. Filmmaker Alix Lambert, who directed *The Mark of Cain*, the outstanding documentary on Russian prison tattoos, also gave me invaluable insights regarding the specifics of that subculture, which I shared with David Cronenberg and his makeup artist, Stephan Dupuis.

Roger Ebert compared your naked knife fight in the steam bath to the car chase scene in The French Connection. Each, he said, set a standard by which others will be judged. How difficult was that scene compared to the physical confrontations in A History of Violence?

Apart from the unavoidable physical discomfort resulting from being thrown and throwing myself around a tiled bathhouse without the benefit of pads, the scene was no more and no less challenging than the stunt work I did in *A History of Violence*.

38 THE FRIENDS OF EDDIE COYLE

(1973–R)

STARS: ROBERT MITCHUM, PETER BOYLE, RICHARD JORDAN, STEVEN KEATS, ALEX ROCCO | DIRECTOR: PETER YATES

Low-level mobster Eddie Coyle is a stand-up guy in a world where he thinks that matters.

It doesn't.

That's the message in director Peter Yates' fascinating and often overlooked gangland morality tale, *The Friends of Eddie Coyle*.

Based on a novel by former organized crime prosecutor George V. Higgins, the movie offers a realistic account of the treachery, betrayal and mistrust that are part of everyday life in the underworld. Higgins knows the story. He also knows Boston, where the movie is set. His dialogue—captured in the screenplay written by Paul Monash—is right from the streets.

Robert Mitchum gives one of the best performances of his stellar career as the title character—an aging gangster who is frustrated, angry, weary and awaiting sentencing for a hijacking conviction that could send him back to jail for five years.

"Look, I'm gettin' old, ya' hear?" he says to Jack Brown (Steven Keats), a young, cocky gunrunner with whom he is doing business. "I spent most of my life hangin' around crummy joints with a bunch of punks, drinkin' the beer, eatin' the hash and the hot dogs and watchin' the other people go off to Florida while I'm sweatin' out how I'm gonna pay the plumber. I done time and I stood up, but I can't take no more chances. Next time, it's gonna be me goin' to Florida."

Even as Coyle says it, you know there's a part of him that doesn't believe it. There is not going to be a happy ending in Florida. Not with "the friends" he has around him.

Those friends include Dillon (Peter Boyle), the local bar owner who set up the hijacking of a liquor truck in New Hampshire that led to Coyle's arrest and conviction. Coyle hasn't given up Dillon and remains a close friend, even as he tries to squirm out

from under the sentence that hangs over his head.

And there's Dave Foley (Richard Jordan), the ATF agent who is willing to go to bat for Coyle with the prosecutor up in New Hampshire prior to sentencing if Coyle can help him make a few cases in Boston—if, the agent says in the vernacular of the streets, Coyle can give something "to uncle."

Finally, there's Jimmy Scalise (Alex Rocco), a local wiseguy and the leader of a small group of bank robbers who have been staging a series of heists in broad daylight with guns Coyle has supplied by way of the gunrunner Brown.

The interconnections mimic those in real life. There is a fine line between the underworld and the law enforcement agents who troll it trying to make cases. Information, connections, gossip and innuendo are what it is all about. And *The Friends of Eddie Coyle* captures that perfectly.

Coyle is being a stand-up guy for Dillon, but Dillon is a $20-a-week snitch (this is 1973 don't forget) for Foley. At the same time—and unbeknownst to Foley—the bar owner also works as a hit man for the mob. Boyle plays the character with just the right combination of arrogance and sincerity. For him, it's all business.

"No money, no hit," he tells a mobster who wants to contract out an assignment without paying in advance.

"And no credit cards whatsoever," he adds.

Coyle, with a wife and three school-age kids depending on him, can't go back to jail. So he decides to work for Foley. But he can't quite deliver enough. He gives up Brown when he's about to sell some machine guns to a pair of hippie radicals driving around in a dilapidated van. But Foley says he needs more than that before he'll put in a word for Coyle with the authorities in New Hampshire.

"I shoulda known better than to trust a cop,"

Coyle says in frustration. "My own goddamn mother coulda told me that."

"Everybody ought to listen to his mother," Foley replies.

Coyle finally decides to give up Scalise for the bank robberies. But when he meets with Foley, he learns that Scalise and his associates have already been arrested.

Dillon, we know, has given them up. But the word on the street is that Coyle has ratted them out in order to get out from under the hijacking case.

As a result, the mob decides Coyle has to be killed. The contact goes to Dillon.

With friends like these. . . .

◉ **HIT:** There is no glamour in the underworld of Eddie Coyle, nor is there any attempt by the director to pretend that there is. This is a gritty, realistic look at "the life." And while those who love the movie compare it favorably to *The Departed*, this film's hard-luck lead protagonist and his inevitable fate are more reminiscent of Al Pacino's role in *Donnie Brasco*. But either comparison is high praise.

⊗ **MISS:** While most of the storyline stays true to the petty saga of crime and punishment that is the world of low-level wiseguys, the gun dealing doesn't make sense. Scalise and his associates want new guns for each bank heist. But a gun gets fired in only one heist. A gun used in a crime—especially a murder—is always discarded. No one wants to be caught holding a gun "with a body on it." But if the guns aren't fired, there is no reason to replace them. So why does Scalise keep buying more guns from Coyle?

☺ **GOOF:** In the scene at the Boston Garden during a hockey game, Coyle gets up to buy beer wearing a sports jacket over a sweater and shirt. When he returns with the beer, he is in the sweater and shirt, and the jacket is hanging over the rail in front of his seat.

✎ **WHAT THEY WROTE AT THE TIME:** "Mitchum has perhaps never been better. . . . Give him a character and the room to develop it and what he does is wonderful. Eddie Coyle is made for him: a weary, middle-aged man, but tough and proud; a man who has been hurt too often in life not to respect pain; a man who will take chances to protect his own territory."—Roger Ebert, *Chicago Sun-Times*

👝 **BET YOU DIDN'T KNOW:** George V. Higgins, author of the novel on which the movie is based, had a multifaceted career. He was a prosecutor who worked organized crime cases. He was a journalist who, at different times, wrote for the Associated Press, the *Boston Globe*, the *Boston Herald American* and the *Wall Street Journal*. As a defense attorney later in his life, his clients included left-wing radical Eldridge Cleaver and right-wing zealot G. Gordon Liddy. He also was a professor at Boston College (his alma mater) and Boston University.

✔ **REALITY CHECK:** Some media types speculated that Peter Boyle's Dillon was fashioned after notorious Boston gangster James "Whitey" Bulger. They also pointed out that Eddie Coyle's situation was not unlike that of Boston bank robber and Bulger associate William "Billy" O'Brien, who was murdered while awaiting trial amidst underworld gossip and speculative news reports that he might have been cooperating with authorities.

◉ **REPEATED WATCHING QUOTIENT:** This is a movie worth revisiting from time to time, if only to see Mitchum at the top of his game.

❞ **BEST LINE:** Gunrunner Jack Brown succinctly explains the facts of life to an associate as he bobs and weaves around Boston making deals with bad guys and staying one step ahead of the authorities: "This life's hard, man. But it's harder if you're stupid."

🏴 **VIOLENCE LEVEL:** Low-key and limited. Lots of guns, but not much shooting.

🔪 **BODY COUNT:** Two.

39 LOCK, STOCK AND TWO SMOKING BARRELS (1998–R)

STARS: JASON STATHAM, JASON FLEMYNG, NICK MORAN, DEXTER FLETCHER
DIRECTOR: GUY RITCHIE

As we noted in the *Pulp Fiction* chapter, Quentin Tarantino's success burst open doors worldwide for young screenwriter-directors touting concepts for black comedies and stylized crime capers. Most of their scripts, sad to say, turned out to be nothing more than poor imitations.

One particularly notable exception was *Lock, Stock and Two Smoking Barrels*. The twisting, amusing heist movie was written and directed by Guy Ritchie, a 29-year-old Brit who never went to film school and learned his craft by creating music videos and TV commercials.

Unfortunately, as we see it, this feature-length debut also serves as the high point of Ritchie's career—unless you count his eight-year marriage to Madonna. One of his later films, *Snatch*, also makes it into our Top 100. But like Orson Welles and M. Night Shyamalan, Ritchie peaked early.

But we digress. *Lock, Stock* owes a lot to Tarantino, as well as to the genre of Asian gangster films that influenced the great master. It features a large cast of oddball rogues whose lives enmesh in unexpected ways. It's got a knotty plot that may require more than one viewing to fully comprehend. There are flashes of brutality, prominent drug use and enough F-bombs to make Joe Pesci cringe. Even the out-of-place Samoan-themed bar in London's hardscrabble East End seems a tribute to *Pulp's* quirky Jack Rabbit Slim's.

What saves it from being a mere Tarantino ripoff is that it works. The dialogue is terrific, the acting adroit and the plot twists engrossing. All of that helps you look past the fact that *Lock, Stock* has no center and no message.

No matter. There are plenty of films in this book looking to make a point. This one does not try to hide that it is merely trying to entertain.

The plot focuses on four gangs of crooks all trying to outsmart one another. We are supposed to root for the group we meet first—a quartet of 20ish lads who are not exactly criminals, but are willing to delve into that business to improve their lot as street vendors and chefs.

The boys agree to pool 25,000 pounds each to stake the smartest among them, Eddy (Nick Moran), in a can't-lose high-stakes poker game hosted by Hatchet Harry, the local porn king and crime boss. (On a side note, you may recognize the actor playing Hatchet, P. H. Moriarty, as the tough guy Razors from 1980's *The Long Good Friday*. Ritchie lists that movie, No. 34 in this book, as his all-time favorite.)

Anyway, what the boys don't know is that the poker game is rigged. Eddy ends up losing 500,000 pounds (more about his playing prowess in a minute). If it's not paid in a week, Hatchet's petrifying henchman, Barry the Baptist, will start chopping off our four boys' fingers as collateral, at the rate of one digit per day.

That sets into motion a series of schemes and swindles involving, by our count, more than 20 characters in London's criminal ranks. We don't have the space here to recount all the anarchic plotline offshoots, and to be frank, we probably couldn't make sense of it if we tried. We can tell you that the various capers include an apartment full of high-grade marijuana, two antique muskets and enough money to fill the trunk of a van.

What you'll remember most clearly are the Tarantino-esque characters populating *Lock, Stock and Two Smoking Barrels*. Like enforcer Big Chris, who travels with his identically dressed 10-year-old son, as if it's "Bring Your Child to Work Day." Big Chris bangs a car door on one poor victim's head and then gently reminds Little Chris to strap on his seatbelt.

Or Rory (Vas Blackwood) the Jheri-curled drug dealer and Jules Winnfield lookalike who sets some poor sap on fire for switching off his soccer game on the pub TV. Or the aforementioned porn entrepreneur Hatchet Harry, who, in a pique of anger, beats a man to death with a rubber dildo. Or a drugged-out young woman who gets mistaken for a sofa cushion. Truth be told, with a collection of losers like this, it's amazing that London's underworld gets anything accomplished.

Did we mention that this is a comedy? Like Quentin-You-Know-Who, Ritchie keeps you going with some throwaway jokes, goofy subtitles and a dynamite soundtrack, which includes bouzouki music from *Zorba the Greek*. As a bonus, *Lock, Stock* leaves you with a cliffhanger of an ending that may have you debating our boys' fate long after you've returned the DVD.

◉ **HIT:** You'll get a kick out of the characters' use of Cockney rhyming slang—a manner of speaking in which words are replaced by other well-known phrases they rhyme with. So "face" becomes "Chevy Chase" and pub becomes "nuclear sub." It's not always easy to pick up (Ritchie even provides subtitles for one scene), but it is fun to listen to.

✖ **MISS:** The quality of the film. No, not the script or the acting, but the actual film. *Lock, Stock* was shot in 16mm, rather than the standard 35mm, giving it a grittier, shallower look. This was Ritchie's first full-length feature and he worked with a budget of just $1.6 million. Clearly, the money was not spent on equipment and film.

✎ **WHAT THEY WROTE AT THE TIME:** "It's supposed to be visually exciting, but the result is more like a corpse-strewn Gap khakis ad than a triumph of technique. At least, based on the film's grainy texture and amber lighting, it's nice to know that the guy who shot every porn movie released in the '70s appears to be working again."—Mary Elizabeth Williams, *Salon.com*

☺ **GOOF:** Throughout the movie, Tom, one of the quartet of lads, sports close-cropped hair. But in the final scene, he has suddenly grown shaggy locks, which he tries to hide under a ski cap. Turns out the actors were called back to reshoot the ending long after the movie wrapped. And actor Jason Flemyng didn't want to clip his hair for one day's work.

☻ **"I KNOW THAT GUY":** Eddy's father, the bar owner J.D., is played by Gordon Matthew Sumner. You may also know him as Sting.

✔ **REALITY CHECK:** We are told that Eddy is a brilliant poker player, but the evidence suggests otherwise. He misreads his opponent, bets more money than he actually has and goes all in on one subpar hand (a pair of sixes). This level of "genius" wouldn't win a Friday night pot down at the local VFW post.

◉ **REPEATED WATCHING QUOTIENT:** With all the plot twists and mumbled dialogue, the film requires two or three viewings just to understand what's going on.

➡ **DON'T FAIL TO NOTICE:** The commentary while that soccer game is televised in the Samoan pub scene. The broadcasters mention players "Guy Ritchie" and "Matthew Vaughn"—the director and producer of this movie.

🔫 **VIOLENCE LEVEL:** One scene demonstrates how Barry the Baptist got his nickname—by holding deadbeats' heads under water until they see the light. Another shows the hoodlum character Dog torturing a poor soul by hanging him upside down and using him as a target while Dog drives golf balls. So we'd say the violence level is high.

🍎 **BET YOU DIDN'T KNOW:** Vinnie Jones, who makes his film debut here as henchman-with-a-heart Big Chris, was a professional soccer player in Great Britain for 16 years. Known as a "hard man" (soccer's equivalent of a hockey goon), Jones set an English Premier League record by getting hit with a yellow card just three seconds into a match.

His trademark move was to grab an opponent by the testicles—and twist.

🗨 **BEST LINE:** Eddy warns his pal Soap that the men they're about to encounter are likely to be armed.

Soap: "Armed? What do you mean armed? Armed with what?"

Eddy: "Bad breath. Colorful language. Feather dusters. What do you think they're gonna be armed with? Guns, you tit!"

🔗 **BODY COUNT:** Sixteen.

40 MILLER'S CROSSING (1990–R)

STARS: GABRIEL BYRNE, ALBERT FINNEY, MARCIA GAY HARDEN, JOHN TURTURRO
DIRECTOR: JOEL COEN

Miller's Crossing is one of those movies that critics love more than audiences do. It's full of metaphors and cryptic symbols and elaborate plot twists. It gets a 90 percent approval rating on *Rotten Tomatoes*, the website that distills the opinions of dozens of professional movie reviewers. On the other hand, the movie garnered a measly $5 million at the box office.

This book is not for film critics. It's for regular guys (and gals) who enjoy gangster movies. Our verdict? We enjoyed *Miller's Crossing* as a tribute to the noir classics of the 1940s. But we don't share the enthusiasm of renowned film historian David Thomson, who called it, "a superb, languid fantasia on the theme of the gangster film that repays endless viewing."

Perhaps if we could have just followed the story a little better.

The movie was produced, written and directed by Joel and Ethan Coen, which may be all you need to know. The brothers are known for their quirky style, gloomy setups and witty dialogue. Sometimes, it works (*Fargo, No Country for Old Men, The Big Lebowski*). Sometimes, it just comes across as self-impressed thumb twiddling (*Intolerable Cruelty, The Ladykillers*).

This one's right in the middle. There's a lot of wit and style, but much of the detail and dense plot seems to be there for the sake of impressing. Don't watch this movie alone, because at regular intervals you'll need to ask your popcorn buddy, "What the hell's going on here?" As Sheila Benson of the *Los Angeles Times* wrote, "A bit of clarity wouldn't hurt *Miller's Crossing*. Even here in Gangsterland, where random characters are cherished and non sequiturs are considered wisecracks, there is a difference between complications and impenetrability, and this plot is a bloody thicket."

That said, we'll aim for a lucid synopsis:

Tom Reagan (Gabriel Byrne) is a cold-hearted Irish mobster with a vague code of ethics and a gambling problem. He works as the confidante to big city boss Leo O'Bannon (Albert Finney), who trusts Tom for his ability to "see all the angles" in advance. Had this movie been made a half-century earlier, a young Humphrey Bogart could have played Tom and Edward G. Robinson would have been ideal as Leo (well, maybe except for the Irish part).

Leo runs an unnamed Prohibition-era big city, but his rule is being challenged by Italian rival Johnny Caspar (Jon Polito). Caspar chafes at Leo's protection of a small-time bookie, Bernie Bernbaum (John Turturro), who has double-crossed him.

Of course, there's a woman involved. Bernie's sister Verna (Marcia Gay Harden) is the seductive moll who maintains an affair with Leo, ostensibly to protect her brother. Plus, she secretly sleeps with Tom on the side. There's not much romance in that relationship, which mostly consists of them insulting each other before heading to bed. "The two of us," notes Tom, "we're about bad enough to deserve each other."

Eventually, Tom divulges his affair to Leo and gets promptly beat up (not the first or last time the poor guy will be assaulted in this movie). It all happens within the larger conflict of a gangland war and leads to Tom switching sides to work for Caspar and being forced to undergo a tough loyalty test.

Internecine violence, blackmail, more double-crossing and lots of machine-gun fire follow. There's also a subplot about homosexuality, a few violent ambushes and a final offer of reconciliation.

It's all pretty pessimistic, which jibes with Tom Reagan's philosophy: "Nobody knows anybody. Not that well." Motivated by that bleak outlook, Tom wanders through the film, more amoral than immoral.

And that's part of our problem. We don't expect the protagonist in gangster movies to be heroic, but we do expect him to have dreams or, at least, emotions. Consider, by contrast, *The Godfather*'s Michael Corleone. He starts out with plans of saving his family and ends up lost and corrupt. We're invested in the character. Tom Reagan never clues us in on his hopes in *Miller's Crossing*. As a result, we never get fully drawn in.

The Coens created *Miller's Crossing* to pay their respects to what Ethan called "dirty town movies," the kind of gangster stories that haven't been made in decades. For that, we admire them. The story evokes Raymond Chandler and Dashiell Hammett—for our money the top pulp fiction mystery writers from back in the day.

Miller's Crossing serves up a stew of many tasty ingredients, but perhaps a few could have been left in the fridge. You'll enjoy the throwback dialogue ("He's just a cheap political boss with more hair tonic than brains") and you'll appreciate the fine actors in small roles (Steve Buscemi, notably). But—at the risk of taking our food metaphor too far—at the end, you may feel like you ate a large, lushly prepared meal but left the table unsatisfied.

◉ **HIT:** In a cast as deep as the 1998 Yankees, two performances stand out. Character actor Jon Polito is riveting as Johnny Caspar, the perspiring old-school gangster who also serves as *Miller's Crossing*'s street-level philosopher. And John Turturro steals scenes as Bernie, the double-crossing bookie at the center of all the trouble.

✖ **MISS:** Gabriel Byrne is a terrific actor. We loved him in *The Usual Suspects*. But he seems bored here. More than once, we turned to each other and asked, "What did he say?" as Byrne mumbled through another line.

"To play enigma, you can't give away much," Byrne explained to the *New York Times*. Perhaps, but it might have helped if he at least took the marbles out of his mouth.

✔ **REALITY CHECK:** Tom gets beat up eight—count 'em eight—times in the movie, sustaining kicks to the ribs and a right cross that splits open his lip. Somehow, he always manages to fully recover by the next scene. The guy has better healing powers than Wolverine.

🎬 **PIVOTAL SCENE:** With so many key plot turns, it's tough to choose just one. But the best moment comes when Tom—after he has switched his allegiances to Caspar—is driven into the woods with two of Caspar's thugs and Bernie. Tom assumes Bernie will be killed; but he doesn't know he'll be assigned to carry out the execution. "Put one in his brain," orders one of the thugs, handing Tom a gun. "The boss wants *you* to do it."

The car is parked at Miller's Crossing. Tom marches Bernie deeper through the trees, as Bernie panics. "You're not like those guys," Bernie implores. "I'm just a grifter. I don't deserve to die for that."

They keep walking, traveling what seems like a half-mile from the car. Tom orders Bernie to his knees as Bernie whimpers, "I'm praying to you. Look into your heart."

Finally, Tom aims and shoots—into the ground. He spares Bernie's life, but orders him to leave town. "You're dead, get me?" Tom says. "You have to disappear for good."

Bernie flees, and Tom heads back to the car to tell Caspar's men he has done the deed. But in his eyes, you can see Tom is already having second thoughts about sparing Bernie's life. Those doubts will turn out to be legitimate.

◎ **REPEATED WATCHING QUOTIENT:** Watch it twice—once just to take it in, and a second time to try to better comprehend it.

➡ **DON'T FAIL TO NOTICE:** The use of men's hats as a symbol throughout the movie. They float through the air, they get knocked off, they get pulled over furrowed brows. And the meaning? Even the actors did not know what the Coens were getting at.

"I asked Joel, 'What's the significance to the hat?' " Byrne told the *New York Times*. "And he said, 'Oh, that hat is very significant.' " In our opinion, if the lead actor doesn't know, it's unclear how the audience is supposed to figure it out.

✎ WHAT THEY WROTE AT THE TIME:
"A noir with a touch so light, the film seems to float on the breeze like the Frisbee of a fedora sailing through the forest."—Richard Corliss, *Time*

(Yeah, sure. Anyway, in 2005 *Time* chose *Miller's Crossing* as one of the 100 greatest movies produced since the publication debuted in 1923.)

☺ GOOF:
Watch for the scene where Verna dials 9-1-1 to call the cops. In fact, the three-digit emergency system didn't begin until 1968, and didn't reach any major American cities until 1976.

◀ CASTING CALL:
Trey Wilson was cast to play Leo, the Irish mob boss. You may recall Wilson as the manager in *Bull Durham* or as furniture tycoon Nathan Arizona in the Coen Brothers' *Raising Arizona*. He died shortly before shooting, so Albert Finney was hired.

🔫 VIOLENCE LEVEL:
Moderate. The best moments come during an attempted hit on Leo, in which the savvy boss mows down his attackers with a Thompson M1928 submachine gun. It's all choreographed to Irish tenor Frank Patterson's beautiful rendition of "Danny Boy."

🍎 BET YOU DIDN'T KNOW:
The portrayal of cops as bought-and-sold commodities was partly influenced by the Coen Brothers' dealings with police while filming the movie in New Orleans. That city's police continually held up shooting, Joel Coen said, to assess fines (or take bribes) for permits the crew had already procured.

🗨 BEST LINE:
Johnny Caspar lamenting the lack of a moral code among his peers—one of whom has sold inside knowledge of a rigged boxing match: "It's getting so a businessman can't expect no return from a fixed fight. Now, if you can't trust a fix, what can you trust? For a good return, you're gonna have to go betting on chance, and then you're back with anarchy. Right back in the jungle,

on account of the breakdown of ethics. That's why ethics is important. It's the grease makes us get along, what separates us from the animals."

🎭 "I KNOW THAT GAL":
Joel Coen's real-life wife, Frances McDormand, makes a brief appearance as the corrupt mayor's secretary. Under all that pancake makeup, it may be tough to recognize her as small-town police Chief Marge Gunderson from *Fargo*.

⊛ IF YOU LIKED THIS, YOU'LL LIKE:
The Glass Key, the 1942 film noir based on the novel of the same name written by Hammett, a book that clearly inspired *Miller's Crossing*.

⚰ BODY COUNT:
Fourteen. Or fifteen, if you want to count the bad toupee left askew on one poor victim's head.

41 INFERNAL AFFAIRS (2002–R)

STARS: TONY LEUNG, ANDY LAU, ANTHONY WONG, ERIC TSANG
DIRECTORS: WAI-KEUNG LAU AND ALAN MAK

Martin Scorsese used this movie as the framework for *The Departed*. And while *Infernal Affairs* has received high praise and dozens of awards, the feeling here is that Scorsese took an interesting plot and made it into a classic film.

Maybe that's cinematic jingoism.

But we like to think it's why Scorsese is Scorsese.

Think of *Infernal Affairs* as a beautifully detailed line drawing. Scorsese took that outline and turned it into a colorful and layered Impressionistic painting.

The tension and absorbing plot twists that made *The Departed* such a great film are all here. The action scenes and murders are recreated almost verbatim. The botched drug deal, the fall from the roof, the meeting in the movie theater and subsequent chase and the finale on and off the elevator play as virtual mirror images—one in Chinese and the other in Bostonian.

Because both films are so highly regarded among film fans, there is an ongoing—and sometimes bitter—debate about them. Go online and you'll find moviegoers backing one film over the other with an aggressive fanaticism normally associated with rival sports fans.

The makers of *Infernal Affairs* came away with dozens of prizes from the Hong Kong Film Awards in 2003, including Best Picture, Best Director, Best Screenplay, Best Actor (Tony Leung) and Best Supporting Actor (Anthony Wong).

The film, released with a limited run in the United States in 2004, has been credited in many cinematic circles with reviving the then-floundering Hong Kong film industry by pumping new life and creativity into what had become a staid and predicable business.

A prequel and a sequel were subsequently made, with all three parts serving as scripture for an almost cult-like *IA* following in the United States and other countries.

But to argue over which is the better film is similar to debating whether Tom Brady or Peyton Manning is the better quarterback. Both play the game of football at the highest level; both movies are superior contemporary crime films.

Still, the argument doesn't stop.

While Wai-keung Lau seemed pleased with the success of *The Departed* after it won Best Picture at the 79th Academy Awards, his codirector Alan Mak helped fuel the controversy with comments he made at the time to the *South China Morning Post*.

On the one hand, Mak sounded snide when noting that since *The Departed* was almost a carbon copy of *Infernal Affairs*, he was pleased *his* film had won the top Academy Award. But in the same interview, he complained about changes that had been made in the script, particularly to its ending. Mak, according to the newspaper article, pointed out that in *Infernal Affairs*, the Triad mole inside the police department survives at the expense of the undercover cop.

"With the death of Matt Damon's character, the symbolism in the film is gone—it was designed so that the opportunist lives and has to face a life led on false pretenses," Mak said.

Two other changes jump out. While *The Departed* had the same love interest for the two undercover operatives, *Infernal Affairs* has the rogue cop living with a novelist and the undercover investigator falling in love with his psychiatrist. This made it easier to incorporate some introspection and foreshadowing, two developments that were implied, but not so obvious, in *The Departed*. The novelist at one point complains about character development in the book she is working on and asks her lover to help her sort it out. She says she doesn't know if she wants her character to be "a good guy or a bad guy" and wonders if, in real life, you get to choose between the two.

Ming (Andy Lau), the Triad member who has infiltrated the police department, finds himself facing the same dilemma—more so than Matt Damon's Colin Sullivan did in *The Departed*, Ming appears to believe he can wipe the slate clean and become a real police officer.

When Ming kills Hon Sam, the Triad leader, it's clearly with that in mind. When Sullivan takes out Frank Costello, it's because he believes Costello is cooperating and might expose him. Sullivan is driven by self-preservation, a theme that occurs again and again in *The Departed*. Ming has a more noble, albeit twisted, goal.

The other big differences between the films, in our opinion, are the importance of their respective mob bosses and the level of performance achieved by the actors playing those roles. Eric Tsang is effective as Sam, but doesn't get the screen time or bring the same presence as Jack Nicholson, who created one of the all-time gangster film bad guys with his portrayal of the diabolical, philosophical and homicidal Frank Costello.

There's just no comparison.

That being said, *Infernal Affairs* is a good movie. But if you've seen *The Departed* first, you probably won't be as impressed.

✎ **WHAT THEY WROTE AT THE TIME:** "No wonder Martin Scorsese wants to remake it. . . . Co-director Andrew Lau, a onetime cinematographer . . . has time and again breathed life into the Hong Kong film industry with slickly produced yet irresistibly human and entertaining action films. With *Infernal Affairs*, which he codirected with writer Alan Mak, Lau has outdone himself. The directors walk a fluidly edited tightrope between character study and action tour de force."—G. Allen Johnson, *San Francisco Chronicle*

👁 **REPEATED WATCHING QUOTIENT:** If you're into making comparisons between originals and remakes, then back-to-back screenings of *Infernal Affairs* and *The Departed* would be an interesting undertaking and a great way to fuel dis-

cussion on which of the two is better. If you just want to be entertained, either movie is worth revisiting.

🎬 **PIVOTAL SCENE:** Ming and Yan finally come face to face, but Yan still doesn't realize Ming is the mole within the police department he has been chasing. They have a discussion about Yan's undercover work and his desire to finally come in from the cold. Yan says he's been at it 10 years. Their exchange is ironic and sets the stage for the movie's blistering conclusion.

"I just want an identity, I want to be normal, man," says Yan.

"Getting tired?" Ming asks.

"You've never been a mole," Yan replies. "You won't understand. Too bad I still can't find the stooge. I'll take him down if I find him."

👊 **BET YOU DIDN'T KNOW:** When *The Departed* won the Academy Award for Best Picture, there was a reference made to *Infernal Affairs* as the film on which it was based. However, *IA*, as its fans like to call it, was incorrectly identified as a Japanese film. This, no doubt, has added to the debate among film fans over real or perceived slights by those involved in making each film.

💬 **BEST LINE:** "What thousands must die so that Caesar can become the great?" asks Triad leader Hon Sam as he initiates a young group of gangsters into his organization and lays out his plan to infiltrate the police department.

🔫 **VIOLENCE LEVEL:** Intense.

☠ **BODY COUNT:** Seven.

Underworld, U.S.A. is a piercing, unsentimental look at revenge, corruption and organized crime in American cities.

Ahh, but what might have been.

The film was shot during the last days of the Eisenhower Administration when Hollywood's priggish self-censorship panel, the Production Code Administration (PCA), was still minding the morals of grown-up filmgoers.

Writer-director Samuel Fuller (*The Big Red One*) drafted a script that sounds, in hindsight, like a cross between *American Gangster* and *Death Wish*.

"If you have a story about gangs, you must show how they live and operate and how they use violence to terrify people," he argued at the time. The same year that *One Hundred and One Dalmatians* was the nation's top-grossing movie, Fuller believed that Americans were ready for a realistic film about an adult topic.

Perhaps Americans were, but the prudes governing the industry were not. For more than a year, Fuller cajoled and argued and compromised with the PCA. There were four script revisions and dozens of post-production edits.

Underworld, U.S.A.'s original opening—in which prostitutes joke of starting a union and holding a "stand-up strike"—was deleted, according to author Lisa Dombrowski's book, *The Films of Samuel Fuller: If You Die, I'll Kill You!* Shots of hardcore drug use were edited out, as was a pioneering nude scene. The number of killings was sliced from 18 to five. Overall, according to Dombrowski, more than 20 pages of script were blue-penciled.

In the end, we applaud Fuller for fighting the fight. For one, his efforts—joined by those of directors like Otto Preminger and Michelangelo Antonioni—helped lead to a scrapping of the PCA. It was replaced in 1968 by the ratings system still in use today.

Beyond that, Fuller's toughness helped him win at least some of the battles. As a result, *Underworld, U.S.A.* is a taut, gritty film noir that still holds up after 50 years.

You get a sense of its bleakness from the onset, when 14-year-old Tolly Devlin rolls a drunk outside a New Year's Eve party. He, in turn, is mugged by a tougher teen who bashes Tolly's eye with a beer bottle. Later that night, Tolly sees his father—a low-level gangster—get beaten to death by four men. It's a jarring scene, shot in a shadowy alley and accompanied by a dirge-like version of "Auld Lang Syne."

In the darkness, Tolly can identify just one of the four killers, a mobster named Vic Farrar. He refuses to tell the cops because, he boasts, "I ain't no fink. I'll get those punks myself."

We learn that Tolly has no mom (she died in prison giving birth to him), so the hapless teen is sent to the state orphanage, where he learns the trade of cracking safes and dreams (literally) of avenging his dad.

Fast-forward a decade. Tolly is now an adult, played by Cliff Robertson with all kinds of tough-guy tics. His obsession with evening the score has not waned. When he learns that Farrar is in prison, he deliberately botches a crime so that he gets sentenced to the same institution.

That sets up the second half of *Underworld, U.S.A.* With Farrar dispatched after blabbing the names of his accomplices (more about that coming up), Tolly finishes his five-year term. By coincidence, the three other men who killed his father have risen to be the underbosses of a ruthless syndicate that controls drugs, prostitution and labor rackets in our unnamed big city. They work for a smarmy capo named Earl Connors (Robert Emhardt), who hides his mob connections by operating behind a legitimate business front (obliquely named National Projects), and by paying off the cops and making large charitable donations.

Connors also spends most of his days swaddling his obese body in a white bathrobe and hanging out by his syndicate's Olympic-sized swimming pool. "I picked the swimming pool location because I wanted a hollow, clean atmosphere," Fuller said in the book *The Director's Event: Interviews with Five American Film-Makers*. "I had this crime organization hold meetings there, rather than in a pompous office or a pool hall or the dingy little room where gangsters usually hang out. I wanted to get that contrast to what they're talking about; it's so vile and low."

Fuller, a newspaper crime writer at age 17, based his portrayal of the mob on a series of exposé articles in *The Saturday Evening Post*. The film also gained box-office buzz when its release coincided with a lurid conspiracy trial stemming from the notorious 1957 mob summit in Apalachin, N.Y.

Underworld, U.S.A. is helped by a quirky supporting cast. There is Beatrice Kay as Sandy—Tolly's surrogate mother and a saloon keeper (in the original script she was a madam suffering from VD) who has a doll fetish because she cannot have children. There is Dolores Dorn as Cuddles, a drug courier for the mob (she was a hooker in the original) who becomes Tolly's girlfriend as well as his point of access to the bad guys he wants to kill. And there's Richard Rust as a hit man named Gus, who is as creepy and emotionless as Javier Bardem in *No Country for Old Men*.

Robertson, who was largely a television actor when this was filmed (check out old episodes of *The Twilight Zone*), does a great job of creating a single-minded character trying to play every angle to gain his revenge. Smarter than the people around him, Tolly feigns loyalty to both a federal crime commission and the local syndicate to set up his victims.

You won't feel a lot of sympathy for his character by the end of the film. But you're not supposed to.

⊙ **HIT:** Fuller did a pioneering job of presenting organized crime as a corporation 13 years before Hyman Roth boasted, "Michael, We're bigger than U.S. Steel." Back when *Underworld, U.S.A.* was made, mobsters were typically presented as slang-talking, unshaven, gun-toting stereotypes.

"I liked working against the clichéd gangster idiom of hoodlums," he said in *The Director's Event.* "These guys sit around on sunny afternoons and cold-bloodedly plan who they're going to bribe, who they're going to rub out—all in a middle-class, upscale day's work."

⊗ **MISS:** We admire Fuller for trying to show the underbelly of police corruption. But did every single cop have to be either on the take or a bumbling moron?

◀ **CASTING CALL:** Humphrey Bogart originally bought the rights to the *Saturday Evening Post* serial, but died of cancer in 1957 before having a chance to film it.

✔ **REALITY CHECK:** When he gets out of prison, Tolly goes to see Sandy, his mother figure. She asks if he has identified the other guys who killed his father. Tolly picks a newspaper up off the desk and—amazingly—the three men are featured in a front-page story with huge mug shots and a headline screaming how they now run the city's crime scene.

Now that is one hell of a coincidence.

✎ **WHAT THEY WROTE AT THE TIME:** "A slick gangster melodrama made to order for filmgoers who prefer screen fare explosive and uncomplicated."—*Variety*

◉ **REPEATED WATCHING QUOTIENT:** Probably worth reviewing once every new presidential administration.

🎬 **PIVOTAL SCENE:** Tolly deliberately botches a crime and goes to prison so that he can confront the only killer of his father he was able to identify the night of the murder. He learns that the man—Vic Farrar—is gravely ill. So he angles to get a job in the prison hospital and, alone one night, confronts Farrar on his death bed.

Farrar peers up through delirious eyes. He seems to recognize Tolly, even though he saw him for just a second back when Tolly was 14. I think I know you, Farrar rasps.

Tolly draws in close and whispers: "That's because I'm a dead ringer for my father, Tom Devlin. Yeah, you beat him to death that night. You and your three pals. Remember, Vic?"

Farrar begins to cry over his old sin. "Don't worry," Tolly calmly says, "you will go to heaven if you reveal the names of your partners." Farrar gasps them out, feels absolved and dies in Tolly's arms.

A little cheesy, we'll grant you. But good stuff.

→ **DON'T FAIL TO NOTICE:** How that scary mob enforcer, Gus, dons sunglasses every time he's about to carry out a job.

"That switches on the killer," explained Fuller. "Afterwards he takes them off and he's a regular guy—good to his mother, pets his dog."

🔫 **VIOLENCE LEVEL:** Moderate, because of Fuller's losing battles with the PCA. In one scene, the corrupt police chief commits suicide when his fealty to the mob is exposed. Originally, Fuller planned a shot of the chief putting his gun in his mouth. The censors wouldn't allow that. So instead, we see the cop pick up the gun, and then the camera shifts to a wall in his office where the bullet (presumably after passing through his head) ricochets off a photo of the once-proud chief smiling in his uniform.

🍎 **BET YOU DIDN'T KNOW:** The revenge angle of the film is based on the Alexandre Dumas novel *The Count of Monte Cristo*. There's a copy of the book on display in Tolly's apartment.

🙿 **BEST LINE:** "There will always be people like us. As long as we don't have any records on paper, as long as we run National Projects with legitimate business operations and pay our taxes on legitimate income and donate to charities and run church bazaars, we'll win the war. We always have."—Underworld boss Earl Connors.

✪ **IF YOU LIKED THIS, YOU'LL LIKE:** *Pickup on South Street*, Fuller's equally gritty 1953 movie about a subway pickpocket who inadvertently ends up snatching top-secret microfilm from a Russian agent.

🚲 **BODY COUNT:** Five, including a nine-year-old girl who gets run over while riding her bike to silence her father as a witness against the mob.

AN INTERVIEW WITH CLIFF ROBERTSON

Actor Cliff Robertson's distinguished career began with roles on classic TV shows of the 1950s and continued through the massively popular *Spider-Man* trilogy in the 2000s. He is perhaps most famous for playing John F. Kennedy in 1963's *PT 109* and for his 1968 role in *Charly*, for which he won a Best Actor Oscar. He shines as revenge-driven Tolly Devlin in *Underworld, U.S.A.*

What do you remember about making Underworld, U.S.A.?

We wanted to make a movie that didn't fall in with the stereotypical Hollywood concepts of gangsters. We wanted to show how the bad guys were hiding behind kind of a corporate persona, coming off as good citizens when they were actually criminals. A lot of big people involved in crime were considered respectable back then—as it is now.

Director Sam Fuller was not a real Hollywood insider. What do you recall about working with him?

We got along great. We were both Hollywood outsiders, which helped. And we were both former newspaper people. I was a would-be journalist back when I started out in Ohio, and Sam came from that field. He was obsessed with two things—reading Mark Twain and talking about his days in the Army during World War II. He was very proud of that, which is why he worked so hard on the movie *The Big Red One*. Anyway, Sam was an old short guy following behind a big cigar. A little, feisty, screw 'em all kind of guy, and a tremendous talent.

There were a lot of censorship battles during the filming of Underworld, U.S.A. What impact did that have on the film?

It really changed the script. It's a terrific movie, but certainly would have been better if the censors left it alone. One of the reasons I appreciate Sam is he fought that losing battle. He had courage. In those days you kept your mouth shut. There was a firmament of fear in Hollywood, a place where people had—still have—inordinate power. The moguls would say, "I can ruin your career," and they were right.

Given that it was a groundbreaking movie, what was the public reaction to the movie?

It was not as popular as it should have been. Columbia Studios didn't spend much money to promote the film. They didn't sell it, and that can really hurt. Listen, a lot of tough guys were in the business then. Some of those guys knew the gangsters. They weren't all interested in the movie doing well.

Your character in Underworld, U.S.A., Tolly Devlin, spends his life obsessed with revenge against the gangsters who killed his father. Was he the grittiest character you ever played?

Tolly was a persistently angry guy, but he had good reason. And it wasn't just revenge. It was also genetics. He had that seed of a rebel. He was his father's son, and his father was a criminal. But I admire Tolly because he was the little guy who didn't give in. In a country where the big guys invariably win out, I think the little guy is a hero.

Why do you think gangster movies have always done well?

Well, America has always had that same sense of being the little guy, back to the Colonial days. America was the rebel, the upstart who spit in King George III's eye. So although we're now the big guy, we still have the affection for the underdog who's not going to be put upon, not going to be shafted by the rich guy. That seed has stayed with us. And gangsters fill that role, at least in the movies.

Any particular actors you admire from those movies?

I always loved Edward G. Robinson. He was a little Romanian Jewish guy playing a tough Italian mobster. Cagney was tough to beat. And he started out as a dancer from Hell's Kitchen. And Bogart. How do you not love Bogey?

Other than Underworld, U.S.A., it doesn't seem like you've played a criminal very often.

The closest I got was playing a villain named Shame in the old *Batman* series on TV. Playing the bad guy is fun because it leaves room for excess. You can let it all go. Oh, I would love to play a real gangster. Tell them I'm still available.

43 TRUE ROMANCE (1993–R)

STARS: CHRISTIAN SLATER, PATRICIA ARQUETTE, DENNIS HOPPER, GARY OLDMAN, CHRISTOPHER WALKEN | DIRECTOR: TONY SCOTT

This is an old-fashioned boy-meets-girl love story, filtered (perhaps scrambled is a better word) through the artistic lens of Quentin Tarantino, who wrote the screenplay for director Tony Scott.

Clarence Worley (Christian Slater) is a blue-collar kid from the mean streets of Detroit. He works at a comic book store, loves kung fu movies and occasionally has conversations (usually while he's taking a piss in the bathroom) with his mentor, Elvis Presley.

Alabama Whit man (Patricia Arquette) is a call girl with a heart of gold, just up from Florida and learning her way around the city. One of her first gigs is as a surprise birthday present for Clarence.

Somewhere between the kung fu triple feature where they meet, the pie that they share at a local diner and the sex in his bed, they fall in love.

From there, the story gets really bizarre.

Tarantino, who actually worked in a comic book/video store, borrows heavily from the SLAM! BANG! POW! imagery of that genre to create a violent buddy movie of sorts. It is sprinkled with memorable performances by a host of actors who were, or were soon to become, members of Hollywood's A-list.

"Everyone shines . . . but it's Tarantino's gutter poetry that detonates *True Romance*," wrote *Rolling Stone*'s Peter Travers in a review praising the film. "This movie is dynamite."

Samuel L. Jackson, Gary Oldman, Christopher Walken, Dennis Hopper, Brad Pitt, James Gandolfini and Val Kilmer (barely seen as the "mentor" we know is Elvis) all make appearances. Some are on screen longer than others, but none goes more than a scene or two.

These are more than cameo roles, though. In some ways, the movie is a series of vignettes, each of which could stand alone as a short film worth watching. We might even argue that the pieces are better than the whole.

There's Jackson as Big Don, going on at length and in detail about how he likes oral sex with women. His sexual monologue ends abruptly when he's blown away by a shotgun-wielding drug kingpin named Drexl (Gary Oldman). We're never quite clear why Big Don has drawn Drexl's ire, but no matter. That's the way Drexl rolls.

The dreadlocked kingpin—"He's white, but he thinks he's black," Alabama tells Clarence—is Alabama's pimp. Needless to say, he is less than pleased with her decision to leave his employ.

Clarence's confrontation with Drexl is another comic book-inspired scene of mayhem and violence sprinkled with tough guy dialogue and the standard Tarantino movie references.

"Ya' know what we got here?" Drexl asks his associate Marty after Clarence shows up at the brothel. "Motherfuckin' Charles Bronson. *Mr. Majestyk*."

Clarence has brought along his gun. And, buoyed by words of encouragement from his "mentor" ("Every pimp in the world gets shot. Two in the back of the fuckin' head. Cops'd throw a party, man."), he has no intention of backing down.

"I ain't scared of you," he tells Drexl. "I just don't like you."

A violent fight scene ends with Drexl and Marty dead and a badly beaten Clarence leaving the brothel with what he thinks is a suitcase packed with Alabama's belongings.

What he really has, however, is $500,000 worth of cocaine.

From there, *True Romance* becomes a twisted road movie with Clarence and Alabama on the run from the mobsters Drexl worked for. Not surprisingly, those wiseguys want their drugs back.

Walken, as Sicilian mobster Vincenzo Coccotti, has a great scene with Dennis Hopper, who plays

Clarence's father, Clifford. The confrontation, inside a trailer in a freight yard where Clifford lives and works as a security guard, is a movie within a movie. Both Walken and Hopper shine in a scene that became one of the signature moments in *True Romance*.

From there, the action shifts to Hollywood, where Clarence hopes to reconnect with his friend Dick Ritchie (Michael Rapaport), who is trying to make it as an actor. Clarence figures Dick can help him unload the half-million dollars worth of coke, which he's willing to sell for the bargain basement price of $200,000.

Gandolfini is Virgil, one of the mob hit men sent to Hollywood to track down Clarence, Alabama and the cocaine. His brutal fight scene with Alabama—"You got a lot of heart, kid," he tells her while smashing her face and literally tossing her around a motel room—ends with another comic book-like blast (literally) of violence involving a can of hair spray and a cigarette lighter.

Brad Pitt—as a stoner who never really understands what's going on—helps direct traffic during the manhunt, as assorted characters show up looking for the love pair. Pitt's character, Floyd, is high in each scene and never leaves the couch of the rundown apartment he shares with Ritchie.

Drugs, the movie industry and heavily-armed cops and gangsters all converge for a final confrontation that ends with bodies strewn about a swank hotel room.

SLAM! BANG! POW!

Just a boy-meets-girl love story.

⊙ **HIT:** The frenetic action never stops. This is a movie where you never get a chance to catch your breath. One crazy scene spins into another. There's a roller-coaster ride in Hollywood that's emblematic of the entire movie. It's up and down and going in circles. Fans will enjoy the ride.

⊗ **MISS:** This is hinted at several times by characters involved in the drug deal, but anyone attempting to sell $500,000 worth of cocaine for $200,000 is going to be met with skepticism. The drug underworld is built around fear and paranoia. This was a deal too good to be true, and it is one of the major flaws in an admittedly entertaining, but flawed, plot.

✎ **WHAT THEY WROTE AT THE TIME:** "*True Romance* aims to be a *Bonnie and Clyde* for the '90s, but its aim isn't true—it's just *Bonnie and Clyde* for an MTV generation with a short attention span and an even shorter emotional range. Despite its noir references and evocations, this slick film, directed by Tony Scott from Quentin Tarantino's script, is a preposterously bloody mess, as is the plot."—Richard Harrington, *Washington Post*

◉ **REPEATED WATCHING QUOTIENT:** The best way to revisit this movie is in pieces. Any one of a dozen scenes involving the stellar supporting cast is worth viewing at any time. Small doses, in fact, may be more fun.

🙾 **BEST LINE:** "I'm the anti-Christ. You got me in a vendetta kind of mood," Coccotti (Walken) says to Clifford Worley (Hopper) as their confrontation in the trailer begins.

Worley's responses, leading to an "eggplant" reference, are also classics, but to repeat them here would spoil their effect.

➡ **DON'T FAIL TO NOTICE:** In typical Tarantino fashion, the word "fuck" and its derivatives are used more than 200 times.

🔫 **VIOLENCE LEVEL:** Filled with bloody and brutal fight scenes and characters with swollen faces, blackened eyes and lots of other damaged body parts.

🐾 **BODY COUNT:** Twenty-four, most piling up during the climatic shootout in the hotel room.

✸ **IF YOU LIKED THIS, YOU'LL LIKE:** Three other stories of murder and mayhem that are part of the Tarantino playbook: *Natural Born Killers* (1994), *Kill Bill, Vol. 1* (2003) and *Kill Bill, Vol. 2* (2004).

44 A PROPHET (2009–R)

STARS: TAHAR RAHIM, NIELS ARESTRUP, ADEL BENCHERIF
DIRECTOR: JACQUES AUDIARD

We've seen this story before. The reluctant nice guy gets pulled into working for the mob and grows into a cunning, ruthless leader of organized crime. It was Michael Corleone in *The Godfather* and Vito Corleone in *The Godfather: Part II*.

And we've seen *this* story before. Prison is a Darwinian society where brutal attacks are necessary for survival. Think *Bad Boys*. Or *American Me* (reviewed later in this book). Or even *The Shawshank Redemption*.

A Prophet, a French movie nominated for the Best Foreign Language Film Oscar in 2010, is not particularly original. It combines those two plotlines in presenting an inside look at the Corsican gangs operating in Gallic prisons. It just happens to

tell those stories very well.

As a prison movie, it would rank in our all-time Top 10. As a gangster movie, not as high, but we do heartily recommend it.

The film is directed by Jacques Audiard, whom critics delight in calling "The French Scorsese." That certainly seems an overstatement. We will say that *A Prophet* does carry some of the same raw intensity seen in Scorsese's earlier works, like *Taxi Driver*, if not the master's craftsmanship.

A Prophet tells the story of Malik El Djebena, a 19-year-old French Arab sent to prison for six years for assaulting a cop—a charge he denies all the way. It's been a tough life for Malik, an illiterate street urchin. He's small and shy, and during his first day in the yard he gets beaten for his sneakers. This prisoner is more victim than criminal.

He soon meets Cesar Luciani (Niels Arestrup), an aging Corsican mobster who looks like Don Corleone in sweatpants. Cesar runs dirty casinos on the outside and everything on the inside. Cesar sees value in the new kid because he provides an entry into the wing housing Arab prisoners. (On a side note, it's interesting to learn that French prisons feature the same tribal battles as American prisons, just with different tribes.)

Cesar needs to get to an Arab prisoner who is scheduled to testify against the Corsican mob. So he orders Malik to seduce the man and then slash his throat. "But I can't kill anyone," Malik sobs in protest. Then you will die, he is coldly told.

The mission is accomplished in a clumsy and violent scene. And Malik, like Michael Corleone—after his infamous visit to the Italian restaurant—is on his way.

Tahar Rahim, the young French actor portraying Malik, does a good job of transforming his character. After a few more missions, you see the boy's face hardening and his posture rising. Malik learns to read—not just books, but also the people around him. Hanging around the Corsicans in prison, he picks up the nuances of their language, without them ever suspecting he can understand them. All good skills in crime or any other vocation.

Now that he is under Cesar's wing, Malik earns special privileges from the corrupt prison officials. He is granted 12-hour leaves, ostensibly to earn a few bucks at an auto shop, but actually to run outside errands for Cesar. There's one frightening kidnapping scene as well as a bloody shootout on the streets of Marseilles. The business is never neat.

By this point, our aspiring mobster has learned enough to set up his own side enterprise. So Malik spends much of each 12-hour leave running a nascent drug operation with his buddy—a cancer-stricken former prisoner named Ryad (Adel Bencherif).

You know where this is going because you've also seen this part of the story before. Ever since 1931, when Paul Muni gunned down his capo in *Scarface: The Shame of a Nation*, movie mob underlings have been overthrowing their bosses.

And that's what happens here.

The rise of Malik's outside drug enterprise coincides with Cesar's fading influence inside. Seems that most of the Corsicans have been transferred, leaving the remaining gang as weak as the prison coffee. Meanwhile, Malik makes inroads with the Arab prisoners, overcoming their resentments toward him for his ties to the Corsicans.

The malevolent Cesar becomes increasingly desperate. Malik, meanwhile, learns to get things done through guile rather than violent coercion.

"Cesar is an ogre, a father who eats his children," Thomas Bidegain, who cowrote the movie with Audiard, told the *New York Times*. "But Malik is smart, so his objectives are always changing and expanding. . . . If he hadn't gone to prison, he would never have found out that he is smart. Instead he would have been absolutely wasted, killed or OD'd at 22."

We won't give you the blow-by-blow (hell, the movie is 155 minutes long). But we will tell you that Audiard describes his lead character as "the anti-Scarface"—a reference to Al Pacino's immoral, drug-crazed Tony Montana rather than to Muni's classic character, Tony Camonte. You'll certainly feel more empathy for Malik than you did for either of those two.

That's especially true at the end of the movie.

Malik, who once had nothing, ends up with everything. By this point his pal Ryad is dead of cancer. But the man's wife and son meet Malik upon his release from prison, suggesting he may finally get the family he never had. And as they stroll away from the gates, the camera pulls back to show a line of black cars following them for protection.

The kid, now a man, has put together an organization. He's got the money, he's got the power, he's got the woman.

⊙ **HIT:** In a surreal touch, Malik is literally haunted by his first murder victim, the Arab prisoner. The dead man's ghost—sometimes smoldering in flames—comes back to serve as Malik's muse, giving him counsel and guidance. Rather than coming across as hokey, the device suggests a permanent bond between the dead man and his killer.

⊗ MISS: Perhaps a few things get lost in translation, but there are moments when *A Prophet* gets downright difficult to follow.

✎ WHAT THEY WROTE AT THE TIME: "If Malik doesn't remind you of Al Pacino's Michael Corleone on his journey from innocence to corruption in *The Godfather* saga, well . . . he should. *A Prophet* is similarly, startlingly momentous."—Steven Rea, *Philadelphia Inquirer*

◉ REPEATED WATCHING QUOTIENT: This is a two-and-a-half-hour, subtitled French film. If you're the kind of person who enjoys rereading the works of Camus or Sartre, view it again. If not. . . .

▤ PIVOTAL SCENES: Malik is ordered by Cesar to rub out that fellow Arab prisoner. Malik has never killed anything. He's petrified, and tries to avoid the job—first by blowing the whistle, then by getting thrown in solitary. But there is no refusing the powerful Cesar.

The mobster's aides give Malik murder lessons (teaching him to hide a razor blade in his mouth and flip it with his tongue to slash another man), he gets close to the Arab and they meet in the man's cell.

The unknowing victim is gracious to the younger Malik, offering tea and reading lessons. Malik does not want to harm the man, but he knows he must. The attack is clumsy and downright gory. Its brutality shocks Malik, as it will likely shock you. Malik then puts the razor blade in the dead man's palm to make it appear the man killed himself. He steps away, drenched in blood.

The kid who spent most of his life being bullied is now a killer. And killing comes easier the second time. Having to choose between his soul and his life, Malik makes the only real choice he can.

✔ REALITY CHECK: Let's see now. A key witness in a mob trial is found with his neck slashed one week before he's set to testify. Because the razor blade is found in his hand, everyone believes it's a suicide? Yeah, sure.

➡ DON'T FAIL TO NOTICE: The food in French prisons appears to be far superior to the fare offered by the American penal system. We were especially impressed with the fresh-baked loaves of bread handed to each prisoner at every meal.

♟ BET YOU DIDN'T KNOW: Director Audiard originally wanted to entitle the film, *You Gotta Serve Somebody*, as a nod to Bob Dylan's song about choosing between God and the devil. "But that was too difficult to translate into French," Audiard told the *New York Times*. Audiard said the final title was not picked for religious reasons, but because the lead character "is a prophet in the sense that he designs a new kind of gangster."

🔫 VIOLENCE LEVEL: High and gruesome. If you were ever curious what occurs after a man's carotid artery gets sliced, *A Prophet* is for you.

❞ BEST LINE: Cesar, the godfather, knows his authority comes through intimidation. So when he senses he is losing his grip over the increasingly confident Malik, he tries to impress the younger man with his power.

"No longer scared of me?" Cesar asks Malik. "If you can walk around this place, it's because I had you made a porter. If you eat, it's thanks to me. If you dream, think, live—it's thanks to me. . . . You live off of me."

Cesar digs a spoon into Malik's eye to stress the point.

⊕ IF YOU LIKED THIS, YOU'LL LIKE: *Midnight Express*, a classic 1978 film showing the horrors that occur after an American drug smuggler winds up in a Turkish prison.

🔪 BODY COUNT: Eight, plus one unlucky deer that strays into traffic.

A child murderer is terrorizing the city. The police hunt is intense, but fruitless. So the cops redouble their efforts—rousting bars, hassling citizens walking the night streets, turning a bright spotlight on the creatures of the back alleys.

The killer still remains at large, but there's an unexpected side effect: with every flophouse and crime den being raided on a nightly basis, the underworld pimps, thieves and pushers cannot operate. "There are more police on the street tonight than whores," complains a pickpocket, who can't find a john's pocket to pick.

What are the criminals to do? A meeting is called of the city's underworld leaders. Until the monster is captured, they agree, their business will suffer. Therefore, they decide, the job must be theirs. The gangsters must find the killer, if only so that things can return to normal.

That's the setup for director Fritz Lang's 1931 masterpiece *M*, which is based on the true story of German serial killer Peter Kurten, the "Vampire of Dusseldorf." It stars 26-year-old Peter Lorre, whom you're more likely to know from his portrayal of weasely characters in *Casablanca* and *The Maltese Falcon* (or, more recently, as the inspiration for the voice of hyperactive Chihuahua Ren in *The Ren & Stimpy Show*).

Here, the young Lorre is all bug-eyed and sweaty, kneading his chubby fingers as his twisted desires kick in. He's loathsome and, for one very brief moment, sympathetic, as he wanders among citizens oblivious that such a pipsqueak of a man could be the monster among them.

But the audience knows from the start. In the first few minutes, Lorre's character buys a balloon for a young girl playing on a city street. The camera cuts to the girl's family apartment, where her mother sets a table for lunch. Time passes. Now the mother, frantic, calls the girl's name out the window. There is silence, as we see the balloon floating away. We know the girl is gone.

The drama comes in catching the killer. In Lang's eyes, the cops are fat and inept. There's a great scene that sets up the second half of the movie; it shows frustrated police officials and the city's underworld leaders holding parallel meetings on opposite ends of town.

"Maybe we should offer more reward money," one cop suggests. "No, we need to crack down harder," offers another. "We need more raids."

Meanwhile, the mobsters—a smart collection of counterfeiters, safecrackers and club owners—need to get the law off their backs. "You can't do business anymore without tripping over cops," says one. "An outsider is ruining our reputation."

Another notes that with the cash tap turned off, "We can't even afford to pay the expenses for the wives and children of our members who are currently boarding at state expense." Meaning prison, of course.

The gangsters make it clear that murdering a child violates their code. It's evocative of the drug summit scene in *The Godfather*, where the dons draw the line at selling heroin near schoolyards.

The camera shifts from one meeting to the other. The cops pace the table, scratching their heads and smoking (including one corpulent detective who puffs a cigar stuffed into a pipe stem). The gangsters, too, wring their hands, until the cleverest among them devises a plan.

To catch the child murderer themselves, the gangsters employ an army of the city's beggars to act as a spy network. Each is assigned a block, and it quickly becomes clear that the underworld is better equipped for this manhunt than the police are.

Needless to say, Lorre's monster is captured, and Lang employs a great device to make it happen. The killer unconsciously whistles the same tune every time he stalks a child. A blind balloon salesman hears it, recalls it from the day of one of the murders and notifies the gangsters. The device has been imitated many times over the years, but never to such great effect.

Lorre's creepy killer is hauled into a vacant distillery, where he stands trial before a kangaroo court of more than 100 hardened thieves and hookers. He initially denies the murders, but breaks down when shown photos of the missing young girls. His face becomes a fright mask, his words impassioned.

"I can't help myself," he moans. Then he turns on his jury. "Who are all of you? Criminals and proud of it. . . . But I have no control over this cursed thing inside of me. The fire. The voices. The agony."

We won't tell you how the story ends, but it's well worth sticking around for the full 110 minutes to find out.

M opened in 1931 and was banned in Germany in 1934 by the Nazi Party for its negative portrayal of police. It disappeared for more than 30 years, before a few old muddy copies were found. The movie was masterfully restored for its Blu-Ray release in 2010.

⊙ **HIT:** Lang was way ahead of his time in his use of sound and shadow to set mood. In an early scene, schoolchildren jump rope while reciting a singsong nursery rhyme about a bogeyman who "will make mincemeat out of you." Lorre's killer makes his entrance as a shadow, cutting across a streetlight poster promoting a reward for his capture. Eerie stuff.

⊗ **MISS:** If you can't hack subtitles and the slower pace of old movies, this one's not for you. But we recommend you try.

❞ **BEST LINE:** The gangsters rationalizing their plan to capture the child stalker:

"We conduct our business to survive, but this monster must not survive. He must be killed, eliminated, exterminated."

"Yes, he's not even a real crook."

✎ **WHAT THEY WROTE AT THE TIME:** "It is regrettable that such a wealth of talent and imaginative direction was not put into some other story, for the actions of this Murderer, even though they are left to the imagination, are too hideous to contemplate."—Mordaunt Hall, the *New York Times*

➡ **DON'T FAIL TO NOTICE:** Lorre's pained expression as he is thrown down the steps by his captors. That's because he really is in pain after Lang directed him to take the tumble more than a dozen times. Lang, who was accused over the years of displaying sadism toward his actors, thought it imperative that Lorre's trapped murderer felt genuine terror in the scene.

⌐ **VIOLENCE LEVEL:** Not much, other than that stair toss. Although this is the first movie ever made about a serial killer, all of the bad stuff happens off screen.

✪ **BET YOU DIDN'T KNOW:** Lorre had been a comedic actor before *M* and saw the movie as his chance to expand his career. Decades later, he said he regretted taking the role because people always associated him with being a child murderer. Beyond that, Lorre, who was Jewish, fled Germany soon after the film's release. A still shot of his face from *M* was put on a 1940 Nazi propaganda poster above the words: "Typical Jew."

⊕ **IF YOU LIKED THIS, YOU'LL LIKE:** See the following chapter.

FRITZ LANG AND GERMAN GANGSTER MOVIES

Truth be told, writer-director Fritz Lang probably deserves more mention than we give him in our Top 100. He's in there twice—for the pioneering 1931 *M* and for *The Big Heat*, made in 1953, two decades after he fled Nazi Germany.

Over a span of 38 years, Lang directed four films centered on the character of Dr. Mabuse, an early pulp fiction villain created by German novelist Norbert Jacques. In the movies, as in the books, the evil doctor employs a network of criminals he blackmails, hypnotizes or psychically manipulates to carry out crimes on his behalf. Either of the first two films could have fairly found their way into our Top 100.

In the silent feature *Dr. Mabuse: The Gambler* (1922), Lang shows the evil doctor and his gangster pals doing their best Gordon Gekko by stealing information to manipulate the stock market. Mabuse also gets inside the head of a young millionaire, luring the callow rich kid into a card game where he loses his fortune. In the end, Mabuse sees the ghosts of his many victims and goes insane. A fascinating movie, although it has lost a little of its lucidity over the years.

The Testament of Dr. Mabuse (1933) opens with our antihero presumably having died in the insane asylum. But he has left behind writings full of master criminal plans for his band of gangsters. Turns out that Mabuse is still lurking around in two forms: as an ethereal visage that speaks with the psychologist running the asylum and as a voice behind a curtain that directs his underworld underlings. It's complex and confusing stuff, especially if you don't speak German and need to read the subtitles.

Adolf Hitler's government hated the movie. Nazi Propaganda Minister Joseph Goebbels banned it, saying Lang's film aimed to erode confidence in the government among German citizens. It is no coincidence that Lang had his evil doctor mouth dialogue straight from the mouths of Nazi leaders.

Soon after that, Lang—whose mother was born Jewish but later converted to Catholicism—fled the country and relocated in Paris. His ex-wife and fellow *Dr. Mabuse: The Gambler* screenwriter, Thea von Harbou, stayed behind and even joined the Nazi Party.

Lang ended up back in Germany in his latter years. His final film as a director was *The Shadow vs. the 1000 Eyes of Dr. Mabuse* (1960), which is as goofy as its title suggests. To call it a gangster film may be a reach, but it does combine elements of crime, evil Nazi intrigue and a clubfooted bad guy named Hieronymus B. Mistelzweig. We don't necessarily recommend watching it sober.

Director Wim Wenders' *The American Friend* (1977) is the story of an American gangster (Dennis Hopper) who convinces a terminally ill picture framer (Bruno Ganz) to act as a hit man so that he can leave behind an inheritance for his family. Some critics called it Hitchcockian; others deemed it murky.

Renamed *Short Sharp Shock* for its American release, *Kurz und Schmerzlos (1998)* tells the tale of three buddies who immigrate to Hamburg from other parts of Europe, hoping to rise out of poverty. One joins the Albanian mob, one becomes a car thief and the third—fresh from jail—tries to keep his friends from a life of crime. The film was a box-office flop that deserved a better fate.

46 ANGELS WITH DIRTY FACES
(1938–NR)

STARS: JAMES CAGNEY, PAT O'BRIEN, HUMPHREY BOGART, ANN SHERIDAN
DIRECTOR: MICHAEL CURTIZ

Some movies hold up well over time. This one doesn't.

We wanted to like *Angels with Dirty Faces* as much as we did the first time we saw it. But it just wasn't happening. Maybe some movies play better in our memories than they do on DVD.

It is still worth watching, however, mostly due to the acting. As protagonist Rocky Sullivan, James Cagney delivers one of his great tough-guy performances. His classic shoulder roll and "whaddaya hear, whaddaya say" line has probably been mimicked more than any other, and his final scene still resonates.

Pat O'Brien, as Father Jerry Connolly, does the goodly Catholic priest thing to cinematic perfection. It's a role that he and Bing Crosby (remember Father O'Malley in *Going My Way*?) should have had patented. Humphrey Bogart is good as corrupt lawyer Jim Frazier. And Ann Sheridan has her moments as Laury Ferguson, the would-be moll who knows better.

But the storyline in this Warner Brothers gangland melodrama seems contrived and overly moralistic. And the Dead End Kids (remembered as humorous) are six annoying, overacting caricatures—the Three Stooges times two.

Cagney got a Best Actor Academy Award nomination for this performance, which is understandable. However, the film's two other nominations—for Best Director and Best Writing, Original Story—are hard to believe. But then maybe we're unfairly applying 21st-century sensibilities to 1938 cinema.

Rocky Sullivan and Jerry Connolly are boyhood friends growing up in the slums of New York City. As teenagers, they hang on fire escape landings, harass cute neighborhood girls and look for ways to get into trouble.

A plan to steal boxes of fountain pens from a freight car at a train loading dock leads to a police chase and Rocky saving Jerry's life by pulling him off the tracks after he slips and falls in front of an approaching steam engine. It ends with Rocky being captured and Jerry, the faster runner, getting away.

Rocky takes the rap, never gives up his friend Jerry to "the coppers" and heads off to reform school. Flashing newspaper headlines chronicle the highlights of the era ("Harding Nominated for President" screams one; "Flier Circles the World" hollers another) and track the next 15 years of Rocky's criminal life. When he finally returns to the old neighborhood after a series of arrests for more serious crimes, Rocky has become a renowned gangster.

In the meantime, his childhood friend and juvenile crime partner Jerry has become the parish priest. He works to set the teenage boys in the 'hood on the straight and narrow. And Laury, whose first husband was killed in an underworld dispute, is now into social work and setting things right.

But both still love Rocky. And he loves them back.

"Somehow I feel Rocky could be straightened out," the good priest tells Laury after Rocky gets the Dead End Kids to come to the gym to play basketball—something the priest had failed to get them to do.

Rocky falls for Laury, even though an associate warns, "That dame's a jinx."

Against her better judgment, Laury returns his affection and takes a job as a hostess at a nightclub/casino in which Rocky has an interest.

But this is a crime-doesn't-pay tale, so it's not going to end well.

Rocky is double-crossed by Bogart's sleazy lawyer character, Frazier, who has become a mover and shaker in the corrupt world of politicians and gangsters—the people who really run the city. At first, demonstrating the bravado and street savvy on which his underworld reputation has been built, Rocky gets the upper hand on the lawyer and his business partner Mac Keefer (George Bancroft).

Unfortunately, his old pal Jerry, out to expose the evildoers, launches a crusade to clean up the city, warning Rocky that he will take him down as well if he is involved.

"Priest Declares War on Underworld Vice" screams the wood on another flashing headline.

Rocky spreads his cash around, giving a wad to the Dead End Kids, who use it to buy zoot suits, gamble and drink beer at a pool hall instead of showing up at the gym. He also sends an anonymous $10,000 donation to Father Connolly for the youth center he wants to build. But the priest turns down the cash and turns up the heat, joining forces with a newspaper to publicize the city's corruption.

"Don't be a sucker," Rocky tells Connolly when he returns the cash.

But the good Father won't take the money and instead asks Rocky to stop associating with the neighborhood kids.

"Don't encourage them to admire you," he implores.

Rocky saves Connolly's life one more time, bumping off Frazier and Keefer after learning they intend to put a hit out on the priest. But those murders lead to yet another police chase—bringing the story full circle—that ends with several dead cops and Rocky's arrest.

Facing the electric chair on death row, Rocky gets an 11th-hour visit from Father Connolly, who has one last favor to ask.

Given that Rocky has saved his life twice and is in jail in part because of the priest's moral crusade, this seems a bit much. But this is a morality play as much as it is a gangster movie.

The beauty is: we never really know if Rocky grants the favor.

⊙ HIT: The cramped, desperate and dirty life of the 1930s in New York City's tenements is captured perfectly.

⊗ MISS: Father Connolly's moral crusade comes out of nowhere. It feels like a forced plot device.

✎ WHAT THEY WROTE AT THE TIME: "Should do fair business, but the picture itself is no bonfire. . . . In at least one instance, the same set is used for two supposedly different locales." —*Variety*

➡ DON'T FAIL TO NOTICE: When Rocky slaps around the Dead End Kids during the raucous basketball game—which is more like a rugby match—the action strays beyond the script. Apparently the Kids were running wild on the set and Cagney, returning to his own New York roots, set them straight. He wasn't afraid to get physical and continued while the cameras were rolling.

❚❚ BEST LINE: "What we don't take, we ain't got," a teenaged Rocky says to Jerry, who at first is reluctant to go down to the freight yards and look for swag.

✔ REALITY CHECK: The mob hit in the pharmacy phone booth was modeled after the murder of mobster Vincent "Mad Dog" Coll, who was targeted by Dutch Schultz during a New York gang war. Coll hid out in an apartment that was over top of a pharmacy. But he would use the phone booth in the pharmacy each day to call his girlfriend. Schultz learned of this and sent two hit men to snuff him.

◀ CASTING CALL: Frankie Burke, the teenage actor who portrayed the young Rocky Sullivan, looked, sounded and moved like Cagney. He had the actor's speaking cadence down perfectly and his "whaddaya hear, whaddaya say" is hardly distinguishable from Cagney's. Burke, born Francis Aiello in Brooklyn, had minor roles, many uncredited, in about 15 other movies, including *Shadow of the Thin Man* in 1941, before dropping out of the business.

☺ GOOF: One of the newspaper headlines after Sullivan kidnaps Frazier misspells the word "kidnapper," dropping a "p." Where's the copy editor when you need him? (Back then it was almost certain that the editor was a he, and that he was wearing a green eye visor.)

♟ BET YOU DIDN'T KNOW: Cagney, in his biography *Cagney by Cagney*, said he grew up in a New York tenement neighborhood where a local pimp and hustler used to hang out on the corner, greeting everyone with "whaddaya hear, whaddaya say." Cagney said he stole the line and the shoulder roll/neck twitch from that neighborhood corner boy. "I did those gestures maybe six times in the picture," he wrote. "Impressionists have been doing me doing him ever since."

⚰ BODY COUNT: Six.

47 DINNER RUSH (2000–R)

STARS: DANNY AIELLO, EDOARDO BALLERINI, KIRK ACEVEDO
DIRECTOR: BOB GIRALDI

Ever since James Cagney smashed a grapefruit into Mae Clarke's face in *The Public Enemy*, food has been an integral part of mobster movies.

There are an estimated 60 eating references in *The Godfather*, including two of its iconic lines: "Try the veal, it's the best in the city" and "Leave the gun, take the cannoli."

In *GoodFellas*, the boys stop at Tommy's mother's house after midnight needing a knife, and end up staying for a full Italian feast. And, of course, Henry Hill learns to slice garlic with a razor in prison, where, "Dinner was always a big thing. We had a pasta course and then we had a meat or a fish."

In *Little Caesar*, Edward G. Robinson dines on spaghetti and espresso. In *Pulp Fiction*, Jules and Vincent settle for Big Kahuna Burgers and $5 milkshakes. In dozens of other gangster flicks, the bad guys fill their guts before emptying their guns.

But no movie in the genre portrays food as lovingly as *Dinner Rush*, a story about a New York City restaurateur/bookmaker trying to protect his properties against rival gangsters. In truth, the film focuses more on the cuisine than the crimes. But don't underestimate it; *Dinner Rush* is a solid mob movie.

The story is set in a trendy TriBeCa trattoria named Gigino, owned by patriarch Louis Cropa (Danny Aiello). He presides from a corner table and protests—unconvincingly—that he has nothing to do with the underworld. "I've never even held a gun," he insists.

Perhaps, but he's got problems with the wrong people. Louis' bookmaking partner is gunned down by a pair of thugs from Queens known as Black and Blue (you may recognize Mike McGlone from *The Brothers McMullen* as one of them). Now those hoods are muscling for a "partnership" in his bookmaking operation and his beloved restaurant. He's willing to give them the first—but never the second.

The hoods come to Gigino for their meals and their quarry. "We're not leaving without our deal," one threatens Louis over a plate of roasted artichokes. "You take it, or you leave."

But on this, a typical Tuesday night, many other stories are unfolding at the restaurant. And we, as viewers, get to sample a diverse menu of customers. There's a snooty art dealer (Mark Margolis) and his table of acolytes; a mean-spirited restaurant critic (Sandra Bernhard); an enigmatic Wall Street yuppie (John Corbett); and a city police detective (Walt MacPherson) whose invitation to dine that night appears anything but coincidental. Each table features a story, loudly played out.

"When did eating out become a Broadway show?" wonders Corbett's yuppie, who observes it all from the restaurant's bar. As it turns out, his character has a surprise twist, just like the pisco sour he orders.

All are there to sample the nouvelle cuisine of Louis' son Udo (Edoardo Ballerini), who has become a celebrity chef by concocting seemingly ridiculous dishes that combine elements like lobster, truffles, vanilla bean and wasabi. There is tremendous tension between Udo and his old man, who simply wants to run a traditional red-sauce joint. "There's nothing left to eat here," Louis moans in despair. "Can't I just get some sausage and peppers?"

All of the action in the dining room is matched by what's going on in the kitchen downstairs. Udo is trying to take over the restaurant from his dad. Each server has his or her own story. And sous chef Duncan (Kirk Acevedo) has a compulsive gambling problem that Louis is trying to cure. Yes, Louis is a bookmaker, but he's that rare one with a heart.

Duncan, like any problem gambler, goes elsewhere for his fix, making a bad bet on St. John's basketball. And by the end of the night, he owes those Queens mobsters $13,000. Lucky them, now they've got two scores to settle.

There's a whole lot going on in *Dinner Rush* and director Bob Giraldi (best known for directing videos such as Michael Jackson's *Beat It*) does a deft job of juggling the interlocking plotlines. Aiello serves as the center of gravity, stepping into each of the stories with a weighty nobility. His character, Louis, is not daunted, even as his livelihood—and perhaps his life—gets threatened.

Before dessert is served, you assume Louis has a plan to stave off the bad guys. Will he handle it himself? Is he going to call on that detective at Table 33 enjoying a complimentary bottle of champagne?

The act of vengeance arrives before the check. And you probably won't see it coming.

◉ HIT: The portrayal of life behind the scenes in a bustling restaurant is terrific. In the kitchen, the chef acts as a tyrant and the workers as his slaves. The speed and detail of the prep work, the cooking, the plating and the serving are more impressive than anything seen on a Food Network reality show. It should be no surprise that director Giraldi is actually a New York restaurateur and owns the eatery where *Dinner Rush* was filmed.

✖ MISS: While the movie enjoyably washes over you for 99 minutes, you may find yourself asking questions at the end. There are a few plot holes and things wrap up a bit too tidily.

✎ WHAT THEY WROTE AT THE TIME: "Effortlessly graceful and burnished to a glow, *Dinner Rush* is surely as satisfying as any of the delicious-looking food served at Louis' restaurant—and is as full of surprises as any dish Udo ever concocted."—Kevin Thomas, *Los Angeles Times*

✔ REALITY CHECK: Bernhard's critic character, Jennifer Freely, demands a better table, insists on comped wine and announces, "I don't like waiting." Any legitimate food reviewer we've ever met is adamant about going undercover to restaurants and keeping a low profile.

◉ REPEATED WATCHING QUOTIENT: Complex and rewarding enough for multiple viewings. Just be sure to have dinner plans afterward. This movie will make you hungry.

➡ DON'T FAIL TO NOTICE: Louis' doomed partner, Enrico, laughingly announces his plan to open a website called BookmakersAreUs.com. In 2000, that might have sounded like a joke. These days, a British site called Bookies.com lets you compare odds on thousands of events.

🍎 BET YOU DIDN'T KNOW: This is one of at least four movies in which Aiello had a close relationship with Italian food. In *Do the Right Thing*, he owns Sal's Famous Pizza. In *2 Days in the Valley*, he's a down-on-his-luck hit man working in a pizza parlor. And in *The Professional*, he is a Mafia don operating behind a front called The Supreme Macaroni Company.

🗩 BEST LINE: Food critic Freely: "Only in New York will a double murder triple your business."

😀 "I KNOW THAT GUY": The maître d' at Gigino Trattoria is played by Ajay Naidu. You may recognize him as Samir Nagheenanajar, the fidgety computer programmer who gets laid off and then plots revenge in *Office Space*.

✱ IF YOU LIKED THIS, YOU'LL LIKE: *Big Night*, the story of two Italian immigrant brothers who strive to keep their underdog Jersey Shore restaurant afloat by having singer Louis Prima come to eat there to generate publicity. Like *Dinner Rush*, that movie will prompt you to raid the fridge.

🔪 BODY COUNT: Three—one at the beginning, two at the end.

48 GET CARTER (1971–R)

STARS: MICHAEL CAINE, IAN HENDRY, BRITT EKLAND, JOHN OSBORNE
DIRECTOR: MIKE HODGES

After launching his career with star turns in *Alfie, The Ipcress File* and *Funeral in Berlin*, Michael Caine wanted to play a bad guy. In writer/director Mike Hodges' *Get Carter*, he got to play one of the baddest.

A bleak, angry underworld story of brotherly love, vengeance and betrayal, *Get Carter* opened to mixed reviews and a lukewarm box office. But like a good wine, it has improved with age.

In 1971, one British reviewer called it a "revolting, bestial horribly violent piece of cinema." Another likened it to "a bottle of neat gin swallowed before breakfast." (In a country where a typical breakfast consists of fried eggs, bacon, sausage, fried bread, mushrooms and baked beans, a little gin might not be a bad idea. But we digress.)

Nearly 30 years after its release, the British Film Institute listed *Get Carter* at No. 16 on its list of the Top 100 British films of all time. And in 2004, film critics in a survey conducted by *Total Film* magazine chose it as the greatest British film ever.

We rate it somewhere in between those two extremes and give it extra credit for creating a genre that has become part of the British cinematic canon. Films like *The Long Good Friday, The Krays* and *Sexy Beast* owe a nod to what Caine and Hodges created.

Caine plays Jack Carter, a hit man totally in control of his passions. But at the same time, Carter conveys that those passions—anger, lust, pride and envy—are constantly simmering just beneath his surface. Part of the fun in watching the film is waiting for Carter to act on those feelings.

He doesn't disappoint.

Carter is a mercenary whose loyalty to his London crime boss Gerald Fletcher (Terence Rigby) is questionable at best. His decision to head north to Newcastle to look into the circumstances surrounding the death of his brother Frank, despite Fletcher's suggestion that it wouldn't be a good idea, is the first indication that Carter is his own man.

A few scenes later, when Carter engages in phone sex from Newcastle with Fletcher's wife, Anna (Britt Ekland), there is no longer any doubt.

Carter's quest to find out how and why his brother died is the driving force behind all the action. He's told that Frank was drunk, lost control and drove his car into the river—an explanation that he rejects.

Finding out what really happened puts him in conflict with local mob boss Cyril Kinnear (John Osborne), former associate Eric Paice (Ian Hendry) and shady businessman Cliff Brumby (Bryan Mosley). Brumby tries to manipulate the London hit man. Paice tries to match wits with him. And Kinnear tries to kill him.

All three men come to bad ends.

Along the way, Carter gets to reconnect with Doreen (Petra Markham), his niece who may actually be his daughter. And he ends up in bed—at different times—with both a boarding house landlady, Edna (Rosemarie Dunham), and Glenda (Geraldine Moffat), a mob moll and part-time porn actress.

In one scene that captures his multifaceted persona, Carter emerges naked from bed with the landlady to confront two mobsters sent up from London to end his adventure in Newcastle.

Waving a shotgun and totally in the buff, Carter orders the mobsters out of the boarding house.

"Put that away, you know you won't use it," says one of the gangsters as he retreats.

"The gun, he means," adds the other.

Long hair, thick sideburns and shiny miniskirts establish the movie as a period piece. So do the frequent and clearly dated references to pornography. In the opening scene, Carter and his London mob friends are watching a pornographic slide show—

black-and-white pictures popping up one after the other on a living room wall. Later, in Glenda's apartment, he watches a grainy porno movie from an eight-millimeter film reel she has set up in her bedroom. (Today, it's all in color and, thanks to the Internet, available to almost anyone with a computer.)

Carter gives up bits and pieces about himself as he interacts with his brother's old friends and associates. But his most telling line comes after his brother Frank's prostitute girlfriend, Margaret (Dorothy White), makes a disparaging remark about her late boyfriend.

"Frank wasn't like that," he says. "I'm the villain in the family."

The porno movie ends up being an important plot device. It helps Carter understand who killed his brother and why. Once he's certain, it's simply a matter of tracking them down and sending them on their way. Employing cold, calculating but controlled fury—along with a gun, a knife and a hypodermic needle loaded with enough heroin to snuff out one of his targets—Carter becomes a one-man hit machine.

Totally focused and completely amoral, he is never in doubt about what he will do and remains unfazed as he goes about doing it.

◉ **HIT:** The pub scenes in the film are perfect. Anyone who has spent time in England can practically smell the dank, smoky and boozy atmosphere that the settings expertly convey.

✖ **MISS:** Carter is a tough guy. We get that. But there are just too many scenes in which he puts himself at risk and other tough guys pass on the chance to take him out.

🎞 **PIVOTAL SCENE:** After Carter beds Glenda, he watches a porno movie in her apartment. The movie, *Teacher's Pet*, shows a young girl being seduced. The girl is his niece Doreen, Frank's daughter. Carter then surmises that his brother was killed because he found out about the film and went after those who had forced his daughter into it.

🗨 **BEST LINE:** When Carter confronts Paice at a racetrack, his old acquaintance asks what brings him back to town. Carter says he's visiting relatives. Paice says that's nice, to which Carter replies coldly, "It would be . . . if they were still alive."

✎ **WHAT THEY WROTE AT THE TIME:** "There is nobody to root for but the smoothly dressed sexual athlete and professional killer (Michael Caine) in this English gangland picture, which is so calculatedly cool and soulless and nastily erotic that it seems to belong to a new genre of virtuoso viciousness."—Pauline Kael, *New Yorker*

☺ **GOOF:** During a foot chase leading up to his murder, Paice loses a shoe in the mud along the waterfront. In the next shot, with Carter in hot pursuit, he has both shoes on.

➡ **DON'T FAIL TO NOTICE:** When Carter is riding in the train from London to Newcastle at the start of the film, he is reading *Farewell, My Lovely*, the Raymond Chandler novel that became one of the best film noir movies of all time.

🍮 **BET YOU DIDN'T KNOW:** There were two remakes of *Get Carter*, neither very good. Sylvester Stallone starred in the 2000 version, set in America, with Michael Caine making a cameo appearance. A less-than-memorable 1972 movie, *Hit Man* starring Bernie Casey and Pam Grier, also retold the story, only this time within the blaxploitation genre.

🎬 **CASTING CALL:** Director Mike Hodges originally wanted Ian Hendry for the role of Carter, then decided on Caine. Hendry, who played Paice instead, was never happy with the switch. The tension between the two characters in the film reflects the friction between the two actors on the set.

⚰ **BODY COUNT:** Seven. Eight if you count the murder of Frank Carter, which happens before the movie begins but is the driving force behind all the action.

49 THE BIG HEAT (1953–NR)

STARS: GLENN FORD, LEE MARVIN, GLORIA GRAHAME | DIRECTOR: FRITZ LANG

There's a popular character in film noir efforts—the femme fatale, or deadly woman. She's the vamp who ensnares all men she encounters, eventually destroying their lives.

The Big Heat, the last outstanding film by Austrian expatriate director Fritz Lang, takes that character and turns it over in several ways. In this case, the character is a guy—big-city cop Dave Bannion (Glenn Ford). And he isn't trying to destroy all the women he encounters; it just turns out that way.

Bannion is a tough-talking homicide detective investigating the suicide of another cop. He ques-

tions the dead man's widow, who makes up a phony story of how her husband shot himself because he had been suffering from an undiagnosed illness. Her tale sounds fishy.

We learn, well before Bannion does, that the dead officer had actually been racked with fear and guilt about being on the mob's payroll. Turns out, his unsympathetic widow has used his tell-all suicide note to blackmail the gangsters into continuing those payments to her.

As Bannion probes the case, he's told to slow down by the chief of police. When he goes to visit the city's most-influential businessman—who also runs the local crime syndicate—he's told that he'll lose his job and his life if he doesn't back off.

Of course he doesn't. And the bodies start dropping.

There's clip joint singer Lucy Chapman, who's seen talking with the detective at a bar. Next thing we know, she's tossed from a speeding car and found dead on the side of the road.

There's Bannion's wife, Katie (played by Jocelyn Brando, sister of Marlon). She goes to turn on the car and—BOOM!—she's like Ace Rothstein in the opening scene of *Casino*. Except that she doesn't survive.

There's Bertha, the venal widow, also shot dead after a visit from the detective. Considering her miserable demeanor, that might be a relief to everyone.

And there's Debby the gun moll (Gloria Grahame), who turns to our good cop after her mob boyfriend scalds her face with a pot of boiling coffee. Later, she gets shot four times, right through the mink coat.

As we said, Bannion wasn't aiming to harm these ladies (well, he does admit that he considered offing the cop's wife). But he does bear some responsibility in each case. Two are killed because they trust the rackets-fighting detective. A third dies because he blabs about their meeting. And his wife? Being married to Bannion was her death sentence.

Turns out, it's all a big conspiracy. The mob runs the entire town. The police commissioner plays poker with the thugs. A viscous, silk-pajamas-wearing boss named Mike Lagana (Alexander Scourby) gives orders to everyone, from the city council on down.

Except, of course, for our inviolable detective. Initially, Bannion is investigating the suicide as a professional cop. After his wife's murder, his motive becomes revenge.

The brilliant director Lang is also in this book for his 1931 film *M*, which actually portrays gangsters in a favorable light. This time, Lang said his objective was different. "I wanted to expose organized crime for what it is," he said, "the enormous parasite that threatens to devour everybody."

In one strong scene, Bannion pushes his way into Lagana's mansion as the mob boss's daughter is hosting a socialite dance. As Bannion tries to ask questions about one of the murders, Lagana dismisses him by saying he doesn't "like dirt dragged into my home."

"Oh, we don't talk about those things in this house, do we?" chides Bannion. "No, it's too elegant, too respectful. No place for a stinking cop. It's only a place for a hoodlum who built this house out of 20 years of corruption and murder. You couldn't plant enough flowers around here to kill the smell."

Then he punches out one of Lagana's bodyguards for good measure.

Throughout, *The Big Heat* boasts that kind of hard-boiled, if now clichéd, tough-guy dialogue. Ford, with his perfect Ronald Reagan hair and nice-guy face, is outstanding as the straight-arrow cop who evolves into a reactionary. He remains unmindful of the fact that his own habit of rushing in is responsible for the deaths that surround him.

Actually, that obliviousness strengthens the film. Regardless of the cost, he just presses on with his mission.

◉ **HIT:** Lee Marvin, at 29, is menacing in his breakout role as Vince Stone, the misogynist hood who snuffs out a cigarette on one young woman and splashes that boiling pot of coffee on his girlfriend. "He's a scary foil," wrote critic Roger Ebert, "with his long, lean face and his ugly-handsome scowl."

⊗ **MISS:** Lang aims to contrast the hard-edged clean cop vs. underworld theme by showing slices of Bannion's idyllic suburban home life. But the domestic scenes, with the perky apron-clad wife and sugary young daughter, come across like a lame 1950s TV show—*Leave it to Beaver*, if Mrs. Cleaver were to get firebombed.

✎ **WHAT THEY WROTE AT THE TIME:** "The present vogue for sadism and violence reaches some kind of apex in *The Big Heat*, a truly gruesome crime thriller. There is, of course, no excuse at all for a film like *The Big Heat*."—Robert Kass, *Catholic World*

✔ REALITY CHECK: Several people get shot in this film, but there's not one visible drop of blood. In the most egregious example, the suicidal cop holds a gun to his own temple, fires and drops dead at his desk. When he's discovered, there's no splatter and no apparent tissue damage.

◎ REPEATED WATCHING QUOTIENT: There are enough other great noir films that you probably won't get around to this one a second time.

🎬 PIVOTAL SCENE: After a few days of tension, highlighted by some threatening phone calls from mobsters, our hero and his wife decide what they need is a night on the town.

Bannion's wife heads out to pick up the babysitter while he puts their daughter to bed. Just as he begins reading a story ("Three little kittens have lost their mittens. . . ."), the bedroom window fills with a flash and there is a loud explosion offscreen.

The car bomb meant to kill the nosy cop has instead killed his wife. Bannion mourns—for an extremely short period of time—and then redoubles his efforts to squash the mob. Now it's not just business; now it's personal.

➡ DON'T FAIL TO NOTICE: Many of the scenes are shot from Bannion's point of view. Fritz Lang said he filmed it that way so that the audience involuntarily followed Bannion and identified with him.

◀ CASTING CALL: Columbia Pictures executives wanted Marilyn Monroe (who was under contract to 20th Century Fox) for the role of Debby, the tart with the heart of gold. They balked when they heard Fox's asking price.

The role instead went to Gloria Grahame, who forged her career playing a floozie (town hottie Violet in *It's a Wonderful Life,* Ado Annie—the girl who can't say no—in *Oklahoma!*). In other news, Grahame was married four times, including once to director Nicholas Ray and later to his son (her stepson), Anthony Ray.

🔫 VIOLENCE LEVEL: There's no blood, as we said. And the really violent stuff—the car bombing, the hurled hot coffee—all takes place offscreen.

🎩 BET YOU DIDN'T KNOW: William P. McGivern's original *Saturday Evening Post* serial, on which the movie is based, had several black characters. All were removed for the film, an unfortunate nod to the prejudice of the times. McGivern, by the way, later wrote for the TV cop show *Kojak.*

❞ BEST LINE: Vince: "Hey, that's nice perfume."
Debby: "Something new. It attracts mosquitoes and repels men."
Vince: "Well, it doesn't chase me."
Debby: "It's not designed to."

🎞 "I KNOW THAT GAL": Doris, the unfortunate B-girl who has a cigarette extinguished on her wrist, is played by Carolyn Jones. She would later don a black fright wig and witch's costume to play the sexy Morticia on the 1960s TV hit *The Addams Family.*

✵ IF YOU LIKED THIS, YOU'LL LIKE: *The Salton Sea* (2002), the story of a man whose wife is murdered, causing him to drift into a world where he is antagonized by both drug dealers and undercover police agents.

⚜ BODY COUNT: Four on-screen, another two offscreen.

50 MIDNIGHT RUN (1988–R)

STARS: ROBERT DE NIRO, CHARLES GRODIN, DENNIS FARINA, YAPHET KOTTO
DIRECTOR: MARTIN BREST

This is *The Odd Couple* on the run from the mob.

And it works primarily—if not entirely—because of the pairing of Robert De Niro, as bounty hunter Jack Walsh, and Charles Grodin, as the nerdy accountant Jonathan "the Duke" Mardukas. The story line is outrageous and the twists and turns along the way consistently challenge our credulity. But De Niro and Grodin are so good together that we happily go along for the ride.

Director Martin Brest took a screenplay from George Gallo and was smart enough to let the actors run with it. Some of the best scenes are built around their improvisations. The "litmus configuration" routine, which Walsh and the Duke use to

scam a bartender out of a stack of $20 bills so that the broke duo can continue their journey, came out of the heads of the actors.

So, too, did most of the dialogue when they are in the boxcar of a freight train discussing whether they could ever be friends. The conversation about having sex with a chicken and the back-and-forth between Walsh and the Duke sound so natural because the two actors were just winging it.

Their laughter, at their situation and at one another, comes across as spontaneous and genuine. And it apparently was.

Walsh is an ex-Chicago cop who becomes a bounty hunter because he finds the work more honorable. His back story, which comes out slowly and provides the Duke with lots of conversational fodder, is that Walsh had to leave the Chicago PD after he was set up by a local heroin dealer and a bunch of corrupt cops. Walsh was one of the few men in blue not on the take from the dealer. He lost both his career and his marriage, then headed for Los Angeles where he hooked up with bail bondsman Eddie Moscone (played to frantic perfection by Joe Pantoliano).

the Duke is another matter. He was an accountant who unknowingly went to work for the mob and helped Las Vegas wiseguy Jimmy Serrano (Dennis Farina) launder millions in dirty money. When he finally realized what was going on, the Duke started playing fast and loose with the mob's cash, embezzling $15 million and giving a lot of it to needy causes.

The movie opens with the Duke in hiding. Arrested for embezzlement, he has skipped out on a $500,000 bond posted by Moscone. The bail bondsman has five days to find the Duke and get him to Los Angeles, or he's out his half-million.

Looking to finance his dream of changing careers and opening a coffee shop, Walsh takes the assignment after Moscone promises to pay him $100,000 if he can locate and return the Duke.

Both the FBI and the mob also are interested in finding the loquacious accountant, but for decidedly different reasons. The FBI wants the Duke to testify for the government in a racketeering case being built against Serrano. The mob, on the other hand, wants the Duke dead.

Walsh finds the Duke in New York, handcuffs him and begins what he figures will be a quick trip home and a fast 100 grand.

But the Duke's fear of flying—"I have aviaphobia," he says—scuttles Walsh's plan to take the red eye to L.A. and sets the road movie in motion. Instead of first class on a jet, they spend a week on the run, ducking bullets, mobsters, Feds and a rival bounty hunter.

They travel by train, by car, by bus. They shoot the rapids near a Texas border town, have a brief encounter with a crop duster and hotwire a pickup truck.

De Niro, who chose *Midnight Run* because he

wanted to do a comedy, is perfect as the cynical, seen-it-all tough guy who just wants to cash in. He doesn't quite know what to make of the Duke, but a part of him is fascinated by the financial felon. Against his better judgment, he ends up telling him most of his life story, including his plans for the future.

"As your accountant, I would strongly advise against it," the Duke says when Walsh mentions that he wants to open a coffee shop.

"You're not my accountant," says Walsh, shaking his head at the matter-of-fact audacity of the guy he has in handcuffs.

Grodin, in a performance that underscores how good he is as a character actor, turns the Duke into the perfect sounding board for the pent-up anger and frustration that drives Walsh. In a review that appeared in the *Washington Post*, Hal Hinson hailed the brilliance of Grodin's work in *Midnight Run*.

"Grodin functions as a kind of kvetchy Greek chorus; he comments on the action as it's taking place," Hinson wrote. "As the Duke (has anyone in the movies ever been more inappropriately nicknamed?), Grodin is a kind of actor-alchemist. He does more with less than perhaps any movie actor working. He's a genius at minimalistic embroidery, and his performance exists almost entirely in the tiniest inflections, in half-whispered line readings that seem like thought balloons floating over the actor's head."

The trip from New York to Los Angeles takes all of five days. And along the way, Walsh and the Duke become buddies. *We* see their friendship develop, but *they* don't really know it until the final scene.

That scene, in the LAX Airport, caps a series of plot twists that involve all the principle players, including Serrano, FBI Agent Alonzo Mosely (Yaphet Kotto) and rival bounty hunter Marvin Dorfler (John Ashton).

Walsh succeeds in what he set out to do. He gets the Duke back to L.A. before Moscone's deadline has expired. And he also extracts revenge on the drug dealer who cost him his job, his career and so much more back in Chicago. That dealer was Serrano, the mobster whose money the Duke had stolen.

What Walsh doesn't do is collect the bounty. And that adds a nice twist to a buddy movie that works despite its outrageous plotline.

◉ **HIT:** One of the movie's most telling and touching subplots is foreshadowed with Walsh's continual attempt to get his broken wristwatch to work. He is constantly tapping it and shaking it to get it to work, but he never takes it off. The idea was De Niro's—another example of the great improvisation here—and without giving away too much, it's a highly effective visual that says a lot about the character.

✪ **MISS:** The embezzlement charge against the Duke is never clearly explained, nor does it make sense. If he's cooking the books for the mob, then the front companies he worked for would never want the exposure that a criminal case would bring, so they'd never press charges. Conversely, the Feds would move in once the Duke's role as an embezzler was uncovered, using that crime as the leverage to get him to cooperate. So the premise for the entire movie is flawed. But without it, of course, there is no bail, no bail bond, no bounty and no road trip. So we just go with it.

❞ **BEST LINE:** During one of several conversations in which the Duke is clearly driving him nuts, a frustrated Walsh looks at his bounty and says, "I have two words for you: Shut the fuck up."

☺ **GOOF:** After the Duke convinces Jack that he can't fly, they decide to head to Los Angeles by train. But they pick up the train at Grand Central Station in New York. Westbound trains out of New York leave from Penn Station.

◀ **CASTING CALL:** Paramount Pictures, which originally had the rights to the movie, wanted to change the gender of the accountant and suggested Cher, with an eye toward romantic tension between Walsh and his bounty as they head west. Brest rejected that idea and also chose to go with Grodin over Paramount's suggestion that Robin Williams get the role of the Duke. Brest was right on both scores. *Midnight Run* was remade as *The Bounty Hunter* in 2010 with a female, Jennifer Aniston, cast as the bail jumper. Gerard Butler, playing her ex-husband, was the bounty hunter bringing her in. The movie bombed.

✎ **WHAT THEY WROTE AT THE TIME:** "A buddy movie brim full of thrills, spills and honestly affecting pathos. . . . Grodin is the perfect straight man for De Niro, whose remarkable range as an actor allows him to switch instantly from knock-about farce to moments of painful insight or an emotionally wrenching encounter with his ex-wife and the daughter he scarcely knows. The last great screen actor who could work such magic without skipping a beat was Spencer Tracy."—Bruce Williamson, *Playboy*

🔫 **VIOLENCE LEVEL:** Lots of shooting and punching, but most of the action is more comic-book than graphic.

☠ **BODY COUNT:** Four.

51 MESRINE: KILLER INSTINCT
MESRINE: PUBLIC ENEMY #1
(2008–R)

STARS: VINCENT CASSEL, CÉCILE DE FRANCE, GÉRARD DEPARDIEU, ELENA ANAYA, LUDIVINE SAGNIER, MATHIEU AMALRIC | DIRECTOR: JEAN-FRANÇOIS RICHET

Jacques Mesrine (pronounced MAY-reen) was one of the most notorious criminals in France during the 1960s and 1970s. Part John Dillinger, part John Gotti, the egotistical bank robber, kidnapper and escape artist became a hero in the French tabloids and in the working class slums of cities like Paris and Marseilles despite his penchant for violence and cruelty.

Early in his career, he fashioned himself a Robin Hood, although all indications are that the only people with whom he shared his ill-gotten gains were his criminal associates and a string of beautiful mistresses.

Later, he postured as an urban revolutionary, spouting the ideology and striking a pose in support of the Red Brigade in Italy, the Baader-Meinhof gang in West Germany and the Palestinians in the Mideast.

In fact, Mesrine never robbed from the rich to give to the poor. And his politics, at best, were muddled.

But much like Billy the Kid or Al Capone in America, he captured the populist imagination of the French, becoming a larger-than-life character—a rogue and bandit admired for flaunting authority and living life on his own terms. Like those two

American outlaw icons, he was a darling of the media. His life also served as the subject of this four-hour, two-part biopic from director Jean-François Richet, which, for the purposes of our book, we will consider as one film.

The French director's work is somewhat familiar to American audiences. Richet did the 2005 remake of *Assault on Precinct 13*, starring Laurence Fishburne and Ethan Hawke. He also directed several French films before taking on the subject of Jacques Mesrine.

This two-parter is loosely based on the autobiographical novel *Killer Instinct* written by Mesrine during one of his many prison stays. But as reviewer Julien Allen is quick to point out, Mesrine was "a man whose recollection of the events of his life was as distorted by a need to please his readership as it was by his own colossal ego."

Vincent Cassel stars in the title role and his performance is the best part of both episodes. Even when the plot falters, Cassel's Mesrine remains mesmerizing. We may not always have a clear understanding of why something is happening or what has motivated him to act, but it is always fascinating to watch Cassel as the archcriminal.

The French star had a key role in *Eastern Promises*, playing Kirill, the dysfunctional son of a Russian mob boss in London. He also played Baron François Toulour, The Night Fox, in *Ocean's Twelve* and *Ocean's Thirteen*.

Another familiar face for American audiences is Gérard Depardieu, who plays Mesrine's mob boss and mentor Guido. Like most of the characters who get close to Mesrine, Guido is gunned down in one of the dozen or so shootouts that take place in the films. The Paris underworld of the 1960s and 1970s was, at least as depicted here, not unlike Chicago in the 1920s.

Cassel, in an interview before the American release in 2010, was asked how he thought the movies would be received in the United States.

"There are two different factors that might seduce an American audience," he said. "It's violent and it's French."

The movies won three Cesars (the French equivalent of Oscars)—including Best Director and Best Actor. But critics have complained that *Mesrine* is, in fact, too Americanized; that the savoir-faire and sang-froid that are the marks of earlier French gangster films like *Breathless* and *Touchez Pas au Grisbi* have been sacrificed here. Richet, those critics argue, chose action over character and plot development.

It's a valid point.

There is, without doubt, plenty of action, and that, coupled with Cassel's performance, makes both films worth watching.

Part One opens with some tricky camera angles and, without using any dialogue, sets up the 1979 ambush in Paris in which Mesrine was killed. But before the shooting starts, the movie goes into flashback and we're in Algeria where a young Mesrine, a French soldier, is forced to take part in the torture and murder of suspected Algerian terrorists.

The Algerian war is an emotional and political touchstone for the French and audiences in France would clearly draw conclusions and begin to frame a mental picture of Mesrine from the events depicted there. We're not sure an American audience would draw the same picture.

The movie bounces from place to place, not only geographically but also intellectually.

"Times change, a man doesn't," Mesrine tells Guido early in the evolving story. But the narrative never backs up that platitude.

There are murders, bank robberies and kidnappings—most based on actual events—as Mesrine embraces a life of crime. He goes on the lam in Canada, where he is jailed and escapes from a horrific prison. He and a fellow inmate then try to break other prisoners out in a frontal assault that seems outlandish, except that it, too, is based on fact.

A brief foray into the United States, more robberies and then back to France for Part Two and a series of escapades as Mesrine and his associates crisscross the country, robbing banks and casinos. Mesrine was known as the "man of a thousand faces" because of the many disguises he used in pulling off his heists. For one caper, he and an associate pose as police detectives from Paris in order to scope out a small police station in the south of France where they plan a casino heist.

This heist, like so many others, ends with bullets flying and bodies dropping.

There is also an interview with a reporter lifted almost verbatim from an actual transcript. Mesrine wines and dines the female journalist and offers insights into his philosophy and his motivation.

"Why are you doing this?" the reporter asks, referring to a crime spree Mesrine has launched.

"Because . . . I don't like laws and I don't want to be a slave of the alarm clock my whole life," he replies.

Then borrowing a line from Willie Sutton, he smiles and very charmingly says, "I'm looking for the money in the places where they are—in banks."

At the end of the interview, he offers the reporter a glass of champagne.

But not every relationship with the media turned out as well for either the reporter or for Mesrine.

Toward the end of his run, there is a gruesome scene after he lures another reporter from a right-wing conservative publication to a meeting. The reporter, Jacques Tillier, had written a less-than-flattering piece about the bandit. Inexplicably, Tillier thinks he is going to be granted an exclusive interview. Instead, he is taken to an abandoned quarry where he is ordered to strip and then is brutally beaten, shot and left for dead. Two scenes later, we learn that the reporter has survived, which seems to be a cinematic device.

In fact, it actually happened that way.

In its October 22, 1979 edition, *People* magazine detailed the assault with a story headlined "Fugitive Killer Jacques Mesrine Teaches a Grisly Lesson in Cruelty." The article described Mesrine as "an ex-soldier turned killer and stick-up man" who "has courted the spotlight like a preening jambon." ("Jambon" is French for ham.)

The beating and attempted murder of Tillier, *People* wrote, had turned public opinion against Mesrine, noting that "France's romanticization of its Robin Hood was over."

Two weeks later, police in Paris set up the trap that was supposed to lead to Mesrine's arrest. Instead—and the portrayal in the movie seems to support this theory—France's leading criminal was brutally gunned down by a team of police riflemen who fired repeatedly and without provocation as the elusive bandit sat helplessly behind the wheel of his car stopped at a traffic light.

⊙ **HIT:** If you're looking for the typical French existential gangster film, this isn't it. But it's one hell of an action story and the fact that most of it is true makes it well worth watching. Richet also does a great job recreating the mood of 1970s France.

⊗ **MISS:** We like the typical French existential gangster film and, in that sense, *Mesrine* fails to deliver. But *vive la différence*.

🍎 **BET YOU DIDN'T KNOW:** Cassel gained 44 pounds before filming began and Richet shot the nine-month production in reverse chronological order because Cassel knew that he would lose weight during filming. Both he and Richet wanted a heavier, stodgier Mesrine at the conclusion.

❞ **BEST LINE:** "No one kills me 'til I say so," Mesrine boasts during one of several outbursts early in Part One. The line captures the arrogance and fatalism that run through both movies. Mesrine knew how his life was going to end, he just didn't know where or when. But his enormous ego led him to believe he could determine his fate.

✏ **WHAT THEY WROTE AT THE TIME:** "Mr. Cassel's monumental performance fuses the cobra-like menace of the young Robert Mitchum with the whipsaw, shape-shifting (from wiry to bulbous) volatility of classic Robert De Niro, and lightens it with a cat burglar's grace and agility. . . . The movie is a virtual ode to a bad boy's fatal attraction for women who should know better but can't resist the thrill of dangerous attachment to a man who devotes the same intensity to sex that he does to robbing banks, killing policemen and escaping from prison."—Stephen Holden, *New York Times*

🔫 **VIOLENCE LEVEL:** Extremely high.

🔪 **BODY COUNT:** Twenty-plus. A series of major shootouts, in which bodies dropped from various angles, made it impossible to get an accurate count.

FRENCH GANGSTER FILMS

Back in 2010, *The Daily Beast* asked Martin Scorsese to list the gangster films that had the most significant impact on his work. Scorsese, one of America's greatest directors, talked about 15 films. Two of them were French.

Scorsese praised the style and the craftsmanship that French directors brought to their work. We've listed four French movies (*Mesrine, Parts I and II* count as a single entry) in our book's Top 100. But we'd be remiss not to recommend several others.

Gangster films play a rich part in the history of French cinema and most of the country's greatest directors and actors—from François Truffaut, Claude Lelouch and Claude Chabrol to Jean Gabin, Alain Delon and Yves Montand—have contributed to the genre.

The French underworld, however, is portrayed somewhat differently than the underworld we see in American or British films. There is less edge and more elegance.

The movies tap into the film noir heritage that is also so much a part of French cinema, but add twists from Jean-Paul Sartre's existentialism and André Malraux's *condition humaine*.

French gangsters are, by and large, introspective outlaws. And that introspection is often their undoing.

Here are five French films that ought to be seen by anyone interested in the gangster movie genre.

Touchez Pas au Grisbi (Don't Touch the Loot, 1954).

Jean Gabin (who starred in *Pepe le Moko*, which we rank in our Top 100) has been called the French Bogart and this film is one of the reasons. Gabin is Max, an aging and cynical wiseguy who has pulled off one of the biggest heists of his life and is now sitting on 50 million francs in gold bars.

He and his partner, Riton (René Dary), figure to retire. But Riton's ambitious girlfriend, Josy (Jeanne Moreau in one of her first films), has other ideas and other gangster loves.

Kidnapping, extortion and murder quickly follow as Max's retirement plans literally go up in smoke. The movie relaunched Gabin's career, which had waned following World War II. A review for a film retrospective in San Francisco captured the essence of the gangster character that Gabin made his own. Gabin, the reviewer wrote, "meshes suave elegance with tough-guy weariness."

Touchez Pas au Grisbi was one of the two French movies Scorsese singled out as having had a profound effect on his work.

Bob le Flambeur (Bob the Gambler, 1956).

Cards, dice, horses, casinos and Montemarte—that's the world of Bob Montagné (Roger Duchesne), an easygoing underworld gambler who is battling a streak of bad luck.

But he has a plan. He wants to rob the casino at Deauville and enlists his young protégé Paolo (Daniel Cauchy) and several other associates. Paolo is one of several men attracted to the young and easily bedded Anne (Isabella Corey), although Bob—being the gentleman gambler that he is—manages to resist her charms.

Anne, like so many of the women in French gangster films of this period, is there to be either seduced or ignored. And like so many of those women, she talks out of turn and undermines the heist.

Director Jean-Pierre Melville adds a nice twist to the denouement, however. As Bob waits for the planned 5 a.m. robbery, he begins to gamble. And he wins and wins and wins.

The police, tipped off about the heist by an informant who heard about it from Anne, swarm the casino parking lot as the robbers arrive. A shootout leaves several of them, including Paolo, dead. As Bob is put into a police car under arrest, two men from the casino come out and hand him his winnings.

Is his losing streak over, or has another just begun?

A Bout de Souffle (Breathless, 1960).

Directed by Jean-Luc Godard and based on a screenplay he wrote that was built around a story by Truffaut, this was the breakthrough movie for Jean-Paul Belmondo, who rode the New Wave French cinema to fame and fortune.

Belmondo built his career playing the quintessential rogue who chases money and women with equal gusto. Here, he is a small-time crook and sociopath who kills a motorcycle cop while stealing a car and then goes on the run through the streets of Paris as he woos an American journalism student (Jean Seberg) studying at the Sorbonne.

Belmondo's Michel Poiccard is conniving, reckless and oozes the blasé nature that defines French gangsterism. He bobs and weaves away from detectives and the media while trying to convince his young American love to flee with him to Italy.

They make it to bed, but not to Milan.

Le Doulos (The Snitch, 1962).

Scorsese called this film his "personal favorite" among French gangster movies and compared the code of conduct that its cops and its gangsters followed to "a code of honor like knights in the age of chivalry."

It's another Jean-Pierre Melville film, and this time the director tells the story from the perspective of his two central figures, Maurice (Serge Reggiani) and Silien (Jean-Paul Belmondo). Just released from prison, Maurice kills a friend and steals the jewels the friend had stashed from an earlier heist (jewelry robberies are a big part of the French underworld, if the cinema is any reflection of reality). He then teams with Silien to plan a break-in and robbery at a wealthy estate.

But Silien is both a crook and a police informant.

Le Doulos explores that code of honor that Scorsese mentioned and plays Silien's friendship and loyalty against his instinct for self-preservation. Melville described the underworld he created as one populated by characters who are "two-faced" and characters who are "false."

Le Cercle Rouge (The Red Circle, 1970).

This police procedural teamed Alain Delon with Yves Montand in a jewel heist caper that, as in so many other French gangster films, goes awry. There's a dogged police inspector, Mattei (André Bouvril), who comes right off the pages of *Les Misérables* and a cynical chief of police who has no time or tolerance for thieves or, it seems, the rest of humanity.

"All men are guilty," he says. "They're born innocent, but it doesn't last."

The movie starts slowly. The first half of the film is more character study than action drama. But it picks up steam as Delon and his associates move to Paris, set up the heist and then are betrayed by a fellow gangster who doesn't want to go to jail. The exquisitely coordinated robbery is reminiscent of the one in *Rififi*, a film in our Top 100.

Lots of trench coats, cigarettes and meetings in Paris nightclubs.

52 HIGH SIERRA (1941–NR)

STARS: HUMPHREY BOGART, IDA LUPINO | DIRECTOR: RAOUL WALSH

Before *High Sierra*, Hollywood's gangsters were not just black-and-white on celluloid; they were equally definitive in their morality—or, rather, immorality. There was nothing sympathetic about Paul Muni as Tony Camonte in *Scarface* and no doubt where James Cagney's Tom Powers stood in *The Public Enemy*.

This movie, a star vehicle for Humphrey Bogart, helped change all that. Adapted by John Huston from a novel by W. R. Burnett, *High Sierra* depicts Bogart's character of Roy "Mad Dog" Earle as a bank robber and, yes, a killer. But there's another side to this career criminal—decency, compassion, a yearning to reform.

We've since seen it dozens of times in more recent years, from young Michael Corleone's dream of taking the family legitimate to Jules Winnfield talking of giving up the life to walk the earth in *Pulp Fiction*. But it started here.

The movie opens with Earle, who's been

serving a long sentence for bank robbery, gaining a pardon from the corrupt governor of Illinois (we think his name was Blagojevich). The mobster who sets up the release, Earle's old boss Big Mac, summons him to California for a heist. There is a poorly guarded resort near Los Angeles full of wealthy patrons who are dripping money and jewelry.

Earle doesn't hesitate to accept the job. Robbing people is what he knows. But on his drive west he meets a sweet elderly couple—identified only as Ma and Pa—and their 20ish granddaughter, Velma. Earl and Pa hit it off. The old man explains how he lost his farm in Ohio and is relocating to Los Angeles. You get a sense from the conversation that Earle's family was also dispossessed in his youth.

More than that, Earle finds himself falling for Velma, an innocent young thing who limps because she was born with a clubfoot. Our tough guy is both sympathetic and smitten. He decides to fund an operation to mend her with his potential earnings from the L.A. gig. And before long, he's holding her hand under the starry California skies.

(On a side note, actress Joan Leslie, who plays Velma, was 16 years old when *High Sierra* was filmed. Bogart was 41. Hollywood sure had a different attitude toward romance with minors back then.)

Anyway, Earle checks into a California fishing camp to set up the heist. He is joined by two small-time twits, Red and Babe, and a dime-a-dance gal named Marie (Ida Lupino) whom they picked up along the way. (What ever happened to taxi dancers anyway?) To be honest, the movie bogs down in the middle, with Marie falling for Earle despite his ambivalence about her. As love triangles go, this does not rank with Bogey's later effort in *Casablanca*.

More importantly, you get the sense that Mad Dog Earle has lost his zest for crime. Something about those rubes from Ohio apparently has him thinking about buying a plot of land and settling down with their perky granddaughter. Very *American Gothic*.

From there, things go awry. Earl funds Velma's successful foot operation, but she rejects his romantic overtures after her jackass of a boyfriend from back home shows up in California. The resort robbery goes off, but during the getaway, Red and Babe get killed in a car crash. The inside man on the job blabs to the cops. And Mad Dog Earle becomes a hunted man.

Director Raoul Walsh (*White Heat, The Roaring Twenties*) makes use of the great scenery around Mount Whitney during this part of the movie. With police in pursuit, Roy drives up into the Sierra Nevada Mountains until a barricade blocks his way. He continues on foot, hiding behind a boulder as the cops draw near.

Of course, Earle's got to die. He spends his final moments talking to his loyal mutt (more about that in a moment) and writing a note that would exonerate Marie from any of his crimes—except the note blows away as he is gunned down by a sharpshooter.

"Well, well, Big Shot Earle," says one of the cops after his lifeless body tumbles down the mountain. "He ain't much now, is he?"

Perhaps not. But because of the way Huston wrote the role and the way Bogart plays it, you'll find yourself mourning Big Shot Earle's failed attempt at redemption.

⊙ **HIT:** The final 10 minutes of *High Sierra* set the early standard for movie pursuit scenes. The car chase—while not up to, say, *The French Connection* or *Bullitt*—was ahead of its time in 1941. And the two-day standoff in the mountains, with crowds gathering and radio broadcasters setting up shop, really builds the tension.

⊗ **MISS:** Hollywood's treatment of African Americans in the 1940s was downright despicable. The film's only black character, a fishing camp aide named Algernon (Willie Best) is portrayed as a shuffling, napping, subservient Stepin Fetchit, whose eyes go crossed when they aren't popping out of his head in panic.

✎ **WHAT THEY WROTE AT THE TIME:** "What makes *High Sierra* more than a Grade B melodrama is its sensitive delineation of Gangster Earle's character. Superbly played by Bogart, Earle is a complex human being: A farmer boy who turned mobster, a gunman with a string of murders on his record who still is shocked when newsmen call him 'Mad Dog.' He is kind to the mongrel dog that travels with him, befriends a taxi dancer who becomes his moll and goes out of his way to help a crippled girl. All Roy Earle wants is freedom. He finds it for good on a lonely peak in the mountains."—*Time*

CASTING CALL: Bogart coveted the role, believing that playing this multifaceted character would help move him into the upper echelon of stars. Warner Brothers had other ideas. Paul Muni was first cast for the lead, but hated the script and dropped out. The studio next turned to George Raft. Bogart, hearing that news, secretly went to his pal Raft and suggested that the movie would hurt Raft's chances of changing his gangster image. Raft agreed and declined the role, which left it for . . . Bogart. As he anticipated, *High Sierra* ended up being the movie that made him a star.

BET YOU DIDN'T KNOW: As *High Sierra* was being filmed in 1940, Bogart was called before the House Un-American Activities Committee to explain his so-called Communist leanings. His sin? Donating a few bucks to striking lettuce workers. Bogart's name was cleared. He went back to shooting with a rage that, according to director Walsh, released itself in his acting.

DON'T FAIL TO NOTICE: Pard, the stray terrier mutt that Earle adopts at the fishing camp. The dog comes with a warning: everyone who has owned him has come to a bad end. Pard is listed in the credits as Zero the Dog and was, in fact, Bogart's pet in real life.

REPEATED WATCHING QUOTIENT: Anything with Bogart is worth a second look but, to be honest, this film doesn't make our Bogey Top 10.

BEST LINE: "Doc" Banton (Henry Hull), the mob's faux-physician, on greeting Earle: "Hello, Roy. Last time I saw you was when I was taking slugs out of Lefty Jackson's chest. Boy, those were the good old days."

REALITY CHECK: We're lacking medical degrees, but we're awestruck by how a girl can live 20 years with a clubfoot, undergo surgery by a shady nonlicensed doctor and be up and dancing the Lindy in what appears to be a matter of days.

VIOLENCE LEVEL: Very low. A couple of punches, a few shootings. Not a drop of blood.

"I KNOW THAT GUY": The kindly grandpa of clubfooted Velma is played by Henry Travers, best known as Clarence the angel from *It's a Wonderful Life*. He's still working on getting those wings.

IF YOU LIKED THIS, YOU'LL LIKE: *They Drive by Night*, a 1940 murder story involving wildcat truckers that first teamed up Bogart, Lupino and Walsh.

BODY COUNT: Five. The hoodoo dog survives, ready to spread his bad luck on someone else.

53 SNATCH (2000–R)

STARS: BRAD PITT, BENICIO DEL TORO, DENNIS FARINA, JASON STATHAM, ALAN FORD
DIRECTOR: GUY RITCHIE

This is the second of Guy Ritchie's madcap mob capers.

And Brad Pitt's performance as Mickey O' Neil, the Irish gypsy, is the biggest reason for watching it.

Pitt is a damn good actor, especially when he is portraying a slightly off-center character. He demonstrated this with his performance as a stoner in *True Romance* and his turn as a whacked-out, paranoid apostle of doom in *Twelve Monkeys*. We also liked him in *The Mexican*, but that's another story.

One of the pretty-boy actors who came on the scene in the 1990s along with Christian Slater and Johnny Depp, Pitt has succeeded in spite of his looks, not because of them. Pitt brings a cockeyed, can-you-freakin'-believe-it attitude to the screen. And he delivers it here with the often-incomprehensible accent of an Irish pikey, a vagabond traveler who lives life on his own terms.

But that's part of the joke in *Snatch,* a comic book-like story of a jewel heist, an illegal boxing match, a gangster who feeds body parts to pigs, violent mobsters, bumbling bookies and a dog.

Told rapid-fire (Ritchie is clearly aiming for the MTV generation) with time overlaps and occasional flashbacks, *Snatch* works because it doesn't try to be more than it is.

It's silly. It's funny. Sometimes it's downright hilarious.

The performances by the lead actors—and given the way the story meanders, it's sometimes hard to say exactly who has the lead—are almost stand-alone pieces. There are dozens of scenes that could be clipped, put up on a website and offered as five-minute comedy spots.

Alan Ford, as Brick Top, the yellow-toothed, pig-feeding crime kingpin, brings a sinister cynicism to his role. His matter-of-fact explanations of life in the underworld are humorous and chilling at the same time.

Take, for example, his ruminations on pigs, told to some hapless bookies who may or may not end up as pig feed.

"They will go through bone like butter," Brick Top says with a knowing glint in his eye. "So beware of any man who keeps a pig farm."

Jason Statham, as Turkish, the would-be boxing promoter who narrates the story, brings just the right mix of bravado and naïveté to his character. And several other members of the ensemble cast take turns in the spotlight.

Dennis Farina, as Cousin Avi Denovitz, is the New York hustler clearly out of place in London and totally lost in the city's turbulent—and to him, incomprehensible—underworld.

Rade Serbedzija is perfect as Boris the Blade, the Russian gangster whose quest for a stolen diamond creates the chaos.

And then there is Benicio Del Toro as gangster and jewel thief Franky Four Fingers.

The movie opens with the theft of an 84-carat diamond in Antwerp.

Franky and his associates dress as Hasidic rabbis to pull off the heist. Along the way, in the character of the rabbi, Franky explains the "error" that led to the virgin birth story in the Bible. The result, he says, is the Catholic Church.

There is no reverence in *Snatch*, but again, that's part of the movie's charm.

Sit back and enjoy.

This is not *The Godfather*.

But it never tries to be.

◉ **HIT:** The pacing is frantic, so don't try to dissect what's happening. Just let it flow. You can figure it out later.

⊗ MISS: The hit above is also the miss. Those who like to follow along and understand all the whys and wherefores as they unfold may find the overlapping plotlines and periodic flashbacks disconcerting.

✎ WHAT THEY WROTE AT THE TIME: "Ritchie began in music videos, and he brings a barreling energy to the whirligig; each sequence seems choreographed for maximum charge. And yet nothing slows a picture down more than non-stop relentlessness. A lot of the exhilaration in this film is indistinguishable from exhaustion. Ritchie's problem isn't a lack of ideas; it's a lack of discrimination. After a while, the various convoluted subplots begin to run into each other and it doesn't much matter whose head is being bashed in, or who's on the wrong end of a meat cleaver. Ritchie is so carried away by his facility that he loses sight of why we should bother looking at this spectacle in the first place. This may be one of the hazardous offshoots of the music-video-trained generation of moviemakers; they confuse a diet of eye candy with a full meal."—Peter Rainer, *New York* magazine

✔ REALITY CHECK: Those who have been there say that Pitt and the other actors who play the Irish gypsies have captured their accents, their body language and, most importantly, their attitude.

◉ REPEATED WATCHING QUOTIENT: There are enough laughs to make this worth revisiting, either at full length or just to catch a scene or two.

▣ PIVOTAL SCENE: The fire at the gypsy camp that kills Mickey's mother is Brick Top's attempt to keep everyone in line. It sets in motion a chain of events that carry the kinetic plot full circle. The first time through, we didn't see it coming.

◀ CASTING CALL: Ritchie makes a cameo appearance as a man reading a newspaper in one of the bar scenes.

⌐ VIOLENCE LEVEL: Very high, but hard to take seriously because the movie is constantly going for the laugh.

☺ "I KNOW THAT GUY": Stephen Graham, who plays Turkish's sidekick Tommy, portrayed Shang in *Gangs of New York*. But he is probably best known to Americans as the young Al Capone in HBO's latest gangster saga, *Boardwalk Empire*.

❝ BEST LINE: A toss up between Bullet Tooth Tony's take on the madness going on around him—"You should never underestimate the predictability of stupidity"—and New York-based Cousin Avi's take on London—"Yes, London. You know: fish, chips, cup 'o tea, bad food, worse weather, Mary Fuckin' Poppins. London!"

⊕ IF YOU LIKED THIS, YOU'LL LIKE: *Lock, Stock and Two Smoking Barrels* (1998), which Ritchie also wrote and directed and in which he used some of the same actors, including Ford, Statham and Vinnie Jones.

⚔ BODY COUNT: Nineteen.

54 THE KILLING (1956–NR)

STAR: STERLING HAYDEN | DIRECTOR: STANLEY KUBRICK

There are two great reasons to see *The Killing*, Stanley Kubrick's 1956 caper film about a botched racetrack heist. First off, the movie served as inspiration for Quentin Tarantino's *Reservoir Dogs*, a film you should have spotted earlier in this book. And second, *The Killing* stands up as a solid work on its own.

It's a quick (85 minutes), suspenseful story with few wasted words or actions. It's got all the essential elements of a potboiler—plot twists and double-crosses, strong men and weaklings, sharp-talking crooks and one evil temptress.

First things first. Tarantino was turned on to *The Killing* as a young man working behind the register at a movie rental store. He fell in love with the film, especially for its time-arcing plotline that shows the robbery scheme from each participant's perspective. Years later, when Tarantino wrote the screenplay for *Reservoir Dogs*, he said, "I didn't go out of my way to do a rip-off of *The Killing*. But I did think of it as my *Killing*, my take on that kind of heist movie."

The similarities are certainly there. Both films, as we said, shift forward and backward in time, requiring a viewer to pay careful attention. Tarantino, by the way, had freer reign to time travel. Kubrick's bosses at United Artists sent his original version back, saying he needed to make it more linear and add a narrator for clarity.

Both films center on a crime gone wrong and show some of the participants after the fact, trying to figure out what happened. And both feature a group of gangsters, most of whom never met before, participating in a caper where they don't all get to learn each other's roles.

In *The Killing*, Mr. Blonde, Mr. Pink and the others are replaced by a crew of former cons and disaffected racecourse employees who come together for one crime—the multimillion dollar stickup of a California horse track. Their master-mind is the hardened Johnny Clay, who has just finished a five-year stint at Alcatraz and figures that if he's going to chance doing time again, the rewards ought to be worth the risk.

Clay is played by Sterling Hayden, an actor you'll immediately recognize from his portrayal of Capt. McCluskey in *The Godfather*. You know, the corrupt cop who breaks Michael Corleone's jaw and later ends up face down in his plate of veal at that Italian restaurant? He doesn't get shot in the throat in this movie, but things don't turn out much better for Johnny Clay.

His plan requires six men to act independently but in exact synchronization. One, a former wrestler, must create a distraction for police by starting a fight at the track's bar. Another, the bartender, must be part of that fake brawl, and also smuggle and hide a rifle into the track's storeroom. There's a Caspar Milquetoast betting-window teller who opens the door to let Johnny into that storeroom. And there's a psycho sniper whose job it is to create panic at the track by shooting the lead horse in Race 7.

Of course, there's also Johnny, who collects the hidden gun, forces his way into the office where track receipts are kept and emerges with $2 million in hard cash. The sixth plotter is a corrupt cop, whose role is to wait at a window below that office as Johnny hurls out the duffel bag of bills.

It all seems to work perfectly. But, of course, the movie's more fun if things unravel. And so they do.

We won't reveal all the details, but suffice it to say there's a woman involved. One of the basic tenets of 1950s gangster movies seems to be that no matter how brilliantly planned a caper might be, there's always a dame around to screw things up. In this case, the harlot is Sherry Peatty (Marie Windsor), the sexbomb wife of nerdy track teller George (Elisha Cook Jr.), who spends her days lounging around in lingerie and emasculating her mouse-like spouse with lines such as, "Sure you'll get rich, honey. Did you put the address on the envelope when you sent that letter to the North Pole?"

Anyway, Sherry is not to be trusted. And as good as Johnny's plan might be, he certainly would have been smart to do deeper background checks on the families of his makeshift crew.

The Killing is based on a suspense novel by Lionel White, a pulp-fiction author who had at least four of his books converted into films. Most of the taut dialogue was written by Jim Thompson (a.k.a. "The Dimestore Dostoevsky"), author of six books, including *The Grifters* and *The Getaway*, that were later translated into popular movies.

⊙ **HIT:** Actor Timothy Carey steals the show as Nikki, the seemingly stoned beatnik sociopath hired to shoot the racehorse. Carey spent his career portraying crazies and heavies. His twisted on-camera presence prompted big-time talents Elia Kazan and Marlon Brando to hire him; and his warped, real-life personality compelled both to fire him. Carey turned down roles in both *The Godfather* and *The Godfather: Part II*. In this movie, his glee at the chance to murder a horse is downright chilling.

⊗ **MISS:** The movie's ending—which we won't give away—is a real letdown. It's as if the scriptwriters, after carefully plotting the first 80 minutes, ran out of ideas and had the main character step off a curb and get run over by a taxi. He doesn't, but what you get isn't much better.

✎ **WHAT THEY WROTE AT THE TIME:** "At 27 Writer-Director Stanley Kubrick, in his third full-length picture, has shown more audacity with dialogue and camera than Hollywood has seen since the obstreperous Orson Welles went riding out of town on an exhibitors' poll. What's more, Director Kubrick made his entire movie for a price ($320,000) that would hardly pay for the lingerie in an Ava Gardner picture, with the result that *The Killing* seems likely to make a killing at the cash booths."—*Time*

🍎 **BET YOU DIDN'T KNOW:** Forget that cash-booth bonanza, this movie was a box-office dud. Still, its pace and originality gained its young director a reputation as a Hollywood comer. Actor Kirk Douglas especially liked his work and helped Kubrick land his next two jobs, directing Douglas in *Paths of Glory* and *Spartacus*.

◉ **REPEATED WATCHING QUOTIENT:** Watch it once on its own. Then watch it a second time, right before or after *Reservoir Dogs*.

➡ **DON'T FAIL TO NOTICE:** The cheap suitcase Johnny buys to transfer the stolen cash from the duffel bag. Hey, if we were trying to sneak around with $2 million, we wouldn't stow it in a $15 valise.

◀ **CASTING CALL:** Jack Palance and Victor Mature both vied for the lead role that went to Hayden.

🔫 **VIOLENCE LEVEL:** Pretty low, other than seeing a horse get shot.

❞ **BEST LINE:** Johnny Clay, sizing up the scheming Sherry: "Sure, you like money. You've got a great big dollar sign there where most women have a heart."

😀 **"I KNOW THAT GUY":** One of the spectators watching the racetrack brawl is a 34-year-old Rodney Dangerfield. He has no lines and is on-screen for about five seconds. Look two men to the left of Johnny Clay and you'll spot him popping his head out of the crowd.

⊕ **IF YOU LIKED THIS, YOU'LL LIKE:** *The Hard Word* (2002), an underrated Australian film starring Guy Pearce about three brothers out on bail coerced into committing a heist at a Melbourne racetrack.

🏍 **BODY COUNT:** Eight.

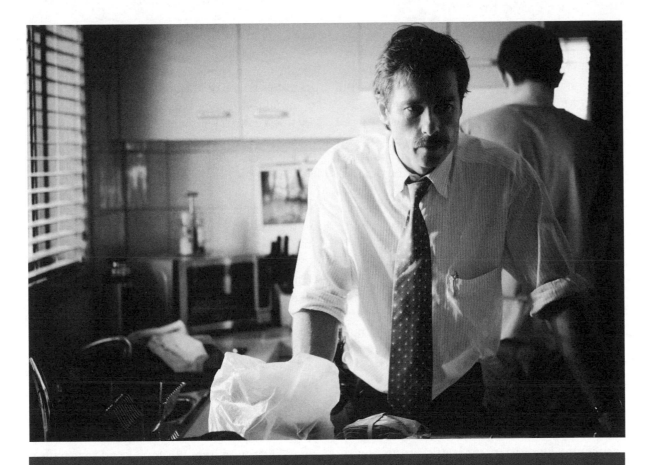

55 ANIMAL KINGDOM (2010–R)

STARS: JACKI WEAVER, GUY PEARCE, BEN MENDELSOHN
DIRECTOR: DAVID MICHOD

In the pantheon of evil movie mothers, Janine Cody has no peer. Overseeing a criminal family of bank robbers and drug dealers, the diminutive, 60ish charmer is, as Stephen Holden of the *New York Times* wrote, "a magnetic, seductive hybrid of Lady Macbeth and Ma Barker in the camouflage of a cheery suburban grandmother."

Cody, played by veteran actress Jacki Weaver, is the matriarchal centerpiece in this Australian crime drama, and she's the character you can't take your eyes off. Nicknamed "Smurf" by her three gangster sons, she cheerfully dotes on her boys, pulls another casserole out of the oven and bats blue eyes at suspicious detectives.

Moments later, there she is, blackmailing cops and ordering a hit that's as cold-blooded as Michael Corleone taking out his brother Fredo. "He's got to go," she says with an innocent smile and a shrug.

She's the queen bee. The puppeteer. The five-foot-tall, bleach-blond monster. And this den mother is the most dangerous predator in the jungle that is *Animal Kingdom*.

The first full-length feature by writer-director David Michod, *Animal Kingdom* is based on the story of Kath Pettingill (a.k.a. "Granny Evil") and her three sons—a criminal family that terrorized Melbourne in the 1980s. The Pettingills were involved in drug trafficking, arms dealing, prostitution and armed robbery. They were also tried but acquitted of the ambush murder of two policemen, a crime that is mimicked in the film.

Beyond that, we can't tell you how faithful *Animal Kingdom* is to real life. But the Pettingills—here the Codys—are portrayed as one warped brood. There's Pope (Ben Mendelsohn), a rodent-faced psychopath who's alternately laconic and bullying. There's Craig (Sullivan Stapleton), the tattooed, paranoid cokehead. And there's Darren (Luke Ford), the youngest and dimmest of the crew, who spends most of the movie nervously chewing his fingers.

Into this pack of wolves stumbles poor 17-year-old Josh (James Frecheville), whose mother—the daughter/sister of these sociopaths—opens the film by OD'ing on the couch. Her death places him in the care, if that's the word, of Grandma Smurf, whom he hasn't seen in years. Turns out Josh's mother, for all her problems, tried hard to keep him away from her side of the family.

Josh seems like a good-hearted, if sullen, teen. But what chance does he have in this lion's den? On his first day, he's goaded into aiming a loaded pistol at a mouthy motorist after a traffic dustup. Such is day-to-day life with the Codys.

Josh's uncles are eager to teach him the ropes. And to this end, *Animal Kingdom* does a good job of showing how the young really cannot question their circumstances. In this suburban household, crime is the norm. Josh is in no position to change that.

Compounding his difficulties, the timing of his entrance into the family (or Family) could not have been worse. The Codys are at war with Melbourne's out-of-control police armed robbery squad. Within days of Josh's arrival, Baz Brown (Joel Edgerton)—the conscience of the gang, if there is one—is shot point-blank by the rogue cops as he sits in his car.

That episode shifts the movie into a story of tit-for-tat revenge. As the bodies fall, Josh tries to stay neutral, until one particular killing forces him to take a side.

The troubled teenager draws the attention of Detective Nathan Leckie (Guy Pearce), a rare decent cop who wants to save Josh while also using him to ensnare his criminal family. Leckie earns the movie its title by giving Josh an interview-room speech about the hunter and the prey, the weak and the strong, the jungle's laws of survival. The cop starts to sound like Marlin Perkins after a while.

Animal Kingdom sets a languid pace and there are times in its 113 minutes when your interest may wane. It's a slow boil, but some dishes simmer best over low heat. Things get increasingly charged, right up to the film's tense and shocking ending.

◉ **HIT:** We place Jacki Weaver, as Grandma Smurf, on the Mount Rushmore of female movie gangsters, along with Faye Dunaway (*Bonnie and Clyde*), Helen Mirren (*The Long Good Friday*) and Gena Rowlands (*Gloria*). Except that Weaver gets to occupy the highest point of the peak. Weaver spent most of her career doing television work in her native Australia. She received a 2011 Best Supporting Actress Oscar nomination for her work in *Animal Kingdom*. Here's hoping it makes her a late-arriving film star.

⊗ **MISS:** We understand that Josh's character is written to be an affectless bystander to the horror going on around him. But too often Frecheville's deadpan delivery and blank stare seem almost catatonic. We felt like snapping our fingers to see if the young man was awake.

✎ **WHAT THEY WROTE AT THE TIME:** "The strength of *Animal Kingdom* is its slow-building fatalism; the criminals' luck runs out, but then finds depressing extension via an out-of-left-field collaborator. It's a movie that has very little faith in authority, not even in Guy Pearce's righteous detective. The only law here is Darwin's."—Joshua Rothkopf, *Time Out New York*

◉ **REPEATED WATCHING QUOTIENT:** Any scene with the monster granny deserves another look. You can fast-forward through the rest.

➡ **DON'T FAIL TO NOTICE:** The overly affectionate way that Grandma Smurf kisses her three sons. Downright creepy.

PIVOTAL SCENE: Midway through the film, Josh has already been questioned by the police. He is unsure where his loyalties lie, and his uncles grow increasingly suspicious of him.

Josh's girlfriend, Nicky, goes to the Cody house one night looking for him. Josh isn't there, but Darren and Pope ask her in. Pope invites her to shoot heroin with him, and the vulnerable girl doesn't have the strength to say no.

Pope injects Nicky, who goes into a soporific daze. He begins to question her: Have you been talking to the cops? Has Josh? What have you told them?

Nicky issues weak denials, but is too drugged to respond to Pope's satisfaction. Fearing any loose ends, Pope proceeds to smother the helpless girl to death. It's the most gut-wrenching scene in the film.

The next day, police find Nicky in an alley. They take Josh to show him the body. If there was any doubt which way he would go, it is over now.

BEST LINE: Josh, looking at the events in hindsight: "My mother kept me away from her family because she was scared. I didn't realize at the time that they were all scared, even if they just didn't show it."

"I KNOW THAT GUY": Take away his bouffant of a haircut, and you may recognize the actor playing sleazy lawyer Ezra as Dan Wyllie, the guy who also played Cackles the skinhead in Russell Crowe's 1992 thug drama *Romper Stomper*.

BET YOU DIDN'T KNOW: Michod and producer Liz Watts' original script called for a younger, more innocent-looking actor for the part of Josh. When they chose Frecheville, who appears older and larger than his 17 years, they rewrote the role so that the character actually plays more of a part in his uncles' crimes.

VIOLENCE LEVEL: There are no gun battles, car chases or beatdowns. *Animal Kingdom's* violence comes in quick, unannounced flashes that do more to build a deepening sense of dread than glamorize the criminal life.

BODY COUNT: Six—three crooks, two cops, one innocent.

IF YOU LIKED THIS, YOU'LL LIKE: *The Boys*, a 1998 Aussie drama about three criminal brothers facing impending doom as their plans go awry. Toni Collette plays the weak mother of the dysfunctional brood.

56 DRUNKEN ANGEL (YOIDORE TENSHI) (1948–NR)

STARS: TOSHIRO MIFUNE, TAKASHI SHIMURA | DIRECTOR: AKIRA KUROSAWA

This one, we know, is a tough sell. *Drunken Angel* is a 60-plus-year-old, black-and-white, subtitled Japanese movie with virtually no action and not a single gun shot. It focuses on the mercurial relationship between a cranky, alcoholic doctor and a brazen young yakuza dying of tuberculosis.

Your instinct here is probably to turn the page. Not exactly *GoodFellas*.

But if you give it a chance (the movie, actually, not this essay), you'll be rewarded with a moody look into the seamy society that was post-World War II Japan. You'll enjoy a close-up view of the psychology of a young gangster struggling with his choices. And you'll see one of the first important works of Akira Kurosawa, the legendary Japanese filmmaker whose style impacted nearly every other director in this book.

But don't believe us:

"His influence on me and other filmmakers throughout the entire world is so profound as to be almost incomparable," said Martin Scorsese.

"One thing that distinguishes Akira Kurosawa is that he didn't make one or two masterpieces," said Francis Ford Coppola. "He made, you know, eight masterpieces."

Drunken Angel falls short of being one of those

masterpieces (if you're looking for the best of them, we'd recommend *The Seven Samurai*). But it was Kurosawa's first critical success, as well as the first movie in which the director says he really found his way. It works as a portrait, a period piece, a gangster film and—in a weird way—as a buddy movie.

It focuses on a disillusioned doctor named Sanada (Takashi Shimura), who runs a clinic in a crime-ridden Tokyo slum. When a thug named Matsunaga (Toshiro Mifune) visits him late one night after being shot in the hand, the doctor notices the young man's cough and diagnoses him with tuberculosis. Sanada tries to convince the gangster to undergo treatment, especially after an X-ray shows a hole in his lung. But the callow Matsunaga refuses, joking that the hole "is good for ventilation" and snapping that, "Yakuza are not afraid of death."

Thus begins a push-pull between the two men, in which their relationship veers between tender and violent. Like any young gangster, Matsunaga tries to mask his fears and weaknesses. The doctor, meanwhile, believes that if he can heal this one man's body and soul, he can recover a bit of his own humanity.

"I was like him once," he tells a nurse. "In medical school I would pawn my own clothes to pay for brothels. But his heart isn't yet frozen over with evil."

The good doctor's office is not exactly the Mayo Clinic. He sucks on bottles of medicinal alcohol, smokes while standing over a patient and spits on the floor to punctuate a point. He's constantly got a three-day growth of stubble and his hair and clothes are a mess. Nothing pretty here.

Still, in this slum—bordered by a huge black-market plaza on one side and an oozing, noxious pool of garbage on the other—he shows compassion to the pan-pan girls and hustlers.

"You think angels all come looking like your dance hall girls," the doctor tells the reluctant Matsunaga in one of their volatile meetings. "But I'm your angel. Your drunken angel."

The young tough aims to reform. But things devolve when his gang's former boss returns from prison and begins to bully his ill underling into smoking, drinking and shoving around the local cit-izenry. And just to show who's in charge, the boss steals Matsunaga's girlfriend. The ailing young man is eventually tossed from the gang.

This is not going to help his recovery.

The movie builds up to a three-sided tug of war among the doctor, the yakuza boss and the terminally ill, now-ostracized gangster. And it culminates with Dr. Sanada's moral lesson, which was really Kurosawa's message to his audience:

"Yakuza will always do the wrong thing at the end. That's why they are so pointless and senseless."

⊙ **HIT:** *Drunken Angel* was the first of 16 collaborations between Kurosawa and Mifune, Japan's version of Scorsese and De Niro. You can see the early chemistry between director and actor, but you should know that it matures like a great wine in their future films.

Kurosawa loved Mifune's cat-like movement on-screen and his animal grunts and intensity. He encouraged Mifune to "act like a panther," even showing him films of the big cats to help him mimic their actions.

⊗ **MISS:** There's a hokey dream sequence (in which Matsunaga is chased by his own ghost) clumsily stuck into the movie. It wouldn't get a passing grade in a freshman film class. Kurosawa later called that hackneyed scene "part of my learning process."

✎ **WHAT THEY WROTE AT THE TIME:** "Kurosawa creates . . . a world of more than healer and hoodlum, girls and gangsters. His is an environment of disease, where the fateful bacilli of corruption lurk in every dancehall and gambling dive—puddles of social consumption—to be battled by the weak power of man's will."—Bosley Crowther, *New York Times*

🐾 **BODY COUNT:** Just one.

⬛ **BET YOU DIDN'T KNOW:** The screenplay was originally written with the doctor as a young idealist, to counter the hardened gangster. Kurosawa didn't like the character, but wasn't sure how to change him. Later, while scouting filming sites in Yokohama with writer Keinosuke Uekusa, he met an older physician.

"This man fascinated us with his arrogant manner, and we took him with us to three or four bars to listen to his stories while we drank," Kurosawa said in his memoir, *Something Like an Autobiography*. "He operated without a physician's license, and his patients were the streetwalkers of the slums. His talk about his illegal gynecology practice was so vulgar it nearly made us sick, but every so often he said something bitterly sarcastic about human nature that gleamed with aptness.

"Uekusa and I looked at each other and simultaneously felt, 'This is it!' "

📽 PIVOTAL SCENE: The first few meetings between doctor and gangster end in confrontation because of both men's tempers and Matsunaga's refusal to accept his own illness. Late in the movie, the gangster—drunk himself—begins to cough up blood. He stumbles to the doctor's home in the middle of the night. At first, Sanada refuses to see him, saying he is done wasting his time. Eventually, the doctor relents, and comforts the seriously ill man.

"Go to sleep," Sanada says, putting a blanket over his pained patient. "Dream about your childhood."

Their battling is now over.

➡ DON'T FAIL TO NOTICE: The film was shot during the post-World War II occupation of Japan, when all movies had to be cleared by American censors. Kurosawa still managed to slip several anti-Western images into *Drunken Angel*. The pinstriped gangsters and their girlfriends all dress and wear their hair like Westerners (the so-called "big boss" resembles George Raft, down to the detail of him flipping a coin). And the nightclub scene designed to show their decadence features a lampoon of American jazz, called *Jungle Boogie*, (no, not *that* version), for which the director himself wrote the mocking lyrics.

🔫 VIOLENCE LEVEL: Very low and very unrealistic. The highlight is a fight between two mobsters who, for tough guys, sure don't know how to duke it out. They end up tripping over an open can of paint and slapping each other around like the Three Stooges.

◉ REPEATED WATCHING QUOTIENT: Watch it once and move on. But really, you ought to watch it once.

❞ BEST LINE: A drunken Dr. Sanada to a disinterested dancehall girl: "Don't fall for him, fall for me. I may be kind of scruffy, but you'll get free medical care."

Given how things are, that pickup effort might stand a better chance these days.

IF YOU LIKE THIS, YOU'LL LIKE: Any of the great collaborations between Kurosawa and Mifune. You may actually want to start by checking out Stuart Galbraith IV's book *The Emperor and the Wolf*, which documents the actor and filmmaker's long relationship.

57 KILL THE IRISHMAN (2011-R)

STARS: RAY STEVENSON, VAL KILMER, CHRISTOPHER WALKEN, VINCENT D'ONOFRIO
DIRECTOR: JONATHAN HENSLEIGH

Chances are you've never heard of the Cleveland Mob Wars. They began with the death of Mafia boss John Scalish in 1976, leaving control of the city's criminal enterprises and corrupt labor unions up for grabs.

Soon enough, the power struggle began. By the end of the year, 36 bombs had exploded around northeast Ohio and more than a dozen men were killed. The Cleveland wars sparked a chain reaction that shook the underworld structure in Milwaukee, Kansas City and other organized crime outposts. It led to acting Los Angeles boss Jimmy "the Weasel" Fratianno—who knew the inner workings of La Cosa Nostra across the country—flipping to become one of the government's most-important witnesses against the mob.

A central figure in that combat was Danny

Greene, known to all as "The Irishman." All these years later, Greene has become a legend to certain constituencies, a charismatic mythical figure.

Greene's story is told in the excellent 2011 biopic, *Kill the Irishman*, which covers his rise from lugging boxes as a stevedore to running a corrupt union to working as a mob enforcer to standing up to the new Mafia boss—Scalish's replacement—looking to grab a percentage of Greene's operation. There's a lot packed into two hours.

Along the way, *Kill the Irishman* borrows from some of the best gangster movies ever made. The opening shot—a flash forward to Greene surviving a car bombing that actually occurs later in the story—is a direct nod to the attempt on Ace Rothstein's life at the start of *Casino*. The scenes where beleaguered longshoremen try to rise against corruption in their union will take you back to *On the Waterfront*. And Greene's turn as an FBI informer who uses that status to enhance his criminal power will certainly remind you of Frank Costello in *The Departed*.

So you've seen these plotlines before. But they don't just feel like copies of the originals, in large part because the movie stays true to Greene's real story.

The movie is based on the book *To Kill the Irishman: The War that Crippled the Mafia* by Rick Porrello, a suburban Cleveland police chief and author of three books on the mob. The script takes very few liberties with Porrello's book, which traces Greene's life from his impoverished youth to his exalted status as "the Robin Hood of Collingswood."

Lead actor Ray Stevenson, a native of Northern Ireland best known for his role as Titus Pullo in the HBO series *Rome*, plays Danny Greene as a complex figure—both a thug and a visionary. He goes on TV to recklessly challenge his enemies to kill him, but at the same time worries about cholesterol in his diet. He's the high school dropout who reads hardbound books, the cold-blooded murderer who celebrates Thanksgiving by handing out free turkeys to cops and neighbors. And in an industry that values silence, he's the chattiest guy on the block.

Kill the Irishman is helped by an outstanding cast. Christopher Walken, who is all over this book's Top 100, is his usual kooky-scary self as Jewish mobster Shondor Birns. At first, Birns serves as Greene's sponsor and mentor. But after a three-way money dispute among Birns, Greene and New York's Gambino Family, Birns puts out a contract on his former protégé's life. It is Birns, however, who gets blown to bits by a car bomb.

Vincent D'Onofrio (*Law and Order: Criminal Intent*) is more understated than usual as John Nardi, the labor racketeer trying to claim power after Scalish's death. Nardi first meets Greene when the young Irishman has the brass ones to stand up to him for a friend. The two eventually form a partnership, which lasts until Nardi, too, is the victim of a firebomb.

Val Kilmer (*Batman Forever, The Doors*) is also here as the good-guy cop who never solves a crime but is in the movie to serve as a counterbalance to all those bad guys. Kilmer—who has put on so much weight that he appears to have swallowed both The Riddler and Jim Morrison—gets to fire off one of *Kill the Irishman*'s best lines. Responding to a veiled threat by Greene, he says, "I will cut your heart out with a rusty butter knife and eat it while it's still beating."

You've probably figured out how it ends for Danny Greene (What's one more Cadillac up in flames?). Right before his grisly end, though, The Irishman is greeted by a pack of young boys on their bikes.

"My cousin says you've got balls like no one else," says one of the kids. "He wants to be just like you."

"Ah, you don't want to be like me," Greene tells the lad. Then, as Irish pipe organ music swells up, he removes a Celtic amulet from around his neck and slips it over the boy. For a guy professing not to be a hero, the movie sure allows him to go out like one.

⊙ **HIT:** Beyond the main characters, *Kill the Irishman*'s smaller roles are populated by a gangster movie all-star team. As Walken said in an on-set interview, "A lot of the actors in it are guys I know from New York, whom I worked with before. In that sense, it's a family picture."

We don't know about the family aspect. But we'll pay attention to any film boasting Paul Sorvino (*GoodFellas*), Vinny Vella (*Casino*), Vinnie Jones (*Snatch*), Mike Starr (*GoodFellas*), Steve Schirripa (*The Sopranos*) and Tony Lo Bianco (*The French Connection*).

⊗ **MISS:** Greene's romance with flower-power nature girl Ellie doesn't ring true. What's the innocent veggie vendor doing with the hardened mobster? How is she so oblivious to his well-publicized criminal activities? Why is she unconcerned with the multiple attempts on his life? None of this is ever explained. We couldn't figure out any purpose for this subplot other than the opportunity to show actress Laura Ramsey's breasts.

✎ WHAT THEY WROTE AT THE TIME: "While *Kill the Irishman* isn't a great movie, it's a juicy one, full of action, big dramatic moments and humor. . . . Stevenson is such a free-swinging force of nature that he pulls you into the story, making it an enjoyably involving tall tale that has the advantage of being improbably true."—Marshall Fine, *Huffington Post*

✔ REALITY CHECK: *Kill the Irishman* features more than a half-dozen scenes of car bombings. And yet victims continue climbing into their Caddies, which keep exploding. We were waiting for someone to smarten up and take public transportation.

◉ REPEATED WATCHING QUOTIENT: Definitely worth multiple viewings. There are great actors here working with a well-crafted script. We watched *Kill the Irishman* three consecutive days and kept picking up new details.

🎬 PIVOTAL SCENE: Through his connections as an FBI informant, Greene learns that a close friend, Art Sneperger, has been blabbing about him to the cops. Greene has boasted that he regards his crew members as brothers. Now he must decide what to do.

"Maybe we could let him go, Danny," pleads another gang member. "I've known him all my life."

But Greene knows better. He sets up an operation where Sneperger—unaware he's been found out—is told to plant a bomb under the car of a gang enemy. As Sneperger backs under the automobile in the dark, Greene and the gang watch from a block away. Just as Sneperger affixes the bomb, Greene flicks a switch, exploding both the rat and the car of his enemy.

Murdering his friend is a hard pill to swallow. But Greene now knows he can trust no one. The lesson comes in handy as things move along.

➡ DON'T FAIL TO NOTICE: *Kill the Irishman* is interspersed with actual television news footage from the 1970s. You'll see Brian Ross, who later became chief investigative reporter at ABC News, as a young local correspondent covering Cleveland's mob wars. And, at the end, you'll see the real Danny Greene falsely predicting that "the luck of the Irish" would continue to keep him alive.

⚔ VIOLENCE LEVEL: High. In an early scene, a teen gets pierced through the hand with a No. 2 pencil. Later, a helpless parking valet—his body bound with duct tape and tossed in a car trunk—gets repeatedly stabbed as a show of loyalty. Those are just two of the highlights.

🍎 BET YOU DIDN'T KNOW: The real-life fallout from Greene's assassination led to an unsuccessful mob murder plot against Cleveland Mayor Dennis Kucinich, as well as bribery charges against nearby Sheriff James Traficant (who was acquitted). Both went on to become U.S. Congressmen. In 2002, Traficant was convicted, in a separate case, of bribery, racketeering and tax evasion. He served seven years in federal prison.

❞ BEST LINE: New boss Jack Licavoli (Tony Lo Bianco) informs Greene that the mob wants a 30 percent take of his action.

"Do you understand?" Licavoli asks.

Greene nods. Then he offers his own spin on Licavoli's business plan: "Let's see. A gang of hairy, greasy wops who came into existence when a Greek fucked a goat want to extort hard-earned money from a band of noble Irish stock. How's that?"

Needless to say, his interpretation of things does not go over well.

☻ "I KNOW THAT GUY": Bob Gunton, who plays the corrupt and authoritarian president of the longshoremen's local, is best recognized for playing the corrupt and authoritarian Warden Norton in *The Shawshank Redemption*. He also was a regular for three seasons on the TV series *24*. As a young man, Gunton won a Bronze Star for valor for his service in the U.S. Army in Vietnam.

☠ BODY COUNT: Thirteen, plus a whole lot more unseen carnage in all those bombed-out cars.

58 JACKIE BROWN (1997–R)

STARS: PAM GRIER, SAMUEL L. JACKSON, ROBERT FORSTER, BRIDGET FONDA, MICHAEL KEATON, ROBERT DE NIRO | DIRECTOR: QUENTIN TARANTINO

Film fans and critics wondered where Quentin Tarantino would go after his highly praised and wildly successful *Pulp Fiction* (covered earlier in this book), a 1994 underworld film that some thought established a new form of crime cinema.

Whether by design or because it was the safe move, Tarantino chose a more standard form of storytelling with *Jackie Brown*. It's a good movie, but certainly not in the same league with Tarantino's two preceding films, *Pulp Fiction* and *Reservoir Dogs* (1992).

This is more a character study built around an intriguing heist-con-double-cross-triple-cross. There's plenty of the trademark Tarantino asides, quips and street corner philosophy. But sometimes all the talk gets in the way of the narrative. And sometimes you get the feeling that Tarantino is just trying to show how clever he is.

The cast is major league. Pam Grier reestablished her career playing the title character and Robert Forster got an Academy Award nomination for Best Supporting Actor for his role as Max Cherry, the soft-spoken and world-weary bail bondsman.

But it is Samuel L. Jackson, over-the-top as the gunrunner and principal bad guy Ordell Robbie, who steals this picture. His character can't utter a sentence without incorporating the word "nigger" or "nigga," but he says it in such a matter-of-fact manner that it hardly sounds offensive.

His take on life is built around making money and eliminating anyone who might get in the way of his enjoying it. He's got a long ponytail, a narrowly braided Chinese-like goatee and an attitude. He's also got a half-million dollars in cash stashed in Mexico that he wants Jackie Brown, a stewardess on a small airline, to bring back to him.

It's Jackson's Robbie who has the most Tarantino-esque lines, whether it's complaining about the customers and the advertising in the illegal gun dealing business or dismissing the violence and betrayal that are routinely part of his life.

"The AK-47, the very best that there is," he says as he and his longtime friend Louis Gara (Robert De Niro), just out of prison after a four-year stint, watch a video called *Chicks Who Love Guns*. "When you absolutely, positively got to kill every motherfucker in the room, accept no substitutes."

Gara is both bewildered and impressed with the video, Robbie's spiel and, it seems, life in general. Four years behind bars have taken a lot out of him. "What happened to you, man? You used to be beautiful." Robbie cries in one pivotal scene with his former partner in crime.

De Niro does a good job in a minor role. Gara is what Johnny Boy from *Mean Streets* would have been like had he lived to be 50 and spent a big chunk of his adult life in prison.

When Robbie shows Gara the body of a former associate he has recently killed and stuffed in the trunk of his car, Gara asks, "Who's that?"

"That's Beaumont," Robbie replies.

"Who's Beaumont?" asks Gara.

"An employee I had to let go," says Robbie.

Robbie also has the perfect take on his surfer-girl mistress Melanie (Bridget Fonda) who Gara also ends up in bed with.

"You can't trust Melanie," Robbie says, "but you can always trust Melanie to be Melanie."

Trust, or the lack thereof, is a big part of the story here. While Robbie has the guns and the money, it's Jackie Brown who, in the vernacular of the movie, has the balls. She's been running cash up from Mexico to Robbie, but after getting jammed up in an investigation in which he is the primary target, she manages to turn the tables on the bad guys, the good guys and the hapless women caught in the middle.

Several of them end up dead along the way, although not at Jackie's hand.

The only time she pulls a gun is when she confronts Robbie in her apartment, in the dark. He has come, she knows, to kill her because, like Beaumont, he believes she is cooperating with the authorities.

After Robbie has backed her into a corner and is holding her by the neck, he pauses.

"Is that what I think it is?" he says as the two stand face-to-face in the dark apartment room.

"What do you think it is?" Jackie asks.

"I think it's a gun pressed up against my dick," Robbie says.

Jackie manages to convince Robbie that she is playing the authorities, pretending to cooperate, when in fact, what she wants to do is help him get his half-million dollars out of Mexico. She'll do it, she says, for $100,000.

That sets the plot in motion and, like a dealer in a game of three-card monte, Jackie Brown is always two steps ahead of everyone who thinks they are following the cards.

Cherry, of course, has no stake in the game, but because he is falling in love with the principal player, agrees to help her pull off the ultimate scam. When she assures him the money won't be missed, his reply captures the tired cynicism that defines his character.

"Half a million dollars will always be missed," he says.

There's a quasi-happy ending, but only Jackie gets to ride off into the sunset.

⊙ **HIT:** The music is a big part of setting the mood, whether it's a love song by the Delfonics or Bobby Womack's "Across 110th Street." These are echoes of the blaxploitation films that Grier starred in earlier in her career, but this movie heads her in a different, more entertaining and sophisticated direction.

⊗ **MISS:** Chris Tucker's brief appearance as the doomed Beaumont is more cartoon than character. And while there is a cartoonish nature to parts of what Tarantino does in almost every film (*Kill Bill*, anyone?), Tucker overplays it here.

🍎 **BET YOU DIDN'T KNOW:** Tarantino based the movie on Elmore Leonard's novel *Rum Punch*, but changed the locale from Florida to Southern California and made the heroine an African-American woman. Both changes were fine by Leonard, who is not always happy about the way his novels are translated to movies. Of *Jackie Brown*, he told *Time* magazine that Tarantino "surprised me. I thought he might be all over the place; but he stayed very, very close to the plot and used quite a bit of the dialogue."

➡ **DON'T FAIL TO NOTICE:** The closing credits include "special thanks" to "Bert D'Angelo's Daughter." This is a reference to Mira Sorvino, Tarantino's girlfriend at the time. She is the daughter of actor Paul Sorvino who in the 1970s starred in a TV detective series in which he played Bert D'Angelo.

This is either the kind of hokey, insider stuff that Tarantino fans love or an example of the self-indulgent name dropping that reinforces critics' opinion of Tarantino as an obnoxious blowhard.

Take your pick. We're staying on the sidelines on that one.

✎ **WHAT THEY WROTE AT THE TIME:** "*Jackie Brown* has the makings of another, chattier *Get Shorty* with an added homage to Pam Grier, the Annie Oakley of 1970's blaxploitation. That could well have been enough, since Mr. Tarantino shows such obvious affection for his leading lady and for the cheerful, greedy lowlife in Mr. Leonard's stories. But for all its enthusiasm, this film isn't sharp enough to afford all the time it wastes on small talk, long drives, trips to the mall and favorite songs played on car radios. And although Ms. Grier makes an enjoyable comeback, she isn't an actress well served by quiet stretches of doing nothing before the camera."—Janet Maslin, *New York Times*

👁 **REPEATED WATCHING QUOTIENT:** This is a highly entertaining film and almost any scene with Samuel L. Jackson is worth revisiting.

PIVOTAL SCENE: The cash transfer in the women's dressing room. It's played three times from three different perspectives and sets the stage for the big-time violence that leads to the film's conclusion.

CASTING CALL: Michael Keaton plays the same ATF agent, Ray Nicolette, in another Elmore Leonard novel adapted for the screen, *Out of Sight* (1998). In that movie, he gets to flirt with Jennifer Lopez instead of Pam Grier. Both seem like fine options to us.

VIOLENCE LEVEL: Typical, but not over the top, for a movie dealing with gunrunners and drug dealers.

BEST LINE: This movie is loaded with them, in no small part because of the aforementioned loyalty to the dialogue in Elmore Leonard's book. Leonard has one of the best ears in the business when it comes to crime writing and this translates easily to film.

Here are two to consider:

"My ass may be dumb, but I ain't no dumbass," says Robbie as he and Cherry discuss the ebb and flow of the dangerous game they're playing.

"You know, a good cop will never let you know he knows you're full of shit," Cherry tells Jackie as she outlines her plan to double-cross the agents who want her to cooperate.

⊕ IF YOU LIKED THIS, YOU'LL LIKE: Almost any of the other movies based on the novels of Elmore Leonard, including the aforementioned *Out of Sight*, *Pronto* (1997) and *Killshot* (2008).

BODY COUNT: Four.

59 HEAT (1995–R)

STARS: ROBERT DE NIRO, AL PACINO, VAL KILMER, JON VOIGHT
DIRECTOR: MICHAEL MANN

Back in the 1980s in South Philadelphia, there was a woman named April who was married to a mobster named Cuddles. No kidding, Cuddles.

April had serious information about a couple of murders her husband allegedly had been involved in and came to believe that he planned to kill her. So she went to the Feds and became a cooperating witness. For a time, she lived in a safe house under FBI protection and hung out with a lot of guys in law enforcement serving in a rotating task force assigned to guard her. April eventually testified against her husband, whom she divorced. Then she married one of the FBI agents.

At one point, someone asked April what the difference was between the cops and the wiseguys.

Without missing a beat, she said, "The cops have badges."

That's the point that Michael Mann makes dramatically in this slick and sophisticated cops-and-robbers movie that paired Robert De Niro and Al Pacino for the first time.

This is an organized crime movie in the literal sense of that term. It's not about the mob, but about a gang of well-organized professional thieves. They know their business and work it very well.

They, in turn, are tracked by a group of police detectives who also take their work very seriously. Neil McCauley (De Niro) heads the gang of outlaws; Lt. Vincent Hanna (Pacino) directs the LAPD unit that is tracking McCauley.

Both put their jobs ahead of their personal lives. And every other relationship they have suffers as a result. Hanna is on the down side of his third marriage.

"This is not sharing, this is leftovers," his wife Justine (Diane Venora) says during one of several arguments about Hanna choosing his work over their marriage.

McCauley lives alone in a sparsely furnished luxury apartment with a breathtaking view of Los Angeles.

"I'm alone, I'm not lonely," he tells an associate asking about his lifestyle.

Both men define themselves by what they do. Nothing else matters.

Mann, who wrote the script and directed the movie, takes nearly three hours to tell the story. Along the way, he gives us lots of the action scenes that were the trademark of his *Miami Vice* television series. But he also includes scenes that lend themselves to the kind of introspective character study more typical of French gangster films.

McCauley and Hanna only have three scenes together, all in the second half of the film. But each is aware of the other as the game of cat-and-mouse unfolds. Each, in fact, has an almost animal-like instinct for the game and the other's presence.

They finally come face-to-face when Hanna pulls McCauley over after tailing him through the streets of Los Angeles and invites him to have a cup of coffee in a nearby restaurant. They already seem to know one another.

McCauley, who has spent time in prison, tells Hanna he has no intention of going back. Hanna says the best way to avoid prison is to stop doing scores. Both know that's not an option. Then they each talk about their work and how it has impacted their lives.

"I don't know how to do anything else," Hanna says.

"Neither do I," says McCauley.

"I don't much want to, either," says the cop.

"Neither do I," replies the robber.

Heat moves in several different directions at once and provides back stories that flesh out many of the characters, especially the women in the lives of the central figures.

Amy Brenneman's Eady is both attracted and

fearful of McCauley and Ashley Judd is both loyal and disloyal as the wife of Chris (Val Kilmer), McCauley's top associate.

At one point, Mann has both groups—the gangsters and the cops chasing them—out partying with their wives and girlfriends. The events take place at two different locations, but we see the same things going on at each locale.

These are multidimensional cops and robbers. Highly armed and dangerous—and often literally explosive. Both the good guys and the bad guys bring their A games. And sometimes, it's hard to tell one group from the other, which is the point both Mann and April were making.

⊙ **HIT:** Too often, gangster movies use action and violence to define character. Michael Mann has plenty of both here, but also spends the time—some critics argued too much time—showing his characters operating in their domestic worlds to give us a glimpse of who these people really are.

⊗ **MISS:** The armored truck heist that opens the movie goes awry because one of the robbers, Waingro (Kevin Gage), is trigger-happy. Waingro is new to the McCauley group and is clearly a loose cannon. Given the caution and detailed planning that are the hallmarks of McCauley's operational style, it makes no sense that he would bring someone like Waingro into the group.

✎ **WHAT THEY WROTE AT THE TIME:** "This is the first time De Niro and Pacino have acted together . . . and each gives a strong, water-tight performance. The problem is, they've both appeared in high-energy crime yarns before, and Mann's story doesn't require them to do anything new, or to show new facets to their talents.

"The other problem is that *Heat* peaks too early. . . . You think the film is ready to end. Instead, it has more than an hour to go. It's a monster of a movie and it gets unwieldy."—Edward Guthmann, *San Franciso Chronicle*

✔ **REALITY CHECK:** Some of the events and De Niro's character were based on an investigation in Chicago into a band of robbers headed by an underworld figure named McCauley.

After the movie's release, authorities cited armored car robberies in South Africa, Colombia, Denmark and Norway that had mimicked the robbery at the start of *Heat*.

☻ **"I KNOW THAT GUY":** Jeremy Piven, who plays the obnoxious agent Ari Gold in HBO's popular series *Entourage*, is the rogue doctor who appears in one scene, patching up Chris (Val Kilmer) after the big shootout outside the bank. Natalie Portman also makes a limited appearance as Hanna's troubled teenage stepdaughter.

🍎 **BET YOU DIDN'T KNOW:** The movie was a remake of *L.A. Takedown*, a made for TV movie that Mann wrote and directed. It aired in 1989. The television version was a pared-down account of the same story, one that Mann had been trying to get to the big screen for more than a decade.

❞ **BEST LINE:** "You wanna be making moves on the street, have no attachments. Allow nothing to be in your life that you cannot walk out on in 30 seconds flat if you spot the heat around the corner," says McCauley while he and Chris discuss Chris' problems at home with his wife (Ashley Judd). The line captures the underworld philosophy of the De Niro character, a philosophy that is challenged when he falls in love with Eady (Amy Brenneman).

🔫 **VIOLENCE LEVEL:** Highly potent weaponry and lots of characters who know how to put it to use.

⚰ **BODY COUNT:** A minimum of twenty-one—although so many bodies keep dropping during the bank shootout, an accurate count isn't really possible.

60 BUGSY (1991–R)

STARS: WARREN BEATTY, ANNETTE BENING, HARVEY KEITEL, BEN KINGSLEY
DIRECTOR: BARRY LEVINSON

"That kid's name was Moe Greene. And the city he invented was Las Vegas. This was a great man, a man of vision and guts. And there isn't even a plaque or a signpost or a statue of him in that town."—Hyman Roth, *The Godfather: Part II*

Moe Greene, of course, did not invent Las Vegas. But the real-life mobster on whom his character is based—Benjamin "Bugsy" Siegel—did. Well, sort of.

And while Siegel suffered the same, sad fate that Moe Greene did (namely, a bullet through the eye), we are pleased to report that there is a plaque honoring him on the Vegas Strip, right on the site where he built the original Pink Flamingo Hotel & Casino in 1946.

There is also a movie honoring his life—*Bugsy*,

starring Warren Beatty. The film portrays Siegel as both a visionary and a gangster. An innocent dreamer and a cold-blooded killer. An optimist and a cynic.

Beatty and director Barry Levinson go a little over the top at times trying to convince you what a lovable guy Siegel was. But the dichotomy of mobster/family man generally works, as it did so brilliantly in *The Sopranos*. Here is "Benny," in his kitchen, wearing a goofy chef's toque and icing a cake for his daughter's birthday. Suddenly, the family celebration is interrupted by his partners—most notably Meyer Lansky (Ben Kingsley)—to discuss their nefarious business. With frosting smeared on his face, "Bugsy" explains to them how the mob can own Nevada.

This is a solid biopic, though, like most biopics, it bends the facts a bit. Bugsy Siegel did not really discover Las Vegas, as the movie portrays. His hotel was not the first on the Strip, but the third. And he did not build that from scratch, but rather took over an unfinished project started by a degenerate gambler.

But what Siegel did was to envision Vegas with all the neon and naughtiness that would eventually define Sin City. Before he came along, casinos were Western saloons with sawdust on the floor and slot machines by the men's rooms. Siegel installed wall-to-wall carpet, hired statuesque showgirls and lured big-time acts like Al Jolson and Jimmy Durante from Hollywood.

That he robbed, cheated and murdered trying to realize that dream, well. . . .

Bugsy opens with Siegel's move to California during World War II to run the New York mob's interests, assisted by the vicious Mickey Cohen (Harvey Keitel). He visits a film set with an actor friend named George played by Joe Mantegna.

"My character is modeled after George Raft," Mantegna said in an interview for this book. "I studied his work to get him down. In *Bugsy*, I'm reenacting a scene from *Manpower*, which Raft did with Marlene Dietrich. We studied that movie and tried to stage it exactly the same."

As Mantegna's character recites his lines, Siegel mouths them. He is smitten by the movies. He wants in.

He is also smitten by a bit-part actress, Virginia Hill, played by Annette Bening. For what it's worth, Beatty and Bening fell in love filming this movie, resulting in their 1992 marriage and four children. Indeed, their on-screen chemistry appears convincing.

Anyway, Ms. Hill becomes more than Mr. Siegel's paramour (his wife and children are back in Scarsdale, N.Y.). She becomes his business partner as they grow the Los Angeles operation and, soon enough, expand to Nevada. You're not sure at times whether she's really with him or just using him to further her own interests. In fact, you get the sense that she's not really sure herself.

The back half of *Bugsy* focuses on Siegel's grand vision for the Flamingo (named, by the way, in honor of Hill's leggy figure) and the extraordinary cost overruns he accrued trying to get it built. His partners initially funded him $1 million for the project; in the end, it cost $6 million.

We don't have to tell you what happens when you squander the mob's money. And we've already given away how it ends for Siegel. Sitting in his Los Angeles living room, reading a newspaper, he is hit from behind by nine rifle shots fired from outside—the last of which passes through his left eye. By all accounts, it happened just that way in real life.

There's a wonderful scene near the end when Bugsy senses what's about to go down. On the phone with Lansky, his friend since childhood, he doesn't beg for his life. Rather, he implores Lansky to never sell his own shares of stock in the Flamingo. The doomed man knew something. According to the movie's postscript, "By 1991, the $6 million invested in Bugsy Siegel's dream had generated revenues of over $100 billion."

⊙ **HIT:** Director Levinson does a terrific job of showing the fashion, music and lifestyle of Los Angeles in the 1940s, a place that appears so glamorous you almost forget there was a world war going on. We put Bugsy up there with *Chinatown* and *L.A. Confidential* in terms of recreating that city back in the day.

⊗ **MISS:** As breathtaking as Bening is as Virginia Hill, the character's constant tantrums grow tiresome. Every other scene she's stalking off in anger at some perceived indignation.

✎ **WHAT THEY WROTE AT THE TIME:** "It would be easy to dismiss *Bugsy* as a phony Hollywood movie. Beatty seems an unlikely choice to play a Jewish gangster. The script is riddled with the kind of clever dialogue that happens only in movies. And Oscar-winning filmmaker Barry Levinson directs with a studied slickness. But *Bugsy*'s artifice has a seductive resonance. The film is, after all, about contrivance—about the folly of a man who lived and died for delusions of grandeur. The story is compelling. At times, it is wickedly funny."—Brian D. Johnson, *Maclean's*

➤ DON'T FAIL TO NOTICE: What happens every time some unknowing fool refers to Siegel as "Bugsy." Apparently, he always resented the nickname, which was given to him as a teenaged hood for being "as crazy as a bedbug." His violent reaction does nothing to shake the moniker.

🎬 PIVOTAL SCENE: Siegel, Hill and Mickey Cohen take their first trip to Nevada to visit the mob's only casino. It's a dusty, ramshackle joint, prompting Hill to crack, "We drove five-and-a-half hours for this canker sore?"

Siegel, too, is mortified, asking aloud, "Do we really want to be associated with this kind of dump?" He orders it closed down. "Looks matter," he insists.

They bicker during the drive home, and Siegel becomes so infuriated that he skids the car to a halt and stomps into the desert in anger. Suddenly he stops and looks around. Raising his arms toward the setting sun, he appears to be drawing a skyline in the cactus-filled wilderness.

The Vegas Strip has come to his mind, "like a vision, like a religious epiphany." Back home on the East Coast, he tells Lansky, "What do people always fantasize about? Sex, romance, money, adventure. I am building a monument to all of them."

🗨 BEST LINE: Bugsy tries to explain the above concept to his cohorts:

Vito Genovese: "What are you talking about? A whorehouse?"

Bugsy: "No . . . I am talking about a place where gambling is involved, where everything is allowed. The whole territory is wide open. I'm talking about a palace, an oasis, a city. Do you know when the Hoover Dam is finished, electrical power is going to be available on a massive scale in Las Vegas?"

Vito: "I don't get it. The Hoover Dam and fucking are connected how?"

Bugsy: "By air-conditioning. It's the wave of the future."

😀 "I KNOW THAT GUY": Mobster Charlie "Lucky" Luciano is played by legendary West Coast rock promoter Bill Graham. Two months before the film's release, Graham was killed in a helicopter accident.

✔ REALITY CHECK: As we said, most biopics take liberties with reality. And we're not here to pick nits. But the postscript tacked onto the end of *Bugsy* states that "Virginia Hill committed suicide in Austria," making it sound that her distraught gesture followed Siegel's assassination. Sure it did—except it was 19 years later. Somehow that makes us believe the two acts were not connected.

🎥 CASTING CALL: Keitel, who plays Mickey Cohen here, actually portrayed Bugsy Siegel in the 1974 TV movie, *The Virginia Hill Story*.

🔫 VIOLENCE LEVEL: Sporadic. We will contend that Bugsy's mauling of gangster Joey Adonis over an insult to Hill may be the top mob movie beatdown this side of Sonny's attack on brother-in-law Carlo in *The Godfather*.

☺ GOOF: Desperate for money to keep funding his hotel, Siegel sells his Los Angeles house and liquidates his furniture. But the movie's final scene shows him getting murdered inside that same house, sitting on the same furniture he had already sold.

🍎 BET YOU DIDN'T KNOW: That house (at 810 Linden Drive, Beverly Hills) was long a fixture on Hollywood tours. Guides were eager to tell stargazers that after Siegel's shooting, police found his intact eye 15 feet from his body.

💀 BODY COUNT: A mere two, plus one more off-screen.

Not many movies in this book can be described as endearing. If you're looking for endearing, wait to pick up *The Ultimate Book of Romantic Comedies*—which *we* certainly won't be writing.

But *Things Change*, an unlikely buddy flick with subplots of bribery, mistaken identity and double-crossing, is also a feel-good yarn—and not just in comparison to *Scarface*. It's a leisurely paced, plot-turning charmer about two guys who pull off a great con, precisely because they have no intention of pulling off a con.

Don Ameche stars as Gino Gotto, a sweet-tempered octogenarian shoeshine man who is a doppelgänger for a Chicago mobster fingered for murder. Gino is taken before the local crime chief and offered a deal—if he steps in to take the bogus rap and serves a three-year prison term, the appreciative bad guys will reward him with anything he wants.

"You must have a dream now," suggests mob chief Mr. Green (Mike Nussbaum). "What is that dream?"

"A boat," says Gino, with a heavy Southern Italian accent. "A fishing boat. In Sicily."

"In three years, you can have that boat," says Mr. Green. "But if you stay in the shoe store, what will you have in three years?"

And so the deal is struck. Gino is assigned a syndicate babysitter who must park him in a hotel for a few days, help him memorize the lines of his false confession ("I shoota the no good summa bitch") and deliver him to the courthouse the following Monday.

Problem is, the job is given to a low-level screwup named Jerry (Joe Mantegna), whose current responsibilities center on washing the dishes and taking abuse from his colleagues ("Hey Cinderella, I hear you really bollixed up that last job.").

Thus begins the buddy caper. Jerry takes an immediate liking to the guileless old man. In a plot device reminiscent of Jack Nicholson's *The Last Detail*, he decides the soon-to-be prisoner needs one last fling. So they fly out to Lake Tahoe for the weekend.

The plan is to keep a low profile—especially since Jerry's already "on probation" with his bosses. But that plan goes awry as soon as they land in Nevada. A limo driver buddy (deftly played by William H. Macy) meets them at the airport and assumes that the foreign-sounding old man is bigtime Mafiosi from abroad. Callow young Jerry further undermines his own secret mission by whispering to the driver that Gino is "the guy behind the guy—behind the guy."

Soon enough, everyone in Tahoe takes Gino for the second coming of Carlo Gambino. The two visitors are comped at the hotel, given unlimited credit at the tables and escorted to the penthouse suite with 24-hour butler service and a sunken hot tub. Even the two showgirls who join Gino and Jerry in that bubbly appear to be part of the deal.

It's all going swimmingly until word gets to Tahoe crime boss Don Giuseppe Vincent (Robert Prosky). How can there be such an important man that the Don doesn't know of? And what is that curious figure doing in *his* town? The Don summons Gino to his mountain estate, figuring he's going to either have to welcome the old man to the family or have him taken out in a body bag.

The scene of their meeting plays out like a beautiful dance, with Don Giuseppe trying to draw out information without insulting his potentially powerful guest and Gino answering (honestly) without really saying anything. Somehow his description of shining shoes becomes a metaphor for running a crime family and the Don ends up embracing him as an equal. It's evocative of the Peter Sellers' film *Being There*, in which the simplest of souls is mistaken for Mr. Big and shielded by his naïveté and decency.

The plot turns from there. There are a few dangerous encounters, a double-cross and a lucky coin that comes to have great meaning. Plus, there's the reward of an ending that you won't likely see coming.

Throughout, writer-director David Mamet and cowriter Shel Silverstein play *Things Change* for charm and sentimentality, plus the occasional laugh. Some of the characters may act befuddled by the ruses, but you won't be. You'll just enjoy being in on the joke. And, if you've made it through the first 60 movies in this book, you could probably use a chuckle about now.

⊙ **HIT:** Don Ameche started in vaudeville as a young man. He became a star in radio, feature films and television. At age 80, he superbly hits the mark as the simple Sicilian-born laborer thrown into extraordinary circumstances.

"I have never played a character like Gino before," Ameche told the *New York Times*. "But I knew I could do it because I understand the Italian mentality. I was around Italians all during my childhood. My father was from Italy. The accent I used for Gino is totally my father's—he had that until he died. And like Gino, he was a man of integrity, according to his standards."

When the courtly Ameche saw that the script required him to curse, he held up the scene for a few minutes to first apologize to everyone on the set for what he was about to say.

⊗ **MISS:** For some reason, Mamet often directs his actors to speak with an unemotional, almost-monotone delivery. It slows everything down and occasionally steals the fun from this comic caper.

✎ **WHAT THEY WROTE AT THE TIME:** "Mamet tells a fairytale for adults; a sweet, funny one about the Mafia. Joe Mantegna is wonderful in the more flashy performance, but Don Ameche steals this picture in his role as the simple man who finds himself in a world of glitz and desire. . . . Ameche's character always answers honestly and warmly. That's the joke of the movie—if you play it straight and decently, you can do it better than if you try to outsmart people." Gene Siskel, *Siskel & Ebert at the Movies*

🎬 **PIVOTAL SCENE:** The meeting where Don Giuseppe tries to ascertain whether Gino is the real deal is to be savored. Watching the scene, you know what answers the Don is looking for. And you also know what the innocent Gino is saying.

Don: "It's good to know one's family."

Gino: "Sure, I gotta big family."

Don: "And still, no matter how big your family, you know all their names."

Gino: "From the little one up."

The beauty is that Gino keeps answering truthfully without blowing his cover. And at the end of the scene, the two men embrace as new best friends—neither really understanding what the other is truly about.

◉ **REPEATED WATCHING QUOTIENT:** Worth seeing once for every 20 other gangster movies you watch, just for an escape from the mayhem.

❞ **BEST LINE:** Gino: "We were gonna go fishing tomorrow. Me and Don Giuseppe."

Jerry: "You were gonna go fishing? If Don Giuseppe finds out who you are, you were going to go fishing as the bait."

🔫 **VIOLENCE LEVEL:** Virtually none. Well, one guy gets punched in the face.

🎭 **"I KNOW THAT GAL":** That leggy Wheel of Fortune spinner in Tahoe? That's 25-year-old Felicity Huffman in her cinematic debut. Many miles away from Wisteria Lane.

⊕ **IF YOU LIKED THIS, YOU'LL LIKE:** *House of Games*, Mamet's dark and twisting 1987 look at con men. No fewer than 15 members of Mamet's troupe of stage actors—including Mantegna, Macy and the always-edgy Ricky Jay—appear in both films.

🍿 **BET YOU DIDN'T KNOW:** Ameche starred as the title character in 1939's *The Story of Alexander Graham Bell*. The film was so popular that for a decade, people used the word "ameche" as slang for the telephone—as in, "You're wanted on the ameche."

AN INTERVIEW WITH JOE MANTEGNA

Joe Mantegna is a distinguished actor who has appeared in more than 50 films—often playing a gangster. He costars in three films in this book—*Things Change*, *Bugsy* and *The Godfather: Part III*.

***Things Change* has a very different approach from most gangster movies....**

Yes, it's sentimental and perhaps charming, and you don't often find mob movies like that. That's largely because of the collaboration between writer-director David Mamet, who has a tremendous feel for people, and Shel Silverstein, who wrote poetry and children's books. So it had a unique sensibility for a mob movie.

Your character in Things Change, *a mob gofer named Jerry, is the perpetual screw-up. How did you view the character going in?*

The way I saw him was like this: A year earlier, I had done *House of Games*. My character in that, Mike Mancuso, was a guy who knew who he was. He was strong and self-assured. So now, I'm Jerry, who thought he was Mike Mancuso—but wasn't. He thinks he's *that* guy, but he's mistaken. He's trying to pretend, but he's not really made for that life. At the end of the day, he's more like Don Ameche's gracious character of the shoeshine man.

What was it like working with Don Ameche?

It was great, and the older I get, the more I appreciate the opportunity of hanging around a Hollywood legend. You know, I paid tribute to him in *Godfather III*. There's a scene where Joey Zasa is talking to reporters, and I ad libbed the line about Italians being a great people. I say that an Italian, Antonio Meucci, invented the phone and that we also have the guy, Don Ameche, who played the guy people mistakenly believe invented the phone. I did that as a shoutout to Don.

You also appear regularly as the voice of mob boss Fat Tony on The Simpsons....

Oh yeah, nothing interferes with my doing *The Simpsons*. It really is my favorite role, because it's so fun. It started right after I'd finished *Godfather III*, and it was going to be a one-shot deal. Next thing I know, he becomes the most-repeated non-cast character on the show. I travel a lot—Australia, England—and the role people always ask me about is Fat Tony. Well, it's nice to be known for something.

Let me ask you about that third Godfather. Did you have any reservations when you were offered the role of mob boss Joey Zasa?

No reservations at all. Yes, the first two might be the greatest movies ever, and going back 18 years later was a huge risk. People joked to me, "You've hit the jackpot, you're making the Italian *Star Wars*." But when Francis Ford Coppola asks, you don't say no.

Honestly, things weren't easy from the start. The original script had Robert Duvall in it. He backed out, so major changes were needed. Then, Winona Ryder dropped out at the last second. They hired Coppola's daughter, Sofia, who was just a young girl visiting from art school who fell into the role. But that wasn't my business or concern. I was just thrilled to be part of the trilogy.

What do you say to fans who were disappointed in that movie?

I get it. But if you look at the movie on its own, it works. In hindsight, it was impossible for it to live up to expectations after all those years. But when I talk to people in their 20s or 30s—who didn't see the first two right when they came out—they appreciate the entire trilogy and say that they loved *Part III*. They may not even know who Brando was, or have lived with the Corleones all those years, or seen the hype. So in a way, that's heartening.

Why do you think the gangster genre has been so successful for all these years?

People are fascinated with those who walk on the wrong side of the tracks—Western gunmen, outlaws, bikers. We're titillated by that. Gangsters are the same. It's a chance to look through the window without living the life, without ending up hanging from a meat hook in an alley.

Plus, the whole Omerta issue makes it intriguing. I have relatives who are borderline into the life. They say in the old days there was this code of honor. Now, for a sandwich they'll rat out their mother. That sense of honor is attractive to viewers just like the old code of the West.

What do you think of criticism that the movies cast a bad light on Italian-Americans?

My thoughts are well documented. For every time I play a Joey Zasa or Fat Tony, I also make sure I play a redeeming Italian-American character. I've done that with David Rossi in *Criminal Minds*, or when I did the HBO series *First Monday*, when I insisted that the Supreme Court justice I played was an Italian-American.

I make no apologies for playing mob characters. Let's face it; most Mafia guys aren't named Smith or Jones. We can't hide from that. And maybe the way to desensitize it is to expose it. The more you laugh at something, the more it becomes less of a thing.

62 LAYER CAKE (2004–R)

STARS: DANIEL CRAIG, COLM MEANEY, KENNETH CRANHAM, JAMIE FOREMAN, MICHAEL GAMBON | DIRECTOR: MATTHEW VAUGHN

Matthew Vaughn was the producer for Guy Ritchie's popular but—some would say—disjointed British gangster films *Lock, Stock and Two Smoking Barrels* (1998) and *Snatch* (2000). It's clear from this twisted saga of London's drug underworld that he was paying attention.

Layer Cake, Vaughn's first crack at directing, moves with much the same rhythm as the Ritchie movies. It also employs the same kind of convoluted plot that viewers either loved or hated in those films. Vaughn also captures Ritchie's trademark blend of style and substance thanks in large part to the performance of Daniel Craig.

Craig, in a pre-James Bond role, plays a businessman/drug dealer who has made his money and now plans to get out. But his mentor and boss, Jimmy Price (Kenneth Cranham), wants one last favor. The result is chaos. Fast-paced and at times terribly brutal, *Layer Cake* doesn't try to moralize and offers few heroes.

"I'm not a gangster, just a businessman," Craig says in one of several voice-overs as the movie opens. "And my commodity happens to be cocaine."

Vaughn and screenwriter J. J. Connolly (author of the novel on which the movie is based) make a not-too-subtle argument for the legalization of drugs early in the movie with a futuristic shot of Craig walking the aisles of a pharmacy stocked with "FCUK" labeled boxes and bottles of over-the-counter cocaine, heroin, meth and assorted other illegal drugs. (FCUK stands for "French Connection United Kingdom," a high-end clothing line whose founder, Stephen Marks, was executive producer of the movie. Talk about product placement.)

The film's point is that branding and legalization may be the only way to get a handle on the billion-dollar drug market and put an end to the cycle of violence that stretches from manufacturer to mass supplier to middle man to street user.

Layer Cake focuses on that cycle with Craig, the West End businessman whose name we never learn (he's referred to only as XXXX in the credits) naively believing that he can stay above the fray.

As his voice sets the story in motion, we see him moving through the streets of London, suave, sophisticated and totally at ease. He has a real estate company as a legitimate front, a money-laundering Pakistani accountant and a team of associates insulating him from the seedier side of the drug underworld.

Or so he believes.

The movie's title refers to the various strata of the chaotically violent, multibillion dollar world of cocaine trafficking. Craig may think he's made it to the top layer of that world, but he is about to learn that he is a lot closer to the bottom. Caught in the switches of a series of double-crosses and never quite sure whom he can trust, Craig eventually becomes the gangster that he claims not to be.

Reviews were mixed when *Layer Cake* was released in 2004, but following Craig's success as the latest incarnation of 007, the movie gained a cult following.

One reviewer called it a "masterly, intricately plotted crime story" while another wrote that it was "lamentably short of narrative coherence." Several reviewers noted Craig's striking resemblance to the late, great Steve McQueen.

Like McQueen, Craig speaks with his eyes and his body as well as his words. And the message he sends, on a visceral level, is "watch me." The film works in large part because when Craig's on screen, he dominates it.

Cranham and Michael Gambon are perfect as drug kingpins Price and Eddie Temple, two players clearly higher on the layer cake than our man. Both manipulate him into doing their bidding in a battle of wits that revolves around Temple's drug-addicted daughter and a stolen shipment of one million ecstasy pills that Price wants Craig's character to put on the market.

The drugs were stolen from Serbian war criminals operating in Amsterdam. A group of scatter-shot drug dealers, led by Duke (Jamie Foreman) pull off the heist, but then bungle their way toward getting the product to market.

Murder and mayhem ensue.

The leader of the Serbians says he wants Duke's head. And he means it literally.

Sienna Miller's Tammy provides Craig with a love interest, although her original attachment to Duke's nephew Sidney (Ben Whishaw) adds to Craig's problems.

Craig's underworld sidekick, Morty (George Harris), seems to be a reasonable bloke until he runs into an old acquaintance in a restaurant. Morty proceeds to brutally beat his old friend and then pours a pot of hot tea (it's a London restaurant, what else would you expect) over the hapless victim. We later learn in a flashback that the "friend" had set Morty up for a fall that led to a 10-year prison stint.

Colm Meaney, as always, is masterful as Gene, another player in the drug world.

In fact, almost everyone we meet is in the drug game. And while they occupy different layers of it, their motivation is the same: money.

"Life is so fucking good I can taste it in my spit," Craig says early on when he still believes he can walk away.

Vaughn, in explaining his approach to the film, said he was aiming for the MTV generation.

"They want it all," he said in an interview. "They want it now. And they want it quick."

The same can be said for those doing business in the drug underworld that *Layer Cake* so accurately portrays.

⊙ **HIT:** Vaughn does a masterful job creating the treacherous, no-one-can-be-trusted drug underworld. And then lets his narrative show how Craig's character slowly comes to realize the rules of the game. The character study makes this so much more than a Guy Ritchie clone.

⊗ **MISS:** The Serbians who are ripped off and seek to get revenge and/or their ecstasy back are Romanian actors. They speak Romanian, not Serbian. Of course, those of us who depended on the subtitles for translation didn't have a clue.

👆 **BET YOU DIDN'T KNOW:** J. J. Connolly's novel *Layer Cake* was 344 pages long. His first draft for the movie script ran 408 pages. Needless to say, a lot of it was cut.

99 **BEST LINE:** "Always remember that one day all this drug monkey business will be legal. They won't leave it to people like me, not when they finally figure out how much money is to be made—not millions, fucking billions. Recreational drugs . . . giving people what they want: good times today, stupor tomorrow."—Daniel Craig's XXXX in a voice-over as the film opens.

➡ **DON'T FAIL TO NOTICE:** In one of the final scenes, when XXXX and his new team gather for a meeting in the country club that he now belongs to, the gangsters are sitting around a table eating . . . layer cake.

✒ **WHAT THEY WROTE AT THE TIME:** "A stylish and classic gangster saga about the clashing of rival empires, where the only thing worse than the killer before you is the killer waiting behind him. There's no escape in this world, only moments of personal courage, grace and luck."—Desson Thomson, *Washington Post*

◀ **CASTING CALL:** Jamie Foreman, the actor who plays Duke, is the son of a London gangster and associate of the notorious Kray twins—the mobster brothers who terrorized London in the 1960s.

☠ **BODY COUNT:** Twelve.

63 THE ASPHALT JUNGLE (1950–NR)

STARS: STERLING HAYDEN, SAM JAFFE, LOUIS CALHERN, MARILYN MONROE
DIRECTOR: JOHN HUSTON

This book is jam-packed with so-called "heist movies"—films that focus on a gang of criminals plotting the perfect caper. *Rififi*, *Reservoir Dogs*, *The Killing* and *The Usual Suspects* are classics of the genre.

Before all of those, there was John Huston's *The Asphalt Jungle*. This tale of a jewel theft gone wrong is credited with resetting the ground rules for gangster films. More than any previous effort, it focuses on the inner lives and aspirations of its criminals. The film lays out, in gritty detail, the financing, planning and execution of a robbery—as well as the inevitable fallout. To steal a sports term, this is a real Xs-and-Os look at the business.

If it all seems familiar, that's because its template has been copied dozens of times. But *The Asphalt Jungle* didn't just come first. All these decades later, it continues to hold up as both a character study and as a spellbinder.

Not that everyone agreed upon its release. Back in 1950, MGM chief Louis B. Mayer panned his studio's own film as "full of nasty, ugly people doing nasty, ugly things."

"I wouldn't walk across the room to see something like that," he said.

Gee, boss. Thanks for the support. We'll be sure to put that on the promo posters.

The movie is based on a novel by W. R. Burnett (a.k.a. the Poet Laureate of American Crime Writing), who also authored *Little Caesar*, *Scarface* and *High Sierra*. It's directed by the great John Huston. Included in the DVD is a brief statement in which Huston addresses the audience and says, "You may not admire the characters in this movie, but I think they will fascinate you."

Indeed they will. The center of the story is aging criminal mastermind Doc Riedenschneider (Sam Jaffe), a scrawny German emigrant just out of prison after a seven-year stint. He apparently spent all that time hatching a foolproof plot to commit the largest jewel heist in the history of the Midwest, from which he expects to net $500,000.

Doc's got the specifics all laid out. He recruits a crew that includes a safecracker (Anthony Caruso), a driver (young James Whitmore), a so-called "hooligan" for muscle (Sterling Hayden) and a well-connected financier (Louis Calhern) to provide seed money and later fence the jewels.

We get to see each man's inner life and motivation for taking part in the heist. The hooligan, named Dix Handley, is tired of getting rousted by big-city cops and wants to return to Kentucky to live on a horse farm, as he had in his youth. The financier, a corrupt lawyer named Alonzo Emmerich, is supporting both a wife and a stunning young mistress played by an actress we guarantee you'll recognize.

And Doc? Well, Doc's got this creepy thing for teenaged girls. He tells everyone that his plan after pulling the heist is to retire to Mexico so he can ogle the young ladies.

"We all work for our vices," Doc explains. In his case, that proves to be his undoing.

This Dream Team of criminals is able to pull off the robbery, but not without slipups. Because *The Asphalt Jungle* was made in 1950 when Hollywood still operated under the Motion Picture Production Code, there was no way the robbers could be allowed to get away with it as they could years later

in, say, *Ocean's Eleven*. (Huston did win one fight with the censorship board, having one of the characters commit suicide rather than face the wrath of the law.)

So the back half of the movie focuses on the pursuit and eventual capture of the gang. Greed, of course, leads to double-crosses and murder. And surrounding these criminals is a society as crooked as they are. You meet dirty cops, shady lawyers and posturing public officials. Gee, who would have thought?

The strength of *The Asphalt Jungle* is in the interaction of its characters, particularly Jaffe's criminal genius and Hayden's simple tough guy. Some of the best scenes carry little dialogue, but are masterful at delineating the gang members with all their faults and attributes.

And despite Huston's warning that "you might not admire the characters," in the end you might instead be surprised how much you end up rooting for them to survive.

◉ **HIT:** In a solid cast, Hayden stands out as the career thug who has got a sense of honor and longs for a return to the peaceful life of his youth. Watch for the tender scene where he reminisces to his sometimes girlfriend (Jean Hagen) about riding his first horse.

The sulking, hulking Hayden was a solid performer with one career problem: he hated acting. "I couldn't stand the work," he said, "because in the final analysis, an actor is only a pawn." He described his films as, "Bastards conceived in contempt of life and spewn out onto screens across the world with noxious ballyhoo; saying nothing, contemptuous of the truth, sullen and lecherous."

Sheesh, and we thought Louis B. Mayer was a tad critical.

⊗ **MISS:** The DVD commentary by film historian Drew Casper (a Woody Allen sound-alike) is a snoozefest. Listen to it only if you're nostalgic for your old 90-minute college lectures.

✎ **WHAT THEY WROTE AT THE TIME:** "Has the authority of a blow in your solar plexus. It leaves you physically tired with sheer tension, participation and belief. It is the crime picture of the decade, and it may be the best one ever made. This picture drives home the corollary thought that criminals are also human beings."—Archer Winsten, *New York Post*

🎬 PIVOTAL SCENE: That sequence showing the jewel robbery is one of the best-staged capers in movie history.

We watch the crew hammer through a brick wall into the store and deactivate the alarm. Three of them then slide under the electric-eye alarm, pick a lock to gain access to the vault and drill through the safe's door.

The yegg carefully opens a bottle of nitroglycerin (called "the soup") and sets off a charge. The explosion opens the safe, but also trips alarms at a nearby business. That alerts police. Their sirens whine in the background as Doc pours the gems into a sack. The thieves escape, but not before another mishap (which we don't want to reveal).

John Huston devotes 11 minutes to this claustrophobic scene, trusting his audience's patience in a way that no director would today. There are few words and no soundtrack music. The silence helps build the tension to near-boil.

✔ REALITY CHECK: Even by 1950 standards, the store security is lame. A fortune of jewels sitting behind a brick wall in a safe that takes all of five minutes to bust open? We don't think so.

☺ GOOF: During the big heist, the gang is careful not to step in the line of the electric-eye alarm—at least for a while. When they debate whether to abandon the plan as the police sirens go off, Dix is clearly standing right in front of the electric eye.

◉ REPEATED WATCHING QUOTIENT: Watch all the noir films in the book, then check this one out a second time.

➡ DON'T FAIL TO NOTICE: Marilyn Monroe, before she was a star, in a small role as the paramour of corrupt power broker Emmerich. Actually, why are we saying this? There's absolutely *no* chance you'll fail to notice the 23-year-old beauty.

By the way, in the DVD commentary, actor James Whitmore says other cast members regarded Monroe as shy and insecure.

◀ CASTING CALL: Georgia Holt auditioned for the sex bomb role won by Monroe. If you don't recognize Holt's name from any other films, that's because she didn't make any. She did, however, make her mark as the mother of Cher.

🔫 VIOLENCE LEVEL: Low. There's one scene where a dirty cop slaps around a bookie, but other than that, not much.

🙶 BEST LINE: "Experience has taught me never to trust a policeman," says Doc. "Just when you think one's alright, he turns legit."

⊛ IF YOU LIKED THIS, YOU'LL LIKE: This is one of three John Huston-directed movies in this book (including *Key Largo* and *Prizzi's Honor*). All of his classics are worth seeing, especially *The African Queen, The Treasure of the Sierra Madre* and *The Maltese Falcon.*

☻ "I KNOW THAT GUY": Fans of *Nick at Nite* might recognize the night clerk Dix robs early in the movie as a younger version of general store operator Sam Drucker in *Green Acres*. Frank Cady is the master thespian behind both roles.

☙ BODY COUNT: Three on-screen, one more offscreen.

64 BULLETS OVER BROADWAY (1994–PG)

STARS: JOHN CUSACK, DIANNE WIEST, JENNIFER TILLY, CHAZZ PALMINTERI
DIRECTOR: WOODY ALLEN

Woody Allen broke out of a directing funk with this classic underworld comedy, a Runyonesque look at the guys and dolls of 1920s Broadway. The film grabbed seven Academy Award nominations, with Dianne Wiest winning an Oscar as Best Supporting Actress.

Wiest gives an over-the-top and totally hilarious performance as Helen Sinclair, a boozy, aging diva who is cast as the leading lady in a play by struggling Greenwich Village writer David Shayne (John Cusack).

Shayne is the neurotic central figure in the movie, the role that Allen would usually play himself. This time, he stuck to directing (and cowriting with Douglas McGrath). It was a wise choice.

While played for laughs, *Bullets Over Broadway* does have a serious underlying theme: how far is an artist willing to go to ensure the integrity of his art? The question is raised early in the film when Shayne and his Village mentor and rival, the bombastic Sheldon Flender (perfectly portrayed by Rob Reiner), are sitting in a café discussing their craft.

This is Woody Allen, the writer and director, taking a not-so-subtle shot at the self-indulgent and self-absorbed actors, writers and directors in the entertainment industry.

"I have never had a play produced," Flender boasts. "That's right. And I've written one play a year for the past 20 years."

"Yes," says Shayne, "but that's because you're a genius. And the proof is that both common people and intellectuals find your work completely incoherent."

Flender then poses the hypothetical: "Let's say there was a burning building and you could rush in and you could save only one thing—either the last known copy of Shakespeare's plays or some anonymous human being. What would you do?"

He and Shayne both agree that you save the Bard's work, everyone else be damned. The artists talk at great length about the value of what they and the greats who have come before them have given the world.

But it is a mobster—from their perspective a "Neanderthal"—who ultimately faces that dilemma and makes the film's life-or-death decision over the integrity of his art.

The gangster faced with the artistic crisis—and who also fires most of the bullets in *Bullets Over Broadway*—is Cheech (Chazz Palminteri). One year after his highly acclaimed performance as mob boss Sonny LoSpecchio in *A Bronx Tale* (which he also wrote) and a year before his role as a U.S. Customs agent in *The Usual Suspects*, Palminteri turned in an understated but dead-on (no pun intended) portrayal of a mobster out of his element but not in over his head.

Cheech is assigned as the bodyguard to Olive (Jennifer Tilly), the Mafia moll and aspiring actress who has been guaranteed a key role in Shayne's play because her boyfriend, mob boss Nick Valenti (Joe Viterelli), has put up the cash to finance the production. (We also have to wonder if Allen wasn't tweaking Jack Valenti, the longtime president of the Motion Picture Association of America, by giving his surname to a mob boss.)

Most of the action takes place during rehearsals as the cast—Helen, Olive, leading man Warner Purcell (Jim Broadbent) and costar Eden Brent (Tracey Ullman)—run their lines and bicker over everything from stage direction and their characters' motivations to Brent's incessantly barking Chihuahua, Mr. Woofles.

Shayne agonizes over having sold his artistic soul to a mob boss and is racked with additional guilt because he is cheating on his long-suffering girlfriend, Ellen (Mary-Louise Parker), with the much older but famous Helen Sinclair.

Sinclair clearly plays to Shayne's vanity, telling him at one point, "We're having dinner Sunday with Gene O'Neill. He's heard your writing is morbid and depressing. He's dying to meet you."

Cheech watches it all unfold while periodically dispatching rivals for his mob boss. But he also begins to make plot suggestions and to rewrite dialogue for Shayne. The play, in fact, finally starts to work because of Cheech's suggestions. Shayne, at first reluctant, quietly agrees to rework his "masterpiece" with the mobster—the ultimate ghost writer.

During a meeting in a pool hall where he hangs out, Cheech tells Shayne that his story is good, but his dialogue is weak.

"Nobody talks like that," he says in thick gangsterese. "You don't write like people talk."

Cheech agrees to fix everything wrong with Shayne's play, taking a paper and pencil and going to work while assuring Shayne that no one will know.

"Where I come from, nobody squeals," he says.

As the play steadily improves, Cheech becomes more invested in the production and more aghast at Olive's show-stopping—and not in a good way—performance.

"She's killing my words," he tells Shayne. "I can't have her ruining my show."

He quickly amends the comment to "our show," but Cheech's point is clear: someone needs to do something about Olive, even if she is his boss's girlfriend.

When Olive has to sit out a performance during a pre-Broadway run in Boston and an understudy takes over her role, the play gets even better. And Cheech gets even more frustrated.

Just how far *will* an artist go to ensure the integrity of his work?

The last straw comes when mob boss Valenti tells the play's producer, Julian Marx (Jack Warden), that he wants Olive to have more lines. With the play about to open on Broadway, Marx tries to explain that last-minute changes and additions could upset the staging and confuse the cast. But Valenti, who meets with Marx in the nightclub where Olive used to dance, doesn't want to hear it.

"Let's avoid confusion," he says. "She gets some new fuckin' lines or I'll nail your kneecaps to the dance floor."

Cheech, of course, has other ideas.

⊙ **HIT:** As with almost any Woody Allen movie set in New York, the music perfectly captures the mood, era and pacing of the story. From Al Jolson's "Toot, Toot Tootsie Goodbye" to Dick Hyman's rendition of "Thou Swell," the soundtrack provides a trip back in time. Other recordings come from Duke Ellington, Bix Beiderbecke and Red Nichols & His Five Pennies.

⊗ **MISS:** Hard to find a miss, unless you're one of those gangster movie purists who believe there's no room in the genre for comedy.

🍎 **BET YOU DIDN'T KNOW:** Dianne Wiest won an Academy Award as Best Supporting Actress twice, each time in a Woody Allen film. The first was for her work in *Hannah and Her Sisters*. For her second Oscar statue, Wiest beat out Jennifer Tilly, who was also nominated for her performance in *Bullets Over Broadway*. Palminteri was nominated for Best Supporting Actor, with that award going to Martin Landau for his work in *Ed Wood*. The movie also got nominations for Best Director, Best Original Screenplay, Best Art Direction-Set Decoration and Best Costume Design.

🗨 **BEST LINE:** A somewhat inebriated Helen predicts that Shayne will be the toast of Broadway once the play debuts. "The world will open to you like an oyster," she says, then has second thoughts. "No, not like an oyster. The world will open to you like a magnificent vagina."

✎ **WHAT THEY WROTE AT THE TIME:** "[Woody Allen] successfully reinvents himself as comic philosopher, finding wicked humor in questions of artistic life or death. . . . *Bullets Over Broadway* is a bright, energetic, sometimes side-splitting comedy with vital matters on its mind, precisely the kind of sharp-edged farce he has always done best."—Janet Maslin, *New York Times*

➡ **DON'T FAIL TO NOTICE:** The name of Shayne's play appears on a theater marquee several times during the film. Its title, *God of Our Fathers*, is a nice twist on the title of what we consider the all-time greatest mob movie.

😎 **"I KNOW THAT GUY":** A hit man who appears early in the movie and is later sent to deal with Cheech is played by Tony Sirico, who will forever be remembered as Paulie Walnuts from *The Sopranos*.

👁 **REPEATED WATCHING QUOTIENT:** Any time you're looking for a laugh. *Bullets Over Broadway* offers a series of vignettes, each one worth watching on its own.

💀 **BODY COUNT:** Twelve.

65 SALVATORE GIULIANO (1962–NR)

STARS: SALVO RANDONE, FRANK WOLFF | DIRECTOR: FRANCESCO ROSI

There is a common refrain among academics and law enforcement officials who have studied the Italian Mafia, arguably the best known and in many ways the seed group for all other crime syndicates.

To understand the Mafia, they say, you first have to understand Sicily.

Francisco Rosi's riveting account of the life, times and death of Sicilian bandit Salvatore Giuliano is a good place to start.

In his excellent commentary included in the movie's DVD package, British film critic Peter Cowie calls the quasi-documentary a "new kind of investigative cinema" and "the first film to strip away the mystique that surrounded the Mafia."

He also offers high praise for Rosi, who shot the entire film in Sicily and used locals to fill all but a few key roles. Cowie called Rosi "an altogether new voice . . . a director stabbing his finger in your face and saying this is the way the world really is today."

Movies like the Brazilian gangster saga *City of God* (reviewed elsewhere in this book) and Costa-Gavras' famous *Z* (1969) built and expanded on the storytelling style developed here by Rosi.

Not unlike Sicily itself, *Salvatore Giuliano* is both fascinating and troubling. It is a story built around lies, betrayals and shifting alliances.

Salvatore Giuliano was a poor peasant who became a bandit during World War II in Sicily. Operating primarily in the hills outside of Palermo, he built a highly effective organization and, at least in some circles, was considered a Robin Hood. But was he a member of the Mafia, or merely used by the secret society? Was he part of their criminal underworld, or had he created his own?

Rosi doesn't pretend to know the answers, but does dramatically pose the questions.

The movie opens with Giuliano's blood-soaked body lying in a courtyard in Montelepre, where he was born. Over the years, the town provided him with protection as he avoided arrest and established his reputation.

His shooting death in 1950 was international news. He had been profiled in *Time* and remained a strong advocate for an independent Sicilian state. But his role in post-war Sicily and his murder have always been the subjects of intense speculation and wild contradictions.

Rosi uses his film to raise significant questions not only about his central character, but also about the institutions—the Italian government, its political parties and the Mafia—that have controlled the island.

For Giuliano's supporters, those institutions are no different than the Greeks, the French, the Spanish and the Moors who over the centuries governed Sicily and oppressed its people.

American actor Frank Wolff is compelling in his role as Gaspare Pisciotta, a key lieutenant in Giuliano's organization who ultimately betrays him. Salvo Randone plays the Italian magistrate charged with overseeing the trial of Giuliano associates accused of the May Day massacre at Portella della Ginestra that did much to taint the image of the bandit leader.

The motivation for the attack, which left at least 11 people dead and more than 30 wounded, is never clear. Was Giuliano manipulated by politicians who feared the rise of Communism in Sicily following World War II? Was he framed by the Mafia, which at first embraced the bandit kingpin, but later found that the intense law enforcement efforts to track him down were impeding its own ability to operate? Or was he simply the kidnapper-extortionist that law enforcement authorities claimed he was, and who saw this as another in a string of violent acts orchestrated by Giuliano to expand his status and influence?

Throughout the film, we never get a close-up

shot of the actor playing the bandit king. Nor do we hear him speak. He is seen only from a distance, usually wearing an off-white trench coat and leading a band of gun-toting associates into the hills or on a raid.

His narrative relayed in flashbacks, Rosi skillfully uses cutaways from the Portella della Ginestra trial to introduce the political intrigue and Mafia treachery that may have been behind much of what Giuliano did.

Pisciotta is a key witness who, along with other members of Giuliano's band, offers insights into the outlaw and hints at a memoir—still undiscovered—in which Giuliano himself allegedly detailed the deals, promises and betrayals that began when he was recruited by politicians to head a separatist Sicilian army in 1945.

Historically, many of these issues were raised by reporters who covered the killing of Giuliano—which authorities originally claimed was the result of a shootout with Carabinieri, the Italian national police tracking him.

One reporter in the film calls in his story with a classic line that has defined the case.

"The only thing we know for certain is that he's dead," the reporter says during a telephone call to his editing desk.

Rosi cleverly uses that same reporter to make one of the fundamental points of the film.

Sweating in the Sicilian sun and moving around the neighborhood questioning locals about the "shootout" hours after Giuliano's body has been removed, the reporter stops at a lemonade stand for a drink and asks the proprietor what he thought of Giuliano.

We only see the back of the lemonade stand operator's head as he speaks.

Giuliano, he says, "took from the rich and gave to the poor."

"That's it?" asks the reporter.

Yes, says the lemonade stand operator, who then asks the reporter where he is from.

"Rome," says the reporter.

At that, the man behind the lemonade stand shakes his head and says, almost disdainfully, "What do you know about Sicily?"

⊙ **HIT:** Great pacing in this black-and-white film and its documentary style create a sense of being there, whether it's in one of the hillside hideouts or on the winding streets of a Sicilian village. Another great touch—and one borrowed by *The Godfather: Part II*—is a town crier beating a drum as he walks through the streets of Montelepre announcing curfews, rationing and other restrictions imposed on the town as authorities try to ferret out Giuliano.

⊗ **MISS:** There's not much to dislike here if you buy into the documentary style. But the film lacks a central figure and consistent narrative. This is not your typical gangster movie and, if that's what you're looking for, you'll be disappointed.

✎ **WHAT THEY WROTE AT THE TIME:** "Though the pic has many moments of suspense and excitement as it tells the Giuliano story and all that went with it, it is by no means the usual bandit-gendarme yarn. In fact, one rarely if ever catches a close-up of the notorious outlaw who made national and international headlines in the post-war years."—*Variety*

✔ **REALITY CHECK:** The Portella della Ginestra massacre scene opens with a rousing speech from one of the local Communist leaders to the villagers gathered for the annual May Day celebration. In fact, the shooting began before any speeches did, and the attack was believed to have been designed to break up the rally before it got going.

◎ **REPEATED WATCHING QUOTIENT:** History buffs and anyone with an interest in the contradictions that are Sicily will find this movie worth a second, or even a third, viewing.

♟ **BET YOU DIDN'T KNOW:** Giuliano had little faith in Italian politicians, whether from the mainland or Sicily. He once wrote a letter to President Harry Truman asking him to annex the island as an American state.

CASTING CALL: Frank Wolff struggled to make it in America, but found success in Italy after his portrayal of the conflicted Gaspare Pisciotta. He had appeared in several Roger Corman films, but made his mark in Europe. He played key roles in several spaghetti westerns and is perhaps best known to American audiences for his role as farmer Brett McBain in *Once Upon a Time in the West* (1968), the Sergio Leone classic.

BEST LINE: In one of the many voice-overs used to propel the story forward, the movie's narrator describes the villages in the hills outside Palermo as, "Giuliano's kingdom, protected by omerta, passion and terror."

IF YOU LIKED THIS, YOU'LL LIKE: *The Battle of Algiers* (1966), director Gillo Pontecorvo's excellent account of the French-Algerian civil war, or *Gomorrah* (2008), a movie based on a book by the same name that details organized crime's violent and disheartening control of present day Naples.

If you want to go in another direction, one of Mario's Puzo's last books, *The Sicilian*, was based on the life of Salvatore Giuliano. Christopher Lambert starred in the 1987 Michael Cimino movie based on the book. It's a more traditional and somewhat melodramatic film, and lacks the edge of Rosi's classic.

VIOLENCE LEVEL: Massacres and shootouts throughout the film, although none of the high-tech, up-close violence that is prevalent in more recent gangster movies.

BODY COUNT: Fifty and counting. It's impossible to get an accurate total because of the battle scenes.

THE ORIGINS OF THE WORD "MAFIA"

The word "Mafia" has become part of the American lexicon and is now used to describe almost any organized crime group. There's the Russian Mafia, the Asian Mafia, the Black Mafia, etc. The media also use the word to describe loose confederations of people participating in some type of collective, unsavory behavior. So we see and hear references to the financial mafia, the waste-hauling mafia, the political mafia, etc.

The word, like the island of Sicily that spawned it, is difficult to define. And tracing its origins is next to impossible.

Not that academicians haven't tried.

Luigi Barzini, the author of two fascinating books on Italy (*The Italians* and *From Caesar to the Mafia*) says flat out that no one knows where the word came from. Other scholars have offered interpretations that generate debate, but never lead to a definitive answer.

One theory is that the word is rooted in Arabic slang. The Sicilian dialect, like the island's mouth-watering food, has many traces of Arab influence. In this explanation, the word came from *mahyas*—an Arabic expression that signified aggressive braggadocio—or from the word *marfud*, which indicates some type of rejection.

The word *mafiusi* began appearing in Sicilian literature in the 19th century and usually referred to an individual who was bold, sometimes arrogant, but also looked up to and admired.

Another explanation—but one that most historians now reject—is that MAFIA was an acronym of a slogan dating back to the 13th century when the local population was bristling at French control of the island. A legendary uprising, known as the Sicilian Vespers, sparked a rebellion against the French, using the slogan *"morte alla Francia, Italia anela"*—which translates as "death to France, Italy cries." But since most Sicilians in the 13th century did not yet have a strong sense of their "Italian-ness" (the country wasn't unified until the 1860s), this theory seems strained at best.

The most romantic explanation—one repeated by British film critic Peter Cowie during his excellent DVD commentary on the movie *Salvatore Giuliano*—also dates to the 13th century and the Sicilian Vespers, but features a familial twist. It claims the term mafia sprung from an incident in a small village where a Sicilian woman was raped on her wedding night by French soldiers stationed at a garrison there. Her mother ran through the town square, screaming, "Ma figlia! Ma figlia!" ("My daughter! My daughter!"). In the guttural Sicilian dialect—in which syllables are often swallowed whole—those words can sound like "ma fia." In response to the mother's cries, the men of the village rose up and slaughtered the French soldiers before fleeing into the hills, where they became outlaws known as "mafia."

Salvatore Giuliano director Francesco Rosi offers none of the romanticism conveyed in that explanation in his docudrama, but historians could argue that the Mafia's noble and honorable roots had been bastardized and distorted by greed, corruption and politics when Giuliano took to those same Sicilian hills in the 1940s.

66 STATE OF GRACE (1990–R)

STARS: SEAN PENN, ED HARRIS, GARY OLDMAN, ROBIN WRIGHT
DIRECTOR: PHIL JOANOU

The Westies were an Irish street gang that dominated the underworld in New York City's Hell's Kitchen neighborhood for three decades. T. J. English, a former New York City cab driver, second-generation Irish-American and one-time reporter for the *Irish Times* wrote the definitive book about the gang, *The Westies: Inside New York's Irish Mob* in 1990, about the same time this movie was released.

State of Grace covers some of the same ground as English's book, fictionalizing the names of the characters and adding some dramatic associations. By and large, however, the movie stays true to the core of the story, capturing the wanton violence

and chaos that were two of the gang's trademarks.

This was disorganized organized crime.

English's book is a classic. *State of Grace*, directed by Phil Joanou, doesn't quite reach that level. But it's a good movie with a stellar cast providing mesmerizing performances.

At the top of that list is Gary Oldman, whose character of Jackie Flannery defines both the time and the neighborhood. Jackie's older brother Frankie (Ed Harris) is the leader of the gang.

Terry Noonan (Sean Penn) is Jackie's longtime friend returning to the neighborhood after an absence of more than 10 years. He rekindles his friendship and renews his romance with Kathleen

(Robin Wright), the sister of the two Flannery brothers.

John Turturro has a pivotal role as Nick. And Burgess Meredith makes a brief appearance as Finn, an aging neighborhood relic.

The relationships between the central characters form the backdrop for a story about love, honor and betrayal. And while these themes are frequently explored in traditional Italian-American Mafia movies, here we get an Irish-American underworld take on them.

As a result, there's more guilt, introspection and angst. Some comes from Kathleen, who has moved uptown to get away from her roots. But most of it comes from Terry, whose reason for coming back to the neighborhood forms the major plotline in the movie.

Staying true to the actual history of the Westies—while never defining the gang by that name—*State of Grace* builds tension into a nascent business association between Frankie Flannery and a group of mobsters from Little Italy headed by a Mafioso named Borelli (Joe Viterelli).

In real life, the Westies developed working relationships with both the Genovese and Gambino crime families in New York and sometimes served as their enforcers and hit men.

Violence was what the gang was about. As a History Channel documentary accurately noted, the Westies of the 1970s and 1980s "raised mayhem to a blood sport."

But their roots were on the sidewalks of Hell's Kitchen and in the corner taprooms where they sipped beer and smoked cigarettes while sitting on the same stools that their fathers and their fathers before them had occupied.

Joanou, working from a script by Dennis McIntyre, is able to convey that sense of belonging and the anger and frustration that came with change—whether from the gentrification of the neighborhood or the association with the wiseguys from Little Italy. Oldman's Jackie Flannery voices those sentiments repeatedly.

"They don't even want to call it Hell's Kitchen no more," he tells Noonan shortly after his return. "Renamed it Clinton."

At another point, he says, "Yuppies got to be thicker than the rats and the roaches. Assholes can't live without their dogs. Got dog shit all over the sidewalk. And it didn't used to be that way. It used to be, you dropped a cone, you could lift it up and finish it. People are roaming the streets homeless because of these assholes."

But Jackie's brother Frankie, who has moved to a nice home in suburban New Jersey, sees opportunities in those changes and in emulating the wiseguys. He talks about maturity and discipline to a brother who just wants to fight, drink, smoke and make love. The difference is defined early in the film when Frankie takes his crew into a local bar where they are attempting to shake down the owner.

Before they can grab any cash, the gang members, with Jackie right in the middle of it, start to fight among themselves. Then they all go have a drink.

It's an Irish thing.

Frankie ultimately chooses the guys from Little Italy over his brother and the young brawlers he has around him. But this is only after a tension-filled sitdown in Little Italy.

Frankie meets with Borelli but arranges to have Jackie's crew ready to rumble in the event things don't go well. Jackie is told to set up in an abandoned building on Mott Street near the café where the meeting is to take place. Mott Street is in the heart of Little Italy, maybe a 20-minute car ride from Hell's Kitchen.

As Jackie jumps into a van to head downtown, he asks his associates, "Anyone know how to get to Mott Street?"

Frankie, of course, knows. That's the difference between the two brothers.

After Jackie is killed, Noonan has to choose between completing the job that brought him back to his old neighborhood or confronting Frankie and avenging the murder of his friend.

The climax is a shootout during the St. Patrick's Day Parade in New York City. The gunplay takes place in a neighborhood bar. Where else would you expect a bunch of Irish gangsters to settle their differences?

⊙ HIT: The gritty feel of Hell's Kitchen—old cars, trash-strewn streets, houses in disrepair—sets the mood for the narrative. The point, at the end of the day, is this: You can't go home again. The question is: Why would you want to?

⊗ MISS: The premise, without giving up the film's big plot twist, is a bit of a stretch. Noonan is gone for 10 to 12 years. The explanations of what he's been doing during that time and why he's come back to New York seem unrealistic . . . highly unlikely, in fact.

✎ WHAT THEY WROTE AT THE TME: "Every gangster story needs its loose cannon, the individual scary and erratic enough to take the possibility of danger way beyond the theoretical. Better still if that character, like Sonny Corleone of *The Godfather* or Robert De Niro's Johnny Boy in *Mean Streets,* is also vastly sympathetic, despite his own least enlightened or charitable instincts. *State of Grace* has a comparable figure in Jackie Flannery, the toughest and most volatile of the Hell's Kitchen Irish-American hoods who are this film's unflinching focus."—Janet Maslin, *New York Times*

✔ REALITY CHECK: One of the three unnamed mobsters gunned down in the bar by Jackie is played by Louie Eppolito, the so-called Mafia Cop. Eppolito was one of the most decorated police detectives in New York City history, but left the department under a cloud because several of his relatives were members of the Gambino crime family. He wrote a book about his life called *Mafia Cop.* He denied that he had any ties to organized crime and tried to start a career as an actor and screenwriter.

In 2005, he and his former detective partner, Stephen Caracappa, were indicted on charges that, while on the NYPD force, they took money to funnel information to notorious mobster Anthony "Gaspipe" Casso, helping Casso kill at least eight people. In one instance, authorities allege, they provided bad information, giving Casso the address of a man who had the same name as someone Casso wanted dead. The wrong man was killed. Eppolito and Caracappa were also charged with carrying out one hit for Casso.

◉ REPEATED WATCHING QUOTIENT: Oldman's performance alone makes this worth revisiting from time to time.

🍎 BET YOU DIDN'T KNOW: Both Oldman and Harris portrayed composer Ludwig von Beethoven in different movies. Oldman was the lead in *Immortal Beloved* (1994) and Harris starred in *Copying Beethoven* (2006).

◀ CASTING CALL: Bill Pullman was originally chosen to play Frank Flannery, but was replaced by Harris.

" BEST LINE: "Jesus Christ, I thought you Kitchen guys were tough guys," Nick says during a dispute with Terry.

"We're not tough, Nick," Noonan replies. "We're just crazy."

☞ VIOLENCE LEVEL: Near the top of the charts, wanton and repetitive.

⚰ BODY COUNT: Thirteen.

67 KEY LARGO (1948–NR)

STARS: HUMPHREY BOGART, EDWARD G. ROBINSON, LAUREN BACALL, LIONEL BARRYMORE | DIRECTOR: JOHN HUSTON

This was Bogey channeling Rick from *Casablanca* and Edward G. Robinson doing an updated version of Rico from *Little Caesar*. Both actors are great. Lauren Bacall and Lionel Barrymore—not too shabby casting there—provide good support.

But the storyline is just so-so and too often instead of tension, we feel claustrophobia.

Part of the reason for that, of course, is that *Key Largo* is based on a play. Most of the action takes place in a hotel lobby during a hurricane. In fact, this is probably the only gangster movie where the weather is a genuine character, just as violent and volatile as Robinson's Johnny Rocco.

Rocco is a gangster hiding out in Cuba who has slipped into the Florida Keys to make a "delivery" to a mobster from Miami. He holes up at the Largo Hotel with four of his associates while he waits for the meeting.

Frank McCloud (Bogart), a World War II vet, comes to the hotel to pay his respects to the father and the widow of George Temple, a soldier who died under his command in Italy. The father, James Temple (Lionel Barrymore), owns the hotel. His daughter-in-law Nora (Lauren Bacall) helps him run it.

The clash between McCloud and Rocco—good versus evil writ large—drives a plot that unfolds in stages.

Rocco and his four henchmen at first claim to be tourists looking for a chance to fish the Keys in the off season. They eventually drop that façade, pull their guns and take over the hotel as they wait for the gang from Miami to arrive.

A hurricane complicates the issue. Rocco's bullying of his girlfriend Gaye Dawn (Claire Trevor) and James Temple's attempt to help some local Indians provide secondary story lines that flesh out the characters.

Rocco, despite the hurricane bearing down on the hotel, is nothing if not self-indulgent. The first time we see him, he's taking a bath with a fan blowing on him and a large cigar jammed into his mouth. And despite the heat and the volatile atmospheric pressure, he gets dressed as if he's on his way to a nightclub, putting on two-tone shoes, starched white shirt, floral tie and double-breasted jacket. The tie never is loosened.

McCloud quickly figures out Rocco's true identity and purpose, but shies away from confrontation. Like Rick in *Casablanca*, he claims that he will risk his life for no man.

"One Rocco more or less isn't worth dying for," he says, adding, "I fight nobody's battles but my own."

He takes a slap in the face from Rocco during one dust-up and turns down a chance to draw on the gangster in another. As it turns out, the gun he was offered had no bullets in it.

"But our hero didn't know that," a cackling Rocco says derisively as Nora and her wheelchair-bound father-in-law wrestle with what to make of McCloud, the Army officer George Temple described in his letters home as brave and honorable.

James Temple has no trouble expressing his opinion of the gangster who has taken over his hotel. When Rocco complains about being deported, the old man, from his wheelchair, shouts, "You shouldn't have been deported. You should have been exterminated."

Rocco laughs at the old man who falls out of his wheelchair taking a swing at the gangster.

Later a snarling Rocco turns away the group of local Indians seeking shelter at the hotel—as they always do during a hurricane. Two members of the tribe have recently escaped from jail and are being sought by the Sheriff's Department. This brings the law to the hotel and into Rocco's orbit.

A deputy sheriff and the two escaped Indians end up dead before McCloud and Rocco finally stop circling each other and have their mano-a-mano. This is after Rocco has sold a satchel of counterfeit bills to the hoods from Miami and has forced McCloud to pilot the boat that will take him and his gang back to Cuba.

McCloud, despite his claim of indifference, proves to be the hero that the late—and never seen—George Temple said he was.

We would expect nothing less from Bogey.

◎ **HIT:** The interaction between Bogart and Robinson is classic. These are two actors at the top of their games doing what they do best. The Bogey-and-Bacall chemistry adds another spark to what is, at its heart, a run-of-the-mill melodrama.

⊗ **MISS:** After Rocco kills the deputy sheriff, two of his thugs dispose of the body by taking the corpse out to sea in a rowboat in the face of a building hurricane. The body of the deputy is dumped overboard. In fact, the two hapless thugs should have ended up in the drink as well. No way anyone is going out to sea and coming back in a rowboat during a hurricane.

🍎 **BET YOU DIDN'T KNOW:** The movie was based on a play by Maxwell Anderson, but the storyline was updated by Huston and cowriter Richard Brooks. The play, which ran on Broadway in 1939 and 1940, involved a veteran from the Spanish Civil War confronting a group of Mexican bandits.

🗩 **BEST LINE:** As the hurricane rages and Rocco paces nervously, McCloud tries to get in his head. "You don't like it, do you Rocco, the storm? Show it your gun, why don't ya'? It doesn't stop, shoot it."

✏ **WHAT THEY WROTE AT THE TIME:** "Mr. Robinson's performance is an expertly timed and timbred scan of the vulgarity, corruption and egoism of a criminal man. Mr. Bogart's enactment of a fellow who blows both hot and cold is also penetrating, largely because it's on the acid side. . . . But the script . . . was too full of words and highly cross-purposed implications to give the action full chance. Talk—endless talk—about courage and the way the world goes gums it up."—Bosley Crowther, *New York Times*

◀ **CASTING CALL:** Claire Trevor won an Academy Award for best supporting actress for her portrayal of the over-the-hill nightclub singer and mob moll abused by Rocco. She appeared in more than 60 films in a career that stretched from the 1930s to the 1980s. She was known as the "queen of film noir" in the 1940s because she frequently played the girlfriend or love interest of a bad guy. One of her last films was *Kiss Me Goodbye* (1982), in which she played Sally Fields' mother.

✔ **REALITY CHECK:** The character of Johnny Rocco was shaped from the life stories of two famous gangsters—Al Capone and Lucky Luciano. Like Capone, Rocco was from Chicago and was a major player during the bootlegging era that gave rise to the mob. And as Capone sometimes did, he used the pseudonym "Mr. Brown" when checking into the hotel. Like Luciano, Rocco had been deported and was cooling his heels in Cuba as he tried to maneuver his way back into the United States.

😃 **"I KNOW THAT GUY":** Tom Osceola, one of the two Indian brothers who have escaped from jail and are being sought by the authorities, is played in an uncredited role by Jay Silverheels. Those of us of a certain age will remember Silverheels as Tonto, the loyal and taciturn Indian companion of television's cowboy legend *The Lone Ranger*.

◉ **REPEATED WATCHING QUOTIENT:** A little too slow and wordy. Once is enough, unless you're a diehard Bogey and Bacall fan. This was the fourth and final movie the married stars made together. The others were *Dark Passage* (1947), *The Big Sleep* (1946) and *To Have and Have Not* (1944), which included the classic line from Bacall to Bogey: "You know how to whistle, don't you Steve? You just put your lips together and . . . blow."

🔪 **BODY COUNT:** Eight.

68 ATLANTIC CITY (1980–R)

STARS: BURT LANCASTER, SUSAN SARANDON | DIRECTOR: LOUIS MALLE

Lou was one tough Atlantic City gangster in his time. Says he knew Al Capone, Lucky Luciano and Meyer Lansky. Even was Bugsy Siegel's cellmate for a while.

"I had to kill guys in the day," he wistfully confides to a young drug-dealing wannabe. "Then I'd feel real bad. I'd swim way out into the ocean to clean up. Ahh, you should have seen the Atlantic in those days."

Problem is, none of it is true—unless you count spending one hour with Siegel in a community holding pen as being his cellmate. In truth, Lou was never anything more than a toady for the Atlantic City mob. Never killed anyone. Answered to the nickname "Numb Nuts."

And as the movie *Atlantic City* gets underway,

Lou—now in his seventies—is still the lowest of the low men on the organized crime flow chart. He's reduced to taking 50-cent bets from old ladies for the local numbers runner. He earns a few bucks by walking the yapping poodle belonging to the widow of his boss, Cookie Pinza, and a few more by performing sexual favors for the old crone in her apartment stuffed with kewpie dolls and pink feather boas.

That's the setup for this fine, albeit slow-paced movie. The wonderful Burt Lancaster portrays the schlepper who never made it; he's kind of like Al Pacino's Lefty Ruggiero in *Donnie Brasco*—but even more pathetic. He imagines a past that never was. Even now he lives behind the façade, eagerly buying the nonsense when a young thug patronizes him by saying, "The guys in Detroit said you were the man to see in this town."

Then the mob guy who never was finally gets his chance.

Lou stumbles upon a pile of cocaine and an eager customer. For the first time, he's got real money in his hands, enough to replace his frayed old outfit with a sharp white suit and $200 fedora. He also latches onto Sally (Susan Sarandon), a young and beautiful but weary import from Saskatchewan who wants to be a blackjack dealer but is stuck shucking oysters at a casino raw bar.

Through a series of plot twists, Lou ends up as Sally's protector and, briefly, as her lover. And the bottom-rung bum whose responsibility was once limited to fetching condoms for his boss now gets that late-in-life chance to amount to something.

Without giving away too much, we'll tell you to notice the elation in Lou's eye when he finally gets to gun down a few bad guys. The old man's got a teenager's delight at popping his cherry. And the May-December romance between Sally and Lou—unimaginable at the start of *Atlantic City*—seems to make sense, although you know it cannot last.

Lancaster, as always, is terrific. Even playing this lifelong loser, he carries himself with dignity. In one scene, as he is about to be roughed up by a mobster from Philadelphia, he gracefully brushes away the hood's arm, saying, "Don't touch the suit."

Sarandon is also great in the role of the young woman trying to escape her hick town and bad marriage. She studies French on a tape recorder and dreams that she'll end up as the first female croupier in Monte Carlo. She's desperate for worldliness. "Teach me stuff," she implores Lou at one point.

Sarandon's character of Sally represents the future of Atlantic City, where the first casino opened two years before this movie was released. Lancaster's Lou represents the past, when the mob knew how to inject some vice into the seaside vacation town. "I don't like these new casinos," Lou gripes. "Too wholesome for me. Nuns, for Chrissakes."

Of course, he cannot reverse time. But Lou does get that one last opportunity to stand up and act as he perceives a real man should act. And Sally gets

that chance to escape (in a car stolen from mobsters, no less), although odds are slim that she's going to make it all the way to Monte Carlo.

⊙ **HIT:** Lancaster and Sarandon are great. But the real star of the movie is the actual Atlantic City, the once-bustling tourist town that had declined into decay and destitution—clearly serving as a metaphor for Lancaster's character. All around are vacant lots strewn with debris, graffiti and bulldozers. Tall cranes and construction signs promise a better tomorrow.

Atlantic City was optimistic about that future in 1980. Three decades later, glitzy hotels dot the skyline. But the rubble and poverty remain, making it questionable whether legalized gambling really did much to save the downtrodden town.

⊗ **MISS:** The hippy-dippy character of Sally's sister Chrissie seems an outdated cliché. Weren't flower children gone by 1980? We just roll our eyes when the foot-rubbing mystic spouts about reincarnation or declares that she doesn't use seatbelts because "I don't believe in gravity."

✎ **WHAT THEY WROTE AT THE TIME:** "The film portrays the town of Atlantic City as a place of myth, of legends and dreams, most of them pretty tacky. It's beautiful and squalid and, like the movie itself, sometimes rueful and sometimes funny."—Vincent Canby, *New York Times*

❞ **BEST LINE:** Lou, harkening back to the era when gambling had a little sin to it: "Now it's all so goddamn legal. Howard Johnson's running a casino. Tutti Frutti and cards don't mix."

⊙ **REPEATED WATCHING QUOTIENT:** Given the slow pace and depressing tone, we'd recommend it about once a decade.

▤ **PIVOTAL SCENE:** The one you'll remember comes early when Sally, home from her job at the casino's clam bar, stands in front of her kitchen window, washing off the scent of seafood by rubbing her arms, shoulders and breasts with lemon halves. As the camera pulls back, the viewer becomes aware—as Sally must be—that she is being spied on by Lou from his scruffy apartment across the way.

It's an erotic moment. And it sets up the connection between Sally and old Lou, even though they haven't yet met. Later, as they are becoming friends, he admits to peeping. "What did you see when you looked?" Sally asks, and Lou recounts her nightly routine in stunning detail. When the camera returns to Sally, she has unbuttoned her blouse, initiating their brief love affair.

In more ways than one, Lou gets the opportunity to be the man he never was back in his prime.

➜ **DON'T FAIL TO NOTICE:** Lou and Buddy, the aging men's room attendant, have a nostalgic conversation about the days when they ran errands for Nucky Johnson.

"Remember the time Nucky sent us out to buy 100 boxes of rubbers for the party?" Buddy says. "The look the clerk gave us. A hundred boxes of rubbers for two guys? He couldn't get over it."

Nucky Johnson was the racketeer who ran Atlantic City from 1911-41 under the cover of serving as Atlantic County's treasurer. He is also the model for Nucky Thompson, the character played by Steve Buscemi in HBO's *Boardwalk Empire* series.

◀ **CASTING CALL:** Robert Mitchum was the favorite for the lead. But director Louis Malle reportedly was so put off by Mitchum's recent face lift, that he turned to Lancaster.

🔫 **VIOLENCE LEVEL:** Low, except for a gory stabbing and one scene where a mob guy smacks around Sally.

🍎 **BET YOU DIDN'T KNOW:** *Atlantic City* was nominated for each of the top five Oscars, but won none. It lost Best Picture and Original Screenplay to *Chariots of Fire*. Malle lost Best Director to Warren Beatty for *Reds*. And Lancaster and Sarandon lost the top acting awards to Henry Fonda and Katharine Hepburn in *On Golden Pond*.

😀 **"I KNOW THAT GUY":** The over-attentive restaurant waiter is played by Wallace Shawn, a five-foot-two, rubber-faced bald guy who is rarely confused with Burt Lancaster. You may recognize him as Vizzini the Sicilian, the baddest bad guy in *The Princess Bride*. Your children more likely know him as the voice of Rex the Dinosaur in *Toy Story* and its sequels.

🏊 **BODY COUNT:** Three. And you won't mourn for any of them.

69 LET·HIM HAVE IT (1991–R)

STARS: CHRISTOPHER ECCLESTON, TOM COURTENAY, EILEEN ATKINS
DIRECTOR: PETER MEDAK

On a dank London morning in January 1953, Derek Bentley was hung for murder.

More accurately, he was hung for shouting the words, "Let him have it, Chris" to a 16-year-old accomplice pointing a revolver at a police officer. The cops had surprised the duo during an attempted late-night warehouse break-in.

To the police, Bentley's five words were a command to fire and led to a constable getting shot through the head. The 19-year-old Bentley, however, insisted that his remark was a desperate plea to his pal, Chris Craig, to surrender and hand over the gun.

Director Peter Medak's powerful movie—named after the first four of those words—focuses not just on the tragic events of that night, it also examines everything that led up to them, as well as the heartbreaking aftermath, including Bentley's execution three months later.

Oh, and by the way, it's based on a true case—one that helped turn public sentiment against capital punishment, which was finally banned in Britain in 1969.

Let Him Have It takes place in the gritty London section of Croydon. In an era of poverty and rationing, the local teens idolize the town thug. He drives a fancy car and dates the prettiest girl. When he gets sent to prison for 12 years, they mourn.

Mostly, these impressionable adolescents take their cues from American gangster movies. They name their group The Bogeys and dress in black overcoats and wide-brimmed hats, making them appear as much like Yeshiva students as mobsters. Chris, the punkish 16-year-old leader, watches *Angels with Dirty Faces* and comes out mimicking James Cagney's staccato speaking style and shooting his cuffs. They even refer to police as "the coppers."

They're boys playing men. But this is more than a kid's game of cops and robbers. The lads swap revolvers like baseball cards during recess. England, we learn, is awash with black-market weapons brought back by soldiers from World War II. So when the teens' shoplifting sprees evolve into theft, they're packing heat. And this, of course, leads to the tragic episode that night on the roof of the warehouse.

Derek (Chris Eccleston), the center of the story, is a docile young man with epilepsy and an IQ of 77. He's got a loving and supportive family, but he lacks the will to stand up to bad influences. So when Chris and his crew offer friendship, Derek goes along. He embraces a set of brass knuckles (called "knuckle dusters" in the film) that Chris gives him—not that he ever intends to use them.

You can see where this is going. Derek and Chris end up on a warehouse roof, and the police response leads to the cop getting killed. Chris, as the 16-year-old triggerman, is spared the death sentence because of his age.

Derek is not as lucky. His trial seems less concerned with justice than vengeance. The prosecutor describes the events as "a Chicago-style gun battle." Derek is sentenced to be hanged—even though it's clear that he lacks the mental capacity for responsibility. And, beyond that, the trial reveals that Derek surrendered to police custody on that roof 20 minutes before the gunshot, never made an attempt to escape and credibly appeared to be imploring Chris to surrender his weapon right before the fatal shot was fired.

The back end of the movie covers the desperate campaign by Derek's family to overturn his death sentence before it can be carried out. They gain momentum among the public and the press, as well as the support of 200 members of Parliament. But the British home secretary, who could petition for clemency, turns a deaf ear.

As the days tick down, you'll start to sweat. As the hanging occurs—graphically and efficiently—you may find yourself in tears.

Derek Bentley's case did not end with his trip to the gallows. It quickly became viewed as a miscarriage of justice and emerged as a focal point in the debate over capital punishment. His family continued to seek a full pardon for Derek. It finally was awarded in 1998, years after both of his parents and his sister had passed away.

⊙ **HIT:** In a movie full of strong performances, one worth noting is that of Tom Courtenay, who plays Derek's dad. William Bentley is a loyal, working-class Englishman forced to show astonishing bravery even as the institutions he has always believed in are letting him down. Three decades before *Let Him Have It,* Courtenay played a young man falsely accused in *The Loneliness of the Long Distance Runner.*

⊗ **MISS:** Maybe it's just us, but that double-decker that rumbles by in every scene in every neighborhood appears to be the exact same bus. Maybe the producers could only afford to rent one.

✒ **WHAT THEY WROTE AT THE TIME:** "Medak asks us to imagine what it means to plead for your life before a man dressed in one of those ridiculous wigs, whose manner tells you he's taken the title of 'Lord' all too literally. . . . *Let Him Have It* is a superb piece of craftsmanship. It's also not an easy movie to watch."—Charles Taylor, *Salon.com*

⊛ **IF YOU LIKED THIS, YOU'LL LIKE:** *The Krays,* Medak's 1990 biopic about the sadistic twins who ran London's underground in the 1960s.

◉ **REPEATED WATCHING QUOTIENT:** Once may be all you can handle. The movie will leave you gloomy for days.

◀ **CASTING CALL:** Alex Cox (*Repo Man, Sid and Nancy*) was hired to direct, but was replaced by Medak after Cox insisted on filming the movie in black-and-white.

"" **BEST LINE:** Derek's final thoughts, dictated to a sympathetic guard, are haunting: "Always keep your chin up, Mum, and tell Dad not to grind his teeth. The truth of this story will come out one day, and on that day a lot of people will get into trouble."

🔫 **VIOLENCE LEVEL:** Low, although Derek's hanging at the end is gut-wrenching.

🍎 **BET YOU DIDN'T KNOW:** At least four songs have been written about the Derek Bentley case over the years. The most well known is "Let Him Dangle" by Elvis Costello.

😐 **"I KNOW THAT GUY":** Edward Hardwicke, who plays the principal of the "approved school" (read: reform school) where preteen Derek spends three years, previously costarred as Mr. Watson in a 1986-94 BBC series about Sherlock Holmes. If you haven't watched those shows, starring the late Jeremy Brett, we recommend you check them out.

☺ **GOOF:** Chris Craig's gun, which he proudly shows off, is a five-shot revolver. On the warehouse roof, however, he fires six rounds.

➡ **DON'T FAIL TO NOTICE:** The black kerchief that is placed on the judge's head before he sentences Derek. This was an old English tradition in which judges donned a black cap before invoking the death sentence.

🔪 **BODY COUNT:** Two—an innocent policeman and an innocent young man.

THE VALACHI PAPERS (1972–PG)

STARS: CHARLES BRONSON, LINO VENTURA, JILL IRELAND, WALTER CHIARI
DIRECTOR: TERENCE YOUNG

Joe Valachi literally changed the face of the American Mafia—and for that reason alone, Terence Young's uneven docudrama about him would belong in any discussion about the Top 100 gangster movies.

Valachi, a soldier in the Genovese crime family, was the first Mafioso to publicly testify about the inner workings of the secret society. In fact, he was the one who first disclosed that the organization was known as the Cosa Nostra, literally translated as "Our Thing." His appearance before a U.S. Senate subcommittee in 1963 was covered by both television and radio and captured the imagination of the country.

For years, FBI Director J. Edgar Hoover had downplayed the possibility that a large-scale organized crime syndicate existed in the U.S. Even after the infamous Kefauver Committee hearings in the 1950s—which included an appearance by Mafia boss Frank Costello—many Americans still failed to grasp the scope and power of the Italian-American crime families.

Valachi put it all out there. And this movie does a more-than-adequate job of telling his story.

Set in flashbacks after Valachi agrees to cooperate, *The Valachi Papers* traces the history of the American Mafia, from the Castellammarese War that pitted 1930s mob bosses Salvatore Maranzano against "Joe the Boss" Masseria, all the way up through the emergence of a ruling commission, the dominance of Lucky Luciano, the infamous murder of Albert Anastasia (no relation to one of the authors of this book) and the 1957 Apalachin Conference that was designed to reestablish order in the underworld, but ended up having an entirely different effect.

Discovered by a New York State Police trooper, the conference became an embarrassment for mob leaders who had to scatter through the fields and woods around an upstate New York farm. Many were arrested and their secret society was again exposed publicly.

While the acting is choppy and sometimes overly dramatic in *The Valachi Papers*, the story stays close to actual events. It offers an easily digestible history lesson about Cosa Nostra and its origins in America.

Just as interesting is the back story that led to journalist Peter Maas' book on which the movie is based. Valachi, like his boss Vito Genovese, was serving a prison term for heroin dealing in the 1960s and believed that Genovese had marked him for death because he thought he was an informant. Panicked and paranoid, Valachi mistakenly killed a fellow inmate he thought had been assigned to kill him by beating him with a pipe. The prison intrigue and murder are part of the opening scenes in the movie.

Not an informant before the prison murder, Valachi quickly became one afterward. As he was cooperating, Valachi was told that he would be able to write his memoirs. In fact, Maas, then a young journalist who broke the story about Valachi's decision to become a witness in *Life* magazine, was asked by the U.S. Justice Department to edit what became known as *The Valachi Papers*.

Before they could be published, however, U.S. Attorney General Nicholas Katzenbach went back on his agreement with Maas and sought to block publication. Katzenbach, according to most reports, was responding to complaints from Italian-American groups claiming the memoir would reinforce the ethnic stereotype of Italians as gangsters.

Maas was unable to publish Valachi's memoir, but did write a third-person account based on the information he had obtained through editing the papers and through hours of interviews with the jailed mob soldier. In what remains an historic black eye for the Justice Department, Katzenbach went to court in an attempt to block Maas from publishing his book, but failed.

Still, complaints from civil rights groups and threats from Cosa Nostra resulted in much of the movie being filmed in Italy, with Italian actors playing many of the roles and the English dialogue dubbed.

The result was a less-than-satisfying film. *The Valachi Papers* also had one other thing working against it as a theatrical endeavor. It was released in 1972, the same year as another mob movie that you may have heard about—*The Godfather*.

⦿ **HIT:** Bronson, who built a career around tough-guy characters who spoke with their actions rather than their words, gives a strong performance as a conflicted and introspective gangster whose world has come undone.

⊗ **MISS:** The same cannot be said of Bronson's supporting cast. Even delivering their lines with a credible Italian accent proves too much for some of them, especially Joseph Wiseman, who plays Salvatore Maranzano.

✒ **WHAT THEY WROTE AT THE TIME:** "The movie's life is in a series of fairly nice period pieces, some strong action sequences and the interesting Bronson performance. For the rest, it declines to be a traditional gangster movie and cannot approach the psychological or narrative depth of *The Godfather*. We're not involved enough to really care that much about Joe Valachi, and the movie becomes a series of high points on the road to a labored conclusion."—Roger Ebert, *Chicago Sun-Times*

☺ **GOOF:** During one car chase set in the 1930s, Valachi speeds past parked cars that are clearly from the 1960s. In another New York scene, the World Trade Center towers can be seen under construction in the background.

✔ **REALITY CHECK:** The castration scene takes place offscreen, but still manages to be one of the most brutal in any mob movie. Designed to show the bitter and violent nature of Cosa Nostra, it is actually a fictionalized account of revenge taken on a mobster who had a secret love affair with the boss's wife (never a good idea). Still, it's one of the few elements in the movie that has no basis in fact.

◉ **REPEATED WATCHING QUOTIENT:** There are better mob stories, but few with the same historic backdrop. For that reason, this is a movie worth revisiting occasionally.

🙺 **BEST LINE:** "Always he lived with death. . . . Always he waited for this to happen." Salvatore Reina's wife explaining to her daughter Maria (Jill Ireland) that mob boss Reina's murder was not unexpected and, in fact, was part of Mafia life. Despite the warning, Maria stayed in the "family," marrying Valachi.

⚑ **VIOLENCE LEVEL:** This is a story of the mob at war, so there's plenty of shooting, as well as the aforementioned dismemberment.

⚘ **BODY COUNT:** Eighteen.

A CONVERSATION WITH MOBSTER/ INFORMANT NICK CARAMANDI

Nicholas "Nicky Crow" Caramandi was the Joe Valachi of Philadelphia. So it's no great surprise to find out that his favorite gangster movie is *The Valachi Papers*.

"The story is as true as you're gonna get," the gravelly voiced wiseguy said in a telephone interview from his home somewhere in Middle America.

Caramandi, who testified at nearly a dozen trials in the late 1980s and early 1990s, served five years in prison on murder and racketeering charges after becoming one of the first members of the Philadelphia branch of Cosa Nostra to turn government witness.

Paired with fellow wiseguy Thomas "Tommy Del" DelGiorno who also became a cooperator, Caramandi helped the Feds convict mob boss Nicodemo "Little Nicky" Scarfo and at least 20 other wiseguys.

To this day, however, Caramandi still wonders about his decision.

Now 76 and living under an assumed name (he left the Witness Protection Program after a few years), he said he cooperated to save his own life.

Like Valachi, he was in jail at the time. And like Valachi, he came to believe that his mob boss—in this case Scarfo—had decided to have him killed. Considered one of the most violent Mafia leaders in America, Scarfo had built a reputation for dealing with any problem, large or small, by resorting to violence, usually murder.

While Caramandi can relate to Valachi on a personal and underworld level, he also has good memories of the film's star. Charles Bronson spent time in South Philadelphia after World War II before heading to Hollywood.

In Philadelphia, Bronson befriended Jack Klugman (who went on to star in the television series *The Odd Couple*).

"When I was a kid, maybe 12 or 13, they used to hang at this place around Seventh and Morris (Streets) called Barney's," Caramandi said of his old neighborhood. "Guys used to play gin there. In them

days, that was the big thing. It was right across the street from this pool hall where I spent a lot of time. Bronson and Klugman were like corner guys."

Bronson also worked out at a gym above a police station on Fourth Street, Caramandi said. Ironically, so did local gangster Ralph "Junior" Staino, a wiseguy who some thought could have had a movie career due to his good looks. Staino went one way and spent a good part of his life in jail. Bronson went in a different direction. *The Valachi Papers* was one of his first starring roles.

"I used to have a tape of (the movie) and I would watch it at least once a week," said Caramandi, who was relocated by federal authorities after his release from prison in the early 1990s. "Sometimes, every other day. The thing about it is, it's all true. It's closer to the way things really are than *The Godfather*."

Caramandi said he also came in contact with some of the real-life characters portrayed in another gangland classic, *GoodFellas*, while doing time in a federal prison on a counterfeiting rap in 1976.

"When I was in Lewisburg, I met this kid Tommy from New York who the Joe Pesci character was supposed to be," he said. "He was a little nutty, even in jail. He always had this bitterness in him."

For realism, Caramandi says *GoodFellas* and *Donnie Brasco* come the closest to *The Valachi Papers* for telling it the way it is.

"Them movies are pretty close," he said. "*Donnie Brasco* was pretty good, but I don't know, I just don't understand how these guys didn't pick up on it (that Brasco was an FBI undercover agent) after four or five years. I never understood that."

For pure viewing pleasure, The Crow also likes three films from his formative years: *Kiss of Death* (1947) starring Victor Mature, *Al Capone* (1959) with Rod Steiger —"Not the De Niro, Costner one," he said disdainfully—and *Murder, Inc.* (1960) a movie that earned Peter Falk a Best Supporting Actor Oscar nomination for his portrayal of mob informant Abe "Kid Twist" Reles.

STARS: BURT LANCASTER, AVA GARDNER, EDMOND O'BRIEN
DIRECTOR: ROBERT SIODMAK

Ernest Hemingway hated Hollywood. Or, more to the point, the great American author hated Hollywood's treatment of his literary works. So it's a bit surprising that Papa's favorite adaptation of his writing is *The Killers*, a noir gangster film that takes tremendous liberties with his original short story.

Hemingway wrote *The Killers* in 1927 as a 3,000-word yarn. It's largely set in a diner that two out-of-town hoods walk into one night, seeking to kill a guy who had done their boss wrong years before. Their target, a one-time prizefighter known as Swede, passively accepts his fate as he waits for the assassins to find him. Readers never even learn about his transgression.

And that's Hemingway's entire short story. Not really enough on which to base a full-length movie. But it served as a fine pretext for this 1946 film, which took his setup and added a hard-boiled back story full of greed, desire and double-crosses.

The screenplay (written by Anthony Veiller and an uncredited John Huston) fleshes out Hemingway's one-day narrative by creating a drama that covers six years. Swede, the ex-boxer is there, played by Burt Lancaster in his movie debut. *The Killers,* by the way, made Lancaster an instant star.

The filmmakers added new characters to the story. There's the femme fatale (a steamy Ava Gardner) to bring the boxer to his ruin. There's the big-city mobster (Albert Dekker) to scheme up a quarter-million-dollar heist that leads to Swede's eventual murder. And there's the dogged insurance investigator (Edmond O'Brien) to pursue the hows and whys of it all.

After the movie was wrapped, Universal Pictures' publicity chief traveled to Idaho to give Hemingway a private sneak preview. Expecting to dislike the adaptation, Hemingway watched *The Killers* with a full bottle of gin in front of him. When the movie ended, he smiled, held up the still-sealed bottle and said to the PR man, "Didn't need it."

Hey, if it's good enough for him, it's good enough for us.

The opening scene of *The Killers* will remind you of *A History of Violence*. That menacing duo of out-of-towners shows up at a small-town diner late one afternoon looking for Swede. They terrorize the owner, the cook and the lone patron while waiting for their target to arrive for his usual 6 p.m. dinner special.

When Swede doesn't show, the gangsters go to search for him. The customer (named Nick Adams, in honor of Hemingway's literary alter ego) rushes to Swede's boardinghouse room to warn him. Swede is there in bed, submissively waiting for his hunters. The ex-boxer is drained of any intent to fight back.

"I did something wrong . . . once," Swede sighs. That's all the explanation he gives. Soon enough, eight bullets tear through his body.

Over the next 90 minutes, a complex series of interlocking flashbacks reveal how things got to that point. We see how Swede's boxing career ends and how he falls into crime. We meet his mob boss, his partners and the siren who leads him astray. You will certainly notice Ava Gardner as sex bomb Kitty Collins. Gardner was 23 when *The Killers* came out and this was a star-making vehicle for her as well as for Lancaster.

Pulling it all together is Edmund O'Brien as Jim Reardon, the insurance man investigating Swede's murder. The narrative moves through Reardon's interviews with friends and enemies from the dead man's past. Time shifts backward and forward in a way that would do Quentin Tarantino proud.

The highlight of the film—and the turning point of the story—is a caper to rob a New Jersey manufacturing company of its $250,000 monthly payroll. It's planned by the crew's boss, Big Jim Colfax (Dekker), and designed to make all four of its participants wealthy—at least by the standards of 1940, when it takes place in the film.

The crime, filmed from high overhead in one continuous shot, goes off without a hitch. It's after the getaway that things go awry. In this business, it's best to trust no one.

⊙ **HIT:** If you want a primer in 1940s noir style, *The Killers* is a great place to start. The mood and the lighting are equally dark in scenes set in pool halls and corner taprooms. The women smolder and the dialogue snaps. And there are several terrific background characters who may or may not be there to send you off in the wrong direction. Watch especially for hopped-up hood Blinky (Jeff Corey) and Swede's astronomy-loving ex-cellmate Charleston (Vince Barnett).

⊗ **MISS:** One inherent flaw in *The Killers* is that we're never really told why a sleuthing insurance adjuster is so obsessed with the case. The local cops don't care about Swede's murder and Reardon's boss wants him to focus on bigger matters. Swede's death benefit is a paltry $2,500. So why is our hero so fixated on this one? Beats us.

✎ **WHAT THEY WROTE AT THE TIME:** "...it certainly does not enhance the literary distinction of Hemingway's classic bit. But, as mere movie melodrama, pieced out as a mystery which is patiently unfolded by a sleuthing insurance man, it makes a diverting picture—diverting, that is, if you enjoy the unraveling of crime enigmas involving pernicious folks."—Bosley Crowther, *New York Times*

☺ **GOOF:** The narration during the big robbery says that the factory guard was shot in the groin. But even as those words are spoken, a gun fires and the guard grabs his shoulder. Let's be honest, we'd all rather be shot in the shoulder than the groin.

📼 **PIVOTAL SCENE:** Shortly after one final knockout ends his boxing career, Swede attends a cocktail party with Lilly, his good-girl sweetheart (she even orders a soda pop). As they engage in small talk, the glamorous moll Kitty slinks into the room. Swede becomes fixated the moment he sees Kitty, ignoring his girlfriend. Kitty, aware of his attention, walks over to the piano and starts singing a sultry tune. The sexual tension is palpable.

At that moment, Swede abandons both his woman and the straight life. It's all downhill from there.

🖐 **BET YOU DIDN'T KNOW:** Hemingway was paid $36,700 for the rights to his short story.

😀 **"I KNOW THAT GUY":** The burly hit man in the opening scene is William Conrad, who was 25 when this was filmed. Fans of television detective shows will remember Conrad as the star of *Cannon* in the 1970s and *Jake and the Fatman* in the 1980s.

🔫 **VIOLENCE LEVEL:** Low. But the tough talk is high.

🗨 **BEST LINE:** Kitty, the ultimate bad girl, is asked by a devastated Swede why she has abandoned him for the despicable Big Jim Colfax.

"Maybe it's because I hate him," she says. "I'm poison, Swede, to myself and everyone around me. I'd be afraid to go with anyone I love for the harm I'd do to them. But I don't care harming him."

➡ **DON'T FAIL TO NOTICE:** Lancaster's skill in the ring during the flashback to his boxing days. The 32-year-old actor trained for two months with a former prizefighter. Those punches and knockdowns in the scene are genuine, not staged.

◉ **REPEATED WATCHING QUOTIENT:** *The Killers* shows up about once a year on Turner Classic Movies. It's worth checking out annually.

⊕ **IF YOU LIKE THIS, YOU'LL LIKE:** The 1964 version of the same story, directed by Don Siegel (*Dirty Harry*) and starring Lee Marvin, Angie Dickinson and Ronald Reagan (!) as the evil crime boss. The project was originally commissioned by NBC as a made-for-TV movie, but was kept off the air due to its sexuality and violence. It later had a limited run in theaters.

🔫 **BODY COUNT:** Five.

72 AMERICAN ME (1992–R)

STARS: EDWARD JAMES OLMOS, WILLIAM FORSYTHE, SAL LOPEZ
DIRECTOR: EDWARD JAMES OLMOS

The truly frightening aspect of Edward James Olmos' *American Me* is not watching the film—although that has its moments. It's learning what happened away from the cameras during and after the production of this movie about the Mexican Mafia in Los Angeles.

Olmos tried to forge a truce among rival gangs, in part by casting real gang members to act in the movie. But as *American Me* was being filmed, one of those young men was shot to death away from the set. Olmos started receiving death threats and applied for a license to carry a concealed weapon.

Things got worse when *American Me* came out in 1992. Members of La Eme—the Mexican Mafia—were infuriated with Olmos' final product. Some reports said the gang had cooperated because they expected a Hispanic version of *The Godfather* rather than *American Me*'s scathing portrayal of their way of life. There is no romance in Olmos' vision of barrio warfare.

Within two months of release, two of the film's consultants were executed. One was 49-year-old Ana Lizarraga, a reformed gang member who also had a small role in the film. She was murdered in a drive-by shooting while standing in her driveway.

The movie's biggest offense to La Eme (Spanish for the letter "M") was apparently its blurring of fact and fiction. The opening of *American Me* says its "events are inspired by a true story." Like most filmmakers, Olmos takes liberties with the truth.

Based on the life of La Eme founder Rodolfo (Cheyenne) Cadena, the film's lead character is shown being sodomized on his first night in juvenile jail. Later in the film, he is impotent with a woman and eventually gets murdered by his own clan. Those episodes, true or not, insulted the gang's sense of honor and machismo.

"It may be just a movie, but not to the Mexican Mafia's way of thinking," California Prisons Lt. Leo Duarte told the *Los Angeles Times*. "This is their world, their environment. If they think you did something disrespectful, even if they're wrong, there's going to be repercussions."

For several years, Olmos, who directed, co-produced, and starred in *American Me*, believed there was a contract on his life. Even years later, he declined to talk about events surrounding the film.

The shame is that he went into the project with the best intentions. "I want to show that there's a cancer in this subculture of the gangs," he told the *Times* before the film's release. "They'll say: 'You've taken away our manhood with this movie.' I say to them: 'Either you treat the cancer or it'll eat you alive.' "

In this fictionalized portrayal, Cadena becomes Montoya Santana and La Eme becomes La Primera, a gang that controls drugs, gambling, extortion and prostitution inside and outside of California's prison system.

American Me traces Santana and his cohorts from their childhoods, when they band together to survive the mean streets. A wrong turn in their teens lands them in juvenile jail, where Santana avenges that first-night rape by stabbing his attacker to death. That act keeps him incarcerated into his mid-30s.

But the gang becomes even more powerful behind bars, controlling the drug trade out on the streets. "There was nothing the system could do to stop me," Santana reflects in the movie. "I could run the show from solitary."

The scenes shot at Folsom Prison (again, using real gang members) are fearsome. The ones out on the streets are no gentler. One of the best points made in *American Me* is how gang violence gets handed down from generation to generation, becoming increasingly brutal along the way.

One of the final scenes shows the initiation of a

new gang member—who can't be older than 12. His teenaged companions get him high on an inhalant in a paper bag and then take him out for a drive.

They hand him a gun. Go ahead and fire, one gang member instructs him as they slowly cruise a main drag. With a slight trepidation, the youngster asks, "Who do I shoot?"

"It doesn't matter," he is told. The boy spots a group of people on the corner. With a look of expectation and intoxication, he aims and fires into the crowd.

In an interview with the *Chicago Sun-Times*, Olmos explained the scene: "In the 1980s, they were fighting over turf, over the right to sell drugs. But now it's gotten into a new phenomenon, one that war veterans know very well—the adrenalin that rushes through the body, creating a high when you fire a weapon at somebody. It's like a narcotic."

⊙ **HIT:** Make sure you watch *Lives in Hazard*, the 58-minute documentary included with the film's DVD. It explains how *American Me* was created around the stories of those trying to survive in the barrios of East Los Angeles. If *American Me* is harrowing, this look at boys in gangs and the men they become in prison is downright petrifying.

⊗ **MISS:** Much of the movie is Santana's narration of his thoughts while sitting in a prison cell. Fine. Except that, for some reason, it's mostly done in rhyme, which makes the character sound like an evil Dr. Seuss.

✎ **WHAT THEY WROTE AT THE TIME:** "As a prominent and well-respected Hispanic-American figure, Olmos is commended for not choosing the easy road. . . . He takes his community to task for its self-destructive legacies, for its internalization of failure. To underscore this, he himself plays a most unflattering character, a crime lord named Santana who goes into prison as a young boy and, because he does what he must to survive and maintain respect, becomes a gang kingpin."—Marjorie Baumgarten, *Austin Chronicle*

⊛ **IF YOU LIKED THIS, YOU'LL LIKE:** *Blood In, Blood Out*, the 1993 story of two brothers and a cousin growing up in East Los Angeles. One becomes a prison gang leader, one becomes a cop and one becomes an artist and heroin addict.

☞ **VIOLENCE LEVEL:** Those who cross the Mexican Mafia end up being shot in the genitals, torched with gasoline, stabbed with tattoo needles, strangled with cord and sodomized with a serrated dagger. So we'd say, the violence level is pretty high.

◉ **REPEATED WATCHING QUOTIENT:** See the above paragraph and decide for yourself.

PIVOTAL SCENES: When Santana gets out of prison after 18 years, he and his lieutenant, JD (William Forsythe), move to gain more control over the drug business by challenging the Italian mob. They visit Don Antonio Scagnelli, who's shown tending his garden like Don Vito Corleone.

From now on, JD tells the powerful mob boss, "Your business in the barrio is going to be our business, too." Santana not-so-gently reminds Scagnelli that the don's son is in Folsom Prison, within reach of La Primera's members.

"You listen to me," snaps Scagnelli. "Anything happens to my son and you will regret the day you made that choice."

In the next scene in prison, the Hispanic mobsters pal up to the younger Scagnelli, getting him drunk on homemade rot gut. Then they tie him down, rape him and stab him to death.

Cut to the don's mansion, where you hear him (like Hollywood producer Jack Woltz in *The Godfather*) howl to the heavens after receiving the news. The bottom line is this: Santana and his crew fear taking on no one.

☙ **BET YOU DIDN'T KNOW:** Most of the paid extras (as in non-prisoners) hired for the Folsom scenes quit after one day of shooting. Guards treated the extras exactly as they treated prisoners, making them ask permission to use the bathroom and keeping them penned in a gated area next to an open sewer.

☻ **"I KNOW THAT GUY":** The leader of the Aryan Nation band of hit men is played by legendary Hollywood tough guy William Smith. You may recognize him as Arnold Schwarzenegger's father in *Conan the Barbarian* or as Soviet Col. Strelnikov in *Red Dawn*.

𝟿𝟿 BEST LINE: Santana, reflecting on ordering one of his favorite underlings murdered for turning down a job: "I was proud I didn't let my feelings get in the way of what had to be done to Pie Face that day. Killing one of our own earned us a new respect."

BODY COUNT: Eighteen—the most memorable one being the guy who gets smothered in his own stash of cocaine.

73 ANALYZE THIS (1999–R)

STARS: ROBERT DE NIRO, BILLY CRYSTAL, CHAZZ PALMINTERI, LISA KUDROW

DIRECTOR: HAROLD RAMIS

If not for *The Sopranos*, we would have appreciated *Analyze This* a whole lot more.

HBO's landmark series hit the airwaves in January 1999. It told the tale of a mob boss haunted by mother issues and paralyzed by panic attacks who decides to consult a shrink. Some regard it as the best television show ever.

Two months later, *Analyze This* came to theaters, telling the tale of a mob boss paralyzed by panic attacks who decides to consult a shrink. One change—rather than mother issues, this guy has father issues.

The Sopranos is a storytelling feast. By comparison, *Analyze This* is a bag of French fries.

But you know what? Sometimes a bag of French fries is just fine. *Analyze This* grossed $177 million worldwide, which suggests that a lot of people enjoy an entertaining little trifle of a movie. Or fast food.

The film succeeds because of strong performances by its two stars. Veteran comic actor Billy Crystal is perfectly cast as nebbishy New York psychiatrist Ben Sobel. He's got a roster of whiny patients. His standoffish father (Bill Macy) is a more renowned headshrinker than Ben is. Dr. Sobel's consolation is that he's about to marry a blond television reporter (Lisa Kudrow) several miles out of his league.

Into his life walks Paul Vitti (Robert De Niro, doing an obvious send-up of former New York mob boss John Gotti). Vitti is a feared killer, but he has developed a problem. His hands shake when he's about to club an informer. Then he finds himself bawling uncontrollably at a sappy commercial. Neither is acceptable behavior in his line of work.

De Niro plays Vitti as a satire of his many mob roles. In a comic turn that foreshadows his work in *Meet the Parents*, he's relaxed and subtle, but with a glimmer of menace. He's the peacock in the flashy suits you've seen in *Casino,* and he's still got the trademark De Niro smirk.

Analyze This works best when these two fine actors play off the culture clash between them. When Dr. Sobel invites the Mafia don to release his aggressions by "hitting" a nearby pillow, Vitti takes out a Smith & Wesson and fires six bullets through the upholstery.

"What is my goal here?" the good doctor asks. "To make you a happy, well-adjusted gangster?"

The movie flags a bit when it concentrates on two subplots—one about Dr. Sobel's wedding (which the gangster keeps interrupting with his various emotional crises) and another about internecine mob battles. We did, however, enjoy the always-great Chazz Palminteri as Vitti's main power rival, Primo Sidone.

In one scene, Vitti, all loaded up on psychiatric mumbo-jumbo, tries to make peace with Primo over the phone. The conversation, of course, disintegrates into insults and threats. "Get a dictionary," Primo tells his aide after slamming down the phone. "Find out what this 'closure' thing is. If that's what he's going to hit us with, I want to be ready."

While the general plot may be so-so, director Harold Ramis (*Caddyshack, Groundhog Day*) knows how to play the story for laughs without falling into silliness. The interplay between De Niro and Crystal is terrific and several scenes will prompt you to chuckle out loud. In one, the two men happen to be caught in an ambush when De Niro's Vitti has his emotional catharsis.

"Paul," shouts the panicked Dr. Sobel as he dodges bullets, "you have to channel all this nice grief into a murderous rage."

Good stuff in a frothy film. The trick is to watch it and not compare it to *The Sopranos*.

HIT: The late actor Joe Viterelli is marvelous as Jelly, Paul Vitti's faithful and long-suffering sidekick. Viterelli has a subtle humor, and he certainly has the look and voice of a Mafiosi. A successful New York businessman, Viterelli was coaxed into showbiz at age 52. Before dying in 2004, he appeared in 26 films, almost always as a mobster.

MISS: De Niro has three sobbing fits during the movie. We understand the premise, but there's still something unseemly and unconvincing about watching De Niro blubber.

WHAT THEY WROTE AT THE TIME: "Part of the pleasure of it is the way it carries you along from joke to joke. It's a movie that just doesn't have to try too hard, a dem-dese-and-dose comedy that's also surprisingly—and pleasingly—light." —Stephanie Zacharek, *Salon.com*

GOOF: *Analyze This* makes a point of showing an FBI raid on the infamous 1957 mob summit in Apalachin, N.Y. In fact, while local and state police busted the meeting of more than 100 goodfellas, the FBI was absent. That's because J. Edgar Hoover denied the existence of the Mafia—right up until that summit.

REALITY CHECK: Crystal's character of Dr. Ben Sobel is as obviously Jewish as Jerry Seinfeld. So what's with the conversation about how his son believed in Santa Claus?

REPEATED WATCHING QUOTIENT: It will always elicit a few laughs, but there are probably better options on TV most of the time.

DON'T FAIL TO NOTICE: Dr. Sobel's dream scene in which he imagines himself being gunned down in the street exactly as Don Vito Corleone was in *The Godfather*, while buying oranges at a fruit stand. In the sequence, Vitti represents his hapless son, too inept to save him.

Afterward, the doctor describes the dream to Vitti.

"You mean, I was Fredo?!" the mobster says. "I don't think so!"

CASTING CALL: Martin Scorsese turned down an offer to direct this film.

VIOLENCE LEVEL: Nothing to shock any viewer over age 12.

BET YOU DIDN'T KNOW: Every New York City restaurant location used in *Analyze This* was the site of a well-known, real-life mob hit.

BEST LINE: Dr. Sobel, trying to impersonate a gangster to a roomful of mob bosses: "My name is Ben Sobel . . . -lioni. Ben Sobellioni. I'm also known as, uh, Benny the Groin, Sammy the Schnozz, Elmer the Fudd, Tubby the Tuba and, once, as Miss Phyllis Levine."

"I KNOW THAT GUY": The ER doctor who tells Paul Vitti that he's had a panic attack is played by Aasif Mandvi of *The Daily Show with Jon Stewart*. You might also recognize Mandvi as Mr. Aziz from *Spider-Man 2*.

IF YOU LIKED THIS, YOU'LL LIKE: The dark comedy *Grosse Pointe Blank*. John Cusack plays a freelance hit man who flubs his assignments after developing a conscience. His psychiatrist advises him to get back to his roots by attending his 10th-year high school reunion.

BODY COUNT: Four—one tossed seven stories into a platter of poached salmon at the Sobel wedding.

74 THE ROARING TWENTIES (1939–NR)

STARS: JAMES CAGNEY, HUMPHREY BOGART, PRISCILLA LANE, GLADYS GEORGE
DIRECTOR: RAOUL WALSH

Warner Brothers owned the franchise for gangster films in the 1930s. The studio capped the decade with this Cagney-Bogey crime drama that some consider a classic.

James Cagney is great as Eddie Bartlett and Humphrey Bogart is convincing as treacherous bad guy George Hally. But the rest of the cast is just so-so. And the story is, at times, breathless and, at other times, melodramatic in the extreme.

The tone is set right after the opening credits have rolled. We get a voice-over (with accompanying scroll) from screenwriter Mark Hellinger:

"IT MAY COME TO PASS THAT, AT SOME DISTANT DATE, WE WILL BE CONFRONTED WITH ANOTHER PERIOD SIMILAR TO THE ONE DEPICTED IN THIS PHOTOPLAY. IF THAT HAPPENS, I PRAY THAT THE EVENTS, AS DRAMATIZED HERE, WILL BE REMEMBERED.

"IN THIS FILM, THE CHARACTERS ARE COMPOSITES OF PEOPLE I KNEW, AND THE SITUATIONS ARE THOSE THAT ACTUALLY OCCURRED.

"BITTER OR SWEET, MOST MEMORIES BECOME PRECIOUS AS THE YEARS MOVE ON. THIS FILM IS A MEMORY—AND I AM GRATEFUL FOR IT."

A review in the *New York Times* (see below) labeled the device pretentious. We tend to agree.

Hellinger's short story "The World Moves On" served as the basis for the film's script, which he cowrote. *The Roaring Twenties* tells the sprawling story of one of the most notorious eras in American history by focusing on the lives of a few individuals. But the devices used to connect those characters too often strain credibility.

When the film opens, Bartlett, Hally and Lloyd Hart (Jeffrey Lynn) are soldiers on the front lines during World War I. All three are just trying to survive as they await the long-rumored Armistice that will end the conflict and send them home.

Director Raoul Walsh, borrowing a device that played well in several other Warner Brothers gangster pieces, relies on "newsreels" to move the story along and to hype the era that his film portrays.

Short Skirts. Jack Dempsey. Prohibition. Mob Wars. The Wall Street Crash. Unemployment. Bread Lines. All are detailed in frantic reports as we follow Bartlett, Hally and Hart into civilian life.

Bartlett, unable to get his job back as an auto mechanic, is driving a cab when he is introduced to bootlegging. By the time he has established himself as a rumrunner—and has also invested in a legitimate cab business—Hart is back on the scene as his Ivy League lawyer.

When Bartlett and his gang hijack a shipment of booze, it is his old friend Hally who is the captain of the vessel. They naturally go into partnership. Neither trusts the other, but each knows that together they can make one another very rich.

And they do get rich during one of the most tumultuous and violent periods in American history.

Or as the voice-over in one of the newsreels puts it:

"NINETEEN TWENTY-FOUR . . . AN ERA OF AMAZING MADNESS. . . . THE CHASE AFTER HUGE PROFITS IS FOLLOWED CLOSELY BY THEIR INEVITABLE PARTNERS—CORRUPTION, VIOLENCE AND MURDER. A NEW AND HORRIBLE TOOL APPEARS. THE TOMMY. A LIGHT-WEIGHT WASP-LIKE MACHINE GUN AND MURDER HENCEFORTH IS PARCELED OUT IN WHOLESALE LOTS!"

Bartlett and Hally do their share of parceling, although, as in the foxhole when we first meet them, Hally seems to enjoy the work more than his partner. One of his victims is a security guard at a warehouse where cases of whiskey have been stored. Should we mention that the guard happened to be the obnoxious Army sergeant who gave both Bartlett and Hally a hard time on the front lines during the movie's opening sequence?

Romantic entanglements and predictable double-crossing follow as the money pours in and the country goes crazy. Then comes the stock market crash and the Great Depression—an excuse to roll even more breathless newsreel hype about men staring "wild-eyed at the spectacle of complete ruin" and fortunes "crumbling into nothing before this disaster which is to touch every man, woman and child in America."

Eddie Bartlett loses just about everything, including the cab business that he hoped would make him legit and the young nightclub singer whose career he helped launch. Jean Sherman (Priscilla Lane) is grateful for all Eddie has done for her, but her heart belongs to the young lawyer with the Ivy League pedigree.

Eddie hardly notices Panama Smith (Gladys George), the nightclub moll who has been in love with him forever. But he is with her at the end as he settles a score with Hally while nobly defending the woman who walked out on him.

⊙ **HIT:** This was one of Cagney's last mob movies and he doesn't disappoint. Cagney was to 1930s gangster films what Pacino and De Niro are to the modern classics. Their presence brings the endeavor up a notch or two, even when a film's plot is as conventional and predictable as it is here.

⊗ **MISS:** Of all the cabs on all the streets in all of New York City, she has to step into mine. Bartlett doesn't say it, but you've got to think it when the movie resorts to the highly unlikely coincidence of Jean and Lloyd getting into Eddie's cab several years after they've married and a down-on-his-luck Eddie has been forced to go back to driving a hack to make a living.

✎ **WHAT THEY WROTE AT THE TIME:** "With a grandiloquent and egregiously sentimental forward by Mark Hellinger, with employment of newsreel shots to lend documentary flavor, with a commentator's voice interpolating ultra-dramatic commonplaces as the film unreels, [*The Roaring Twenties*] has taken on an annoying pretentiousness which neither the theme nor its treatment can justify. The dirty decade has served too many quickie quatrains to rate an epic handling now."—Frank Nugent, *New York Times*

✔ **REALITY CHECK:** Cagney's Eddie Bartlett was based on Larry Fay, a 1920s New York City bootlegger who started out as a cab driver. According to a profile of Fay in *Crime Magazine* by Allan May, Fay got his start as a rum runner after picking up a fare in New York who wanted to be driven to Montreal. While in Canada, Fay used some of the money he earned from the trip to buy several cases of whiskey. He took the booze back to New York, sold it at a profit and started to build an empire. Like the Bartlett character, he used his profits to invest in a taxi business and buy several nightclubs. He took a financial hit with the stock market crash of 1929 and was gunned down by an angry employee whose salary Fay had reduced as times got tough.

◉ REPEATED WATCHING QUOTIENT: Fans of Bogey and Cagney might want to go back again from time to time, but once is probably enough for most viewers.

❦ BET YOU DIDN'T KNOW: *The Roaring Twenties* established Walsh as an A-list director, primarily of action and crime films. He would direct more than 130 movies over a 52-year career. He worked with Bogart again in *High Sierra* (1941) and with Cagney in *White Heat* (1949), both of which are profiled in this book. And he directed George Raft and Ida Lupino in the classic *They Drive by Night* (1940).

◄ CASTING CALL: Cagney and Bogart appeared in two other movies together. A year before they teamed up in *The Roaring Twenties*, they starred in *Angels with Dirty Faces* (also in this book), portraying characters with essentially the same kind of relationship. Cagney again played a mobster and Bogey was the corrupt lawyer who double-crossed him. They also appeared in *The Oklahoma Kid,* which came out the same year as *The Roaring Twenties*. The Western did little for either actor's career. Cagney was Jim "The Oklahoma Kid" Kincaid. Bogey was the double-crossing Whip McCord. It seems there's a pattern here. Cagney's the good bad guy; Bogey's the bad bad guy.

❞ BEST LINE: The movie ends with Panama Smith cradling Eddie in her arms on the snow covered steps of a church. When a cop runs up and asks his identity, Smith replies, "He used to be a big shot."

The line is considered one of the best final lines in any crime movie.

☞ VIOLENCE LEVEL: Lots of shooting, beginning with the World War I battlefront scene that opens the movie. But, as noted previously, shoot-'em-ups in movies from the 1930s did not pack the wallop of the more realistic and gory shooting scenes in films of the modern era.

⚷ BODY COUNT: Twelve, not counting two unseen German soldiers who are picked off by sniper fire from Hally on the front lines during World War I.

75 THE GODFATHER: PART III (1990–R)

STARS: AL PACINO, DIANE KEATON, TALIA SHIRE, ANDY GARCIA, ELI WALLACH, JOE MANTEGNA | DIRECTOR: FRANCIS FORD COPPOLA

The problem with *Godfather III* is that . . . it's not *Godfather I* or *Godfather II*. It's a good, not great, gangster movie and certainly deserves to be included in our Top 100.

But it will always be compared with the two movies that preceded it. And in that comparison, it will always come up short.

GF3 has an interesting story and a stellar cast. Coppola and Mario Puzo, who wrote the script together, used real events—the suspicious death of Pope John Paul I and the multimillion dollar scandal at the Vatican Bank—to bring us an updated Michael Corleone, struggling to go legit in a world that, he quickly learns, is as treacherous and cutthroat as the criminal underworld from which he came.

Those storylines gave the writers a chance to offer social commentary, and they didn't hesitate. Their targets: the hypocrisy of big institutions—the Church, banking, politics—and the greed and venality of the men who run them.

"The pope's doing exactly what you said he would," attorney B. J. Harrison (George Hamilton) tells Michael after John Paul I begins to clean up the Vatican mess.

"He should be careful," Michael replies. "It's dangerous to be an honest man."

After meeting with Vatican bankers, Michael offers this take: "We're dealing with the Borgias."

Finally, there is this exchange between Michael and Don Licio Lucchesi (Enzo Robutti), the Sicilian politico with ties to the banks, the Church and the Mafia.

"You are a man of finance and politics," Michael says. "I don't understand either."

"Finance is a gun," says Lucchesi. "Politics is knowing when to pull the trigger."

Pacino brings the right blend of weariness and cynicism to his third turn as Michael. Diane Keaton is back as the long-suffering Kay (although we have always wondered how a volatile Sicilian like Michael ended up with the prim and proper New Englander; God, we miss Apollonia).

Andy Garcia is perfect as Sonny's illegitimate son, Vincent Mancini. He's smoldering and short-tempered like his father, violent and always on the prowl. Who else but Sonny's kid could turn making gnocchi into a sexual dance?

There are several other memorable moments, but not enough of them to elevate this film to the level of its predecessors. Which is the problem.

They say that imitation is the sincerest form of flattery, but for our money, Coppola and Puzo went way over the line in trying to mimic—or revisit—some of the great scenes from the first two films.

For openers—literally—there's the big party after Michael receives the papal award of Commander of the Order of San Sebastian for his philanthropy. Connie (Talia Shire, back and showing more balls than some of the male gangsters) does the Italian folk song right out of the wedding scene from *Godfather I*.

There's also the scene where Joey Zasa (what a great name for the Joe Mantegna character) is walking through Little Italy during a festival as hit men close in on him. This is simply the updated version of the classic scene from *Godfather II* when young Vito Corleone stalks Don Fanucci. This time it's Vito's grandson Vincent stalking the mob kingpin who is about to be murdered.

And the series of murders carried out while Anthony Corleone (Franc D'Ambrosio) makes his operatic debut in Palermo is nothing if not a repeat of the climatic Baptismal scene that puts the stamp of evil on Michael Corleone at the end of *Godfather I*.

The originals were great cinema.

The replays were . . . replays. We've already seen them and there's no way they can be matched.

So why bother?

That, we guess, is the central question for anyone who watches this movie. Why was it necessary?

Clearly, Paramount wanted to dip its beak one more time and Puzo, Coppola and Pacino all realized nice pay days. The film grossed over $66 million in the United States alone and garnered seven Academy Award nominations, including one for Best Supporting Actor for Garcia. But it was shut out on Oscar night—the only film in the trilogy not to win one of the coveted awards.

Puzo originally wanted to call the movie *The Death of Michael Corleone*, but Paramount balked. The story is, however, a morality tale with a basic lesson—evil is punished. Michael Corleone's attempt to repent is too little, too late.

With *Godfather III*, we know how the final chapter in the Corleone saga ends. The Americanization of the family—the goal that Don Vito sought—is completed. But in giving us an ending, Coppola and Puzo have robbed us of imagining how it might have been.

And imagining how it might have been is sometimes better than seeing how it all turned out.

⊙ **HIT:** Andy Garcia brings a spark to his character that is reminiscent of so many performances in the first two Godfather movies. Unfortunately, not too many other actors bring their A-games this time.

⊗ **MISS:** Sofia Coppola's portrayal of Michael Corleone's daughter Mary is a drag on the story. Ms. Coppola has since won praise and built a career for herself as a director, like her father. Her role here was ample evidence that her future lay behind the camera, not in front of it.

She "won" two RAZZIE Awards for her performance: Worst Supporting Actress and Worst New Star. Her father did her no favor by casting her in this film.

✎ **WHAT THEY WROTE AT THE TIME:** "*The Godfather Part III* isn't just a disappointment, it's a failure of heartbreaking proportions. . . . The film completes the story of Vito Corleone and his sons . . . but in supplying the final chapter of the saga, it also sullies what came before. It makes you wish it had never been made."—Hal Hinson, *Washington Post*

✔ **REALITY CHECK:** Several of the characters involved in the Vatican Bank scandal were based, not so loosely, on individuals linked to that financial boondoggle. The Swiss banker in the movie is modeled after Roberto Calvi, chairman of Banco Ambrosiano. Like the character in the film, Calvi was found hanging from a bridge. While authorities first ruled it a suicide, it later was considered a murder. The death of Pope John Paul I from poison in his tea was also based on rumors that swirled around the demise of the Pontiff. And Don Lucchesi, the Sicilian politico with ties to the Mafia was a not-so-subtle reference to former Italian Prime Minister Giulio Andreotti.

◉ **REPEATED WATCHING QUOTIENT:** Only a diehard *Godfather* fan would want to revisit this and since you have the options of instead re-watching *Godfather I* or *II*, why waste your time on this one? But if you must, maybe the best way to take a second look is with the reissued DVD that tells the whole story chronologically.

♟ **BET YOU DIDN'T KNOW:** An early draft written by Puzo was built around a storyline that had Anthony Corleone working with the CIA to rub out a South American dictator. There were several other versions before Puzo and Coppola put this one together. Robert Duvall was originally going to reprise his role as Tom Hagen and would have had a big role in the financial wheeling and dealing and legitimization of the Corleone family. But Duvall balked at the pay he was offered (which was substantially less than Pacino's salary). Instead, the script was rewritten with Hagen dead and his son (John Savage) playing a minor role as a priest who gets assigned to the Vatican.

◀ **CASTING CALL:** Winona Ryder was set to play Mary, but bowed out so that she could appear in *Edward Scissorhands* (1990). Several others were mentioned, including Julia Roberts, Laura San Giacomo and Linda Fiorentino before Coppola settled on his daughter and rewrote the script so that the character of Mary was younger.

Just imagine a scene with Fiorentino and Garcia making gnocchi. It could have gotten the film an X-rating.

⁇ BEST LINE: Everyone knows and repeats the classic lament Michael utters when he realizes he can't get away from Cosa Nostra: "Just when I think I'm out, they pull me back in!"

But there are several other keepers as well.

We especially liked Michael's response to his son Anthony during their argument over Anthony's decision to leave law school and pursue a career as a singer. Anthony tells his father he loves him, but doesn't want to be part of his world.

"I have bad memories," he says.

To which Michael, with a straight face, replies, "All families have bad memories."

Say what?

⁇ VIOLENCE LEVEL: Sporadic, but when it comes, it comes with a rush. Shootings, stabbings, poisoned cannoli.

⁇ BODY COUNT: We figure about three dozen. There were so many bodies dropping during the helicopter assault at the Atlantic City casino that it was impossible to get an exact count.

76 AL CAPONE (1959–NR)

STARS: ROD STEIGER, FAY SPAIN, JAMES GREGORY, MARTIN BALSAM
DIRECTOR: RICHARD WILSON

Long before Don Corleone or Tony Soprano, the face of Italian organized crime in America was Al Capone.

The difference, of course, is that Corleone and Soprano are fictionalized characters based on a type. Capone was the real deal.

Rod Steiger offers one of the best portrayals of the legendary "Scarface" in this straightforward account of the life of perhaps the most fascinating underworld figure in American history. In many ways, Al Capone was larger than life. And he seemed to enjoy it.

Unlike the mob leaders who came before him, Capone did not believe in operating in the shadows. He spoke with reporters on a regular basis, rubbed elbows with politicians and union officials and was a patron of the arts with a real love for both opera and jazz.

While his devotion to opera is captured here, the jazz component is left out. But the clubs and bars he ran in Chicago often served as venues for some of the best jazz performers in the country.

"I'm a businessman, I serve the public," Capone says early in the movie, as his rise from bodyguard for Johnny Torrio (Nehemiah Persoff) to kingpin of Chicago's Southside is tracked.

Steiger captures the persona perfectly. His Capone is both cunning and volatile, not unlike the real-life character. He is the tentative but ambitious Capone, arriving in Chicago with (literally) hat-in-hand, finishing a beer that another patron has left on the bar in one of Torrio's joints, grabbing some lunch meat with his hand and stuffing it in his mouth.

And he is the bold and audacious crime boss, with the fancy suits, big cigars and diamond stickpins who literally shoots his way to the top. He arranges for two hit men to take out Big Jim Colosimo (Joe DeSantis) as he and the mob leader

listen to opera together. And when Torrio loses his nerve after nearly being killed by Dion O'Banion (Robert Gist) and the Irish gangsters from the Northside, Capone takes charge.

One of the best books—and there have been many—written about the man and the era is *Get Capone* by Jonathan Eig. Published in 2010, Eig's book was written years after this movie came out. But both tell the same story, and tell it exceedingly well.

The St. Valentine's Day Massacre, the big mob confab in 1929 in Atlantic City and Capone's retreat to Palm Island in Florida and his ultimate conviction on income tax evasion provide the outline for a story that in many ways defined an era in American history.

James Gregory, as the honest cop Schaefler, provides voice-over narration that offers commentary on both the underworld and the political corruption of the day. He succinctly describes the corrupt nexus of gangsters, elected officials and police that first came together during Prohibition and continued well after beer and liquor again flowed legally. "The underworld invaded the business world. The blackjack and the Tommy gun wore white collars and business suits."

Steiger's Capone never apologized for who he was or what he did. Some called him a Robin Hood. Others described him as the source of all evil in the underworld. In real life, Capone never shied from the publicity and often played off his tough-guy image, once telling a reporter, tongue perhaps in cheek, "You can get more with a kind word and a gun than you can with just a kind word."

As for bootlegging, Capone never missed a chance to highlight the hypocrisy of Prohibition. When he sold liquor, he said, it was a crime. But when his wealthy customers served it in their homes, it was called "hospitality."

Booze and broads and good times. Those were the 1920s in America. And Al Capone was in the middle of it all.

Dozens of actors have portrayed the Chicago gangster in movies based either directly or indirectly on his life and times. There was Paul Muni in *Scarface* and Robert De Niro in *The Untouchables* (both reviewed in this book). Others include Neville Brand, Jason Robards, Ben Gazzara and, most recently, British actor Stephen Graham who plays the young Al Capone in HBO's *Boardwalk Empire*.

But for our money, nobody captured Al Capone's character better than Rod Steiger did.

◉ **HIT:** Voice-over narration was used frequently in 1930s gangster films and too often came across as breathless hype. Here, Director Richard Wilson uses it with just the right touch and James Gregory is effectively matter-of-fact in narrating the story.

⊗ **MISS:** The gang warfare that rocked Chicago during Prohibition was fought partly along ethnic lines, with the Southside Italians battling the Northside Irish. But the movie tends to go over-the-top with the accents. All the Italians speak guttural English with lots of "deese" and "dems" and all the Irish have a lilting brogue

✎ **WHAT THEY WROTE AT THE TIME:** "A tough, ruthless and generally unsentimental account of the most notorious gangster of the Prohibition-repeal era, *Al Capone* is also a very well-made picture. There isn't much 'motivation' given for Capone, at least not in the usual sense. But the screenplay does supply reasons and they are more logical than the usual once-over-lightly on the warped youth bit."—*Variety*

✔ **REALITY CHECK:** Sensitivity and censorship were in play when Schaefler ends his narration of the movie by noting that Capone was released from prison suffering from an "incurable disease." Capone died of cardiac arrest, but it was brought on by advanced syphilis. The movie did not mention the disease, nor was there any depiction of the sexual carousing believed to be the source of Capone's affliction. Several reports indicate that Capone conducted "personal interviews" with each prostitute hired to work in the brothels his organization ran in and around Chicago.

◎ **REPEATED WATCHING QUOTIENT:** While this is one of the best of the movies about Capone, it is not the kind of film that offers the viewer much new in a second, third or fourth look. Once is probably enough unless you're a real Rod Steiger fan.

🍎 **BET YOU DIDN'T KNOW:** The reporter Mac Keeley portrayed by Martin Balsam was based on Alfred "Jake" Lingle, who worked for the *Chicago Tribune*. Lingle was a "leg man," a reporter who gathered information and phoned it in. He worked the crime beat in Chicago and had close ties to both Capone and the police. He was gunned down in 1930 in much the same way that Keeley is rubbed out in the movie. Like the Keeley character, Lingle had gotten entangled in mob business and had become less of a reporter and more of an expediter or go-between for various underworld factions and for the police. Several reports indicate that Capone had decided that Lingle's "head had gotten too big for his hat." But most sources indicated it was not Capone, but other gangsters who put the hit on the journalist.

◄ **CASTING CALL:** Nehemiah Persoff, who plays Johnny Torrio here, had a recurring role as Capone's bookkeeper Jake Guzik in the TV series *The Untouchables*.

❞ **BEST LINE:** "Booze, gambling and broads—a guy could die happy in a place like this," Capone tells Torrio shortly after arriving in Chicago while Torrio is showing him around the club that he owns.

🔫 **VIOLENCE LEVEL:** Lots of shooting, but none of the gory aftermath that dominates gangster movies of the current era.

🐾 **BODY COUNT:** Eighteen.

THE 15 WORST GANGSTER MOVIES EVER MADE

Sylvester Stallone can play a boxer; that much we know. Rocky is one of cinema's iconic characters. And Stallone can sure act the vigilante. He got four star turns out of John Rambo, including one—at age 62—where the HGH-injected old man takes out half of Burma.

But a mobster? Casting Sly as a mobster is always a mistake—bad enough to earn the guy three spots among our 15 worst gangster movies. Could have earned four, had we expanded the list by a few slots.

Beyond violating the Stallone casting prohibition, gangster filmmakers can make three other basic mistakes that all but guarantee they'll end up with a lousy movie. We've highlighted all four rules below, along with 15 movies that ignored them and paid the price.

Rule No. 1: Casting Stallone turns your mob movie into a disaster movie. Or just a disaster.

Consider *Oscar* (1991), a Prohibition Era, suspender-snapping debacle based on a successful French play. Hey, when you think Parisian theater, who springs to mind quicker than Sylvester Stallone? Anyway, Sly plays Snaps Provolone (sounds like a snack food), the heir to a mob throne. He promises his dying father (Kirk Douglas) that he will take the family legit. Of course, his underlings don't get the message. (Snaps: "Don't call me boss!" Henchman: "Uh, sorry boss.")

As Desson Howe of the *Washington Post* wrote: "Stallone is to mob humor what John Goodman is to ballet."

Get Carter (2000) is a remake of a British trailblazer that you'll find in this book's Top 100. The Italian Stallion is Jack Carter, a Vegas hit man who returns home to Seattle to investigate his brother's murder and winds up offing about half the resi-dents of the Emerald City. Watch for Michael Caine, who starred in the original, as the bad guy here. Mostly, watch as Stallone mumbles through 102 minutes, trying to sound weighty while reciting lines like, "My name is Jack Carter, and you don't want to know me." How correct he is.

Avenging Angelo (2002) goes back to the formula of Sly as the meathead with personality. It's kind of a clone of Kevin Costner's *The Bodyguard*, which is not a good enough movie to copy. And while Stallone plays an affable hit man named Frankie Delano, the film comes across more like a bad Lifetime Network soaper, complete with a sappy musical score and an implausible romance between Frankie and the woman he's trying to protect (Madeleine Stowe). *Angelo* marked the last film appearance of the legendary Anthony Quinn, who certainly deserved to go out better.

Honorable mention: *The Specialist* (1994).

Rule No. 2: Unless you've got De Niro and Pacino locked in, don't attempt a remake or follow-up.

The Godfather: Part II is, far and away, the greatest sequel ever made. *The Godfather: Part III*? Well, not a disaster, but the thicket of a plot does nothing to enhance the franchise's legacy.

So there are exceptions. But here are three movies that certainly prove our no-sequel rule.

Be Cool (2005) was an attempt to bring back the great character of Chili Palmer from *Get Shorty*, and also recreate the chemistry between John Travolta and Uma Thurman from *Pulp Fiction* (dance scene and all). How could it fail? Miserably, that's how. There's a solid cast here, including Harvey Keitel and Vince Vaughn, but the story doesn't vary much from Chili provoking people into wanting to kill him, then somehow escaping each time. The basic plot is that Chili wants to leave the film business because he's loath to make a sequel. There should have been a lesson there for Travolta.

Analyze That (2002) took the one-joke pleaser that was *Analyze This* and tried to squeeze another 96 minutes out of it. The first movie worked, because—even though it came out two months after *The Sopranos* hit HBO—the notion of a mobster seeing a shrink carried creative possibilities. The sequel has the same cast and the same jokes and the same basic plot. It seems nothing more than a compilation of skits that weren't good enough to make the original, including De Niro mincing around singing "I Feel Pretty." Hey, there are retreads and then there are bald tires.

Gloria (1999) attempted the old moviemaking trick of stealing the plot from a solid but obscure film and casting a big star in hopes of creating a hit. Shame on director Sidney Lumet, whose effort doesn't come close to John Cassavetes' 1980 original, which starred Gena Rowlands. And good luck buying Sharon Stone (one of film's great seductresses) as a street-smart moll who evolves into a nurturing mom. As Jack Mathews of the *Los Angeles Times* wrote, "It's Damon Runyan in drag."

Rule No. 3: Comedy Can Be Deadly

Yes it can, especially when the humor centers on psychotic folks who kill for a living. *Things Change, Snatch* and *Bullets Over Broadway* pull it off. But for each of those successes, many more have failed miserably.

Somewhere in Hollywood, one creative genius asked another: "Who's the wimpiest guy we can cast in a mob movie?" Answer: British fop Hugh Grant. Result: *Mickey Blue Eyes* (1999), in which Grant plays a sap who proposes to his beautiful girlfriend, only to find out that she's the daughter of a powerful mob don (James Caan, whose facelift looks like someone tightened the screws a few too many turns). We'll admit it—we kept hoping for pretty boy Grant to get whacked.

Joe Pesci is a first-ballot member in our Gangster Movie Hall of Fame. So it's sad that his most recent effort in the genre was *8 Heads in a Duffel Bag* (1997). Pesci stars as a hit man whose airline baggage (including the head-stuffed duffel bag of the title) gets switched with a poor college student's luggage. (Hasn't that happened to all of us?) Needless to say, he spends the film tracking down his cargo, which ends up in Mexico. There's one farcical scene in which the octet of craniums start singing. Hey, what's more fun than a sack full of musical noggins?

Making a solid gangster movie is tough. Making a gangster musical? Close to impossible. A gangster musical with an all-kids' cast? Evidence, we suppose, that Hollywood must have been crawling with some powerful drugs back in the 1970s. *Bugsy Malone* (1976) boasts 13-year-old Jodie Foster, songs by Paul Williams and guns that fire cream rather than bullets. Plus, precocious tweens spouting dialogue like this: "If it was raining brains, Roxy wouldn't even get wet. But he could smell trouble like other people could smell gas."

Gigli (2003) is recalled mostly for sparking a romance between Ben Affleck and Jennifer Lopez (remember Bennifer?). That's a shame, because there are better reasons to abhor it. That includes its plot, which centers on an inept mob enforcer, a lesbian hit woman and the mentally retarded man they attempt to kidnap. It's both vulgar and cheaply sentimental, poorly cast (these two glitzmeisters as cold-blooded killers?) and incomprehensible. Here's all you need to know: Affleck and Lopez were paid a combined $24.5 million for their roles—and that's three times more than the film grossed worldwide.

Honorable mentions: *Wise Guys* (1986), *Corky Romano* (2001), *Kangaroo Jack* (2003).

Rule No. 4: Nobody Likes a Copycat

Clearly inspired by *Once Upon a Time in America*, *Mobsters* (1991) chronicles the rise of four real-life goodfellas (Lucky Luciano, Frank Costello, Meyer Lansky and Bugsy Siegel) from the streets to their stranglehold over organized crime. You'll recognize dialogue, murder setups and entire scenes plagiarized from every decent gangster movie—from Paul Muni's *Scarface* to Al Pacino's *Scarface*. Beyond that, the actors are immature for the roles they're portraying. Christian Slater, at 21, tries to portray a 50ish Luciano, and just ends up looking like a college kid dressed up for a Halloween party.

10th & Wolf (2006) attempts the same ploy as *Mobsters*—tossing every successful gangster movie bit into a blender and hoping to pull out something new. The story is supposedly based on the true accounts of FBI Special Agent Joseph D. Pistone. If that name is familiar, it's because his tale was told before (and better) in *Donnie Brasco*. "This movie doesn't miss a cliché," wrote *New York Post* critic Lou Lumenick. "It ineptly lifts from *The Godfather* and *GoodFellas*, among other classics."

A combination horror movie and urban crime drama, *Urban Menace* (1999) is a horror and a crime only to those subjected to viewing it. The ghost of a crazy preacher (Snoop Dogg) haunts an old warehouse, terrorizing both innocents and the heads of the local crime syndicate. Actually, sometimes he's a ghost. Other times, he's a vampire, a psycho killer or an avenging angel knocking off petty hoods. You won't understand any of it, starting at the opening credits when rapper Ice-T addresses the audience, ending his speech with, "Fuck you." That may be a joke, but the entire film sends the same message.

Wesley Snipes has done a lot of good work over the years, but you won't find any of it in *Sugar Hill* (1993). He stars as a mobbed-up drug dealer who aims to change his life after finding love with a nice girl. He's got $5,000 suits and no apparent job, but she's shocked to learn he's a criminal. "How come every time I go out with you, somebody dies?" she wonders. Truth be told, it's a ponderous, hand-wringing film, and there's less chance that the characters will shoot each other than talk each other to death.

The Whole Ten Yards (2004) breaks nearly every rule in this chapter—it's a vapid comedy, an unoriginal story and a sequel to the slightly better *The Whole Nine Yards*. All it's missing is Stallone. It does, however, boast Bruce Willis as Jimmy the Tulip, a retired hit man who spends his days compulsively cleaning his house and working on his cooking skills. There's more to the plot, but nothing worth mentioning here. Just hope they never decide to make *The Whole Eleven Yards*.

Honorable mentions: *Out for Justice* (1991), *Shottas* (2002), *Rancid Aluminum* (2000).

77 KING OF NEW YORK (1990–R)

STARS: CHRISTOPHER WALKEN, DAVID CARUSO, LAURENCE FISHBURNE, WESLEY SNIPES | DIRECTOR: ABEL FERRARA

A few years ago, a ranking member of the Bloods street gang in Newark, N.J. was picked up on a federal wiretap discussing members of his organization. Everyone was known by their street names, revealed Edwin Spears, whose "gangster name" was "Movelli."

"Red Eye brought me home," he said of the gang leader who had recruited him. "I'm under Red Eye in New Jersey and I'm under Frank White in New York."

Rapper Biggie Smalls (a.k.a. Notorious B.I.G.) referred to himself as the "black Frank White" 10 years earlier. According to some reports, the rapper had checked into a Los Angeles hotel as Frank White a few days before he was killed in a now infamous drive-by shooting.

The name Frank White, it seems, has street cred.

That's part of the bizarre legacy of *King of New York*, director Abel Ferrara's violent, underworld morality tale that wants to be an inner-city Robin Hood story, but lacks the nobility.

Christopher Walken plays—as only Walken can—Frank White, a drug dealer whose release from prison sets the film and the violence in motion. It would be a stretch to say that White has returned from prison a changed man, but he has returned as a man with a mission. He wants to raise $15 million to ensure that a hospital in the South Bronx—earmarked for closure in a fiscal crunch—is refurbished so that it can provide the same kind of medical benefits for the poor that New York City's rich receive.

White and his entourage—including his lawyer and mistress Jennifer (Janet Julian)—hole up in a suite at the Plaza Hotel while his plan is set in motion. It's a simple but logical approach: kill all your rivals and take their drugs and money.

"My feelings are dead," White says after learning that the first of his rivals has been eliminated by his band of not-so-merry-but-oh-so-hopped-up hit men. "I feel no remorse." Walken delivers that line with dry, understated sarcasm, sending out a clear signal that there is much more carnage to come.

Much of that carnage comes courtesy of White's principal shooter, Jimmy Jump (Laurence Fishburne, here billed as Larry Fishburne). Test Tube (Steve Buscemi) is the organization's chemist.

First a Hispanic drug dealer is blown away in a phone booth just outside a brothel he has visited. Then King Tito, a Colombian cocaine supplier, is gunned down in a hotel room along with three associates by Jimmy Jump, Test Tube and a few other White henchmen pretending to complete a drug buy. When Tito opens an attaché case that Jimmy has handed to him, he finds that it's full of tampons instead of cash. He looks up incredulously and asks what they're for.

"They're for the bullet holes, motherfucker," Jimmy replies as he and the others pull out guns and open fire.

It's one of the first of several stylish but overblown shootouts that perhaps helps explain the film's strong following in certain segments of the underworld. A mob clubhouse in Little Italy and a restaurant in Chinatown provide the backdrops for more violence as White consolidates his hold on the city's drug trade.

His reign of terror plays out against his wheeling and dealing with politicos, whom he charms into helping get the hospital project on track. A woman who is introduced to White at a restaurant as he moves between his two worlds says it best: "I've heard a lot about you, and it's all bad."

But several political figures, including a councilman in whose district the hospital is located, don't seem to care where White's money is coming from as long as they can stand up and take credit.

A group of cops see things differently and set out to take White down. Things quickly turn personal. Lead detectives Dennis Gilley (David Caruso) and Thomas Flanigan (Wesley Snipes) eventually decide that to succeed, they have to take the law into their own hands.

Giving a black cop a decidedly Irish name like Flanigan is apparently screenwriter Nicholas St. John's attempt at urban humor—along with having a guy named White lead a band of black gangsters.

While *King of New York* has its moments, they are drowned out by the incessant gunfire that is often a substitute for an actual plot.

⊙ **HIT:** The frustration of the cops trying to bring law and order to the drug underworld is real. That part of the story comes right out of daily headlines.

⊗ **MISS:** There's a car chase across rain-soaked city streets that tries to mimic the classic scene in *The French Connection*. This chase, however, includes lots of gunfire at close range. Yet no one gets hit.

▦ **PIVOTAL SCENE:** Gilley, Flanigan and other cops are in a bar watching a television report about a hospital fundraiser where White is hobnobbing with city power brokers. "Frank is a movie star," Gilley says in disgust. "The King of New York. . . . This whole system favors the scumbag. We make thirty-six-five ($36,500) to risk our lives every night and Frank gets rich killing people."

At that point, Gilley and Flanigan decide to stop playing by the rules.

❞ **BEST LINE:** In a face-to-face with the commander of Gilley's squad, White justifies his existence. "I never killed anybody that didn't deserve it. This country spends $100 billion a year on getting high. That's not because of me . . . I'm not your problem. I'm just a businessman."

✎ **WHAT THEY WROTE AT THE TIME:** "Abel Ferrara's *King of New York* is all soft-core lighting and music video stylings—it's an urban crime story with a Euro-disco flavor. . . . His specialty is a kind of hallucinatory tawdriness, and here he's made a hepped-up film about drugs that plays as if the filmmakers themselves kept a healthy supply of the stuff at hand."—Hal Hinson, *Washington Post*

⌐ **VIOLENCE LEVEL:** Off the charts.

⚶ **BODY COUNT:** Thirty-two, possibly higher. The shootouts are filmed from so many different angles and in so many different shadings that it's impossible to be sure.

78 CHARLEY VARRICK (1973–PG)

STARS: WALTER MATTHAU, JOE DON BAKER | DIRECTOR: DON SIEGEL

Few filmgoers noticed *Charley Varrick* when it came out in 1973. After all, *The Godfather*, that ultimate game-changing gangster film, had been released a year earlier. So who was going to fuss over this nugget about a small-time bank robber fleeing with the mob's money?

Plus, 1973 happened to be an amazing movie year. *The Sting. The Exorcist. American Graffiti. Serpico. Mean Streets. High Plains Drifter*. More than a dozen terrific films debuted in one of the deepest eras ever in American film.

So this little gem arrived in theaters that October and disappeared within three weeks, drawing less than $6 million at the box office. It was quickly forgotten.

Now, thanks to Universal Studios rummaging through the attic and releasing the DVD in 2010, *Charley Varrick* can be enjoyed by new generations of movie fans. This time, we advise you not to miss it. It may not have the breadth of the Top 25 finishers in this book, but it's a gritty sleeper of a crime story, cleverly cast and sufficiently nasty and bleak. (Hey, if you were looking for happy endings, you wouldn't be reading this book, right?)

The story centers on the title character played by Walter Matthau, who strays a long way from his usual grump-with-a-heart-of-gold acting persona. Charley and his crew hold up a bank at a desolate

New Mexico crossroads. But things go awry when a sheriff's deputy gets too curious, and before you know it a pair of cops, the bank guard and two of Charley's accomplices—including his wife—get gunned down in the ensuing shootout.

Charley and his lone surviving accomplice, Harman (Andrew Robinson), escape with a saddlebag they expect to contain a few thousand bucks. To their amazement, the tiny bank has just coughed up $765,000. Harman is elated. Charley, older and wiser, knows better.

Harman: "We lucked out."

Charley: "More like crapped out. It's 10-to-1 this stuff belongs to the Mafia. This is gambling money, skimmed off the top. Whore money. Dope money."

Harman: "What's the difference?"

Charley: "The difference is that the Mafia kills, you moron. No trial, no judge. They never stop looking for you until you're dead. I'd rather have 10 FBIs looking after me."

Charley's instincts are correct. The mob hires an icy, pipe-smoking hit man named Molly (Joe Don Baker). His assignment (delivered in a *Mission: Impossible*-style tape-recorded message) is to hunt down the thieves, kill them and bring back the money.

A tense cat-and-mouse game ensues, with Molly tracking the duo. Charley keeps conniving ways to evade the paid killer and Harman keeps undermining those schemes by blowing his cool or climbing into a bottle of whiskey. We won't give away the double-crosses and triple-crosses that make this movie work except to say that whenever you think you've got it figured out . . . well, assume you probably don't.

Give credit to the film's producer/director—Don Siegel (*Dirty Harry, Hell is for Heroes, Escape From Alcatraz*), who knew how to craft a dark action story and how to create a morally ambivalent hero you end up rooting for. Siegel typically worked with macho leading men like Clint Eastwood, Steve McQueen and Lee Marvin. Casting the droll, hangdog Matthau—better known for his comic roles in films like *The Odd Couple*—in the lead was a risky move. It works because the great actor was smart enough to play the character as a serious, calculating and subdued man—the

anti-Oscar Madison, as it were.

You may recall Andrew Robinson—the actor playing Charley Varrick's cohort Harman—as the maniacal Scorpio Killer from *Dirty Harry*. In that classic, he hires a hood to punch his face into hamburger, hoping to make it appear like he's the victim of police brutality. In this movie, he endures another brutal face mashing. Hey, unlike Matthau, some actors can't escape typecasting.

⊙ **HIT:** Joe Don Baker is downright scary in his role as mob hit man—slapping women, pushing over old men in wheelchairs, stalking his prey with a sneer and a puff of his pipe. It's his most intimidating role this side of Buford Pusser in *Walking Tall*.

⊗ **MISS:** The original movie was filmed in Panavision and boasts beautiful New Mexican vistas. Cropping it to fit the TV screen creates too many pan-and-scan moments and occasional claustrophobia.

◀ **CASTING CALL:** The script was written with Clint Eastwood in mind for the lead, following Eastwood's collaboration with Siegel in *Dirty Harry*. Eastwood reportedly turned down the role because he could find no redeeming qualities in the film's protagonist.

✎ **WHAT THEY WROTE AT THE TIME:** "The casting of Matthau in this key role helps tremendously. Though Charley is tough enough to walk away from his wife's death without showing much emotion, the character is inhabited—maybe even transformed—by Matthau's wit and sensitivity as an actor. If the role were played by someone else, *Charley Varrick* would be something else entirely."—Vincent Canby, *New York Times*

👊 **BET YOU DIDN'T KNOW:** Siegel claimed Matthau contributed to the movie's box office failure by telling everyone that he neither liked it nor comprehended it. One note Matthau sent to the director said, "I have seen it three times, and am of slightly better than average intelligence (120 IQ), but I still don't quite understand what's going on. Is there a device we can use to explain to people what they're seeing?"

We would disagree with Matthau on that one.

☺ **GOOF:** Because the movie was shot out of sequence, the length of Charley's sideburns varies from scene to scene.

☞ **VIOLENCE LEVEL:** Not high, although there's more brutality aimed at women than we're used to. One bleeds to death after getting shot. Another gets slapped in the face and, somehow, finds that a turn-on to have sex with a stranger.

🐍 **BODY COUNT:** Nine—six by gunshot (including one suicide), one by off-screen beating, one by detonation and one by getting run over with a car.

👤 **"I KNOW THAT GUY":** Corrupt bank chairman Maynard Boyle is played by Canadian stage actor John Vernon. You may recognize him from his role as San Francisco's mayor in *Dirty Harry* or as rebel officer Fletcher in *The Outlaw Josey Wales*. We'll almost guarantee you'll spot him as the bullying Dean Wormer from 1978's frathouse comedy classic *Animal House*.

🔊 **BEST LINE:** Maynard Boyle, warning wimpy branch manager Harold Young (Woodrow Parfrey) that the mob will suspect him of being an insider in the heist of his own bank: "They're going to try to make you tell where the money is. They're going to strip you naked and go to work with a pair of pliers and blow torch."

The quote was paraphrased 20 years later in *Pulp Fiction* by Quentin Tarantino, who said he found *Charley Varrick* to be "inspiring." Indeed, Tarantino even borrowed the name Maynard for one of *Pulp's* subterranean characters—the guy who, along with motorcycle cop Zed, gets promised that same "medieval" pliers-and-blow-torch treatment.

👁 **REPEATED WATCHING QUOTIENT:** Neither exciting nor inspiring enough to put into your Netflix queue more than once a decade.

➡ **DON'T FAIL TO NOTICE:** The bank secretary that Varrick seduces and beds is played by actress Felicia Farr. She was the longtime, real-life wife of actor Jack Lemmon, who costarred with Matthau in 10 movies. We can't imagine that Lemmon enjoyed watching that scene.

⊛ **IF YOU LIKED THIS, YOU'LL LIKE:** *No Country for Old Men*, the 2009 Oscar winner for Best Motion Picture, which also centers on a guy reluctantly in possession of mob money and trying to stay one step ahead of an intractable killer. You can decide for yourself who's the more frightening hit man, Javier Bardem or Joe Don Baker. It's close.

79 FEDERAL HILL (1994–R)

STARS: ANTHONY DESANDO, NICHOLAS TURTURRO, LIBBY LANGDON
DIRECTOR: MICHAEL CORRENTE

Writer-director Michael Corrente took the title and setting for his first movie from the Italian-American section of Providence, Rhode Island. Corrente grew up nearby, and he clearly knows his territory.

Originally shot in black-and-white, but available in color on DVD, *Federal Hill* is a middle-class *Mean Streets*. The movie churns some of the same ground as Scorsese's classic, but without the gritty edge. These young wannabe wiseguys are comfortable. Their problem is they're restless.

Nicky (Anthony DeSando) is an excellent mechanic whose father owns a used car lot so he gets to cruise around town each night in a borrowed Caddy or some other hot car.

Ralphie's dad founded a construction company, and while the old man now suffers fits of debilitating depression, he is still a master bricklayer. So is Ralphie (Nicholas Turturro), but he'd rather make his money breaking into homes and stealing cash and jewelry.

"What's with the ninja suit?" Nicky asks when Ralphie shows up one night on the corner dressed in a black hoodie, black sneakers and black jeans.

"I just got off work," says Ralphie, who we watched minutes earlier breaking into a home and making off with a bed sheet full of necklaces, bracelets and other valuables.

Nicky, Ralphie and three friends—including Frankie (Michael Raynor), whose father Sal (Frank Vincent) is the local mob boss—are all struggling in one way or another to find themselves. Nicky deals a little coke on the side. Frankie is an apprentice wiseguy. Bobby (Jason Andrews) works as a valet parking attendant at a fancy restaurant. Joey (Robert Turano) is an ex-con trying to go straight.

Ralphie is the wild card, a short-tempered tough guy who may be having problems with his own sexual identity. Out driving with the guys one night, he stops to brutalize a street-corner male hooker. His friends cringe as he rips out the man's earring and then laughs about it. His intense, over-the-top homophobia hints at an internal conflict. The nature of his affection for Nicky, his best friend, also raises questions that are never answered.

A subplot involving students from Brown University gives Corrente the opportunity to play the Ivy League off these blue-collar ethnics. Nicky's infatuation with a coed he meets when she wants to buy some coke for a frat party brings the two worlds together and into conflict.

"Don't go nuts over her cause it ain't gonna work," Ralphie tells his friend, offering advice that is based on genuine concern . . . and, perhaps, jealousy.

But Nicky won't listen. And after first being rebuffed, he wins her over when he takes her home and prepares a dish of spaghetti *aiolo* that is just perfection. A little wine and before you know it, they're in bed.

She's blonde (of course). Her name is Wendy (Not for nothing, but isn't that the perfect name for a WASP coed?) And she gets Nicky thinking about life beyond The Hill.

We know it can't work. And so, it seems, does she.

Weeks into their relationship, Wendy (Libby Langdon) reluctantly agrees to let Nicky treat her and her parents—who are visiting for the weekend—to dinner at a fancy restaurant in the neighborhood. When Nicky takes charge at the table and orders for everyone in Italian, Wendy's mother asks where he studied the language. The thought that he learned at home from his grandparents is not something she would ever consider.

In his own way, Nicky is just as clueless. He thinks that he might be able to accompany Wendy on a summer archaeological dig in Italy. He could cook, he says, and fix the machines.

Ralphie, for all his anger and pent-up frustration, is the only member of the group who sees things as they are and is prepared to deal with them. Stopped by a cop for speeding and with the stash from a recent burglary in the car, Ralphie "accidentally" drops a $20 bill as he hands the cop his license and registration.

The cash lands on the ground and Ralphie asks, "Is that yours?"

The cop picks up the bill, looks at it and tells Ralphie, "No. It ain't mine. Mine's a fifty."

Life on the streets.

Ralphie also wants to leave The Hill and would like to take Nicky with him. His plan to finance their getaway evolves as he helps Bobby settle a $30,000 debt to wiseguys threatening to bust up Bobby if he doesn't come up with the cash. Ralphie figures out how to get the money—and then some—by breaking into the homes of local mobsters while they dine at the restaurant where Bobby parks cars. This puts Ralphie directly in conflict with Frankie's father, Sal, after the mob boss surmises that his son's young friend is behind the rash of break-ins.

"He's got to have keys, this kid," Sal says. "Either that or he's a ghost."

Ralphie does have keys and the way he gets them and pulls off the heists comes from a story taken from the life of a genuine mobster (see below).

No one in *Federal Hill*, however, gets what he's hoping for, which may be part of the message Corrente wanted to deliver in his first film.

But after settling the score with Sal, Ralphie does get to lay some brick.

◉ **HIT:** A jazz score and some great cinematography set the tone for the movie. *Federal Hill* does for Providence what scores of gangster movies have done for New York. The city becomes a character, part of the story.

⊗ MISS: Some of the dialogue sounds forced. When Sal taps his son Frankie to take care of Ralphie, he tells him, "It's time for you to do a little work." This is genuine wiseguy talk.

But then he adds, "It's time for you to make your bones." The second line is totally unnecessary and seems aimed at the same WASP crowd that gave us Wendy and her parents. Wendy's attempt at sincerity also rings hollow when she tells Nicky, "It's not your cock or your coke. I like you, Nicky Russo." Oh.

✔ REALITY CHECK: Ralphie gets copies of the keys to the houses and security systems of mobsters from the key chains they leave with Bobby after he parks their cars at the restaurant. He provides a press that Bobby uses to make copies. Then, while the wiseguys are out enjoying dinner, Ralphie cleans out their houses.

Philadelphia mobster Nicholas "Nicky Crow" Caramandi, who made his living as a con man and hustler, recounted this same scam in the book *Blood and Honor* (see the interview with Caramandi in this book) that was published in 1991, three years before the release of *Federal Hill*. Caramandi, who became a government informant, had a parking attendant at a garage in Center City Philadelphia working for him. The garage catered to the theater and restaurant crowd—mostly wealthy couples from the suburbs coming into the city for dinner and a show on a Saturday night.

Caramandi would pick out a valuable car, go into the glove compartment to find the registration, which listed a home address, then take the house key from the chain left with the parking attendant and bring it to a nearby locksmith in on the scam. After bringing the original key back to the parking lot, Caramandi and two associates would head to a ritzy suburb, where they would clean out the house. Jewelry, furs and cash were the items of choice he said because they were the easiest to fence. But on any given night, they would take whatever they thought they could get away with.

❞ BEST LINE: Ralphie's attempt to make it with a coed at a frat party he and Nicky crash leads to one of the best putdown lines ever. After Ralphie tells the coed, who is dancing by herself, that he likes her pants and that there seems to be enough room in there for both of them, the young woman gives him a withering stare and replies, "Why on earth would I want you in my pants? I've got one asshole in there already."

✎ WHAT THEY WROTE AT THE TIME: "*Federal Hill* has sincerity on its side and a fair degree of authenticity. You get the feeling the director really has no idea you've heard this story before: neighborhood guys stuck in a rut of crime and squalor. One guy in the group has aspirations to beauty. Another can't see past the sidewalk."— Mick LaSalle, *San Francisco Chronicle*

⌐ VIOLENCE LEVEL: Minimal. Lots of shouting and slapping, but very little gun play. The attack on the male hooker is the most brutal scene.

⚰ BODY COUNT: Two.

⊗ IF YOU LIKE THIS, YOU'LL LIKE: *Brooklyn Rules* (2007), the story of three young Italian-American guys in Brooklyn struggling to find their way, dodging mob connections and looking to make it on their own. Corrente directed this one as well. It stars Freddie Prinze Jr., Scott Caan and Jerry Ferrara.

80 MAFIOSO (1962–NR)

STARS: ALBERTO SORDI, NORMA BENGELL, GABRIELLA CONTI, UGO ATTANASIO
DIRECTOR: ALBERTO LATTUADA

An FBI agent from Philadelphia once tried to explain the difference between the Sicilian Mafia and its American Cosa Nostra cousin, both of which were operating in the City of Brotherly Love in the 1980s.

The agent, since retired, had first been assigned to track suspected Sicilian heroin dealers operating in the area. They were part of what came to be known as the Pizza Connection, an international band of drug traffickers using pizzerias as fronts.

Later the agent was shifted to a unit that built a case against the locals.

It was a lot easier, he said, to gather evidence and prosecute the American gangsters. And by way of explanation, he told a story about a day when he had a Sicilian Mafioso under surveillance in Philadelphia. He followed the mobster as he drove some 45 miles from his home along an extension of the Pennsylvania Turnpike. The mobster pulled into a rest stop, went to a pay phone. Made a call. Spent less than a minute on the phone. Then got back into his car and drove 45 miles home.

There was no way anyone could wiretap that conversation. No way anyone would know what it was about.

"The Sicilians," the agent said, "are very serious about what they do."

We see a lot of that in *Mafioso*, director Alberto Lattuada's dark comedy that says so much about both the criminal organization and the fascinating island of Sicily that gave birth to it.

In a 2010 article in the *Daily Beast*, Martin Scorsese listed the film as one of the 15 gangster movies that had the most profound effect on him as a writer and director. He cited *Mafioso* as "one of the best films ever made about Sicily."

And as we've mentioned elsewhere in this book (see *Salvatore Giuliano*, page 238, for more detail), it is impossible to understand the Mafia without understanding Sicily.

Mafioso appears to be a simple story, told directly. In fact, it is multilayered and full of subtle twists and turns.

Antonio "Nino" Badalamenti (Alberto Sordi) is a native Sicilian who has built a successful career as a supervisor at an auto plant in Milan. Highly efficient and organized, he puts the lie to the stereotype of southern Italians as lazy underachievers.

After 15 years, he has planned a vacation in which he, his northern-born wife Marta (Norma Bengell) and their two young daughters will travel to Calamo, the Sicilian town where he was born. It will be the first time his wife and children have met his family.

Marta becomes the voice of modern Italy, as she asks questions and comments on the people she meets and what she sees. In many ways, the visit is a step way back in time for a modern Italian woman.

As they drive through the village in a taxi, they happen upon a party gathered around an open coffin and a corpse. It is, her husband explains, the way things are done in Sicily. Friends and relatives have come together to see the departed off.

"It's nothing," he tells his wife and daughter. "A man died. His friends are throwing a party for him."

Then, leaning out the car window, he asks one of the men at the party, "How'd he die?"

The man, holding a plate full of food, casually replies, "Two bullets."

Welcome to Sicily.

From there, *Mafioso* heads in two directions.

Marta overcomes a cool reception and wins the hearts of her in-laws while falling in love with the beauty and slower pace of life in Calamo. Helping her sister-in-law Rosalia (Gabriella Conti) get rid of her moustache goes a long way toward thawing the familial ice. Modern depilatory creams and lotions were not in vogue in the village. Rosalia goes from ugly duckling to beauty queen after a simple treatment, leading her brother to quip, "You're like porcelain. Smooth. White. Take my advice. Marry before your moustache grows again."

While Marta's "miracle work" speaks to the naïveté of the village, Nino reconnects with a different Sicily. After getting back in touch with old friends, he finds himself faced with the obligation to repay an old debt to Don Vincenzo (Ugo Attanasio), the local Mafia head and most respected man in town. The debt, not surprisingly, can be repaid only by providing a special service, which Don Vincenzo has only hinted at during his discussions with Antonio.

"Don Vincenzo, what is it that I'm doing?" Nino asks.

"What are you doing?" says the Don. "Something very important. But if you wish . . . you can say no. Do you say no?"

No, of course, isn't really an option. And Nino is well aware of that.

An elaborately planned hunting trip that will explain his absence for two days is organized so that Nino can be hidden in a large crate and shipped to New York City, where he carries out a hit. He is then recrated and flown back to Sicily.

No one is the wiser.

The Mafia, clearly, is serious about what it does.

The *Village Voice*, in a review when the film was reissued in 2007 for American audiences, called *Mafioso* "The Godfather's Godfather." Not a bad description.

The movie ends with Nino and his family back in Milan. At work again at the auto plant, he returns a pen that he had mistakenly taken from a coworker on the day he left for his vacation. The coworker, touched by his honesty, says, "If everyone was like you, it would be a better world."

Don Vincenzo, we can assume, feels the same way. But, in typical Sicilian fashion, we can only assume. Most of what is thought is never said.

⊙ **HIT:** The feel for life in Sicily is captured in several small scenes and moments. Marta, for example, begins to smoke a cigarette after she and her family have been treated to plate after plate of food during their first day at the family home. Everyone stops to look.

She assumes, she tells her husband, that they are surprised to see a woman smoking, adding that she enjoys a cigarette after a meal.

But that's not it, he explains. The food they have eaten was only the appetizers. Several family members then bring out plates full of pasta and other delicacies as the feast continues.

Anyone who ever visited relatives in Sicily can relate. The touch was perfect.

⊗ **MISS:** For those who insist on knowing all the hows and whys, the trip to New York begs several questions, not the least of which is how difficult it would have been to survive the flight in a crate. Likewise, it is never clearly explained why the hit has to be carried out. But while those unanswered questions may count as negatives for some viewers, if you accept the mystery of the Mafia, which *Mafioso* tries to capture, then there is no need to know.

✎ **WHAT THEY WROTE AT THE TIME:** "If you crossed *Meet the Parents* with *The Godfather* and filmed it 45 years ago in Italian, you might come close to *Mafioso*, a black-and-white gem from 1962."—G. Allen Johnson (on the 2007 release of the film in the United States), *San Francisco Chronicle*

✔ **REALITY CHECK:** Alberto Sordi's character is named Antonio Badalamenti. It was an interesting choice for a surname and you have to wonder if Lattuada and writers Rafael Azcona and Bruno Caruso were playing with fire. Gaetano Badalamenti was a real-life Mafia figure who headed an organization based in his hometown of Cinisi, not unlike the town in which most of the movie is set.

By the 1970s, Badalamenti was heading the Mafia Commission in Sicily as the *capo di tutti capi*, boss of bosses, during one of the most violent underworld periods of Mafia history. In the late 1980s he was convicted of being part of the infamous Pizza Connection, a Mafia heroin ring that generated hundreds of millions of dollars. The organization stretched from Sicily, through South America and into the United States. He was sentenced to 45 years in federal prison following his conviction in New York in 1987. He died in 2004.

◎ **REPEATED WATCHING QUOTIENT:** Easy to watch and enjoyable on several levels, it's worth an occasional revisit.

🍴 **BET YOU DIDN'T KNOW:** Lattuada wrote or directed more than 40 movies in Italy, but may be best known to American audiences as the director of the 1985 television miniseries *Christopher Columbus*. The six-hour epic starred Gabriel Byrne in the title role. The all-star, international cast included Rossano Brazzi, Virna Lisi and Oliver Reed.

❞ **BEST LINE:** "The lies of a woman, when softened by grace and courtesy, are always welcome," says Mafia boss Don Vincenzo after a young women pays him a compliment. What he's really saying is that lies are simply a part of life. You recognize them for what they are. You use them. Or you ignore them. Part of the Mafia code of living.

🔫 **VIOLENCE LEVEL:** Hardly a blip, just the one shooting in New York. The violence, reflecting the tenets of the Mafia, is implied and always hovering in the background.

🦶 **BODY COUNT:** Two, if you include the funeral that Nino and his family happen upon, but only one on-screen murder.

Walker just wants his money back.

And he'll go to anywhere and confront anyone to get it.

That's the premise, based on a pulp fiction novel called *The Hunter* by Donald E. Westlake, for this stylized drama—a movie with 1960s sensibilities that doesn't always hold up that well.

There are lots of deliberately out-of-focus shots. Plenty of soap opera-like music to set dramatic scenes. And dialogue that goes for tough guy speak, but comes out as cliché.

Lee Marvin as Walker (we never get a first name) is the best thing in the movie. A young Angie Dickinson, as Chris, shows why she was considered a sex symbol 40 years ago.

But the rest of the cast pretty much phones it in.

As Walker's wife Lynne, Sharon Acker gives a cardboard performance as a woman who betrays him and then, two years later when he confronts her, says, "Walker, I'm glad you're not dead."

By this point, she has been abandoned by Mal Reese (the always-evil John Vernon), Walker's former friend and business associate. Two years earlier, Reese shot Walker and left him for dead in the abandoned prison on Alcatraz Island. The shooting occurred after a money drop from a helicopter. The cash was from "the organization," a business syndicate involved in high-level criminal activity that is never clearly identified.

Reese, a low-level member of the organization, is deeply in debt and needs to come up with cash. He sets up the heist, promising Walker half—$93,000. Instead, he shoots Walker, steals the money and takes Walker's wife, with whom he's already been having an affair.

Somehow, Walker survives and gets off Alcatraz.

The movie picks up two years later as Walker attempts to reclaim his cash and take care of Reese.

Bodies keep dropping as he methodically moves up the ladder, going from one member of the organization to another in search of his money.

Dickinson's Chris is his former sister-in-law. She becomes his love interest after Lynne, distraught over the mess her life has become, commits suicide. Lynne does this shortly after Walker shows up at her doorstep—and after he fires nearly a dozen shots into the empty bed in her apartment, where he assumed she was sleeping with Reese. After she overdoses on that same bullet-riddled mattress, Walker approaches her dead body and places his wedding ring on her finger.

Did we mention the soap opera-like quality here?

From there, Walker becomes a man consumed with his mission. Chris helps him dispose of Reese and, naturally, they fall in love.

But first they fight. She slaps him. She hits him with a pool stick and she ransacks a house where they are lying in wait for another organization member.

Of course, they end up in bed.

"Heh, what's my last name?" she asks after they have spent the night together.

"What's my first name?" Walker responds.

They both then nod knowingly. Only in *Love Story* have we heard that kind of romantic dialogue.

Along the way there are snipers, beatings and car crashes.

Yost (Keenan Wynn), a mysterious character, keeps showing up to offer Walker bits of information that help him peel away the layers of mystery and track the leaders of the organization. Who is he and why does he do this? You have to wait to find out.

Walker eventually gets what he came for, but the premise of the movie seems convoluted.

Ironically, one of the members of the organization makes this point, when he asks Walker, "Good Lord, man, do you mean to say you'd bring down this immense organization for a paltry $93,000?"

And that's the problem. If this organization was as powerful and sophisticated as it was made out to be, somewhere along the blood-strewn road to the story's conclusion, someone would have decided it was cheaper and easier just to give the guy his money.

✎ **WHAT THEY WROTE AT THE TIME:** "As suspense thrillers go, *Point Blank* is pretty good. It gets back into the groove of Hollywood thrillers after the recent glut of spies, counterspies, funny spies, anti-hero spies and spy-spier spies. Marvin is just a plain, simple tough guy who wants to have the same justice done for him as was done for Humphrey Bogart."—Roger Ebert, *Chicago Sun-Times*

✔ **REALITY CHECK:** Located on an island surrounded by a treacherous bay, Alcatraz prison was considered nearly impossible to escape. So it's hard to imagine how Walker survives the initial hit that sets the movie in motion. We see him in the water and the assumption is that he swims to land. But after being left for dead with two bullet holes in him, that's a bit of a stretch. Of course, that would also explain why he's so angry and bent on revenge two years later.

☺ **GOOF:** Chris is wearing a not-particularly-attractive yellow dress when she and Walker end up in bed. The next morning, she is putting on a more stylish white outfit. Unless there was a closet full of women's clothes in the organization's safe house where the tryst took place, how'd she do that?

👁 **REPEATED WATCHING QUOTIENT:** Once is enough.

🍎 **BET YOU DIDN'T KNOW:** This was the first film shot on the site of the famous prison. Alcatraz had closed just three years before the film went into production.

🙶 **BEST LINE:** "You should have stayed an accountant," says Yost (Keenan Wynn) to a dying organization executive at the end of the film, when most of the other leaders of the organization have been killed over the paltry $93,000 that is owed to Walker.

✪ **IF YOU LIKED THIS, YOU'LL LIKE:** *Payback*, the 1999 retelling of the same story, starring Mel Gibson and the always sexy Maria Bello. Set in the drug underworld, the story is in some ways easier to follow and Gibson does a good job as the relentlessly put-upon anti-hero known only as "Porter."

☻ **"I KNOW THAT GUY":** The sniper who makes two brief appearances is James Sikking, a character actor best known for his recurring role as the pipe-smoking Lt. Howard Hunter on the classic TV cop series *Hill Street Blues* in the 1980s.

⚑ **VIOLENCE LEVEL:** High but not unexpected, given the storyline.

⚰ **BODY COUNT:** Seven, including a suicide and a long fall from the balcony of a penthouse apartment.

82 SONATINE (1993–R)

STAR: TAKESHI KITANO | DIRECTOR: TAKESHI KITANO

For decades, Takeshi "Beat" Kitano has been Mr. Everything in Japanese entertainment—comedian, talk-show host, author, painter, video game designer and the auteur responsible for his country's most popular gangster (or yakuza) movies.

He is largely unknown in the United States. His greatest exposure here was Spike TV's re-airing of his schlockiest work, a slapstick-style 1980s game show called *Most Extreme Elimination Challenge*. Not exactly the artistic highpoint of a creative fountain who spends his off days writing poetry.

But in the last decade, Kitano's biggest American devotee—director Quentin Tarantino—has tried to raise his Western profile. Tarantino, who glowingly speaks of how his own work has been influenced by Kitano and other Asian directors, released four of Kitano's yakuza movies on DVD in this country.

The reaction? Mostly shrugs, to be honest.

A lot is lost in translation when watching these extremely violent films. Some of the jokes and dialect meant for Kitano's home audience just doesn't translate. Still, the DVDs are worth checking out if you're a gangster-movie devotee, a fan of Tarantino or just curious about how they execute the genre in the Far East.

And if you plan to give one a try, start with *Sonatine*, which Kitano wrote, directed and edited. He also stars in it as a weary, middle-aged Tokyo mobster.

Kitano's character, Mr. Murakawa, is a yakuza crew boss who tells an associate that he is pondering retirement. He has lost interest in the job and the lifestyle, even though his gang is very successful. "Maybe you're too rich for this business," offers the associate.

Before he can get out, his don—or "overlord"—assigns him to travel to Okinawa to sort out a dispute between two mob factions. He's not eager for the job. He has suspicions that the boss is setting him up. "The last time you sent us out I lost three men," Murakawa says. "I did not enjoy that."

Still, he has no choice. So he and his lieutenant, Takahashi (Ken'ichi Yajima), recruit a band of inexperienced thugs and head to Okinawa. Within a few days, Murakawa and his men get caught in a bloody ambush. His suspicions, it turns out, were correct. He has been double-crossed—sent on a doomed mission so that the boss can muscle in and take over his lucrative territory back in Tokyo.

Now stranded far from home, Murakawa takes his surviving crew and retreats to a remote seaside cabin to plot his next move.

This is where *Sonatine* takes a curious turn. As the men wait it out at the secluded beach house, they play Frisbee, dress up as geishas, practice sumo wrestling and engage in a bizarre version of rock-paper-scissors in which the winner gets to shoot a beer can off the loser's head.

The point, as far as we can see it, is to show the banality of passing time. But Kitano's directing style—which verges on slapstick at times—becomes campy and occasionally downright silly. As Owen Gleiberman of *Entertainment Weekly* wrote, "The picture ricochets from random urban mob hits to horseplay in the sand that wouldn't have looked out of place on *The Monkees*."

To further confuse things, Murakawa begins an extraneous relationship with a gun-loving yakuza groupie (so much for isolation). She is attracted to him, she says, because he has no fear of death. Ah, romance.

There is no room for sentimentality in that relationship, nor any other aspect of Murakawa's life. As Tarantino explains in the DVD commentary, "Takeshi's characters—and his films—are rough, hard and violent. There's none of the romanticism you would find in American gangster movies."

Eventually, Murakawa plots his revenge. We

won't give you all the details, except to say that, by our count, 23 mobsters lose their lives in the film's final five minutes. The last one may surprise you.

⊙ HIT: *Sonatine* does an excellent job of depicting the yakuza code, which apparently requires much more turning the other cheek than in the American mob. In one scene, Murakawa beats one of his boss' deputies into submission in a men's room—but the two remain on speaking terms. In another scene, one impetuous low-level thug stabs another in the gut. The next day, they sit side-by-side on a bus ride, and the slasher even offers his victim an ice cream bar. "You stabbed me in the stomach and it still hurts," explains the wounded man as he declines the treat.

⊗ MISS: Kitano's characters approach murder as their job, he explains in the DVD commentary, making them impassive toward violence. Okay, we get that. But there's impassive, and then there's catatonic. As guns are fired and blood flies, the deadpan shooters (and often the victims) seem bored to the point of stasis. Reportedly, French actor Alain Delon—who starred in the 1967 masterpiece *The Samurai*—watched *Sonatine* and said of Kitano afterward, "What's that? This is not an actor. He's only got three facial expressions and he almost doesn't talk on top of that."

▣ PIVOTAL SCENE: Murakawa's casual approach toward killing is revealed in an early scene in which the stubborn operator of a mahjong gambling house on Murakawa's turf is set up to be frightened into paying protection money. The man is tied and suspended from the arm of a crane and lowered into the harbor. Murakawa, who is supervising the dunking, gets caught up in conversation and forgets how long the man has been under. By the time Murakawa orders the man pulled up, he is dead.

No big deal. Murakawa turns away in boredom and begins another conversation. The victim is forgotten before his body is even cut down from the crane.

◉ REPEATED WATCHING QUOTIENT: Twice—the first time to take it all in, the second time to better comprehend it.

➡ DON'T FAIL TO NOTICE: One year after making *Sonatine*, Kitano was in a serious motorcycle accident that paralyzed half his face. On a bonus interview—included with the DVD—conducted several years later, you can see the difference. The right side of his face sags and twitches.

❞ BEST LINE: Murakawa confesses to his new girlfriend that he often shoots people out of fear.

"But you're not afraid of dying, are you?" she asks.

"When you're scared all the time," he replies, "you reach a point where you almost wish you were dead."

✎ WHAT THEY WROTE AT THE TIME: "No Armani, no marinara, no Joe Pesci. Takeshi Kitano's Japanese mafia flick lacks the quaint iconography of the Sicilian-American fare we were all weaned on. Yet *Sonatine* achieves a cold, manic brilliance all its own that owes nothing to Coppola or De Laurentiis."—Peg Aloi, *Boston Phoenix*

⚸ BODY COUNT: Forty-two, including thirty-seven shooting victims, three dead by bombing, one stabbing victim and that poor guy plunged into the river.

✹ IF YOU LIKED THIS, YOU'LL LIKE: Any of the films in the following chapter.

Ichi the Killer

YAKUZA FILMS

You don't need to enjoy seeing a man get his finger chopped off to appreciate Japanese gangster movies. But it helps.

We watched upwards of two dozen so-called yakuza films while compiling this book and certain themes seem to run throughout: revenge, honor, loyalty to lost values—and the severing of digits. Especially pinkies. Something about penance or apology within the mob. Anyway, it seems to turn up in most films.

As a whole, Japanese gangster movies are far more brutal than their American counterparts. The heroes tend to be stoic but explosive in a Clint Eastwood style. And there's often an underlying plot in which members of the yakuza—Japan's version of the Mafia—serve as "chivalrous outlaws" (machi-

yakko), protecting their villages from more-evil outside forces. Kind of like young Don Corleone (Robert De Niro) in *The Godfather: Part II*.

They can be entertaining (assuming you can accept subtitles or bad dubbing, like in old-time samurai movies or spaghetti westerns or kung fu send-ups). You'll see the influences on Francis Ford Coppola and Jim Jarmusch and Quentin Tarantino. Especially Tarantino, whose *Kill Bill* films pay tribute to Asian cinema.

Beyond *Drunken Angel* and *Sonatine* (which both rated their own chapters as entries in our Top 100), here are the dozen Japanese gangster films that we recommend, although some come with reservations:

Tokyo Drifter (1966) and *Branded to Kill* (1967)

are farfetched dramas directed by Seijun Suzuki, who proudly called himself "the king of B-movies." In *Tokyo Drifter*, a yakuza family decides to go straight and enter the real estate business (insert your own joke here). It works, so well in fact, that a rival gang puts the squeeze on their legitimate venture. Those rivals, headed by a sinister overlord named Otsuka, harass one of the good guys so badly that he has to leave the big city (thus becoming the Tokyo Drifter of the title). He spends much time in self-reflection before returning to blow up everyone.

In *Branded to Kill*, a syndicate's third-ranked hit man botches an assignment, thus making himself a target for assassination. There is lots of strange imagery (a running theme of dead butterflies, for example), and downright weird touches (our protagonist has a fetish for the aroma of boiling rice). But if you don't require narrative clarity in your movies, you should enjoy the over-the-top action sequences.

Battles without Honor or Humanity (1973) is far less outrageous in its storyline, but no less brutal. Set in postwar Hiroshima, the film portrays two gangs battling for control among the ashes. There are no hints of chivalry or anyone trying to cling to an ancient code. Just a lot of street fights and murders (each punctuated on the soundtrack by a trumpet blare), backstabbing and firebombing. If you recognize the title song, that's because Tarantino later used it in *Kill Bill: Vol. 1*. Directed by Kinji Fukasaku, this movie was such a hit in Japan that it led to four sequels.

Takeshi "Beat" Kitano, the creator of *Sonatine*, had his breakthrough with *Violent Cop* (1989), a *Dirty Harry* knockoff that Kitano wrote, directed and starred in. He went on to create three other noteworthy gangster potboilers, shown below in the order of our preference.

Kids Return (1996) is the story of two former schoolyard bullies who have moved on—one to become a boxer, the other to work as a yakuza enforcer. Both aim late to find purpose in their lives, which leads, inevitably, to both returning to that schoolyard. A poignant but downcast movie, which Kitano directed while recovering from a serious motorcycle accident. Maybe that explains his pessimism.

Boiling Point (1990) focuses on a young man who plays baseball and works at a gas station. He makes the mistake of insulting a gangster (think of poor Spider in *GoodFellas*). Despite apologies (and, yes, there is that pesky removal of a pinkie), the violence and reprisals escalate into one bloody massacre. Our kid becomes a man, and a rather frightening one at that.

Brother (2000) was Kitano's attempt to make it in America. Partly told in English and costarring Omar Epps, *Brother* tells the story of a yakuza exiled to the United States, where he and his brother scheme to take over the Los Angeles drug trade. There are plenty of culture clash moments, like when the Japanese basketball player complains that the black guys won't pass him the ball. It's choppy, sadistic (watch for the disemboweling scene) and tougher to understand than Kitano's all-Japanese movies. Among the dozens of murders, our favorite was the guy who meets his end by having chopsticks shoved up his nose.

In recent years, director Takashi Miike has become Japan's most controversial director of gangster films. Consider, for example, his *Ichi the Killer* (2001) about a sadomasochistic enforcer. The film includes a bloody rape, a murder in which our hero severs a man's face, and another scene in which a victim is sliced in half from head to groin. And that's all in the first 20 minutes. When *Ichi* was shown at the Toronto Film Festival, every audience member was handed a barf bag, on which was printed the film's logo.

Miike's other noteworthy films include *Fudoh: The New Generation* (1996); *The Bird People in China* (1998); *Dead or Alive* (1999) and *Gozu* (2003), which features a Chihuahua posing as a yakuza attack dog. Plotlines aren't really important here. Just know that you're in for two hours of gory—albeit creative—murder and kinky stuff, like a murderess who fires a blow gun from her vagina. Kind of makes you long for a nice family film like *Scarface*.

83 DILLINGER (1973–R)

STARS: WARREN OATES, BEN JOHNSON, MICHELLE PHILLIPS, HARRY DEAN STANTON
DIRECTOR: JOHN MILIUS

During the Great Depression, when bank robbers were regarded as rock stars, John Dillinger was Mick Jagger. Portrayed by some of the popular press as a Robin Hood, Dillinger was a failed machinist who was kicked out of the Navy and turned to crime. By accounts of the day, he held up about 20 banks and four police stations, twice escaped from jail and murdered more than a dozen people.

It all ended on July 22, 1934, when Dillinger was caught leaving a Chicago movie theater and shot three times by federal agents. One bullet passed from the back of his neck through his left eye, killing him instantly.

The death scene, the autopsy and the aftermath became a circus. To this day, there are urban legends regarding everything from speculation that the real Dillinger actually escaped the G-men's trap to the size of his sexual organ.

It's all great grist for a movie—well, maybe not the sex organ part. And the story has been told by Hollywood at least eight times, starting with 1945's *Dillinger*, starring Lawrence Tierney in the lead (you probably know Tierney as a much older man, plotting the heist in *Reservoir Dogs*). The roster of actors who've portrayed "The Jackrabbit Gangster" includes Mark Harmon, Robert Conrad and Martin Sheen. The most recent attempt was made by Johnny Depp in 2009's *Public Enemies*, a film you will not find listed in our Top 100. More about that coming up.

The best job, for our money, was turned in by Warren Oates (a veteran character actor best known for Westerns) in 1973's *Dillinger*, a low-budget shoot-'em-up inspired by the success of *Bonnie and Clyde*. The movie focuses on the last year of Dillinger's life, opening with a daring Indiana bank robbery ("I'd like to withdraw my *entire* account," he boasts) and ending with that

movie theater ambush by the United States Bureau of Investigation (forerunner to the FBI).

Dillinger is a B-movie and doesn't attempt to be more than that. There is not a lot of back story, and not much motivation beyond the character's oft-repeated line of, "I like to steal people's money." But the 107-minute string of robberies, escapes and gun fights works because of an excellent cast and because Director John Milius (*Red Dawn, Conan the Barbarian*) knows how to shoot a violent action film.

It opens with that bank stickup, as Dillinger tells petrified patrons, "Don't worry folks. These few dollars you lose here today will buy you stories to tell your children and grandchildren. This could be one of the big moments of your life—don't make it your last."

This is a criminal who clearly enjoys his work. Over time, he amasses a gang, which includes Baby Face Nelson (a young Richard Dreyfuss, before his breakout role in *American Graffiti*), Homer Van Meter (Harry Dean Stanton) and Pretty Boy Floyd (Steve Kanaly). If nothing else, you've got to love this band for its nicknames.

He also collects a girlfriend; prostitute Billie Frechette (Michelle Phillips, formerly of The Mamas and the Papas), who provides the film with a chance to humanize Dillinger.

The movie gives you a good sense of why crime was so rampant in 1933-34, the worst years of the Depression. For one, the criminals owned better cars and weapons than most police departments, which made escape a snap. And local cops were hindered by jurisdiction limits, which meant that a robber often just had to get across state lines to halt the pursuit.

Enter the Feds. The Inspector Javert to Dillinger's Jean Valjean is Melvin Purvis, the lawman who became famous for hunting down public enemies. Another topnotch Westerns regular, Ben Johnson, plays Purvis and is so good that you ignore that he's nearly twice as old as Purvis was at the time of the events.

Purvis is steady and cocksure and downright mean. He has a great ritual in the film (if not in real life) of having an aide pass him a gun and light his cigar right before he enters the fray. You quickly figure that someone's going to die each time that stogie gets fired up. And you edge up on your seat.

Fine art this isn't. But *Dillinger* works because the action is fast-paced and the acting is first-rate. The criminals come across as human beings—ranging from essentially decent folks to sadistic thugs. It's a fun watch.

Unfortunately, we can't say the same about *Public Enemies,* Michael Mann's big-budget 2009 remake of the story. Despite the casting of Depp as Dillinger and Christian Bale as Purvis, despite modern special effects and better sets, Mann's movie comes across as a brooding meditation (and an overly long one at that).

Both films are loaded with historical inaccuracies, but we'll opt for the low-budget effort that brings a sense of humor and doesn't try to be too cool for its own good. The 1973 version of *Dillinger* will give you a sense of the man, his legend and the era that spawned them.

⊙ **HIT:** Warren Oates is ideal for the role, not the least reason being he actually looks like the real John Dillinger (as opposed to, say, Depp). Look up photos of Oates and Dillinger. You'll be amazed at the resemblance.

⊗ **MISS:** *Dillinger* plays fast and loose with the facts. We could recite all the discrepancies, but why ruin the fun? Suffice it to say, you should never attempt to write a school paper off this movie.

▤ **PIVOTAL SCENE:** Speaking of events that never occurred, consider what might be the film's cleverest moment. Dillinger escorts his girlfriend, Billie, to a Chicago restaurant, where Purvis happens to be dining. Rather than ruin his own evening, Purvis (there with his fiancée) just sends Dillinger a bottle of champagne and his business

card. Dillinger accepts the gift and nods back, suggesting the two men are destined to meet again. The scene implies that big-time cops and outlaws had a sense of mutual respect in the 1930s. And, of course, it's complete fiction.

🗩 **BEST LINE:** Dillinger: "All my life I wanted to be a bank robber. Carry a gun, wear a mask. Now that it's happened, I guess I'm just about the best bank robber there ever was. And I sure am happy."

Billie: "Is that what you wanted to be when you were a kid?"

Dillinger: "Yep, my buddies all wanted to be firemen or farmers or policemen or something like that. I just wanted to steal people's money."

➡ **DON'T FAIL TO NOTICE:** The disclaimer read after the closing credits, which was written by J. Edgar Hoover. The FBI chief sent producers a letter of protest during filming in 1972 just weeks before his own death. Although Hoover's demands for script changes were turned down, Milius agreed to have a narrator voice Hoover's words of disapproval.

"Dillinger was a rat that the country may consider itself fortunate to be rid of," Hoover's statement reads. "And I don't sanction any Hollywood glamorization of these vermin. This type of romantic mendacity can only lead young people further astray than they are already. And I want no part of it."

✔ **REALITY CHECK:** Dillinger was gunned down in July on a day the temperature in Chicago reportedly reached 81 degrees. So why are all the G-men shown wearing winter woolen overcoats as they wait for Dillinger to emerge from the movie theater?

👣 **BODY COUNT:** Twenty-eight. Fairly evenly divided between robbers and lawmen, with a few innocent victims thrown in.

🔫 **VIOLENCE LEVEL:** High. Flesh splatters and shooting victims show pain (one bad guy literally cries as he dies). In the cruelest moment, a woman crossing the street is run over and dragged as the gang's getaway car flees a bank robbery.

✎ WHAT THEY WROTE AT THE TIME:
"Against a background of Depression America, where legendary status is bestowed on anyone who can beat the system, Dillinger and his gang rob banks with one eye already on posterity. Milius rightly makes no apology for endorsing the mythic qualities of his characters and setting his film firmly in the roots of American folklore."—*Time Out London*

☻ BET YOU DIDN'T KNOW: Milius, who penned the screenplay for *Dillinger* as well as directing it, left a long legacy in Hollywood as a writer. He thought up the line, "Go ahead, make my day," for Clint Eastwood's *Dirty Harry*, and also wrote the classic USS *Indianapolis* monologue in *Jaws*.

⊕ IF YOU LIKED THIS, YOU'LL LIKE: Any number of old-time gangster biopics that didn't quite make it into this book. One solid effort is B-movie king Roger Corman's *Machine-Gun Kelly*, starring Charles Bronson as the title character. "Without his gun he was naked yellow!" blares the trailer promoting this low-budget thriller.

84 LITTLE ODESSA (1994–R)

STARS: TIM ROTH, EDWARD FURLONG, MOIRA KELLY, VANESSA REDGRAVE, MAXIMILIAN SCHELL | DIRECTOR: JAMES GRAY

This was James Gray's first foray into the world of Russian organized crime. Less commercial and more personal than *We Own the Night* (reviewed elsewhere in this book), *Little Odessa* is more about relationships than underworld mayhem. It's a bleak and troubling character study built around a young Russian-Jewish hit man, the younger brother who idolizes him and their tyrannical father.

Tim Roth brings just the right mix of anger, hostility and cynicism to the character of Joshua Shapira, the mob assassin who has reluctantly come back to Brighton Beach to carry out a hit ordered by his boss. His return is a prodigal son story of sorts, featuring all the moral questions of the Biblical tale, but without the positive ending.

There are lots of cigarettes, cold sidewalks and leather-clad mobsters. And lots of unanswered questions.

The movie opens with Joshua coolly carrying out a hit in an unnamed city. He casually walks up to a man sitting on a bench and blows him away. The first words we hear come after he goes to a pay phone (cell phones were not yet in vogue when this movie was made), makes a call and tells his unseen mob boss, "It's done."

He's then ordered to go to Brighton Beach to murder a jeweler. Joshua at first says he can't go there. We never know why.

But he does go and the rest of the movie revolves around the hit man's attempts at reestablishing connections with his family and his ex-girlfriend Alla (Moira Kelly) while trying to stay one step ahead of the local mobsters with an unexplained old score to settle with him.

Played out against a melancholy musical score heavy on Russian and Jewish religious and folk themes, *Little Odessa* tells the story of ethnic organized crime from the street level. There is no crime kingpin or Mafia boss dominating the action. The one scene in which we do meet some of the local Russian mob leaders is more about family betrayal than wise guys.

Mick LaSalle, in the *San Francisco Chronicle*, wrote that the movie is at times "sodden and sluggish," but praised writer/director James Gray's "undeniable instinct for mood and atmosphere." According to LaSalle, "The scenes shot in the family's suffocating apartment tell you all you need to know about the childhood of these two young men."

In fact, Joshua, his teenaged brother Reuben (Edward Furlong) and their relationship with their father Arkady (Maximilian Schell) provide more drama than any of the action on the streets.

Vanessa Redgrave gives a touching performance as Irina Shapira, the wife and mother who is dying of a brain tumor. Redgrave's role in the film is one long death scene broken up by the interactions of the other characters.

While we never know why Joshua left Brighton Beach, we learn quickly that his father played a role in his banishment and doesn't want him back in the family apartment, even to see his bed-ridden mother.

Joshua and Reuben defy the old man to set up Roth's scene with his dying mother, one of the most compelling in the movie. But how the caring son can be such a cold-hearted killer remains unexplained and inexplicable.

Shortly before dispatching the jeweler he has been sent to kill, Joshua asks the man if he believes in God. The jeweler, kneeling with his hands tied behind his back, says almost in tears that he does.

"We'll wait 10 seconds and see if God saves you," Joshua says. And then, after a short pause, he takes out his gun and blows a hole in the jeweler's head.

The confrontational relationship between Joshua and his father climaxes when he takes Arkady at gunpoint to a snowy field and forces him to undress. The humiliation, the father believes, is a prelude to his murder. But he doesn't say a word.

"You're a big man, is that it?" Joshua asks of his stoic father.

"I don't need a gun to be a man," Arkady replies.

While both the father and the son survive the drama, nearly everyone they love ends up dead.

◉ **HIT:** You can almost feel the cold air whipping across Brighton Beach in winter. Writer/director James Gray paints a bleak picture of the Russian-Jewish underworld and cinematographer Tom Richmond captures the atmosphere perfectly with his camera work.

✖ **MISS:** Reuben has not been going to school for months and makes a point of checking the mail to intercept the letters that the school district sends to his father. But instead of destroying the letters, he hides them in his dresser where—surprise—his father eventually finds them.

✎ **WHAT THEY WROTE AT THE TIME:** "James Gray's smart, brooding debut is only super-ficially a gangster picture. . . . The movie's almost entirely free of bloodshed. When violence does come, it's over almost instantly. Silence rushes back in, and the movie gets back to its primary busi-ness—painting its own atmosphere."—Desson Howe, *Washington Post*

✔ **REALITY CHECK:** Joshua is sent to Brighton Beach to kill a jeweler whom he watches walking to and from his shop. But he plans an elaborate kid-napping before he carries out the hit. At the same time, however, he simply walks up to a rival gang-ster who has spotted him on the streets of Brooklyn and blows the guy away. The jeweler, it seems, could have been dispatched just as easily.

◉ **REPEATED WATCHING QUOTIENT:** The performances are better than the story itself. Once is probably enough.

🍎 **BET YOU DIDN'T KNOW:** James Gray was just 25 when he wrote and directed *Little Odessa*, which won the Silver Lion Award at the Venice Film Festival.

❞ **BEST LINE:** "If there's no body, there's no crime," Joshua matter-of-factly tells his associates, explaining why they have to incinerate their victim's body after they kill him.

☞ **VIOLENCE LEVEL:** Not a lot of shooting, but what there is can be brutal, cold-blooded and heartless.

⚰ **BODY COUNT:** Six.

85 AT CLOSE RANGE (1986–R)

STARS: SEAN PENN, CHRISTOPHER WALKEN, MARY STUART MASTERSON, CHRIS PENN
DIRECTOR: JAMES FOLEY

At Close Range bombed when it came out in the spring of 1986. Despite a stellar cast (which looks even better in hindsight), a No. 1 hit song by Madonna on its soundtrack and a taut, gritty story, it garnered less than $2.5 million in box-office receipts.

Maybe the story was *too* taut and gritty. This is a downcast look at blue-collar crime and teenage tedium. It's punctuated by a nasty rape scene and an attempted filicide. So we shouldn't be surprised that filmgoers at the time preferred more escapist fare (both *Top Gun* and *Police Academy 3: Back in Training* came out within a month).

A quarter-century later, *At Close Range* deserves another chance.

For one, it's worth seeing Sean Penn back when

he was drawing from James Dean (*Rebel Without a Cause*) and Marlon Brando (*On the Waterfront*) to portray the angry but vulnerable bad boy. And any fan of gangster movies will delight in watching Christopher Walken give one of his best performances as a cold, cunning, working-class psycho killer. Walken is Fagan in a pompadour, exuding charm in one scene, menace in the next. We'll rank his work here with his performances in *King of New York* and *True Romance*.

Beyond all that, there's a fine script written by Nicholas Kazan (the son of great director Elia Kazan) and the direction of James Foley, who went on to make *Glengarry Glen Ross*.

The movie focuses on 1970s life in the small towns and farmlands about 30 miles west of

Philadelphia. Nothing much happens there, which is why teenager Brad Whitewood Jr. (Sean Penn) spends his time smoking pot and getting into small-time trouble. Young Brad lives with his half-brother (played by Penn's real-life brother Chris Penn), his mom and grandmother in a shotgun shack where the front yard is dotted with jalopies and the two women spend their nights staring at TV like zombies.

It's all pretty depressing. So when long-gone father Brad Sr. turns up with a Mustang, a devious smile and a roll of $100 bills, well, who can blame the kid for being intoxicated?

Turns out that Dad is the leader of a rural band of outlaws leading a modern-day Bonnie-and-Clyde life. They rob and pilfer (everything from money to tractors to antique guns), and then they party hard. Young Brad is dazzled by the excitement and the promise of more wealth than any honest job could bring, so he becomes an apprentice thief in the gang.

At the same time, he falls for a pretty young thing (Mary Stuart Masterson) whose desperation to escape her family's farm prompts her to ignore Brad Jr.'s increasingly criminal behavior.

It's all going swimmingly for our boy. He even starts up his own crew, known as the Kiddy Gang, which steals farm equipment in the night and passes it up to Brad Sr.'s operation. Make sure, by the way, to take notice of the young actors in the gang, a few of whom went on to greater fame.

And then, of course, things turn. Brad Jr. discovers the truly evil nature of his father and tries to pull away. Soon afterward, the Kiddy Gang is busted. Convinced that the frightened punks are going to blab to the cops, Brad Sr. starts a campaign that uses rape and murder to try to shut them up.

And because any worthy drama requires a final showdown, one occurs between father and son. We don't want to give away the details, but depending on your views on vengeance, you will find yourself frustrated or refreshed by that confrontation.

At Close Range is based on the true story of Pennsylvania's Johnston Gang, a notorious ring led by Bruce Johnston Sr. and his two brothers in the 1960s and '70s. The three men were convicted of murder in 1981. In 2009, Bruce Mowday, a local reporter who covered that trial, wrote a well-reviewed book called *Jailing the Johnston Gang: Bringing Serial Murderers to Justice*. We suggest you see the film before reading the book.

◉ **HIT:** Watching this movie is like scouting a great team of college athletes about to turn pro. Sean Penn was 24 when *At Close Range* was filmed; Chris Penn was 19. Add Masterson (19), Kiefer Sutherland (18) and Crispin Glover (21) and you've got a young lineup that rivals the Brat Pack.

⊗ **MISS:** The song in the closing credits—Madonna's "Live to Tell"—sure sounds dated a quarter-century later. But we could live with that. What becomes downright annoying is that sections of that song are cut up, remixed and milked throughout the movie. Music supervisor Budd Carr created one of cinema's lamest soundtracks by adding a drum machine, stretching out chords and cranking up the Yamaha synthesizer again . . . and again . . . and again.

✎ **WHAT THEY WROTE AT THE TIME:** "It's Walken's Oscar-caliber performance that makes the movie. Not since Robert Mitchum in 1955's *The Night of the Hunter* has there been such a convincing demon prowling the screen. *At Close Range* should come with a warning label: movie dynamite."—Peter Travers, *People*

🎬 **PIVOTAL SCENE:** Young Brad wants to be just like dad—robbing and drinking and driving souped-up hotrods. After a job one night, he joins Brad Sr. and the gang as they celebrate with steak and beers. Life seems fun.

At the restaurant, however, they spot a low-level associate gabbing to a plainclothes officer. Afterward, they take the stool pigeon for a ride, plying him with whiskey and peppering him with questions about what he told the cop. The poor sap assures them he revealed nothing, but they cannot believe him.

He is driven out to the countryside. As Brad Jr. stays by the car and watches, his dad and gang member Dickie (R. D. Call), lead the reeling man into a pond. He is too drunk to know what's coming and too weak to resist. Dickie pushes the snitch down, holding his head underwater with one hand as he calmly lights a cigarette with the other.

As Brad Jr. stares in horror, Brad Sr. gazes up at his son. He places one finger in front of his mouth—a gesture that says, "Tell no one." There are no words. The lesson is obvious.

In that moment, Brad Jr. realizes that his father's evil extends far beyond any act that he could commit himself. He needs to get away. "They're no good," he tells his brother when he returns home. "They're bad people."

☺ **GOOF:** We're still curious why a movie that's supposed to take place in Pennsylvania features a town square boasting a Confederate soldier memorial and a First Tennessee Bank.

◄ **CASTING CALL:** Robert De Niro turned down the role of Brad Whitewood Sr., reportedly because he felt the character was too dark. Too dark for De Niro? How is that possible?

🔫 **VIOLENCE LEVEL:** The really brutal stuff is largely implied or happens offscreen.

✔ **REALITY CHECK:** Shot in the face with buckshot by an armed watchman, Brad Jr. sustains some deep and nasty wounds. But two scenes later—the equivalent of two days in the story—the wounds have completely healed.

🍎 **BET YOU DIDN'T KNOW:** Chris and Sean Penn are not the only relatives in this cast. Their real-life mother, Eileen Ryan, plays their grandmother.

❞ **BEST LINE:** "Most people who drive through here see farms, houses and fields and shit. I see money. I see things, everything with my name writ' on it."—Brad Whitewood Sr., explaining his life philosophy while cruising through rural Chester County.

😀 **"I KNOW THAT GUY":** Tony, the epileptic gang member, is played by taciturn David Strathairn. You may recognize him from *L.A.*

Confidential or *The Bourne Ultimatum*. Perhaps you recall him as the teacher who had a furtive romp with Carmela in Season Five of *The Sopranos*. But we believe Strathairn's best role was as disgraced Black Sox pitcher Eddie Cicotte in *Eight Men Out*.

✪ **IF YOU LIKED THIS, YOU'LL LIKE:** *Rumble Fish*, a 1983 film about a troubled street thug (Matt Dillon) trying to live up to the reputation of his older brother (Mickey Rourke). Dennis Hopper plays the boys' father, and Chris Penn has a small role.

🔪 **BODY COUNT:** Five.

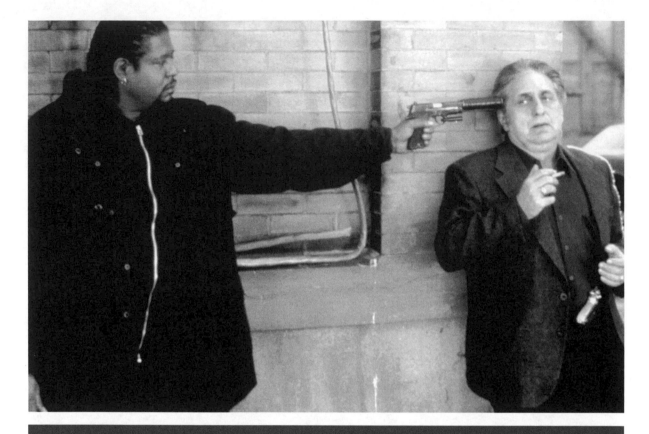

86 GHOST DOG: THE WAY OF THE SAMURAI (1999–R)

STARS: FOREST WHITAKER, JOHN TORMEY, CLIFF GORMAN
DIRECTOR: JIM JARMUSCH

Guys in the hood called him Ghost Dog.

We don't get any other name for this film's protagonist.

He's a hit man with a sense of honor, working for a crime family that doesn't have one anymore. He lives in a shack on a roof next to a pigeon coop. His best friend is a Haitian who sells ice cream in the park and only speaks French, a language Ghost Dog doesn't understand.

Forest Whitaker has created a unique underworld character in this quirky, interesting and sometimes baffling film written and directed by Jim Jarmusch.

Jarmusch (*Lost In Translation, Mystery Train, Night on Earth*) is regarded by many film fans as an acquired taste. *Ghost Dog: The Way of the Samurai* does nothing to dispel that perception.

Absurdist. Existential. Surreal.

Any and all fit the bill in trying to describe what goes on here. Remember Clint Eastwood, the loner without a name, in those spaghetti westerns? There's some of that. And a little bit of *Star Wars*. And a slice of *On the Waterfront*. And a hint of *Léon: The Professional*.

In explaining his approach to filmmaking, Jarmusch once said, "Nothing is original. Steal from anywhere that resonates with inspiration or fuels your imagination. . . . Authenticity is invaluable; originality is nonexistent. . . . Always remember what Jean-Luc Godard said, 'It's not where you take things from—it's where you take them to.' "

Where Jarmusch takes us to is a bleak, unidentified city that is home to a mob family that has lost its way. Honor and loyalty have been replaced by greed and treachery. There is no leadership, just arrogant incompetence. And it's all second-rate.

This is a mob family that falls behind on the rent for its clubhouse and gets hassled by the landlord. Try that in *GoodFellas* and the landlord is history. Here, he's placated.

Whitaker's Ghost Dog is the outsider, partly because he's black, but primarily because he believes in the ancient ways—ways that predate even the storied history of the Sicilian Mafia.

We know this because he is constantly quoting from *Hagakure*, the Japanese classic book of Samurai commentary on life and death. His voice-overs, accompanied by written words superimposed on the screen, are a more somber version of Henry Hill's running commentary in *GoodFellas*. They're also much more philosophical.

Ghost Dog is a true believer. Nothing else matters. How he got to this point in his life is one of the many unexplained—and maybe unexplainable—aspects of a story that, like the main character, is constantly on the move, but never seems to arrive at a destination.

He owes a debt to Louie (John Tormey), a local wiseguy who saved his life during a street fight. This pivotal event is seen in flashbacks. But as in the Japanese classic *Rashomon* (one of several books in our hit man's extensive library), that confrontation is seen differently through the eyes of its various participants. Ghost Dog, as he is being beaten on the ground, sees Louie pull out a gun and blow away one of his attackers. Louie, in recalling the event, sees the attacker turn on him with a gun. He then pulls out his own weapon and shoots the man in self-defense.

In order to repay the debt, Ghost Dog becomes Louie's retainer—his hit man. He goes about his business quietly and efficiently, but circumstances beyond his control create a situation that puts him at odds with Louie's crime family, a bedraggled mob ruled by an aging trio of misfits.

For reasons that don't appear logical, they decide Ghost Dog has to be eliminated.

Ray Vargo (Henry Silva) is the sulking mob boss whose wacko daughter is dating Handsome Frank (Richard Portnow), a mobster Ghost Dog was assigned to rub out. Sonny Valerio (Cliff Gorman) is a rap-spouting mob lieutenant who inexplicably walks with a limp. Gene Ruffini completes the crime family hierarchy as a decrepit, hard-of-hearing consigliere.

The gangsters, by and large, are one-dimensional characters. Several, including the boss and Handsome Frank, spend their time watching cartoons on television.

Ghost Dog, on the other hand, is an erudite shack-dweller who reads *Rashomon* in his spare time. He practices with a sword on the roof next to his birds. Did we mention that he only communicates with Louie via carrier pigeon and that he takes pay for his hits once a year, on the first day of autumn?

Old school traditionalist? Perhaps.

But he makes great use of an electronic gizmo that allows him to override locks on car doors, ignitions and the gates to wealthy residences. He's also got an arsenal of weapons hidden in his shack and knows how to use them.

The body count is high here, but the murders are carried out with a fluid economy that is the mark of a professional. Ghost Dog quickly gets the upper hand in his battle with the mob—fueled in part by his anger over the destruction of his pigeon coop and the bloody annihilation of the flock. (Brando's Terry Malloy was there before Ghost Dog, but lacked the firepower to do much about it.)

The final showdown in the park—with his Haitian friend and a young girl with whom he has shared books looking on—pits Ghost Dog against Louie. Given what's gone on beforehand, Louie shouldn't stand a chance. But as Ghost Dog moves toward Louie, he offers one last piece of ancient warrior philosophy: "A Samurai must always be loyal to his boss."

HIT: While satirical, the depiction of the dysfunctional mob family is a fairly accurate reflection of what's happened to the so-called men of honor over the last couple decades in America. The bottom line is that second- and third-generation Italian-Americans don't make good gangsters. The best and the brightest are now doctors, lawyers, educators and Supreme Court Justices. The guys in the mob? They come from the bottom of the gene pool.

MISS: Two different strangers, an American Indian and a black man, show up on the roof outside Ghost Dog's shack during the movie. Mob hit men confront them each time, killing the black man. Who are these guys and what are they doing there? We have no idea.

WHAT THEY WROTE AT THE TIME: "[Jarmusch] has composed a ruminative, bittersweet visual essay on brutality, honor and tribalism, which may frustrate audiences expecting hyped-up intensity, fast-paced thrills or a story that makes sense. . . . It is drenched in blood and saturated with ambiguity."—A.O. Scott, *New York Times*

GOOF: The hit that takes out Sonny is impossible. Don't believe us? Take a look under your sink. That pipe shaped like an S is called a trap. It's standard. Unless Ghost Dog has one of those magic bullets that took out JFK, there's no way the hit goes down—or up, as it turns out—in the way it's portrayed.

PIVOTAL SCENE: Ghost Dog saves Louie's life by shooting a hit man sent to kill them both. Then he shoots Louie in the shoulder to give him cover with the mob. "Nothing makes sense anymore," Louie says.

BEST LINE: After his cohort Vinny shoots and kills a female cop, Louie is aghast. "You just iced a woman," he says. Vinny's got no problem with that. "You're a male, chauvinist pig," he tells Louie. "They wanna be equal. I made her equal."

"I KNOW THAT GUY": Handsome Frank (Richard Portnow), who exits very early in the movie, played Hal "Mel" Melvoin, the lawyer who consistently managed to keep his client Uncle Junior out of jail during the long-running, Emmy award-winning *Sopranos* series on HBO.

BET YOU DIDN'T KNOW: The soundtrack was composed by Wu-Tang Clan's RZA. The rapper has a cameo as the camouflaged stranger Ghost Dog encounters on his way into the park toward the end of the film.

REPEATED WATCHING QUOTIENT: Once more just to track some of the weird ramblings, but unless you're a big Forest Whitaker or Jim Jarmusch fan, that ought to be enough.

BODY COUNT: Seventeen, not counting the consigliere who collapses with a heart attack before Ghost Dog can take him out.

87 THE JOKER IS WILD (1957–NR)

STARS: FRANK SINATRA, JEANNE CRAIN, EDDIE ALBERT, BEVERLY GARLAND, MITZI GAYNOR | DIRECTOR: CHARLES VIDOR

Sinatra gets to show his acting chops in this biopic based on the life of Joe E. Lewis, the prohibition era singer forced to make an abrupt career change after turning his back on the Chicago mob.

This was an interesting choice for Sinatra, whose career was marked by rumors and innuendo linking him to the wiseguys.

Indeed, Mario Puzo borrowed from one of the classic underworld Old Blue Eyes tales when he wrote *The Godfather*. The "I'll make him an offer he can't refuse" negotiations and the character of singer Johnny Fontane were built around Sinatra underworld folklore.

In reality, it was a similar type of mob-inspired "persuasion" that got bandleader Tommy Dorsey to release Sinatra from his contract with the Dorsey band so that he could pursue a singing career on his own. North Jersey mobster Willie Moretti supposedly offered Dorsey two alternatives. Either Dorsey would sign the release or Moretti would blow his brains out.

Done deal.

Sinatra also showed up in Havana in 1946 with some Chicago wiseguys visiting Lucky Luciano and the mob's Cuban casinos in the pre-Castro days.

In 1963, he lost his Nevada casino license and had to give up ownership of the Cal-Neva Lodge in Lake Tahoe after allowing Chicago gangster Sam "Momo" Giancana to stay there. Giancana was wooing girlfriend Phyllis McGuire, one of the singing McGuire Sisters headlining the casino at the time.

There was also a notorious photo of Sinatra backstage at the Premier Dinner Theater in Tarrytown, N.Y., surrounded by eight avid admirers in his dressing room. The crowd included mob boss Carlo Gambino, his soon-to-be successor Paul Castellano and several other major players in the New York crime family.

The Joker Is Wild offers a dark and violent picture of organized crime. So while Sinatra may have had personal ties to mobsters—both before and after making the film—those relationships apparently did not impact his artistic decisions.

Gangsters are present only during the first third of the film, but none of them is shown in a sympathetic light. These are angry, greedy and treacherous individuals playing by their own set of rules.

The movie opens with Joe E. Lewis, then a hot young singer, performing at a mob-run speakeasy in 1920s Chicago. When he gets an offer to move to the Valencia, an upscale nightclub, he jumps at the chance, raving about the kind of fans he will draw.

"They've got great audiences," he tells his best friend and piano accompanist Austin Mack (Eddie Albert), "not like these reunion clubs from Leavenworth."

Mack realizes that leaving the mob speakeasy might not be the healthiest career move. But Lewis is undaunted. In his first verbal confrontation with the owner of the speakeasy he says, "This is America. I've got a right to work anywhere I want."

To which the mobbed-up club owner replies, "What you got is a right to be buried anywhere you want."

Lewis' decision to go upscale costs him his career, the first indication of which comes when he receives a funeral wreath from the mob in his dressing room opening night. With a record deal in the offing and just three weeks into a successful gig at the Valencia, he is viciously attacked in his hotel room. His skull is bashed in and his throat and vocal chords slashed.

The rest of the movie revolves around Lewis' rebirth as a stand-up comic and how the friends and the women he loves try in vain to support him as he battles alcohol and gambling addictions brought on by the loss of his singing career. Both vices figure prominently in his stand-up routines and both contribute to his personal downfall.

A *New York Times* review accurately calls the movie a "frankly affectionate valentine" that is "disarmingly personable and realistic for about two-thirds of the way."

An attempt to end the story on an upbeat and positive note, however, undermines the personal struggle and tragedy of Joe E. Lewis—a man who thought he could turn his back on the mob.

◎ **HIT:** Any movie in which Sinatra sings has something going for it. In this one, before his character has his throat slit by the mob, Sinatra manages to belt out a few, including "All the Way." Written by Jimmy Van Heusen and Sammy Cahn, it won the Academy Award for Best Original Song and became part of the Sinatra songbook.

⊗ **MISS:** Some of the comedy is forced, especially the censored letters home from Austin Mack as he and Lewis travel on a USO Tour during World War II.

✎ **WHAT THEY WROTE AT THE TIME:** "Sinatra obviously couldn't be made to look like Lewis and Lewis' style of delivery is unique. But these are minor reservations in light of the major job Sinatra does—alternately sympathetic and pathetic, funny and sad. . . . Under Charles Vidor's direction, *Joker* plays out in a well-organized and smooth fashion. But it goes overboard on length."— *Variety*

✔ **REALITY CHECK:** The gangster who sent henchmen to "persuade" Lewis to return to the mob-run speakeasy he had quit was Jack "Machine Gun" McGurn, a member of Capone's Chicago Outfit back in the 1920s. The mobsters were supposed to convince Lewis to return to their club. Instead, they beat Lewis so badly he had to abandon his singing career and leave Chicago. The McGurn character in the movie is named Tim Coogan.

➡ **DON'T FAIL TO NOTICE:** The full name of Mitzi Gaynor's character is "Martha Stewart." But there are no home design or table-setting tips from the young and shapely chorus line dancer.

◉ **REPEATED WATCHING QUOTIENT:** If you like Sinatra in a serious role, this is one worth revisiting from time to time.

🍎 **BET YOU DIDN'T KNOW:** Sinatra bought the movie rights after reading the book *The Joker Is Wild: The Story of Joe E. Lewis* by Art Cohn. Old Blue Eyes was in serious actor mode at the time, having reignited his career with an Oscar-winning performance (Best Supporting Actor) in *From Here to Eternity* (1953).

🗩 **BEST LINE:** Mack first tries to talk Lewis out of leaving the mob speakeasy, warning that the singer could get killed if he did. Lewis jokes about it, but Mack is serious and says he will quit as his piano player.

"Maybe I can't stop you from getting killed, but I'm not gonna provide the accompaniment," Mack says.

Later, against his better judgment, he shows up and continues to play for Lewis.

🔫 **VIOLENCE LEVEL:** The only violence, other than Lewis boozing his way from one personal disaster to another, is the offscreen beating and throat slashing that occurs early in the movie.

💀 **BODY COUNT:** One. A newspaper headline announces the murder of mob kingpin Tim Coogan.

SINGING GANGSTERS

"Singing" has a special connotation in the world of gangsters.

It is not regarded as a good thing.

We recall the story of Abraham "Kid Twist" Reles, a gangster from the New York underworld of the 1930s who decided to cooperate—"to sing"—in an investigation of Murder Inc. and its notorious boss Albert "The Mad Hatter" Anastasia (no relation, by the way, to one of the authors of this book).

Reles was labeled a "canary," another less-than-flattering term from the underworld lexicon of the day.

He was being held in protective custody in the old Half Moon Hotel on Coney Island as he awaited a court appearance in the case against Anastasia. But to the shock and amazement of law enforcement, he took a header—went out the window. None of the six detectives assigned to guard him could explain how it happened.

Was he pushed? Did he jump? Was he trying to escape?

To this day, no one knows for sure.

But the fact that the room was on the sixth floor ensured that Reles would no longer be discussing his life in the underworld. He was dead on impact. And with him went the case against Anastasia.

The word in the underworld following the demise of Abe Reles, canary, was that "he could sing, but he couldn't fly."

This is a look at singers in gangster movies, but not canaries. It's a snapshot of a subgenre. Mob musicals, if you will.

Here are four that we consider among the best.

Guys and Dolls (1955). Based on two Damon Runyon short stories, this classic is a joy to watch and listen to. You've got Frank Sinatra as Nathan Detroit, the beautiful Jean Simmons as Sister Sarah of the Save a Soul Mission and, of course, Marlon Brandon—the handsome, charismatic *On the Waterfront/A Streetcar Named Desire* Marlon Brando—as Sky Masterson.

One of the real treats is hearing Brando sing "Luck Be a Lady," the song that defines the movie. As a crooner, well, he's a great actor.

But it works in a cockeyed kind of way, which is what the story is all about. With music and lyrics by the legendary Frank Loesser, *Guys and Dolls* is full of the characters and character that Runyon mined for years as a newspaper columnist and short story writer covering Broadway.

Nathan Detroit's frantic attempts to find a locale for a high-stakes craps game provides the action; Sister Sarah and Sky are the romantic leads; and Stubby Kaye's Nicely-Nicely Johnson rocks the house with a rollicking version of "Sit Down, You're Rockin' the Boat."

Sinatra wanted the part of Sky Masterson, and his voice was certainly better suited to croon. But the studio wanted Brando for the lead because he was the hot young actor of the day.

Old Blue Eyes leaves his mark, however, with his performance of the title song and three other numbers, including "The Oldest Established, Permanent Floating Crap Game in New York."

West Side Story (1961). An American musical based on Shakespeare's *Romeo and Juliet* but set on the West Side of Manhattan in the 1950s, this is a story of gangsters in their formative years. It's a battle between the Sharks and the Jets, two street gangs who sing and dance as they rumble. We assume everyone knows the Romeo and Juliet plot, so no rehash here.

The movie, like *Guys and Dolls*, is based on a highly acclaimed Broadway musical. And while the dance numbers may be a little too froo-froo for some hardcore gangster movie devotees, the musical score by Leonard Bernstein and Stephen Sondheim can't be matched.

It's Americana. So who cares if Tony (Richard Beymer) and Maria (Natalie Wood) had most of their numbers dubbed by people with real singing voices?

Rita Moreno is smokin' hot as Anita and she lights up the screen with "America," the song that underscores the ethnic pull that young Puerto Ricans in New York were feeling at the time.

"Something's Coming," "Maria," "Tonight" and "Somewhere" are four other songs from this 1961 film that are legitimate entries in the American songbook.

An interesting aside: Elvis Presley was one of several high-profile stars who turned down the role of Tony. Others who were said to be in the running were Warren Beatty, Troy Donahue and the late Bobby Darin.

Robin and the 7 Hoods (1964).

This is not a classic by any stretch, but it's fun. It's Sinatra and some of his Rat Pack buddies playing 1930s Chicago gangsters.

Sinatra is Robbo, a mobster who clashes with cross-town rival Guy Gisborne (Peter Falk). Robbo's band of merry mobsters includes Dean Martin, Sammy Davis Jr. and Bing Crosby. Although not a Rat Packer, Crosby was the crooner that Sinatra most admired when he started in the business (later, demonstrating better taste, Frank called Tony Bennett the best).

They all get to ham it up in this urban—and clearly farfetched—adaptation of the story of a bandit who robs from the rich and gives to the poor. There's a corrupt sheriff (Robert Foulk) and a Marian (Barbara Rush) who turns out to be less a maid and more a mobster than some of the wiseguys.

The songs written by the team of Jimmy Van Heusen and Sammy Cahn include "My Kind of Town," which became a Sinatra standard. But the most enjoyable number is "Style"—performed by Sinatra, Crosby and the always fun-to-watch Dean Martin.

Some Like It Hot (1959).

This buddy-picture from director Billy Wilder is a personal favorite of the authors of this book and has been designated by the American Film Institute as the greatest American comedy of all time.

The infamous 1929 St. Valentine's Day massacre in Chicago sets the story in motion. Tony Curtis and Jack Lemmon, two down-on-their-luck musicians, happen to be in the garage and witness the shootings as they go down. They flee from the mob, posing as women in order to join an all-girl band that is heading by train for a gig in Florida.

George Raft, as "Spats Colombo," is the Chicago gangster on their tail. Spoofing himself, he does the classic coin flip when he shows up at the same hotel where the band is playing.

Colombo is there to attend a conference for "Friends of the Italian Opera," a front for a mob confab. Pat O'Brien is the Chicago detective on his tail.

But it's the band's lead singer and ukulele player, Sugar Kane (Marilyn Monroe) who puts the real heat in *Some Like It Hot*. (The now defunct, thankfully, Catholic Legion of Decency rated the movie a "C" for condemned.)

Monroe, never known for her singing prowess, hits all the right notes when she performs "I'm Through with Love" in a sequined, skin-tight, see-through gown that must have driven the censors wild. The dress and the number define the word voluptuous.

It's one of many reasons to watch the movie again and again and again.

88 LUCKY NUMBER SLEVIN (2006–R)

STARS: JOSH HARTNETT, BRUCE WILLIS, MORGAN FREEMAN, BEN KINGSLEY, LUCY LIU, STANLEY TUCCI | DIRECTOR: PAUL MCGUIGAN

Director Paul McGuigan was channeling British movie-maker Guy Ritchie when he put together this black comedy, a movie with the pacing of an MTV video and DNA that can be directly traced to *Lock, Stock and Two Smoking Barrels* or *Snatch*.

One big difference is the absence of cockney or Irish gypsy accents. So the dialogue is easier to understand.

The plotline is another matter.

We are bombarded with short, snappy flashbacks, some of which are legitimate and some of which are swerves. Lots of quips and clever repartee add to the whimsy of a storyline that has us smiling until it turns dark and sinister. That's when we finally realize what's going on.

This is, at the end of the day, a movie about revenge, brutal revenge for a series of horrific killings. And there's no way to laugh about any of that.

Title character Slevin Kelevra (Josh Hartnett) seems more nonchalant and casual than he ought to be given the dire circumstances he finds himself in. But he knows from the get-go what we only learn much later.

He is mistaken for Nick Fisher, who owes debts and obligations to two crime kingpins—The Rabbi (Ben Kingsley) and The Boss (Morgan Freeman). The identity mix-up puts Slevin in a potentially lethal situation.

Lurking on the fringes of the story is Mr. Goodkat (Bruce Willis, with an awful hairpiece), an international assassin who has been hired by both mob bosses to eliminate Fisher/Slevin after his debts have been settled.

The bosses, once allies, are now bitter enemies who live in bulletproof penthouses in two New York City apartment buildings across the street from one another.

The Rabbi has a gay son. The Boss has a doomed son, one of the first of many characters to be rubbed out as Mr. Goodkat or Slevin or some other unknown force moves about this convoluted and claustrophobic underworld.

There is, of course, a romantic interest.

Lindsey (Lucy Liu) hooks up with Slevin after he unexpectedly shows up in her neighbor Nick Fisher's apartment. Slevin, wearing just a bath towel, tells her he has come to visit Fisher to get over his recent breakup with a girlfriend. In flashback, we see Slevin walking in on his girlfriend having sex with someone else. We see it, but did it really happen? And is Fisher really an old friend, as Slevin claims?

Lindsey is a coroner, so she gets to see a lot of the bodies that pile up as Slevin, Mr. Goodkat, the Rabbi, the Boss and a police detective named Brikowski (Stanley Tucci) play cat-and-mouse with guns blazing.

Fisher (Sam Jaeger) has a life-changing (or ending) encounter with Mr. Goodkat in a bus station early in the movie.

"There was a time," Mr. Goodkat says, apropos of nothing, before offering Fisher a rambling account that includes an explanation of a con called the "Kansas City Shuffle," a story about a fixed horse race from years earlier and the brutal assassination of a family by mobsters looking to make a point.

We get to know those mobsters and one of the family members as *Lucky Number Slevin* unfolds.

◉ **HIT:** The pacing is energizing and the dialogue at times is superb, even when it has little to do with the storyline. This is, in many ways, a cartoon. And it works best when viewed on that level.

⊗ **MISS:** There are several outlandish assassinations. Slevin takes out a bookmaker and his two goonish bodyguards with a pair of glasses and a baseball, for example. But the most ridiculous comes when Willis, armed with two guns equipped with silencers, blows away two former Mossad agents who come at him not through the door of the apartment where he is waiting, but literally through the wall. Somehow, he knows that will be their entry point and has his guns pointed in that direction.

✎ **WHAT THEY WROTE AT THE TIME:** "If *Pulp Fiction* impregnated *The Usual Suspects*, the spawn would look a lot like *Lucky Number Slevin*. Great genes, but you keep wondering when the kid is going to grow up and find an identity of his own. . . . Actually, the performances are juicy, with Freeman and Kingsley hamming it up royally during a double-torture scene. But that's getting too deep into the plot, which is the film's downfall. Director Paul McGuigan keeps the blood splashing. But the convoluted ain't-I-clever script by Jason Smilovic has a cheat ending that makes you want to do a little torturing yourself. Don't you hate it when that happens?"—Peter Travers, *Rolling Stone*

✔ **REALITY CHECK:** The shocked look on Lindsey's face when she returns to the apartment and comes upon Slevin with his bath towel open was for real. According to interviews that both Liu and Hartnett did after the movie was released, he deliberately and unexpectedly flashed Liu when she reopened the apartment door to get the cup of sugar she had originally come for. Lindsey's "Thanks for the sugar, Sugar" line as she leaves the apartment for a second time takes on a whole new meaning in that context.

◉ **REPEATED WATCHING QUOTIENT:** If you're a fan of the quirky, dark-comedy, gangster drama, any Tarantino or Ritchie film would be a better choice for a second look.

☺ **GOOF:** There is a flashback that makes reference to a Mets-Phillies baseball game on the radio in 1979. By way of explanation, Tony Taylor is mentioned as the Phillies second baseman. Taylor retired in 1976. The Phillies starting second baseman in 1979 was Manny Trillo.

😀 **"I KNOW THAT GUY":** Veteran character actor Robert Forster (who has a leading role in *Jackie Brown*) has a very brief part as a cop named Murphy talking on the phone with Brikowski (Tucci).

❞ **BEST LINE:** "I live on both sides of the fence and the grass is always green," says The Rabbi when Slevin asks him how he justifies being both a man of religion and a gangster.

⌐ **VIOLENCE LEVEL:** It's nonstop. There are, in fact, four murders before we hear any significant dialogue.

☠ **BODY COUNT:** Eighteen.

89 PRIZZI'S HONOR (1985–R)

STARS: JACK NICHOLSON, KATHLEEN TURNER, ANJELICA HUSTON
DIRECTOR: JOHN HUSTON

This movie should have been better than it was. The cast is outstanding. The director, John Huston, is a legend.

But the story and the dialogue don't match the talent.

Despite positive reaction from critics when the movie first played in theaters, the view from here on *Prizzi's Honor* is negative.

It makes our Top 100 because of its cast. But of all the movies portraying Italian-American gangsters in this book, we have to say that we'd rank this one as the most offensive to Italian-Americans.

Now we recognize that many Italian-American civil rights organizations get up in arms over everything from *The Godfather* saga to *The Sopranos*. Their arguments are that the portrayal of Italian-Americans as gangsters reinforces an ethnic stereotype and demeans all members of the ethnic group.

We've heard the arguments ad nauseum and usually offer a freedom of speech response. If you don't like it, don't go see it. A movie rises or falls on its artistic merits. There is also a level of whining and a rush to embrace victimhood on the part of many of those groups that too often blurs the issue.

The bottom line—and a point one of the authors of this book has made several times in the past: any ethnic group that can give America Antonin Scalia and Camille Paglia in the same generation doesn't have to worry about Tony Soprano or Vito Corleone being its poster boy.

That being said, *Prizzi's Honor* is offensive both cinematically and from the ethnic perspective.

The dialogue is forced and stilted and the relationships nonsensical. This is cartoonish buffoonery that poses as satire. It's supposed to be a dark comedy that echoes Italian opera. Lots of background music by Puccini and Rossini help make that point.

But there is nothing subtle in the storyline and hardly anything comedic about the way it is delivered.

Unlike a movie such as *Moonstruck*, for example, which in many ways is a love letter to all Italian-Americans, the sense here is that the writer—and by extension his audience—is laughing at, not with, the characters that are portrayed.

And unlike *The Freshman* (movie No. 100 in this book), which spoofs the genre and by extension its Mafia characters, *Prizzi's Honor* holds its characters up for ridicule.

A minor but telling point is that on two occasions Jack Nicholson's character, Charley Partanna, uses the word "wop" to refer to himself and those around him. Italian-Americans may, among themselves, joke about "Guidos," "guineas," even "dagos." In some ways it's the same as African-Americans using the n-word or one of its slang derivatives to refer to themselves.

But "wop" has a different connotation. It's like "coon" or "spic." There is nothing remotely humorous about it. And the fact that writer Richard Condon chose to weave it into his dialogue and Huston decided that it helped define his lead character showed either a lack of caring or understanding.

Prizzi's Honor plays like a story written by someone with no idea how Italian-Americans think, act or relate to one another. These are cardboard Pirandello characters desperately in search of an author.

The love triangle created by Charley, Irene (Kathleen Turner) and Maerose Prizzi (Anjelica Huston) is the wheel around which all the complications flow. Maerose, the granddaughter of Don Prizzi (William Hickey), has been ostracized by her father and sees Charley, her former boyfriend, as a way to get back in.

Irene's husband, Marxie, has scammed the mob and her initial interaction with Charley revolves around his attempts to get the cash back for the family.

And Charley is . . . just Charley. John Huston reportedly told Nicholson repeatedly to remember, "He's dumb."

Murder, kidnapping and betrayal (on several different levels) follow as the romantic entanglements overlap with the "business" problems that face the Prizzi family. The story is driven by Charley's various assignments to straighten them out.

William Hickey is cantankerous but hardly sympathetic as the aging don and Robert Loggia, as his son Eduardo, is serviceable as the lawyer of the family.

While a good opera can be farce, a film satire or dark comedy works when viewers are not hit over the head with what is supposed to be irony. If it is too obvious, then it isn't really ironic. And that, sadly, is too often the case here.

There are some good lines. Charley's take when Irene first mentions her late husband's underworld warning about Sicilians, for example, is classic.

"If Marxie Heller was so fuckin' smart, how come he's so fuckin' dead?"

And his surprise when Irene confesses that she's socked money away by performing three or four hits annually is a setup for one of her best comments. Charley is amazed by the number, but Irene says, "Well, it's not many when you consider the size of the population."

But too often the dialogue sounds like the words of a condescending writer slumming it, if you will, among the goonish Mafiosi. What should be empathy comes across instead as derision.

"When the *merda* hits the fan," a line uttered by Loggia, is ridiculous.

So is Charley's comment when he learns his wife has been given another hit assignment.

"I didn't get married so my wife could go on working."

Much of this is uttered in somber tones and against a phony backdrop of honor that *The Godfather* captured so well, but that *Prizzi's Honor* mocks rather than spoofs. And that, at the end of the day, is the film's principal problem.

Despite glowing reviews at the time of its release and lots of Academy Award nominations, the movie doesn't hold up well against either the gangster classic or most of the other comedies reviewed in this book.

Charley's final choice, between family and THE FAMILY, is one that occurs over and over in mob movies. Even when played for laughs, it has worked better elsewhere.

◉ **HIT:** While Anjelica Huston got the praise, Kathleen Turner steals every scene she's in. A cold, calculating hit woman, this role seemed like a reprise—albeit comedic—of the even more conniving murderess she portrayed in *Body Heat* in 1981.

✷ **MISS:** There's way too much extraneous dialogue with cowriters Richard Condon (on whose novel the film is based) and Janet Roach trying to channel a harder-edged *Guys and Dolls,* but too often coming up empty.

✎ **WHAT THEY WROTE AT THE TIME:** "Marches like weird and gloomy clockwork to its relentless conclusion, and half of the time we're laughing. This is the most bizarre comedy in many a month, a movie so dark, so cynical and so funny that perhaps only Jack Nicholson and Kathleen Turner could have kept straight faces during the love scenes. They do."—Roger Ebert, *Chicago Sun-Times*

✔ **REALITY CHECK:** Charley takes a cab to Marxie Heller's house in a sprawling Los Angeles suburban community to carry out the hit. Then he walks out the door. So how does he get back to his hotel and/or the airport? No way a real hit goes down like that. Taking a cab leaves a trail. A smart hit man, and Charley is supposed to be one, doesn't take a taxi.

🍽 **BET YOU DIDN'T KNOW:** Novelist Richard Condon, whose body of work includes the highly acclaimed *The Manchurian Candidate*, wrote three other Prizzi novels: *Prizzi's Family, Prizzi's Glory* and *Prizzi's Money.* Thankfully, none were made into movies.

◉ REPEATED WATCHING QUOTIENT:
Once should cover it.

◀ CASTING CALL: Al Pacino turned down the role of Charley. Nicholson, who was dating Anjelica Huston at the time, was chosen over Tom Hanks, Dustin Hoffman, Bill Murray and John Travolta. Several top actresses were considered for Maerose, including Rosanna Arquette, Demi Moore, Melanie Griffith and Jessica Lange, but Anjelica Huston got the part. She wasn't a bad choice, even if nepotism was part of the mix. She won an Academy Award for Best Supporting Actress. The film got several other nominations, including Best Actor for Nicholson, Best Supporting Actor for Hickey and Best Director.

❝ BEST LINE: Almost everyone favors the line that captures Charley's dilemma when he first learns that the woman he has fallen in love with is a hit woman and has scammed the family out of $360,000.

"Do I ice her? Do I marry her? Which one of these?"

But our favorite is the exchange between Charley and Irene after the kidnapping. Irene is dumbfounded that the bodyguard she ends up killing didn't try to catch the "baby" she was carrying when she tossed it to him. (The baby was in fact a doll, part of an elaborate plan she had mapped out.)

"I can't get over it," she tells Charley. "What kinda creep wouldn't catch a baby? If it was real, it coulda been crippled for life."

To which Charley sagely replies, "He wasn't paid to bodyguard the baby."

☛ VIOLENCE LEVEL: Very professional and low-key. Strictly business. These are, after all, professional hitters.

⚚ BODY COUNT: Five.

90 THE KILLER (1989–R)

STARS: YUN-FAT CHOW, DANNY LEE
DIRECTOR: JOHN WOO

A "popcorn movie" is, by definition, a fun action flick. Nothing deep or monumental. Just an entertaining waste of time.

There are popcorn movies, and then there is *The Killer*, director John Woo's tale of the unlikely friendship between a Hong Kong assassin and the cop pursuing him. "It's escape-velocity popcorn," wrote *Washington Post* critic Hal Hinson. "Popcorn with a slurp of rocket fuel."

Woo may be the world's top action film director. Born in China, he learned his craft in Hong Kong, starting with martial arts flicks and making Jackie Chan a star. He has since moved to Hollywood, directing thrillers like *Face/Off* and *Mission: Impossible II*.

To some fans, *The Killer* represents the apex of his career—before he went too commercial. It's got a solid storyline and strong acting. But it's mostly a lavishly staged ballet of bullets and blood. Guns blaze in slow motion. Bodies fly through the air. This is high-octane violence in a way that makes your typical Sly Stallone or Steven Seagal fare look like *Mary Poppins*.

The story centers on Ah Jong (Yun-Fat Chow), a hit man for Hong Kong's underworld, known as The Triad. While gunning down eight enemies at a nightclub, Jong accidentally grazes and blinds the club's singer, Jennie (played by Sally Yeh, known as "The Celine Dion of Hong Kong").

For this, he feels great remorse. Jong befriends the pretty singer and she, of course, does not recognize him as the man who shot her. He considers quitting the mob (doesn't *every* movie hit man seem to go through that crisis?) but decides to take one last lucrative job so that he can take Jennie to the United States for a corneal transplant.

To remind you again: You are not watching *The Killer* for any semblance of reality.

In the course of that final assignment (beautifully shot during a dragon boat festival), two bad things happen. First, Jong is spotted by police inspector Li Ying (Danny Lee). And second, he is double-crossed by his own boss—who has set up a deathtrap that Jong barely escapes.

So Jong is on the run. When he goes back to Jennie's apartment to hide, the clever police inspector isn't far behind. There's a great scene where the two men aim guns at each other's face while the sightless woman, oblivious to their standoff and their enmity, tries to serve them tea. Two guys pointing guns at one another became a trademark shot for Woo and makes its way into most of his films.

Anyway, when two enemies are staring down each other's gun barrels, the talk tends to get honest. So cop and killer undergo a rapprochement, realizing that they are both jaded men of honor surrounded by corruption. Each recognizes a bit of himself in his foe. They even make up bogus nicknames for each other—Shrimp Head and Little B—all to convince the pathetic Jennie that they are actually old soccer buddies.

The rest of the movie puts the unlikely trio in precarious situations where Jong and Li tumble around firing Berettas with both hands while Jennie cowers in the corner. The plot becomes secondary to a good half-dozen ambushes, escapes and slaughter scenes. We are pulled back to the focal point when Jong, up against the odds, says to his policeman pal, "Promise me one thing. If I don't make it and my eyes are undamaged, take me to a hospital and have them give my corneas to Jennie. If that's impossible, send her abroad for surgery with my money."

Now that's one honorable mobster.

Together, the new friends face a final confrontation with the gangsters aiming to slaughter them. It occurs in a candlelit church, surrounded by fluttering doves and Virgin Mary statues that explode when hit with gunfire. Again, if you're a fan of Woo's work, you'll recognize many of the visual tricks in his later films.

After Woo went Hollywood in the 1990s, there was talk of an English-language version of *The Killer* starring Richard Gere and Denzel Washington. That didn't happen, but in September 2010, Woo announced plans to remake the film, set in Los Angeles.

◉ **HIT:** If you're a fan of guns, this is the movie for you. According to the website Internet Movie Firearms Database (imfdb.com), no fewer than 25 different weapons make an appearance in *The Killer*.

⊗ **MISS:** There are four differently edited versions of *The Killer* floating around, running from 96 minutes to 124 minutes. In several of those subtitled versions, huge portions of dialogue get mistranslated, including characters' names and the entire point of the movie's ending. We recommend the 104-minute version released by a company called Hong Kong Legends.

✒ **WHAT THEY WROTE AT THE TIME:** "Yun-Fat Chow plays something like a benign Terminator—a wistful, avuncular, superbly tailored murder machine. *The Killer* starts with over-the-top violence and then, like some non-stop cartoon freak out, blasts through the roof."—J. Hoberman, *Premiere*

🎃 **BET YOU DIDN'T KNOW:** All of those guns had to be imported and were strictly monitored because of Hong Kong's tough firearms laws. During one shootout scene, local residents, fearing that a real attack was underway, deluged police with emergency calls. The set was shut down until Woo assuaged the area police chief.

📷 **PIVOTAL SCENE:** It's that sequence where the two main characters nearly kill each other while their blind hostess tries to serve them tea. Afraid to alarm the young woman, the men pretend to be long-lost buddies, even as their trigger fingers twitch.

If that seems cartoonish, perhaps that's because Woo was inspired by *Mad* magazine's "Spy vs. Spy" feature while constructing it. He even dressed one in white and the other in black—a nod, he said, to the yin and yang of cops and gangsters.

☺ **GOOF:** During an emergency room scene, the road sign outside reads "Scared Heart Hospital." We would never want to be treated there.

✔ **REALITY CHECK:** Dozens and dozens of shooters aim at our two lead characters—from sniper's posts, from hunters' blinds, from point-blank range. And yet both men go through most of the movie suffering nothing more than a grazing wound. There sure are some lousy marksmen in Hong Kong.

◉ **REPEATED WATCHING QUOTIENT:** That's a matter of taste. If you delight in shoot-'em-ups, revisit it. If not, move on.

➡ **DON'T FAIL TO NOTICE:** Every time someone drinks a beer in this movie, he reaches for a Budweiser. Being fans of Asian beers ourselves, we'd have thought they'd prefer a Tsingtao or Asahi.

🔫 **VIOLENCE LEVEL:** High, but mostly in a comic-book way. There are two moments that will make you cringe—one where a bullet is removed from someone's back with pliers, and another where a wound is cauterized by pouring gunpowder into it and burning it with a lit cigarette.

✵ **IF YOU LIKED THIS, YOU'LL LIKE:** *Hard Boiled*, Woo's 1992 effort (also starring Yun-Fat Chow) about a detective and an undercover agent who team up to take down a mob crew.

🏃 **BODY COUNT:** We tallied 118. You might get more.

This is a gangster movie without a memorable gangster. But it has one of the all-time great underworld molls in film history.

Gena Rowlands, in the title role, *is* the movie. And that's both a blessing and a curse.

Her depiction of Gloria, which earned her an Academy Award nomination for Best Actress (Sissy Spacek won for *Coal Miner's Daughter*), is the best thing going here.

That may be by design.

Gloria was written and directed by Rowlands' husband, John Cassavetes. He did the film, a departure from the less-commercial, cerebral and artsy work he was noted for, as a favor to his wife, according to Ray Carney in his biography *Cassavetes on Cassavetes*.

"The role deeply appealed to her," Carney wrote. "It tapped into a side of her that captured the way she sometimes thought of herself—the 'sexy but tough woman who doesn't need a man.' "

Critics had mixed reactions to the movie, which didn't do much at the box office.

Most correctly described it as a thin narrative that was designed to provide a stage for Rowlands. She appears in nearly every scene surrounded by a supporting cast that is just so-so.

Buck Henry is Jack Dawn, the nebbish mob accountant whose decision to cooperate with the Feds provides the violent jumping-off point for what amounts to a two-hour game of hide-and-seek. But his portrayal of the panicked FBI informant seems forced.

And the film's young costar, John Adames, gives a stiff performance as Phil Dawn—the overly precocious six-year-old boy Gloria has to save. If you want to see how this should have been done, check out Natalie Portman's performance as a 12-year-old underworld waif in *Léon: The Professional*, a film built around a similar storyline.

Gloria is the ex-mistress of Mafia don Tony Tanzini (Basilio Franchina). She lives comfortably with her memories and her cat in a shabby apartment building in the Bronx. She knocks on a neighbor's door to borrow some coffee and walks out with Phil in her care.

The rest of the family (Jack, his wife, their teenage daughter and her grandmother) have waited—for reasons that are not entirely clear—too long to flee and are about to be visited by a group of angry hit men.

Carnage ensues.

Gloria then goes on the run with Phil and the book his father has entrusted to him. It's a ledger containing all the details of the mob's financial wheeling and dealing—a book that could bury, as it turns out, Tanzini and several of Gloria's other former mob friends.

Using buses, subways and taxis, the intrepid couple traverses the Bronx, often just steps ahead of the mobsters looking to kill the boy and get the book. Bill Conti's jazz score adds just the right mood changes as the chase ebbs and flows.

The late Cassavetes, whose more intense work included *Husbands, A Woman Under the Influence* (which also starred Rowlands) and *The Killing of a Chinese Bookie*, described *Gloria* as "an adult fairy tale" with a message for women.

"I wanted to tell women that they don't have to like children—but there's still something deep in them that relates to children, and this separates them from men in a good way," he said in his biography. "This inner understanding of kids is something very deep and instinctive, in a way, it's the other side of insanity."

That's the instinct roiling beneath the surface as Gloria blows away several gangsters and, despite her protestations, develops a fondness for the boy in her care.

Phil, in turn, goes from angry to sad to belligerent and back again while falling in love with the gun-toting mama who has become the surrogate for all he has lost—mother, father, sister, family.

But his wisecracks, while meant to show a street-smart toughness, ring hollow and often sound like a second-rate Damon Runyan. When a desk clerk at a fancy hotel refuses to give Gloria a room because she is with a Puerto Rican boy, Phil explodes at the slight.

"He don't know the score," he says as Gloria hustles him out of the hotel lobby. "He sees a dame like you and a guy like me. He don't know."

At another point, when Phil says that he wants to go home, Gloria gives him a verbal slap, telling him, "Don't be stupid. You got no home. You got me."

Their goal is to get to Pittsburgh, which from the New York-centric perspective of a Bronx bomber like Gloria, sits at the edge of the earth—a place where the mob won't go.

◉ **HIT:** The movie's depiction of New York is real. This is not Woody Allen's Manhattan. It's the Bronx—chaotic, pulsating and never at rest.

⊗ **MISS:** Not one mobster says anything worth remembering. They are one-dimensional stereotypes.

🎬 **PIVOTAL SCENE:** Shortly after fleeing an apartment ahead of the mob, Gloria has second thoughts about what she is doing and tells Phil to take off on his own. Just then, a car containing four mobsters pulls up. One of the gangsters tells Gloria to walk away, that they just want the boy.

"Frank, what are you gonna do, shoot a six-year-old Puerto Rican kid in the street?" she asks. "He don't know nothing. He don't even speak English."

With that she reaches into her purse, pulls out a gun and opens fire.

After that, there's no turning back.

🗨 **BEST LINE:** In the climatic scene when Tanzini and his associates have a sit-down with Gloria, they tell her that her maternal instincts have kicked in. She denies it.

"I was always a broad," she says. "Can't stand the sight of milk."

✎ **WHAT THEY WROTE AT THE TIME:** "While the script pitches a series of wildly improbable events, the direction remains disruptively attuned to the dark, arrhythmic poetry of anticlimax. Heightened emotion and nagging banal reality fight each other for screen space, doing final battle in a daringly ambiguous ending."—Dave Kehr, *Chicago Reader*

➡ **DON'T FAIL TO NOTICE:** After one lengthy cab ride, Gloria hands the driver a five-dollar bill and emphasizes, "That's a five!" implying that his tip is included. Today, five dollars in a cab in New York will get you about six blocks.

🍎 **BET YOU DIDN'T KNOW:** Cassavetes, according to his biography, got street people and real gangsters for the scene in Tanzini's apartment. In fact, one of the gangsters, a "professional hit man," argued with Cassavetes about the way the scene would play out in real life.

🔪 **BODY COUNT:** Ten.

92 EL MARIACHI (1992–R)

STARS: CARLOS GALLARDO, CONSUELO GOMEZ | DIRECTOR: ROBERT RODRIGUEZ

Fewer people probably saw *El Mariachi* during its run in theaters than any other film in this book. And it was, without a doubt, the lowest-budget movie you'll find on these pages.

The film was written, directed, photographed and edited by Robert Rodriguez, who shot it over the course of two weeks in the Mexican border town of Acuña, across from Del Rio, Texas. You may recognize Rodriguez now as the director of schlock classics *Sin City* and *From Dusk Till Dawn*. But when he made *El Mariachi*, he was a 23-year-old unknown from San Antonio working with a budget of $7,000—or as critic Roger Ebert put it, "about what it costs to cater lunch for a day on a Schwarzenegger picture."

The actors are unpaid volunteers and friends. The sets are whatever street or dusty bar Rodriguez could commandeer for an hour or two. There are no special effects or notable actors or expensive cars that get destroyed in high-speed crashes.

But you know what? This cult movie works in an unpolished way. And the setting—given the increased power of Mexican drug cartels—seems more relevant now that it did when *El Mariachi* was made.

The plot centers on the title character (played by Carlos Gallardo), a wandering guitarist who drifts into a small Mexican town looking for a gig. He dresses in black and, naturally, carries a guitar case.

His timing could not be worse. That same day, a revenge-crazed drug dealer named Azul breaks out of a local jail with the aim of killing his traitorous crime boss, who tried to have him assassinated. Azul, too, dresses in black and carries a guitar case—except that his is loaded with items like automatic pistols and brass knuckles.

That crime boss, named Moco, gives his goons a description of the dealer coming after him. "Don't worry, Moco," says one. "We will find him, kill him and feed him to the dogs."

Thus begins the case of mistaken identity. As the naïve mariachi wanders from tavern to tavern looking for work, an armed hit squad gets on his trail. Soon enough, he is forced to put down his guitar and pick up a gun to defend himself—even though he has no idea why killers are pursuing him.

The transformation is a little abrupt. In one scene, he's the wimpy guitar player bellying up to the bar to order a soda pop; in the next he eludes the posse by riding an electrical wire down from a second-story roof like Tarzan. Trapped on two sides by bad guys, he leaps over a truck, prompting the shooters to kill each other while aiming for him. Where did he learn that? In music school?

That's basically the entire plot. There's a doomed love interest with the mob boss's ex-girl-friend, a half-dozen chase scenes and lots of carnage. Rodriguez doesn't spend much time on character development. You quickly realize, because of his soulful eyes and mellow singing voice, that El Mariachi is a romantic. And you realize as well that Moco is evil because he wears white suits, orders a bikini-clad girlfriend to file his fingernails and enjoys lighting matches off his henchmen's faces.

It all sets up for a great climactic showdown. Reminiscent of *The Departed*, half of the cast gets blown away in the final five minutes.

This is engaging stuff, and you may appreciate it more—rather than less—for the unsophisticated nature of the production. Yes, you sometimes see blood squibs pasted to characters before they explode, and yes, at least a few actors are clearly reading their lines off of cue cards. (You likely won't hear those lines since the current DVD release is dubbed from Spanish to English. See if you don't think the character of Azul sounds exactly like Joe Mantegna with a Mexican accent.)

But there's a lot of energy and creativity in *El Mariachi*. Rodriguez has gone on to become a popular and successful director. Watching this film gives you the sense of watching a rock star back when he was in a neighborhood garage band.

Rodriguez later wrote of his adventures making this movie in the book, *Rebel Without a Crew*. He raised the money to buy film and the one handheld 16mm camera by working as a guinea pig for medical school experiments, most notably taking medication designed to lower cholesterol. That's where he met one of the principal performers, Peter Marquardt, who plays Moco the kingpin. Marquardt's a terrible actor, but we hear his triglyceride level is outstanding.

Rodriguez put the movie on VCR tape and sent it around Hollywood, just hoping to get a foot in the door. Executives at Columbia Pictures liked it so much they bought the rights and spent many times the original budget to convert it to 35mm and add Dolby sound. The movie won several awards, including the Audience Award at the prestigious Sundance Film Festival.

◉ **HIT:** There's actually a lot of humor in this little gem. Watch for the scene where our hero loses a music gig to a one-man band whose electronic keyboard only plays polkas.

✖ **MISS:** For no apparent reason, *El Mariachi* is interspersed with dream sequences, most of which involve a young boy playing soccer with a ball that morphs into a severed head. In his book, Rodriguez conceded that the scenes were meaningless, but said he included them for three reasons: to get the movie up to its 81-minute length, to show some of the beautiful scenery around Mexico, and, in his words, "When in doubt, have dream sequences."

➡ **DON'T FAIL TO NOTICE:** The head in those scenes is modeled after Rodriguez himself. In keeping with the low-budget theme, the cheesy skull looks as much like something taken off an inflatable doll as it looks like the director.

✔ **REALITY CHECK:** Even after the guitarist learns that armed killers are hunting him, he's out at the town's most popular nightclub, leading a crowd in song. For a guy with a price on his neck, he's either too brave or too stupid.

✎ **WHAT THEY WROTE AT THE TIME:** "In a way, the unpolished look of *El Mariachi* and its players is what makes it so refreshing from the standard Hollywood action flick. . . . *El Mariachi* is nowhere near as extravagant as its successors, yet it remains a constant simple pleasure, best enjoyed with a shot of Patron and a cold Corona."—Brian McKay, *efilmcritic.com*

🏃 **BODY COUNT:** Fourteen, plus one poor guy's hand.

🍎 **BET YOU DIDN'T KNOW:** Some media members in Acuña were critical when Rodriguez showed up in town to film his movie. To win them over, the director gave small acting roles to two of them—a TV newsman and a newspaper columnist.

☺ **GOOF:** We're lenient with such a low-budget film, but Rodriguez would have been wise to spend a few bucks in one particular scene. The room where the sympathetic barmaid hides El Mariachi from the posse has a transparent glass door that would conceal no one.

🔫 **VIOLENCE LEVEL:** Extremely high. Of that original $7,000 budget, we suspect that half of the money went for fake blood.

✴ **IF YOU LIKED THIS, YOU'LL LIKE:** *Desperado* and *Once Upon a Time in Mexico*—the second and third parts of the trilogy Rodriguez opens with this movie. Antonio Banderas replaces Gallardo (the director's buddy) as El Mariachi. The sequels have superior sound, multiple cameras, Salma Hayek as eye candy and everything else a studio budget can buy. Still, we'll take this little movie over those two for its heart.

93 YEAR OF THE DRAGON (1985–R)

STARS: MICKEY ROURKE, JOHN LONE, ARIANE KOIZUMI
DIRECTOR: MICHAEL CIMINO

Somewhere in the middle of this overwrought and overwritten gangland shoot-'em-up, there is a decent story. But we're never quite able to get to it. Michael Cimino's direction of a screenplay that he cowrote with Oliver Stone is full of action. But it's built around a narrative that makes little sense.

Year of the Dragon could have done for the Chinese underworld what *The Godfather* did for the American Mafia—offer a plausible and engrossing explanation of how and why it operates. Instead, we get short speeches from several characters that are part history lesson, part political diatribe. We learn of the ancient culture and customs of the Chinese from several individuals who come in contact—and often clash—with Captain Stanley White (Mickey Rourke), a Vietnam vet and the most decorated cop in the city.

The name White is one of several less-than-subtle attempts by Cimino and Stone to make a point about race. The character carries lots of baggage and anti-Asian sentiment from his days in 'Nam—issues that both Stone and Cimino have dealt with much more ably in other movies.

For all his critics and celebrated flops (*Heaven's Gate*, anyone?), Cimino did write and direct one of the most moving and definitive Vietnam movies. But while we cared about the characters in *The Deer Hunter*, we have trouble even getting a fix on the central figures in *Year of the Dragon*.

White is a crusader out to clean up Chinatown after he is assigned to head the police district there. He is not content to maintain the status quo—an arrangement between the businessmen/gangsters controlling the neighborhood and the police and politicians content to ignore the crime and corruption as long as it doesn't spill over into nasty headlines and street violence.

But a push by a group of young Chinese gangsters out to replace the "uncles" in charge of the Triads turns into open warfare, with shootings and stabbings in restaurants and revenge killings on the streets. White is told by his superiors to tamp it down, to get things back under control, to work with the old heads to reestablish what has long passed for law and order in Chinatown. He, of course, will have no part of it. Instead, he wants to root out the corruption and lay bare the international heroin trade that the various factions are really fighting over.

Along the way, White manages to insult or denigrate just about everyone. Turning down a bribe offered by young Joey Tai (John Lone)—the emerging new power broker in Chinatown—White says, "I'm not an Italian. I'm a Polack. And I can't be bought."

"Slant eyes" and "yellow nigger" are two phrases used to describe Asians in the film and Tony, a hardworking Chinese-American, gets to take a shot at whitey in a rant about the young Chinese punks shooting up his neighborhood.

"Young people, no respect," he says in halting English. "Steal. Shoot. Kill. Like white man."

Those kinds of ethnic slurs are rampant in this movie, which attracted strong criticism from Asian-American groups concerned over stereotyping. The arguments were some of the same offered by Italian-American groups protesting films like *The Godfather*.

Our position has always been on the side of free speech. If you don't like the movie, or the message, don't buy a ticket.

The important difference is that *The Godfather* is classic cinema, while *Year of the Dragon* falls well short of that standard.

There are plenty of gangland shootings and one beheading. And there's lots of talk about how the corruption is systemic and so deeply rooted in the culture that it can't be changed.

"This is not the Bronx or Brooklyn" Tai tells White in a meeting to discuss life on the streets. "It's not even New York. It's Chinatown."

White brings his own distorted sensibilities to the conflict, complaining at one point, "This is Vietnam all over again. Nobody wants to win this thing."

That's the kind of simplistic writing that keeps the movie from developing. That and a totally unrealistic romantic subplot that further erodes the film's credibility. White, his marriage on the rocks, takes up with Tracy Tzu (Ariane Koizumi), a young Asian-American television newswoman whose breathless reporting gives us updates on the gang war that drives the main plot. Koizumi's stilted delivery and lack of emotion got her a well-deserved Razzie nomination. But she is nice to look at, especially when she is climbing out of a bathtub.

Tzu is repulsed by White, yet ends up in bed with him. White, in turn, claims to despise everything Tzu represents, yet is happy to use her reporting to enhance his standing and further his increasingly rogue investigation.

Both Tzu and White's wife, Connie (Caroline Kava), pay a price for White's action. Connie is killed and Tzu is raped.

In the end, White gets Joey Tai and his group, but life in Chinatown goes on.

And in a final scene that makes little sense—but is in keeping with the rest of the movie's disjointed narrative— White and Tzu end up kissing in the midst of a Chinatown riot sparked by a funeral for one of the bad guys.

◉ **HIT:** Even though many of the scenes were shot on a sound stage in Wilmington, N.C., Cimino did a good job of re-creating the crowded and often chaotic feeling of the streets of New York City's Chinatown.

⊗ **MISS:** The convoluted plotline goes in several different directions, but takes us nowhere.

✎ **WHAT THEY WROTE AT THE TIME:** "Once again Cimino's ability to handle furious action set pieces is well to the fore: a shootout in a Chinese restaurant and a battle with two pistol-packing Chinese punkettes put him in the Peckinpah class. The connecting material, however, is by turns muddled, crass and dull, amounting mostly to Stanley's interminable self-justification."—*Time Out*

✔ **REALITY CHECK:** There's no way a reporter for a New York television station could be having an affair with the police captain while at the same time reporting on the captain's crusade to clean up Chinatown. Page Six would go nuts.

◎ **REPEATED WATCHING QUOTIENT:** Once is enough.

◣ **CASTING CALL:** Cimino and Stone considered Nick Nolte and Jeff Bridges for the role of Stanley White, but Cimino decided on Rourke after working with him in *Heaven's Gate*. Cimino also had an uncredited role as a director in *The Pope of Greenwich Village*, one of Rourke's best performances.

❞ **BEST LINE:** "This is America you're living in and it's 200 years old, so you better get your clocks fixed," White tells a group of Chinatown leaders after they try to explain the ancient customs that still dictate the way many Chinese operate in both their businesses and personal lives. The line embodies the anger, frustration and xenophobia that drive White.

⚑ **VIOLENCE LEVEL:** Heavy duty and brutal, with guns, knives and explosives.

☄ **BODY COUNT:** At least twenty-four. The shooting in the restaurant, where two hit men spray the establishment with machine guns and bodies fly, made it difficult to get an exact count. There's also the beheading. We don't see it taking place, but we do get to see the head, which Joey Tai pulls out of a sack and presents to an Army general in Thailand he's trying to impress.

94 NEW JACK CITY (1991–R)

STARS: WESLEY SNIPES, ICE-T, ALLEN PAYNE, CHRIS ROCK | DIRECTOR: MARIO VAN PEEBLES

A year after playing the righteous cop out to rid the city of the despicable drug lord in *King of New York*, Wesley Snipes revisited the urban underworld in Mario Van Peebles' morality play about the scourge of crack cocaine.

This time, however, Snipes is wearing a black hat and flashing lots of bling—a braided gold chain, earrings, bracelets and rings—as he delivers an over-the-top performance as bad guy Nino Brown, the central figure in *New Jack City*.

The movie, one of the more popular urban gangster films of the 1990s, is riddled with bullets and clichés.

Brown is an entrepreneurial genius, the kind of guy who others look at and say, "if only he had put his skills to legitimate use." Pookie (Chris Rock) is a street corner hustler who gets strung out on coke, cleans himself up and then goes to work undercover for the cops. But you know trying to do the right thing is going to end badly. And the cops—at least the cops who really understand what's happening—are two misfits, Scotty (Ice-T) and Nick (Judd Nelson) who are thrown together because no one else on the force will work with them.

Scotty's mother was killed long ago in a random act of street violence that you can be sure is going to connect to the cast of characters he is now investigating. And Nick, an Italian-American who talks ghetto, is wrestling with his own demons.

Van Peebles, who made his directorial debut here, also plays Stone, the police lieutenant to whom Scotty and Nick report. He and writers Barry Michael Cooper and Thomas Lee Wright have sprinkled the story's dialogue with lots of 1990s social commentary. There are also plenty of visual comparisons between corporate America and the drug underworld.

Neither the director nor the writers seemed to be going for subtlety. There are, for example, two scenes in which Al Pacino's *Scarface* is playing on a television in the background. Each time—as if you couldn't guess—Pacino is spouting that classic "Say hello to my little friend!" line.

New Jack City does its best to match *Scarface*'s level of violence.

Nino Brown has structured his organization like a corporation and holds periodic board meetings where he discusses business and, on occasion, deals with members who have gotten out of line. One ends up with his hand impaled on the table after Brown pulls a blade from the top of his walking stick to make a point, so to speak.

The movie opens with a disloyal business associate being dropped into the East River from atop the Brooklyn Bridge. Brown gives him a fine send off ("See ya' and I wouldn't wanna be ya' ") before splashdown. Shortly afterward he sets the tone for the film during a meeting in the back room of a dance club. With a half-dozen loyalists gathered around the table, he provides them with their marching orders.

"You gotta rob to get rich in the Reagan era," he says. "Times like this, people wanna get high."

Brown's organization has discovered crack cocaine and he sets up a foolproof marketing plan to take advantage of consumer demand. He and his associates literally take over an apartment complex that covers one city block, driving out the apartment owner and other drug dealers who lived and worked there.

The building is converted into a crack netherworld, with a courtyard populated by zombie-like addicts and a basement room set aside for production. Brown insists that all his workers package product in the nude—to cut down on thievery—which adds a number of gratuitous naked breast shots to the story.

As in *King of New York*, there is the inevitable conflict with the Italian mob, including one biblical confrontation in which Brown, wielding his walking-stick dagger, cuts off the pony tail of a young mobster. Like Samson, the wiseguy no longer has any power. But this humiliation leads him to the cops and sets up an intriguing double-cross that ends in murder and betrayal.

Along the way, Brown also has a falling out with his boyhood friend and top associate, GeeMoney (Allen Payne), over—what else—a woman.

"This is soap opera shit," Brown says in dismissing one confrontation over the hooker that both men want to bed. At another point, in a dispute over cash and drugs, he tells GeeMoney, "Sit your five-dollar ass down, before I make change."

That's what passes for pithy dialogue in what quickly becomes a heavy-handed tale of power and corruption.

Nick, the Italian cop, helps explain it all after acknowledging to Scotty that he, like Pookie, was once a cocaine addict.

"This whole drug shit," he says, "it's not a black thing. It's not a white thing. It's a death thing. Death doesn't give a shit about color."

⊙ **HIT:** Chris Rock's performance as a strung-out coke addict is chilling and is perhaps the best piece of acting in the movie.

⊗ **MISS:** Ice-T's performance, on the other hand, seems forced. He told an MTV interviewer after the movie was released that he hated police because he grew up around gang members. That could explain his reluctance to embrace the role.

✔ **REALITY CHECK:** The story falls apart at a crucial point. Working for the police, Pookie secretly films the drug marketing in the apartment complex with a camera hidden in his belt-buckle. After his cover is blown, the cops say they have no case. Yet they have all the video from the hidden camera, more than enough evidence to bring charges against Brown's top associates. In real life, authorities would certainly use that evidence to pressure one of those associates to "flip" and become a witness

🎬 **PIVOTAL SCENE:** At a New Year's Eve party, Nino toasts the future. "The new American dream . . . life 'til death." That fatalism helps explain the murder, treachery and deceit that follow.

🗨 **BEST LINE:** Just before their final confrontation, the unnamed Old Man from the apartment complex—one of the few civilians to stand up to Nino Brown and his crew—tells Brown, "Idolator, your soul is required in hell."

👤 **"I KNOW THAT GUY":** The aforementioned Old Man is played by veteran character actor Bill Cobbs, who has over 140 film and television credits dating back to 1974 when he was a man on the subway station platform in a scene from the original *The Taking of Pelham One Two Three*. He's played a minister on *The Sopranos,* has appeared in dozens of other television series and has had parts in films as diverse as *Ghosts of Mississippi, Things to Do in Denver When You're Dead, The Color of Money, The Cotton Club* and *The Brother from Another Planet.*

✎ **WHAT THEY WROTE AT THE TIME:** "The stuff of New Jack City is the stuff of a thousand exploitation films; it's the familiar story of cops versus pushers, yet somehow, though the shape of the narrative and a lot of the details are commonplace, Van Peebles penetrates to the reality behind the clichés."—Hal Hinson, *Washington Post*

🍿 **BET YOU DIDN'T KNOW:** Early on, Pookie tries to rob Scotty, not realizing he is an undercover cop. This leads to a chase scene through the city streets, Pookie on his bike and Scotty on foot. The scene was originally written as a car chase, Van Peebles said in an interview, but he decided against that because it would have used up too much of the film's budget. In fact, the bike chase works well and is much more realistic. From our perspective, there are only two car chases worth watching. One is in *The French Connection* and the other is in *Bullitt.* Everything else is derivative.

🔫 **VIOLENCE LEVEL:** At the top of the chart.

☠ **BODY COUNT:** At least twenty-nine. As in many other movies of this genre, the shootouts are so chaotic, they make arriving at an accurate count nearly impossible.

95 BOUND (1996–R)

STARS: GINA GERSHON, JENNIFER TILLY, JOE PANTOLIANO
DIRECTORS: ANDY AND LARRY (LANA) WACHOWSKI

Bound is distinct from the 99 other movies on this list.

For starters, it's the only one featuring lesbian lovers as protagonists. The two gorgeous actresses—Gina Gershon and Jennifer Tilly—wrestle around in several graphic scenes, one of which is regarded among the steamiest ever put on film.

Still with us? We figured so.

For another, *Bound* is tough to categorize. It's a gangster movie, for sure, and an erotic movie. It's also evocative of the classic noir films. And, at times, actor Joe Pantoliano's buffoonish performance makes it a flat-out comedy.

Bottom line, it's an original and entertaining film. Certainly worth your while if you like a little sex with your violence.

Gershon plays an ex-con named Corky who has just completed a five-year stretch for "redistribution of wealth." She takes a job as a Ms. Fix-It in an apartment building controlled by the mob, allowing her to walk around with a tool belt. This immediately arouses the lust of next-door neighbor Violet (Tilly), the kept woman of mobster Caesar (Pantoliano). Violet, who appears to live her life in a negligee, asks the handywoman over to clean out her pipes. This occurs in more ways than one. (Violet's hook-up line: "I have a tattoo. Would you like to see it?")

The two women watch as Caesar has to launder—literally—$2 million in blood-soaked bills recaptured from a rat who embezzled from the family. Caesar washes, irons and carefully hangs the money to dry. The man would make a great domestic.

Caesar is supposed to return the $2 million to his capo, but the women contrive a scheme to steal it from him, skip town and set the nasty Caesar up for the fall. Of course, as soon as they gain posses-

sion, their plan unravels. Bodies begin to fall and snap decisions must be made to deal with new exigencies. The cops show up and miss the evidence right in front of them. And Corky and Violet have to grapple with one of the film's underlying themes—whether the bedroom buddies can actually trust each other.

There's nothing worth taking too seriously in *Bound*, but it is a lot of fun. Pantoliano overplays his character as sort of a Joe Pesci caricature, which makes it easy to root for the two women. Watch for the scene where he confronts rival gangster Johnny, whom he believes stole his money, in front of the mob boss. You know that someone's going to die here, and the scene is masterfully played with a mixture of malice and humor.

We've admired "Joey Pants" from the time we first spotted him as Guido in *Risky Business* back in 1983. He deserves the kind of leading-man break that Steve Buscemi got in 2010 in HBO's *Boardwalk Empire*.

Tilly and Gershon, meanwhile, are smoldering, even if they're playing stereotypes. Tilly is the lipstick lesbian—all legs and little-girl voice—who gets hit on by every single character in the movie. Gershon wraps herself in leather and an Elvis sneer. She drives a 1960s truck and knows how to fine tune the engine. She's both sexy and intimidating.

Since its release in 1996, *Bound* has become an iconic film in the gay community. We agree with *San Francisco Chronicle* critic Barry Walters, who wrote, "*Bound* is a fascinating hybrid—Playboy Channel thriller meets feminist lesbian love story. Without pandering, it attempts to get just about everybody off."

For all of its twists and double-crosses, *Bound* never gets overly confusing. And while the ending may be predictable, it's up to snuff with most of the rip-off-the-mob movies we've seen. If you like a gangster film sprinkled with laughs, sex and violence, you'll enjoy this one.

◉ **HIT:** This is an attractively shot movie, and not just because of its stars. Kudos to chief cinematographer Bill Pope.

⊗ **MISS:** There are a half-dozen mob characters in the movie, each of whom seems to have an IQ under 40. How could the underworld succeed if everyone in it is so dumb?

✎ **WHAT THEY WROTE AT THE TIME:** "Jennifer Tilly, with her oriental eyes, Monroe voice, purple lipstick and sheath dresses, is a perfect modern equivalent for the man-traps who used to be played by Barbara Stanwyck, Jane Greer or Jean Simmons. The radical stroke of *Bound*, however, is that the part that would have once gone to Robert Mitchum is here taken by Gina Gershon. Tattooed, leather-jacketed and smiling crookedly, Gershon may be the first unapologetically gay lead in what is essentially a commercial thriller rather than niche market arthouse erotica."—Kim Newman, *Empire*

☺ **GOOF:** In the early fixing-the-sink scene with Violet and Corky, Violet's shapely legs shift from wearing black hosiery to no stockings, then back to black again.

➜ **DON'T FAIL TO NOTICE:** Joe Pantoliano's apparent Humphrey Bogart imitation at certain points in the movie. That's because the directors told him to watch *The Treasure of the Sierra Madre* and base his character on Bogey's Fred C. Dobbs.

🎬 **PIVOTAL SCENE:** Well, it's the legendary encounter that occurs 12 minutes into the movie, bringing together the two heroines. The scene was choreographed by sexuality author Susie Bright (a.k.a. "Susie Sexpert") and, well, it sure seems a lot more realistic than most sex scenes we've seen on celluloid.

"We had a great time doing that," Gershon told the website *AfterEllen.com*. "We laughed a lot. That was our biggest problem. As soon as I met Jennifer, I thought, 'Okay, this will work,' because we had a chemistry. We ended up with a kind of sisterly love for one another, which made the love scenes easier."

🔫 **VIOLENCE LEVEL:** Over-the-top. One poor sap being questioned by mobsters gets his head repeatedly banged against the toilet. When that doesn't yield information, they start clipping off his fingers, one at a time, with a tree pruner.

🍎 **BET YOU DIDN'T KNOW:** The movie is directed by brothers Andy and Larry Wachowski, who also wrote and produced the three *Matrix* movies and *V for Vendetta*. In 2006, Larry Wachowski left his wife of 15 years and took up with a dominatrix. In 2009, he changed his name to Lana and started living as a woman.

❞ **BEST LINE:** Corky on the excitement of the heist: "Stealing has always been a lot like sex. Two people want the same thing. They get in a room, they talk about it. They start to plan—it's kind of like flirting. It's kind of like foreplay because the more they talk about it, the wetter they get."

😐 **"I KNOW THAT GUY":** Johnnie Marzzone, the dopey and brutal son of a mob chieftain, is played by Christopher Meloni. For 12 seasons through 2011, Meloni played Detective Elliot Stabler on *Law & Order: Special Victims Unit*.

✪ **IF YOU LIKED THIS, YOU'LL LIKE:** *Sex and Fury*, a 1973 Japanese effort about a female gambler and pickpocket (Reiko Ike) who runs afoul of the Yakuza and is aided by a voluptuous and often naked Swedish spy (Christina Lindberg).

🐾 **BODY COUNT:** Four.

96 WE OWN THE NIGHT (2007–R)

STARS: JOAQUIN PHOENIX, EVA MENDES, MARK WAHLBERG, ROBERT DUVALL
DIRECTOR: JAMES GRAY

This is half of a good movie.

The first half.

The set up and premise are intriguing. Unfortunately director James Gray, who also wrote the script, delivers a lot less than is promised. If you want to see Gray at the top of his game, check out *Little Odessa* (reviewed elsewhere in this book).

With *We Own the Night*, Gray again visits the world of Russian organized crime in New York, but this time he has superimposed a family saga involving the NYPD onto the subject. In fact, the movie takes its title from the motto of the department's Street Crimes Unit, which was disbanded in 2002.

Who really owns the night is the central question as the story unfolds and *We Own the Night* offers lots of subtle, contradictory and troubling hints at the answer. Unfortunately, Gray goes for a moralistic and, we would argue, totally unrealistic ending, making the question—which is really unanswerable—moot.

Joaquin Phoenix is Bobby Green, the manager and driving force behind one of the hottest nightclubs in Brooklyn in the late 1980s. Bobby's got a gorgeous Puerto Rican girlfriend, Amada (Eva Mendes), and the full support of the owner of the club, a patriarchal Russian émigré named Marat (Moni Moshonov).

Bobby is warmly received by Marat's family, fawned over by his wife—who constantly wants to feed him—and looked up to by other family members for the job he is doing running El Caribe, a sprawling club/dance hall that is packed with young, hip and fast-living New Yorkers.

Drugs, not surprisingly, are part of the club scene. And Russian gangsters, whether Bobby wants to accept it or not, are big in the drug trade.

All this matters because Bobby's father, Burt Grusinsky (Robert Duvall), is a deputy chief with the NYPD and his brother, Joe (Mark Wahlberg), is a rising star in the department recently named captain and head of a narcotics strike force.

Bobby, we are told, uses his mother's maiden name because of the business he is in and the prominence of his father and brother. To say that the siblings are estranged hardly begins to describe the relationship.

"The whole city is falling apart," Joe tells his brother during one of their early verbal confrontations, which takes place at a beef-and-beer party to celebrate Joe's promotion to captain. "Don't you have any sense of responsibility at all?"

The event, sponsored by the Pulaski Society at a church hall, is nicely juxtaposed with the club scene at El Caribe that Bobby has to leave in order to attend the family affair. One is blue collar. The other cool and sophisticated. Bobby has no trouble deciding which he prefers.

Faced with his brother's question and already bristling at the unfriendly reception his Hispanic girlfriend has received from his family, Bobby pauses briefly, and replies, "Let me think. . . . No."

So it's no surprise when he initially rejects requests by his father and brother to help them by providing information about the Russian drug underworld.

"Sooner or later, either you're gonna be with us or you're gonna be with the drug dealers," Deputy Chief Grusinsky tells his son, setting up the black-and-white moralistic theme that makes the second half of the movie all too predictable.

The target of the drug investigation is Vadim Nezhinski (Alex Veadov), who happens to be Marat's nephew. Vadim's reputation as a ruthless kingpin is established early on when he witnesses an associate being arrested at the club and, with the police in earshot, tells him, "Talk to them, and we go after your mother."

A short time later, while in police custody and before he can be questioned, the Russian thug slits his own throat and bleeds out on the precinct floor.

Vadim's take-no-prisoners approach—an accurate reflection of the wanton violence that is so much a part of the Russian drug underworld—extends to his dealings with the police investigating him. This eventually forces Bobby to choose sides.

After his brother is shot and seriously wounded, Bobby agrees to cooperate and help the police make their case. And the movie begins to slip off track.

Bobby and Amada become protected witnesses. Their relationship is strained. His agreement to testify leads to a rain-soaked car chase in which his father is killed. Then, in a 180-degree spin that challenges credulity, Bobby goes from being a protected witness to becoming a police officer—sworn in under a special department dispensation—and joins his brother in tracking down Alex.

A final showdown, in which Marat's role in the drug underworld is also disclosed, includes a police attempt to literally smoke Vadim out of his hiding place in a marshy, wooded area near a riding stable. Not content to wait for the smoke to do its job, Bobby moves in with his badge and his shotgun.

◉ **HIT:** The movie does a good job capturing the 1980s New York club scene and the subtle but violent nature of Russian organized crime.

⊗ **MISS:** This is New York, right? Home of tabloid journalism at its best? Gossip columns galore? Page Six? How long do you think the son of an NYPD Deputy Police Chief, even one using his mother's maiden name, would go unmentioned as the manager of one of the hottest and most drug-infested nightclubs in the city? And how long after that do you think savvy Russian gangsters would keep him in their employ?

✎ **WHAT THEY WROTE AT THE TIME:** ". . . this is an atmospheric, intense film, well acted, and when it's working it has a real urgency. Scenes where a protagonist is close to being unmasked almost always work. The complexity of Bobby's motives grows intriguing, and the concern of his girl friend Amada is well-used. *We Own the Night* may not solve the question of ownership, but it does explore who lives in the night, and why."— Roger Ebert, *Chicago Sun-Times*

➡ **DON'T FAIL TO NOTICE:** Former New York City Mayor Ed Koch has a cameo as himself in the hospital scene after Joe Grusinsky is shot.

◎ **REPEATED WATCHING QUOTIENT:** There are better movies about cops, gangsters and the Russian mob. Once is enough.

◀ **CASTING CALL:** Christopher Walken was originally tapped for the role of Deputy Chief Grusinsky, but had to bow out because of other commitments.

❞ **BEST LINE:** Lots of tough-guy cop talk, but the best line comes from Chief Grusinsky when he refuses to go along with a plan to bend the law in order to make a case.

"We don't ever play in the dirt here," he says. "Not ever . . . no matter what. If you piss in your pants, you can only stay warm for so long."

✪ **IF YOU LIKED THIS, YOU'LL LIKE:** *The Yards* (1999), another drama directed by Gray that stars Phoenix and Wahlberg. It's based on a true story about politics and corruption set in New York City's train yards.

🏴 **VIOLENCE LEVEL:** Spurts of violence, but they're in keeping with the story. It's all realistic—except for the final showdown.

⚰ **BODY COUNT:** Fifteen.

97 THE YAKUZA (1974–R)

STARS: ROBERT MITCHUM, KEN TAKAKURA | DIRECTOR: SYDNEY POLLACK

Two exciting trends enlivened Hollywood in the mid-1970s. First, Frances Ford Coppola's *The Godfather* reinvigorated the gangster film. Second, Bruce Lee's martial arts mayhem exploded on American screens, creating an enthusiastic audience for kung fu movies.

So why not merge the two?

That was the idea behind *The Yakuza*—a big studio production with a top-flight director, marketable star and expensive screenplay. The result is a mixed bag. Sometimes, this fusion of East and West works. Other times, it's as misguided as cheeseburger sushi.

The Yakuza failed at the box office, and thus did not succeed in launching a new genre. Japanese gangster movies (covered elsewhere in this book) did not find a market in the United States until the 1990s.

Still, accompanied by a bag of microwave popcorn, this movie offers a fine night's entertainment.

Veteran tough guy Robert Mitchum stars as retired American cop Harry Kilmer. He is contacted by desperate former Army buddy George Tanner (Brian Keith, who had previously played the kindly uncle/stepfather of youngsters in the popular TV series *Family Affair*). Tanner is now a sleazy arms trader who has stiffed a yakuza chieftain in a big deal. In return, that mob boss has kidnapped Tanner's daughter and threatened to kill her if the weapons don't show up within four days. Oh my, if Buffy and Jody ever found out what had become of Uncle Bill.

Anyway, Kilmer flies to Kyoto to rescue the girl. He enlists the help of retired yakuza member Tanaka Ken (played by Japanese box-office champ Takakura Ken). You quickly notice two things about Ken. First, he wields a blade better than Bill the Butcher in *Gangs of New York*. Second, he's got a palpable hatred for Kilmer.

This is where things get complicated. We learn that Kilmer was a member of the American occupying forces in Japan after World War II and saved the life of Ken's sister. He also had an affair with her.

Ken, meanwhile, spent six years hiding in a Philippine jungle after the war before returning to Japan. It gnaws at him to know that a former enemy saved his sister. It gnaws at him more that under the Japanese rules of obligation—called *giri*—Ken must spend the rest of his life returning that favor to Kilmer.

There are more twists and double-crosses to the plot, which gets so muddy at one point that Mitchum must provide a voice-over narration to make things comprehensible. There's a decent subplot about Kilmer's rekindling of an affair with the woman he loved but never got to marry. Mostly, you learn about debts of honor and the unbreakable codes of conduct of the Japanese underworld.

And while it doesn't quite evolve into a buddy movie, Ken and Kilmer do come to respect each other as veteran warriors. Their on-screen chemistry works. Takakura brings an intense edginess, which balances Mitchum's typical hangdog performance as a world-weary tough guy.

The Yakuza's fixation with Asian wisdom and social codes grows tiresome after about an hour. But the film is energized by the blood and body parts splattering the screen. There are three great battle scenes, with Ken swinging his sword and Kilmer (unsportingly, we think) firing away with a 12-gauge, double-barreled shotgun. Don't tune out before the final showdown at the gambling parlor, where our two heroes take on 21 heavily tattooed yakuza gangsters. You know who's gonna win.

Director Sydney Pollack, better known for chick-friendly flicks like *The Way We Were* and *Tootsie*, goes a little berserk with decapitations, disembowelments and, as every yakuza movie requires, the chopping off of pinkies. Not that we're complaining.

CASTING CALL: Lee Marvin and Robert Redford were both considered for Mitchum's role. Martin Scorsese wanted to direct this film right after finishing *Mean Streets*, but was passed over for Pollack.

HIT: The over-the-top action scenes in this film are marvelously choreographed. That final showdown featuring two men taking on 21 would do Brian De Palma proud.

MISS: We only notice soundtrack music when it is extremely good or bad. And *The Yakuza*'s soundtrack music is not extremely good. Makes us recall *The Mod Squad* and other dated TV shows from the 1970s.

BET YOU DIDN'T KNOW: The original screenplay by Paul Schrader (*Taxi Driver, Raging Bull*) and Robert Towne (*Chinatown, The Last Detail*) sold for a then-record $300,000.

DON'T FAIL TO NOTICE: The Japanese club singer leading a room full of lounge lizards in "Oh My Darling, Clementine." That's what they regard as American music?

"I KNOW THAT GUY": Veteran character actor Herb Edelman plays Oliver Wheat, the weak-hearted American host who hides behind the stairs whining, "Stop it! Stop it!" during one of the big shootout scenes. If you thought he was a wimp as Bea Arthur's husband in *The Golden Girls*, wait until you catch him in this.

BEST LINE: Kilmer and his American protégé, Dusty (Richard Jordan), debate whether they can rely on Ken, the acerbic retired yakuza, to protect them in an imminent battle. Kilmer explains that under the Japanese system of honor, Ken has that obligation—*giri*—to Kilmer for saving his sister.

Dusty: "You mean he figures he owes you something?"

Kilmer: "Yeah, sort of."

Dusty: "Well, that can work two ways. If you ain't alive tomorrow, he don't owe you shit."

VIOLENCE LEVEL: High, in an outlandish way. The best example comes during a battle at a monastery when a yakuza aims his Smith & Wesson at Kilmer. Ken saves his partner by hurling a samurai sword at the bad guy, whose arm is severed at the wrist. The disembodied hand flies through the air, harmlessly firing the gun at the ceiling.

BODY COUNT: A lusty thirty-one, including eighteen in the final showdown at the gambling parlor.

WHAT THEY WROTE AT THE TIME: "This movie is a cinematic hybrid that crosses American stars, writers and a director with a popular Japanese film form. To come upon it unsuspecting is a little like opening an Almond Joy wrapper and finding inside the arrangement of fish, rice and seaweed."—*New York Times*

REPEATED WATCHING QUOTIENT: Once ought to cover it.

IF YOU LIKED THIS, YOU'LL LIKE: *Kill Bill: Vol. 1*. Quentin Tarantino makes no secret that he cribs ideas from other movies. He must have taken copious notes watching *The Yakuza*. That great moment in *Kill Bill: Vol. 1* when Uma Thurman impales a gangster and then uses his body as a shield against others? It's not the only trick that was done here first.

98 MADE (2001–R)

STARS: JON FAVREAU, VINCE VAUGHN, PETER FALK | DIRECTOR: JON FAVREAU

One of the taglines in the promos for this movie was: "welcome to disorganized crime."

That about says it all.

Jon Favreau and Vince Vaughn, who developed something of a cult following with their 1996 movie *Swingers,* go at it again, reprising their roles, if not their characters. The difference is a grittier, but in many ways less realistic, film.

Favreau, who also wrote and directed, plays Bobby Ricigliano, an aspiring boxer with a big heart, but not much talent. Vaughn is his best friend, Ricky Slade, a screw-up Bobby is constantly bailing out of trouble. Ricky is the incessant motor mouth. Bobby's the long-suffering good guy.

During the day, Bobby works construction. And at night, he's the driver/bodyguard for his girlfriend Jesse (Famke Janssen), a savvy go-go dancer whose bumping and grinding at bachelor parties sends Bobby into a rage.

He shares an apartment with Jesse and her five-year-old daughter Chloe (Makenzie Vega). A scene-stealer, Chloe quietly matches wits with Ricky and clearly steals Bobby's heart. Think *Little Miss Marker*, but with an edge.

The family dynamic is captured in one quick scene. When Jesse offers Chloe a peanut butter and jelly sandwich for dinner, Bobby counters by whipping up a plate of pasta.

"Pasta puttanesca," he says. "Bad girls' pasta."

Bobby knows Jesse's true nature and what she does. He just doesn't want to admit it.

When the guest of honor (Jonathan Silverman) at a bachelor party begins to fondle her, Bobby's had enough.

"No touching," he screams before throwing a right hook that knocks out the bachelor's front teeth. This, of course, is bad for business.

But it sets the plot in motion.

The bachelor party business is one of several enterprises run by Max, a wizened old Jewish gangster played to perfection by Peter Falk. Falk has just a handful of scenes, all sitting behind a desk in his office, and he makes the most of them.

The only sport worth betting on, he tells Bobby, is jai alai.

"Know why I like it?" he asks. "Fixed. It's a sure thing. It's the only way to bet."

And while he's upset with Bobby for punching out the bachelor ("Maybe the last time, with the PRs, but these are nice Jewish boys," he says), Max acknowledges that he has to share some of the blame.

"It's my fault," he says. "I send you to watch scum drool over the love of your life."

To make good on the money that Max had to shell out to repair the bachelor's teeth—and to earn enough cash to buy Jesse out of the go-go business—Bobby agrees to go to New York for Max and help with a financial transaction. Ricky talks his way into the deal.

With that, the action shifts to Manhattan and the Red Hook section of Brooklyn. Bobby and Ricky embark on a convoluted trip through the city as Ruiz (Sean "P. Diddy" Combs) sets up the financial drop and Jimmy (Vinny Pastore) chauffeurs the would-be wiseguys all over the city.

The itinerary includes stops at the Soho Grand Hotel, Spa, Luna and Tavern on the Green. Ricky throws around cash the way he thinks a real gangster might and nearly ends up in a bathtub with Jennifer Esposito.

Along the way, Bobby and Ricky fight, drink, argue and fight some more.

Their faces are scarred and bruised by the time the financial drop takes place in a seedy bar in Red Hook. Bobby gets a knife put to his throat. Ricky comes to the rescue, but he's brandishing a starter pistol. In the end, Jimmy saves the day, but you're never quite sure if the deal was for real or simply a scam set up by Max to test Bobby's mettle.

Bobby earns Max's respect. But then, in a move that nearly leaves Ricky speechless, he turns down an offer to work fulltime for Max. He gives Max a wad of cash that was to be his first payment and, in short order, gives up Jesse as well.

"I never promised you anything, okay," she tells Bobby after he returns to their Hollywood apartment, finds Chloe sitting in front of a television and Jesse snorting coke with a customer in their bedroom.

"I don't think they were expecting me," Bobby says to Ricky as he exits the apartment with Chloe.

⊙ **HIT:** Vinny Pastore doesn't say much as Jimmy the limo driver, but he brings just the right mix of menace and cynicism. Jimmy's a genuine New York wiseguy.

⊗ **MISS:** P. Diddy, on the other hand, mails it in.

✎ **WHAT THEY WROTE AT THE TIME:** "One mug is an uptight worrywart, the other a recklessly loose cannon and the seriocomic account of their misadventures plays like 'Mean Streets Lite.' "—Joe Leydon, *Variety*

➜ **DON'T FAIL TO NOTICE:** The vanity license plate on the limousine that Vinny Pastore drives reads "DBLDN11." This is a reference to a blackjack strategy discussed in *Swingers*—always double down on 11.

☹ **GOOF:** A cut on Ricky's forehead, the result of one of his fights with Bobby, shifts from the center of his forehead to the side and then back again during the final scenes.

◀ **CASTING CALL:** There are four *Sopranos* connections. Favreau made a guest appearance as himself on the popular HBO show shortly before he began filming *Made*. He cast Vinny Pastore, (a.k.a. "Big Pussy") as the limo driver. Drea de Matteo (Adriana on *The Sopranos*) plays a party girl encouraged by her friend Jennifer Esposito to have sex with Ricky. And Federico Castelluccio portrays the doorman who turns Ricky and Bobby away from a hot downtown club. Castelluccio played "Furio"—the mob enforcer imported from Naples by Tony Soprano. Furio, you may recall, nearly had a thing with Carmela, Tony Soprano's wife.

👤 **"I KNOW THAT GUY":** The waiter who sides with P. Diddy in an argument with Ricky over whether Strega is an aperitif or a digestive is Leonardo Cimino, a veteran character actor with credits in dozens of mob movies. He played nearly the same role in *The Freshman*, serving Marlon Brando espresso in his Mulberry Street social club. By the way, Ricky was right. It is a digestive. You drink the witch after dinner.

99 BROTHER (BRAT) (1997–R)

STARS: SERGEY BODROV JR., VIKTOR SUKHORUKOV | **DIRECTOR:** ALEKSEY BALABANOV

In researching this celebration of gangster flicks, we were delighted to learn how many countries have contributed to the genre.

We knew, of course, of the grand tradition of French gangster films, dating back to the 1930s and *Pepe le Moko*. There are seven British entries on our Top 100, from 1971's *Get Carter* to 2004's *Layer Cake*. German and Italian directors created masterpieces of mob life and, more recently, their counterparts from Japan and Hong Kong turned the subject in a whole new direction. In all, projects from 12 different countries crack our Top 100.

But it goes way beyond that. In reviewing hundreds of possibilities for this book, we discovered an International House of Mobster Movies. Among them:

• *Sodoma Reykjavik*, an Icelandic comedy about a teen who becomes embroiled in a conflict between a liquor smuggler and aspiring goodfella while searching for his mom's missing remote control.

• *Cyclo*, the story of an orphaned Vietnamese bicycle taxi operator who gets taken in by a mob queen known as Boss Lady. In one brutal scene, Cyclo witnesses a hit man repeatedly stab a victim while singing lullabies.

• *Kiler*, a funny Polish tale of mistaken identity in which an unassuming cabbie named Jerzy Kiler (which translates to "killer") is believed by both police and the local crime king to be a contract murderer.

• *A Bittersweet Life*, a sadistic South Korean entry combining 1950s noir with 1990s John Woo. The story centers on a gangster caught between loyalty to his boss and affection to his boss's girlfriend.

And this one. *Brother* (which reads as *Brat* in Russian) is the portrait of an Army veteran who sets out to start a new life in St. Petersburg, but winds up as an icy contract killer.

Point is, as long as organized crime exists, creative people around the world will find new ways to tell stories about it. And we, as viewers, will continue to be both shocked and entertained.

The conflict in *Brother* is not between gangsters and the law, since no law appears to exist in 1990s Russia. Rather, it pits the local gangsters against invading Chechens trying to take their territory. There is an irony, of course, since the movie was filmed exactly as the Russian military had overrun the breakaway Republic of Chechnya.

The title has a double meaning. *Bratva*, or Brotherhood, is the name for the Chechen criminal subculture that landed in Moscow and St. Petersburg in the 1990s. And the subject of the story, Danila Bagrov (Sergey Bodrov Jr.), is a bored young man who goes to visit his role model of an older brother in the big city, unaware that Viktor (Viktor Sukhorukov) is now a mobster.

Although, truth be told, Viktor is not a very good mobster. He wears the requisite flashy clothes and silk underwear of an up-and-coming crime boss, but he's got all the cool and cunning of Fredo Corleone. It's clear that neither he nor his muscle men can hold off their Chechen challengers. So Viktor puts his hopes on his younger brother, just released from military service.

"Did you learn to shoot in army?" Viktor asks hopefully.

"Not really," says Danila.

"Were you a hero in the war?"

"No. I was just a clerk at headquarters."

No matter. Viktor gives his kid brother a gun and some cash and sends him out to hunt down the enemy. And, as it turns out, the boy's a natural. Within days, dead Chechens are falling all over town. And, for good measure, young Danila shoots a few of his brother's underlings when they threaten to rub out an innocent witness.

There's a strange dynamic here. Baby-faced Danila is sometimes portrayed as a sweet, naïve kid. He's quick to fall in love, which he does twice. His treasured possession is a Sony Discman, and he's obsessed with the music of a real band of the era named Nautilius Pompilius. (Their songs, by the way, sound like a bad cross between country and klezmer. They're horrid enough to make anyone want to leave Russia.) In many ways, Danila is a typical overeager teen.

At the same time, he immediately takes to the role of hardened killer. Danila embraces the power he commands when he flashes a gun. And he shows no remorse—not even a change of expression—as he shoots his way through the city's underworld.

You wind up not knowing whether to root for or against him. At the end, after conquering St. Petersburg, he heads for Moscow, where you expect he'll create as much damage.

Brother was directed by Aleksey Balabanov, who's been called Russia's David Lynch. The movie created a stir in that country, not unlike earlier controversies in the United States over movies like *A Clockwork Orange* or *Natural Born Killers*, which were said to glamorize violence. We don't think it reaches the level of those movies, artistically or in its level of brutality.

⊙ **HIT:** The strongest element of *Brother* is its portrayal of Boris Yeltsin's 1990s Russia. This is a country in social and economic freefall. The skies are always gray or raining, the infrastructure is decaying (as are everyone's teeth) and there's a general bleakness of mood. Needless to say, this is not a real pick-me-up film.

⊗ **MISS:** Some of the dialogue doesn't translate well to English. Like this line: "Bite off more than you can chew and you end up at the zoo." Somehow, that's supposed to be a witticism.

☺ **GOOF:** There's a scene midway through the film in which the Chechens come searching for Danila at his girlfriend's apartment. She's supposed to be home alone, but you can see a member of the film crew duck down in the hallway trying to get out of the way of the camera shot.

✎ **WHAT THEY WROTE AT THE TIME:** "Young Bodrov is a primal throwback to Cagney in *The Public Enemy* and Edward G. Robinson in *Little Caesar*, a charismatic killer with a wan smile, a goofy, junior-high-bully's voice, a dim intelligence, and a disquieting sweetness, which can appear on display just moments after he's saturated a seedy enemy with hot bullets."—Gerald Peary, *Boston Phoenix*

🔫 **VIOLENCE LEVEL:** Moderate. Most of the victims fall off screen.

➡ **DON'T FAIL TO NOTICE:** While the dialogue is in Russian (with haphazard subtitles) the words "business" and "money" are in English. And when a big contract is paid off, it is paid in American dollars.

👁 **REPEATED WATCHING QUOTIENT:** See it once and then see the four other foreign films highlighted at the start of this chapter.

✺ **IF YOU LIKED THIS, YOU'LL LIKE:** *The Battleship Potemkin* (1925) by Sergei M. Eisenstein. Nah, just kidding. Try *The Wounds*, a 1998 film about two teens in war-torn and decaying Serbia, fighting to survive as gangsters.

🔗 **BODY COUNT:** Eleven.

Smokin' Aces

GUILTY PLEASURES

Not every gangster movie is a masterpiece. But that doesn't mean we haven't enjoyed a few that defy credibility or lack artistic merit. Here are some of our favorite guilty pleasures.

Gun Crazy (1950). Young Bart loves his weapons, but he's never shot anything larger than a chicken—and feels remorse over having done that. He attends a carnival and falls for the sharp-shooting sideshow girl, Annie (B-movie bombshell Peggy Cummins). They marry and all's well, except that Annie's not satisfied with their modest, small-town life. So the couple embarks on a nationwide string of robberies, sharing their love and their lugers.

The St. Valentine's Day Massacre (1967). There's a terrific ensemble cast, led by Jason

Robards as Al Capone. And, of course, there's the real-life story of Capone's February 14, 1929 machine-gun mow-down of rival Bugsy Moran's gang. All of which suggests a great movie. Well, this ain't that. Directed by schlockmeister Roger Corman at a time when no one was making gangster movies, *Massacre* comes across as an unsuccessful attempt to recreate the classics of the 1930s. It doesn't, but it's still a fun watch.

Prime Cut (1972). Lee Marvin plays a Chicago mob enforcer who travels to Kansas City to collect a debt. Gene Hackman plays a lowlife named Mary Ann who sells drugged-out young prostitutes in the equivalent of cattle auctions (they're even lying on top of straw in locked pens). There's a gangster who grinds his enemies into sausage. And there's a classic wheat-field chase scene in which Marvin and Sissy Spacek are pursued by a giant reaper. A high body count and lots of naked breasts. What's not to like?

The Lady in Red (1979). Written by John Sayles (who went on to *Eight Men Out* and *Lone Star*), this feminist flick looks at the life of the mystery woman who briefly crossed paths with John Dillinger in the 1930s. "There's real artistry alongside the violence and nudity in this one," wrote *Entertainment Weekly*. Artistry? Not so much. Violence and nudity? By the shovelful. It stars Pamela Sue Martin in the title role, with Robert Conrad as Dillinger.

Dead Men Don't Wear Plaid (1982). Young Steve Martin and director Carl Reiner create a spoof of the classic noir films by splicing old black-and-white clips into a farfetched storyline built around Martin as a hard-boiled detective. Martin plays it deadpan, whether he's romancing Lana Turner, bossing around Humphrey Bogart or dressing as an old woman to extract information from James Cagney. It's all pretty inane, but you'll laugh at the over-the-top silliness and enjoy spotting scenes from other movies in this book.

Married to the Mob (1988). This goofy sendup stars Michelle Pfeiffer as Angela de Marco, a gum-popping Long Island princess who's the unhappy wife of mobster Frankie the Cucumber (Alec Baldwin). When Frankie gets hit in a hot tub, Angela aims to go straight. But the Feds think she's hiding something and Frankie's don wants her for his own. It's pure schlock played for broad laughs. And it's worth watching for Pfeiffer, who takes quite a different approach to playing Angela than the one she used for her role as Tony Montana's wife in *Scarface*.

My Blue Heaven (1990). Steve Martin is cartoonish as a Brooklyn mobster who turns state's evidence and relocates to a prefab California suburb. Rick Moranis is well cast as the joyless FBI agent overseeing his case. It's basically a comedy sketch overextended into a 97-minute movie, but it has its moments—most notably Martin's super-

market seduction of a suburbanite woman (Carol Kane) in heat. "You know it's dangerous for you to be here in the frozen food section . . . because you melt all this stuff."

Coldblooded (1995). This is a black comedy about a bookie (Jason Priestley) who has no goals, no people skills and no talents. His break comes when his boss (Robert Loggia) promotes him to hit man and, suddenly, our boy finds his niche. You may ask how a teenybopper heartthrob from *Beverly Hills, 90210* pulls off playing a ruthless killer. Not all that well, to be honest. But there is some ironic humor here and a good supporting cast, including cameos by Peter Riegert and Michael J. Fox.

Smokin' Aces (2006). We're not going to argue that this is a great movie—or even a good movie. Truly, it's a confusing mess with more holes than a kitchen sponge. So our advice is to stop trying to follow the plot and just enjoy a cast that includes Jeremy Piven (as an unbearable Vegas lounge singer), Wayne Newton (*not* in that role), Alicia Keys, Ray Liotta (Henry Hill!) and Alex Rocco (Moe Greene!). A missed chance for greatness, but still a fun time.

100 THE FRESHMAN (1990–PG)

STARS: MARLON BRANDO, MATTHEW BRODERICK, BRUNO KIRBY
DIRECTOR: ANDREW BERGMAN

In 1990, the long-awaited third movie in *The Godfather* trilogy was released to an eager public—which was promptly disappointed. *The Godfather: Part III* was dismissed by audiences and critics as implausible, poorly cast and—as Neil Smith of the BBC wrote—"a pale shadow of its predecessors.... This was an offer director Francis Ford Coppola should have refused."

Another, smaller sort of spinoff of *The Godfather* series was also released in 1990. And despite being even more implausible, the screwball comedy *The Freshman* sneaks into our Top 100.

The Freshman has one thing that *The Godfather: Part III* does not—Marlon Brando. While Brando reprises his role as Don Vito Corleone (well, sort of) for laughs, it's not a cheap trick. Instead, it's a funny, recurring joke. And you, as a member of the audience, are in on the gag.

Brando plays Carmine Sabatini, an apparent New York crime boss working out of Little Italy. He has the *Mona Lisa*—the real *Mona Lisa*—hanging above the mantel in his living room. His appearance and voice are so evocative of Don Corleone that those meeting him for the first time are nonplussed.

"You know, your resemblance to the Godfa—" blurts out young Clark Kellogg (Matthew Broderick), before being cut off by Sabatini's aides. No one must state the obvious.

Brando reprises Don Corleone's air of authority. He raises his eyebrows like the Godfather, folds his hands, scratches his face with the backs of his fingers. You've seen these gestures before, but here they're played for comedy. And it works. To further the parody, Broderick's character is a student at NYU, where his freshman film class studies *The Godfather: Part II*.

The plotline is almost superfluous. Clark, through a series of mishaps, finds himself working for Sabatini as a highly paid "delivery boy." His task is to hand off an imported Komodo dragon to a mad Teutonic chef (Maximilian Schell) eager to butcher it for a diners' club that specializes in endangered species. Meanwhile, Clark becomes unwittingly engaged to Sabatini's daughter (Penelope Ann Miller) and is chased by corrupt agents of the Justice Department. He wants no part of any of this, but doesn't have the gumption to stand up to mobsters, cops or a willing and attractive young woman.

In one scene, Brando's Sabatini seals a deal by kissing Clark on the mouth. "Do you know how big this is?" says an awed Victor Ray (Bruno Kirby), Sabatini's nephew. "*Bacio di tutti baci*. The kiss of all kisses. That's the highest. Now you're in for life."

All Clark wants to do now is go home to Vermont.

Broderick is fine in his role as the reluctant young man caught in events far beyond his control. He is the straight man to the lunacy swirling around him and to a cast of accomplished actors who make this parody worth 102 minutes of your time.

Along the way, there are all kinds of quirky little moments: Bert Parks singing "Maggie's Farm" in a style we're sure Bob Dylan never envisioned. The pompous, tweedy professor (Paul Benedict) who believes he *is* Michael Corleone as he shows the film in class. Brando on ice skates—that alone is worth the price of the rental.

And there are several inside jokes that any fan of gangster movies should enjoy. Don't miss the moment when Brando talks privately to the Komodo dragon, riffing on the "I could have been a contender" monologue from *On the Waterfront*.

◉ **HIT:** The late Bruno Kirby (born Bruno Giovanni Quidaciolu Jr.) is a hoot in his role as Victor, Sabatini's pushy, streetwise nephew. In fact, we always enjoyed Kirby—as a small-time mobster in

Donnie Brasco, as Billy Crystal's buddy in *When Harry Met Sally,* and—of course—as young Clemenza in *The Godfather: Part II*. Bet you didn't know that the five-foot-six actor was a close high school pal of seven-foot-two basketball legend Lew Alcindor (later known as Kareem Abdul-Jabbar).

⊗ **MISS:** Sometimes, the screwball comedy gets a little too screwball, such as when the Komodo dragon leads a sitcom-level chase scene through a suburban shopping mall.

✎ **WHAT THEY WROTE AT THE TIME:** "Mr. Brando serves in this film not only as an unexpectedly deft comic actor but also as a magnificent piece of found art, presenting himself quite matter-of-factly as a character any filmgoer of the last 20 years will recognize. When the resemblance is remarked upon, Mr. Brando makes things even better by delivering one of the character's drowsy-eyed, infinitely philosophical shrugs."—Janet Maslin, *New York Times*

➡ **DON'T FAIL TO NOTICE:** The sideways glance that Clark gives to a stack of oranges when he goes to meet Sabatini in a produce market. In *The Godfather*, the presence of oranges was used at least a half-dozen times to foreshadow an impending death.

👁 **REPEATED WATCHING QUOTIENT:** Not as high as *The Godfather*, obviously, but good for an occasional laugh.

🍎 **BET YOU DIDN'T KNOW:** Soon after *The Freshman* was shot in Toronto, Brando called the city room of the *Toronto Globe and Mail* and asked to speak to a reporter—any reporter.

"It's horrible," he said of the movie. "It's going to be a flop, but after this I'm retiring. I'm so fed up. . . . I wish I hadn't finished with a stinker."

A few weeks later—perhaps after realizing his paycheck was tied to box office take—the 65-year-old actor flip-flopped. In a stilted press release, he said, "The movie contains moments of high comedy that will be remembered for decades to come."

🗩 **BEST LINE:** Victor, explaining the Big Apple's cultural strata to newcomer Clark: "Here in New York, we have three distinct social classes: A—people who make a billion dollars a day and get laid in some tower every night; B—people who live in Times Square and eat Yankee Doodles on the sidewalk; and C—guys like me; guys I like to call the glue of society."

☺ **GOOF:** The costar of the movie, that so-called Komodo dragon, is actually a Nile monitor. Wise move swapping it out though, since Komodo dragons cannot be trained and their bites are sometimes fatal.

👤 **"I KNOW THAT GUY":** The maitre d' (Gianni Russo) who shows Brando into the Gourmet Club should be familiar to him. That's because Russo played Brando's son-in-law, the violent and stupid Carlo, in *The Godfather*. Things didn't turn out too well for him in that movie, either.

🔪 **BODY COUNT:** Not a one. What kind of way is that to end this book?

INDEX